D1496408

LOGOS AND CIVILIZATION

SPIRIT, HISTORY, AND ORDER IN THE WRITINGS OF BAHÁ'U'LLÁH

Nader Saiedi

UNIVERSITY PRESS OF MARYLAND

LIBRARY OF CONGRESS CATALOGING-IN-PUBLICATION DATA

Saiedi, Nader, 1955–
    Logos and Civilization : spirit, history, and order in the writings of
        Bahá'u'lláh / Nader Saiedi.
      p. cm.
    Includes bibliographical references and index.
    Clothbound: ISBN 1-883053-60-9.
    Softcover: ISBN 1-883053-63-3.
    1. Bahá"lâh, 1817–1892. 2. Bahai Faith—Doctrines. I. Title.

BP392.S25 2000
297.9'363—dc21

                          00-061454

Cover design by Duy-Khuong Van

Clothbound: ISBN 1-883053-60-9.
Softcover: ISBN 1-883053-63-3.

Copyright © 2000 Nader Saiedi. All rights reserved. This book may not be repro-
duced, in whole or in part, in any form (beyond that copying permitted in
Sections 107 and 108 of the U.S. Copyright Law and except by reviewers for the
public press), without written permission from the publisher, University Press of
Maryland, P.O. Box 34454, Bethesda, Md. 20827.

BP
392
.S25
2000

041601-499858

CONTENTS

PREFACE

Logos and Civilization is an attempt to demonstrate the unity and creativity of the message of Bahá'u'lláh through the analysis of a few works selected from the vast ocean of His writings. But it is not an exhaustive or definitive analysis even of those texts. It is simply a tentative and preliminary exploration of possibilities. It represents only my own personal understanding of the writings of Bahá'u'lláh.

It would be impossible to adequately acknowledge here all the many people who have helped me in this project. The new provisional translations included in this volume were made possible through the indispensable assistance of the Research Department of the Bahá'í World Centre. I am grateful to Carleton College and Landegg Academy for providing me with opportunities to pursue my own independent research and to the Association for Bahá'í Studies–North America for the publication of this book. Special thanks are owed to my teachers and friends Hossain Danesh, Muhammad Afnan, Shapour Rassekh, Iskandar Ha'i, Amin Banani, Roohollah Khoshbin, Manoochehr Manshadi, and Dariush Lamy for their various contributions. I am also indebted to my wife Bita for her support and unconditional encouragement of my work in Bahá'í Studies. Lastly, I wish to express my gratitude to Arden Lee for her perpetual unbounded affection and hope showered upon me. I dedicate this book to the memory of my teacher, the martyred scholar, Dr. 'Alí-Murád Dávúdí.

ABBREVIATIONS

The following abbreviations are used within the text for the English edition of works by Bahá'u'lláh that are frequently cited.

Epistle	*Epistle to the Son of the Wolf*
Kitáb-i-Íqán	*The Kitáb-i-Íqán: The Book of Certitude*
Gleanings	*Gleanings from the Writings of Bahá'u'lláh*
Arabic Hidden Words	*The Hidden Words of Bahá'u'lláh* (cited by number)
Persian Hidden Words	*The Hidden Words of Bahá'u'lláh* (cited by number)
Seven Valleys	*The Seven Valleys and the Four Valleys*
Four Valleys	*The Seven Valleys and the Four Valleys*
Tablets	*Tablets of Bahá'u'lláh Revealed after the Kitáb-i-Aqdas*

INTRODUCTION

OURS IS AN AGE of structural transition and intellectual and moral chaos. Modernity, critics assert, is in collapse, while "postmodern" solutions have shown themselves equally unable to provide a vision of self, society, history, and ethical ideals that can meet the challenges of global realities at the threshold of the twenty-first century. As the world continues "contracting into a neighborhood" and the destinies of all its races, nations, and peoples become ever more "inextricably interwoven," the conscious search for a blueprint for global order that will justly reflect those transformed relations becomes ever more desperate and urgent.[1] The spiritual and structural disorder that had elicited nineteenth-century complaints of anarchy, cultural anomie, and nihilism has yet to be alleviated by an integrative vision of society and culture; that failure typically has led to either a sense of despair and relativism, or narcissism and worship of violence.

In the middle of the nineteenth century Bahá'u'lláh, the Prophet-founder of the Bahá'í Faith, summarized the condition of modern human society in these words:

> Behold the disturbances which, for many a long year, have afflicted the earth, and the perturbation that hath seized its peoples. It hath either been ravaged by war, or tormented by sudden and unforeseen calamities. Though the world is encompassed with misery and distress, yet no man hath paused to reflect what the cause or source of that may be.... No two men can be found who may be said to be outwardly and inwardly united. The evidences of discord and malice are apparent everywhere, though all were made for harmony and union. (*Gleanings* 218)

He offered, in words of revelation, a vision of a global order intended to unite the religions, races, and nations of the world:

> The tabernacle of unity hath been raised; regard ye not one another as strangers. Ye are the fruits of one tree, and the leaves of one branch. We cherish the hope that the light of justice may shine upon the world and sanctify it from tyranny. If the rulers and kings of the earth, the symbols of the power of God, exalted be His glory, arise and resolve to dedicate themselves to whatever will promote the highest interests of the whole of humanity, the reign of justice will assuredly be established amongst the children of men, and the effulgence of its light will envelop the whole earth. (*Gleanings* 218–19)

In His writings He outlined the structure of that spiritual vision of world unity, declaring that

> The distinguishing feature that marketh the preeminent character of this Supreme Revelation consisteth in that We have, on the one hand, blotted out from the pages of God's holy Book whatsoever hath been the cause of strife, of malice and mischief amongst the children of men, and have, on the other, laid down the essential prerequisites of concord, of understanding, of complete and enduring unity. (*Gleanings* 97)

This book is devoted to an analysis of some of the writings from the treasury of Bahá'u'lláh's revelation. But it is impossible to speak of the revelation of Bahá'u'lláh without also talking about that of His forerunner the Báb, Whose spiritual and metaphysical message constitutes an integral aspect of the Bahá'í dispensation and an essential feature of the context necessary to understand Bahá'u'lláh's own writings.[2]

The Báb was born Siyyid 'Alí Muḥammad in 1819 in Shíráz, Iran. It was a time of messianic anticipation in Islam as well as in Christianity and Judaism. Shaykh Aḥmad-i-Aḥsá'í (1743–1828) and his successor Siyyid Káẓim-i-Rashtí (1793–1843) taught their disciples that the advent of the promised Qá'im ("He who ariseth"), the Twelfth and "hidden" Imám of Shí'ih Islam, was at hand. In 1844 (1260 A.H.), Siyyid 'Alí Muḥammad proclaimed Himself to be the Promised One and ultimately the Qá'im and a new Prophet or *Manifestation of God.* He designated Himself the *Báb,* the gate to divine knowledge, to paradise, and to One even greater than Himself, Whose imminent coming He proclaimed. Another title of the Báb is the Primal Point, a reference to the divine creative Word through which all other letters and words—all created things—are generated. Of the many books and tablets He revealed during the six years of His ministry, the most important is the Persian Bayán. In a sense, however, all the writings of the Báb are also His *Bayán* (exposition or Word). After years of imprisonment, the Báb was executed in 1850 by order of the Muslim divines and state authorities in the city of Tabríz.

The Báb's writings are characterized by a theological and philosophical analysis of life and reality. It may be argued that His works are novel explications of the principle of divine unity and sovereignty. According to the Báb, divine unity can only be beheld through the mirror of the Manifestations of the divine attributes—the Messengers and Prophets of God—who are the mediators between the divine and human realms. Recognition of these Manifestations of God is the supreme duty, the perfection, and the very purpose of human existence itself. The Báb spoke of the appearance of the Promised One, "Him Whom God shall make manifest" (*Man Yuẓhiruhu'lláh*) as the supreme focus, meaning, and intention of all His writings. He defined Himself as the herald of that Promised One, often referring to the "year nine" after the inception of His own revelation as the time when the Promised One would appear. He frequently identified the Promised One as the "Glory of God"—in Arabic, *Bahá'u'lláh*.

In His writings the Báb affirmed the dignity of all human beings and prohibited any act which might cause sorrow to others. He summoned the monarchs of the time to recognize the Cause of God and defined their rule as fundamentally illegitimate unless they did so. Although the real intent of His message was the elimination of all forms of violence from the world, and He never permitted open insurrection against state authorities, during His dispensation He did not formally abrogate the Islamic concept of holy war, or the principle of the "sword" in the defense of the Faith.[3] For that reason, when His followers were subjected to systematic and brutal military campaigns and sieges, they responded with heroic defensive measures in battles such as those at Fort Ṭabarsí, Nayríz, and Zanján.[4]

After the martyrdom of the Báb, the Bábí community was left without a formal successor. In fact, this was no accident but a delib-

erate and intentional action by the Báb. Knowing that the advent of
the Promised One was near, the Báb had eliminated the possibility of
any successor other than the Promised One Himself. Among the several Bábí leaders who emerged in the succeeding few years, two half-
brothers were particularly prominent. The younger, Mírzá Yaḥyá,
known as Azal, was, in accordance with the Báb's instructions, the
nominal leader of the Bábí community, but it was his elder brother,
Mírzá Ḥusayn 'Alí, known as Bahá, who stood out above all others for
His spiritual and moral leadership of the Bábí community. The prom-
inence of Mírzá Ḥusayn 'Alí, Bahá'u'lláh, became increasingly obvious to the Bábís and state authorities alike.

In 1852 a few of the Bábís, on their own, made an attempt on the
life of the king of Iran, Náṣiri'd-Dín Sháh, in revenge for the execu-
tion of the Báb. Their uncoordinated and poorly planned attempt
failed, but it galvanized the state and religious authorities to react
against the Bábí community and led to the martyrdom of about ten
thousand Bábís that same year. Bahá'u'lláh, by then a recognized
leader of the Bábí community, was arrested and incarcerated in the
subterranean prison in Tehran known as the Síyáh-Chál (the Black
Pit). In the middle of His four-month imprisonment there, in the first
days of the year 1269 A.H./1852, in the beginning of the year nine after
the declaration of the Báb, Bahá'u'lláh experienced the descent upon
Him of divine revelation and thereafter began to disclose, although in
a veiled way, His station as the Promised One of the Bayán. The year
1852 represents a turning point in sacred history. Bahá'u'lláh was
thirty-five years of age at the time.

Although it was proven that Bahá'u'lláh had played no part in the
assassination plot on the shah, He was exiled to the city of Baghdad in
the Ottoman Empire. A year after taking up residence there, He withdrew to the mountains of Sulaymáníyyih in northern Iraq for a period
of seclusion, largely due to the actions of His enemies within the Bábí
community, who resented His increasing authority. After two years
Bahá'u'lláh returned to Baghdad and, by Himself, began the task of
regenerating the Bábí community. While He did not yet publicly proclaim Himself to be the Promised One of the Bayán, He effectively

abrogated the principle of the sword and called for the Bábí community to rise to a new standard of egalitarian and moral conduct. His many writings during the Baghdad period, addressed to the community of Iranian Bábís in exile, elaborate His universalistic ethics and theology. As He later recorded in Epistle to the Son of the Wolf, He enjoined upon them honesty, piety, and upright conduct, decreeing that henceforth

> war shall be waged in the path of God with the armies of wisdom and utterance, and of a goodly character and praiseworthy deeds. Thus hath it been decided by Him Who is the All-Powerful, the Almighty. There is no glory for him that committeth disorder on the earth after it hath been made so good. Fear God, O people, and be not of them that act unjustly. (*Epistle* 24)

Forbidding His followers contention, conflict, and bloodshed, He bid them instead to:

> "Unsheathe the sword of your tongue from the scabbard of utterance, for therewith ye can conquer the citadels of men's hearts. We have abolished the law to wage holy war against each other. God's mercy hath, verily, encompassed all created things, if ye do but understand...."
>
> "Strive, O people of God, that haply the hearts of the divers kindreds of the earth may, through the waters of your forbearance and loving-kindness, be cleansed and sanctified from animosity and hatred, and be made worthy and befitting recipients of the splendors of the Sun of Truth." (*Epistle* 25–26)

Bahá'u'lláh's regeneration of the Bábí community and infusion into them of a new ethical standard of behavior increased His renown. His half-brother Yaḥyá remained a nominal leader who followed Bahá'u'lláh but always disguised himself for fear of public recognition and played no real leadership role. However, Bahá'u'lláh's leadership and His courageous and creative message caused increasing malice among His enemies, who began to intensify their opposition to Him and to spread rumors that Bahá'u'lláh had denied the station of the Báb. Bahá'u'lláh publicly rejected these lies in categorical terms, while disclosing to only a few of the Bábís His true station as the Promised

One whose coming had been foretold by the Báb. For this reason, Bahá'u'lláh's writings in the Baghdad period are characterized by a certain ambiguity—while they do not explicitly acknowledge His station as the Promised One, they contain subtle allusions to the extraordinary and sublime station of their author.

Bahá'u'lláh's growing fame and influence led again in 1863 to His banishment from Baghdad to Istanbul. Before His departure, in the encampment of the exiles known as the Riḍván Garden, He announced to some of the prominent Bábís gathered there that He was none other than the One promised by the Báb, "He Whom God shall make manifest." It was exactly nineteen years after the inception of the Cause of the Báb.

Bahá'u'lláh remained in Istanbul for four months before being exiled once more by the Ottoman authorities to Edirne (Adrianople) in European Turkey. During His five-year residence in that city, He formally announced His Cause to the Bábí community in various lands, a development which was met with strong opposition from Yaḥyá and his followers. Finally, a decisive severance of relations took place between Bahá'u'lláh and His half-brother, which would be known as the Most Great Separation.

In 1867, in the last year of Bahá'u'lláh's stay in Edirne, He began to proclaim His Cause to the entire world, sending letters to the political and spiritual leaders of various countries and communities. In these messages, He summoned them to recognize the new divine revelation and adopt the principles of the oneness of humankind, universal peace, social justice, and a spiritual culture and ethics. He continued this universal declaration after His final exile in 1868 to the fortress city of 'Akká (Acre) in Palestine. During His twenty-four years of imprisonment in 'Akká and environs, Bahá'u'lláh expounded His vision of a New World Order in an extensive body of books and tablets.

Unlike previous divine revelations, Bahá'u'lláh's revelation is uniquely distinguished by both the quantity of revealed scripture as well as the unequivocal authenticity of His tablets and books, many of which bear His own signature. Another unique feature of Bahá'-

u'lláh's revelation is the explication, within the texts themselves, of the rules of interpretation, or *hermeneutics*, for those texts. According to the covenant He created with His followers, the appointed interpreters of His writings have privileged, that is, sole, access to the true meanings of His texts, and their interpretations are authoritative and binding on all Bahá'ís. Those interpreters were Bahá'u'lláh's son 'Abdu'l-Bahá, whom He designated in His writings as His successor, and 'Abdu'l-Bahá's grandson Shoghi Effendi, whom 'Abdu'l-Bahá designated as the Guardian of the Bahá'í Faith. After the termination of the line of authorized interpreters, the leadership of the international Bahá'í community passed to the Universal House of Justice, an institution created by Bahá'u'lláh and upon which He conferred authority to legislate on matters not explicitly contained in the Sacred Text, to elucidate obscure matters, and to resolve conflicts and disputes.

The works to be analyzed in this book have been chosen as representing three stages of Bahá'u'lláh's revelation. The first of these stages (1852–1860) begins with Bahá'u'lláh's imprisonment as a Bábí and His revelation in the Síyáh-<u>Ch</u>ál, and includes most of His exile to Baghdad and His solitary retreat to the mountains of Sulaymáníyyih. The second stage (1860–1867) opens shortly before His public declaration to His companions in the Garden of Riḍván on the eve of His departure from Baghdad and includes the Istanbul and Edirne periods. The third stage (1867–1892), beginning in Edirne with Bahá'u'lláh's letters to the rulers of the world, comprises His final exile to Palestine and His remaining years in the prison of 'Akká and environs until His passing in 1892.

Chapter 1 sketches the background, in Islamic Sufism, of Bahá'u'lláh's early mystical writings and discusses methodological issues in reading Bahá'u'lláh's texts. Chapters 2 and 3 explore the structure of the Four Valleys and the Seven Valleys, revealed in Baghdad, in which Bahá'u'lláh sets forth a spiritual view of life and existence and outlines the stages in the spiritual journey of the soul. Chapters 4 and 5 discuss the Kitáb-i-Íqán (The Book of Certitude), also from the Baghdad period, explicating Bahá'u'lláh's manifestation theology and His historical approach to spirituality, culture, and society. Chapter 6 dis-

cusses the Kitáb-i-Badí' (The Wondrous New Book), revealed in
Edirne, in which Bahá'u'lláh reaffirms the foundational principles set
forth in the Kitáb-i-Íqán in the context of refuting the arguments of
His Bábí opponents. Chapters 7 and 8 are dedicated to an analysis of
the constitutive principles and the order of the Kitáb-i-Aqdas, revealed in 'Akká. Chapters 9 and 10 analyze the philosophical premises
of the concepts of order and governance contained in Bahá'u'lláh's
writings in light of recent controversial readings of His texts.

A major thesis of this book is the creative, revolutionary, and
unprecedented character of Bahá'u'lláh's spiritual and social vision.
The history and teachings of the Bahá'í Faith have barely begun to be
the subject of systematic analysis. A recent wave of attempts to analyze
the Bahá'í writings, however, has been characterized by hasty conclusions, premature speculations, and a general methodological reductionism which insists on trying to make the message and vision of
Bahá'u'lláh fit into the mold of traditional Eastern categories from
Neoplatonism to Islamic Sufism, or modern Western ones from liberalism to postmodernism. However, it will be argued here that
Bahá'u'lláh's complex vision transcends all of the given Eastern or
Western categories, whether traditional or modern, and that His writings must be read on their own terms and in light of their own hermeneutical principles and creative and novel approaches to metaphysics,
mysticism, historical dynamics, ethics, and social/political theory.

Bahá'u'lláh designates His revelation as the fulfillment of all the
prophecies and millennial expectations recorded in the Sacred Scriptures of the past, and as the inception of a qualitatively new stage of
spiritual and material existence for humanity through a universal revelation shed upon all created things. Given the integrative and universal character of His revelation, Bahá'u'lláh's metaphysics and theology resolve the traditional conflict between what Max Weber
termed *asceticism* and *mysticism*, with their dichotomy of transcendence
versus immanence, and inaccessibility versus anthropomorphism.[5]
The traditions of Judaism, Christianity, and Islam, for instance, have
been primarily understood as religions of asceticism and the doctrine
of the transcendence of God. In this view, it is normally assumed that

the transcendental sacred realm of the divine and the profane realm of nature are opposed to one another. In contrast, the traditions of Hinduism and Buddhism are normally understood as religions of mysticism and the doctrine of the immanence of God in nature. In these religions the opposition of sacred and profane is assumed to be replaced with harmony and unity.[6]

Bahá'u'lláh's theology of revelation is a creative synthesis of the profound truths underlying these two traditions and cannot be adequately captured by either of the Weberian categories. In Bahá'u'lláh's explanation, while the world is not God, it is the mirror of God. Both the transcendence of God and the harmony of the sacred and nature are affirmed in His metaphysics of being and revelation. This unveiling, revelation, and manifestation, Bahá'u'lláh declares, is the ultimate logic and meaning of reality and of history. In His manifestation theology, the traditional opposition between the world and the sacred is overcome, while the Supreme Reality is not reduced to the level of an empirically accessible phenomenon.

But Bahá'u'lláh's manifestation theology is no mere synthesis of asceticism and mysticism. The doctrine of progressive revelation explains the unveiling of the divine in the realm of human history as itself a historical process: religion both interacts with society yet is not reducible to a social construction. All the religions have one and the same source, and divine revelation renews itself perpetually in accordance with divine purpose. Divine revelation is not a static, absolute, and unique event; and spiritual journey is a feature not only of individuals but also of humanity as a collectivity. The recognition of God, the attainment of the presence of the Divine, the reflection of the Transcendental Reality in the mirrors of human hearts, is always a historically specific process mediated by the perpetual and progressive revelation of God throughout human history in the form of the Supreme Manifestations—the Prophets and Messengers of God. There is no termination to this process of revelation or the logic of divine unveiling in the realm of creation.

Relating this process of spiritual journey to the logic of historical dynamics, Bahá'u'lláh articulates a critique of both historical reason and what I have called "spiritual reason." In both cases He offers fundamentally novel outlooks which open new horizons in the study of religion. The Kitáb-i-Íqán explicates this critique of spiritual reason, which is reaffirmed in the foundational discourse of the Kitáb-i-Badí'. In the form of the principle of "heart" it appears again as one of the constitutive principles of the Kitáb-i-Aqdas. The critique of spiritual reason becomes simultaneously a method of spiritual knowledge as well as an affirmation of the logic of scriptural interpretation or hermeneutics—that is, the divine covenant—as well as of human epistemic equality and social justice. Bahá'u'lláh's critique of historical reason emphasizes the dynamic nature of both human history and the revelation of the Word of God, unveiling a theology in which the traditional concepts of "revelation" and "return" become transformed into expressions of a multidimensional, progressive, and dynamic concept of religion and society.

However, Bahá'u'lláh's metaphysics of manifestation and progressive revelation presents yet another new turn. According to Bahá'u'lláh, although all beings are mirrors of God, it is through Bahá'u'lláh's revelation that the radiance of all the divine Names and attributes has been shed over all created things, ushering in the "Day of God." This event creates the basis for a fresh approach to social and political theory. Since all beings have thereby become the recipients of this universal divine revelation, the concrete imperative of human civilization is none other than the realization of the oneness of humankind, and this principle is itself a reflection and affirmation of the sacredness of all beings. The revolutionary implication consists not only in the egalitarian and democratic principles that follow from it, but also in the unifying, holistic, and global logic of Bahá'u'lláh's vision.

Bahá'u'lláh articulated an organic theory of society, but one in which all humanity is defined as that organic whole—not simply the nation-state. In His vision the ideas of equality, democratic governance, human rights, and social justice are inseparable from a global conception of citizenship. Bahá'u'lláh not only rejected the traditional forms of inequality and oppression, but He also disclosed the hypocrisy of the limited and particularistic democratic and egalitarian theories of the modern West that were based on the unit of the nation-state. The profundity of this insight becomes more evident when we consider that at present the chief factor determining social and economic condition and access to resources is none other than the accident of birthplace and citizenship. In the context of an extremely unequal international economic and political order, the exclusion of any group of people from rights and opportunities on the basis of purely nationalistic citizenship can be seen to constitute the essence of oppression, injustice, and inequality. Bahá'u'lláh's emphasis on the unity and sacredness of all human beings as mirrors of all the names and attributes of God and as the constitutive elements of an emerging organic human society discloses the immoral and unjustifiable character of such, in effect, arbitrary notions of differential entitlement to rights, opportunities, and resources.

It should already be obvious that such a multidimensional, creative, and complex vision cannot be subsumed under any of the traditional or modern worldviews of either West or East. Any such analysis of the writings of Bahá'u'lláh will be reductive and therefore incapable of understanding the message of His revelation. An example of such reduction is the attempt to analyze Bahá'u'lláh's theology and social theory in terms of the categories of exclusivism and pluralism.[7]

One can approach the different religions' claims to truth in a number of different ways. The materialistic approach rejects all religions as a set of superstitions and/or reduces them to nonreligious phenomena like society (for Durkheim), the father figure (for Freud), an alienated human nature (for Feuerbach), a linguistic habit of animism (for Müller), an ideological apparatus for control of the masses (for Marx) or for the control of elites by the masses (for Nietzsche), ignorance of the causes of natural phenomena (for Russell), and so on. This approach, while denying the existence of an ultimate supranatural spiritual reality and ignoring the complexity of human beings and of religion itself, at the same time (often unconsciously) elevates some other principle—whether science, reason, nature, society, community, nation-state, sex, or race—to the status of the sacred or the ultimate cause.

Another approach is the fundamentalist and exclusivist approach to religion. In this approach, the believer finds other religions to be delusions, fabrications, and distortions of religious truth. The fundamentalist and exclusivist religious person rejects other Prophets as impostors and only recognizes the truth of one's own religion. Such an approach insists on the absoluteness of divine revelation and the finality of its own religion. It is static, intolerant, and frequently employs a literal method of scriptural interpretation.

A third approach is that of the postmodern pluralist. This approach recognizes no particular significance for any religion. On the other hand, it considers no religion superior to any other. Its relativism of truth and value becomes compatible with an eclectic, arbitrary, uncommitted, and fragmented approach to religion. In this approach, validity is purely conventional, and there exists no objective source of validity or authority outside the mere fact of the existence of certain beliefs and traditions among a given group of people. Religions are not regarded as particularly privileged expressions of divine truth, or they are not connected to one another through the same underlying divine will. For some who adhere to this view, religion is a matter of subjective preference. For others, religion is subordinate to ethnic and cultural categories, making it a self-sufficient and closed system. But exclusivistic and relativistic positions ultimately contradict the explicit claims made in the revealed Scriptures themselves, because those Scriptures mutually confirm each other's statements about universal validity and authority, millenarianism, and a systematic cycle of prophecy and fulfillment. Alternatively, postmodern pluralism views religions as random expressions of reality without any real logic, internal meaning, or divine purpose—one may choose different elements from different religious and nonreligious cultural phenomena in accordance with one's culture, taste, or a consumer orientation to a commodified religious market.

Bahá'u'lláh's approach to religion does not coincide with any of those alternatives or categories. In fact, there is no existing theory adequate to capture or encompass Bahá'u'lláh's approach, and the very act of interpreting it in terms of such categories inherently contradicts and distorts the heart of Bahá'u'lláh's message itself with its central thesis of progressive revelation.

The materialistic logic is obviously rejected by Bahá'u'lláh. But Bahá'u'lláh equally rejects the exclusivism of fundamentalist religion by affirming the unity of all the Manifestations of God. All the divine Messengers and Prophets are likened to the different horizons from which the sun shines upon the earth—the horizons are different but the sun remains the same. Even while they all express the will of God and the same inner spiritual truth, the teachings they reveal differ in accordance with the varying conditions and requirements of the time and the level of human spiritual and social development. That is why Bahá'u'lláh emphasizes both the validity and the unity of all the religions, describes religious teachings as historically specific, and rejects any notion of the finality of divine revelation, while declaring the equality of all human beings and enjoining fellowship among all the religious communities.

However, the fact that Bahá'u'lláh's teachings do not fit the exclusivist model of religious fundamentalism does not mean that His vision corresponds to a version of postmodern pluralism. Unlike the postmodernist assumption of the randomness of religion, progressive revelation assigns a clear purpose, meaning, direction, and logic to the divine revelations in relation to each other and in religious history. Religions are neither random expressions of human cultural construction, nor static and closed reflections of a chaotic, nonbinding, and random divine reality. They are not merely different and incommensurable ways of approaching or experiencing the divine. On the principle of progressive revelation, all religions are equally true and valid precisely because they are all successive expressions of one and the same divine Reality and of the same divine plan for humanity. The diverse revelations of the specific Manifestations of God are not insular or unrelated or culturally determined but inseparable, progressive, and teleological. That interrelationship and sequence of all the divine revelations becomes the very logic of the divine plan for the collective advancement of humankind. In this logic, acceptance of one Manifestation implies acceptance of all the others, and rejection of one implies rejection of all. The essential truth expressed in all the religions becomes accessible through the recognition of the most recent Manifestation of God.

And yet, even while Bahá'u'lláh asserts His message to be the fulfillment of all the scriptural prophecies for the expected universal revelation of God, the attitude Bahá'u'lláh prescribes for His own followers to take toward all people and all religious communities is one not only of respect and equality but of love, fellowship, and unity. Declaring the sacredness of all human beings in the context of universal egalitarian principles, Bahá'u'lláh eliminates any differential social status between believers and nonbelievers. Neither the categories of exclusivism and fundamentalism nor those of pluralism and postmodernism are adequate to capture the complexity and novelty of Bahá'u'lláh's message, a message which is simultaneously an announcement of the unity of all religions, a rejection of relativism, and an exposition of the spiritual foundations of universal human rights.

Part I

THE DYNAMICS OF SPIRITUAL JOURNEY

Chapter 1
MYSTICISM AND METHODOLOGY

THE FOUR VALLEYS and the Seven Valleys, together with the Qaṣí-diy-i-Ra<u>shḥ</u>-i-'Amá', revealed in the Síyáh-<u>Ch</u>ál, the Qaṣídiy-i-Var-qá'íyyih (Ode of the Dove), the Lawḥ-i-Kullu'ṭ-Ṭaʿám (Tablet of All Food), the Hidden Words, and Javáhiru'l-Asrár (Gems of Mysteries), constitute the preeminent mystical writings of Bahá'u'lláh. Like the early revelations of Muḥammad and the Báb, these early texts of Bahá'u'lláh are written in a predominantly poetic language. In this chapter I will briefly sketch the background context of the Four Valleys and the Seven Valleys in the history, concepts, and symbolism of Islamic mysticism and will discuss the problem of methodological reductionism in some approaches to Bahá'u'lláh's writings. I will argue that recent readings of His early writings which contend that they merely reiterate traditional Sufi ideas and symbols fail to discern the ways Bahá'u'lláh radically reinterprets and redefines those conventional concepts and symbols.

THE BACKGROUND OF ISLAMIC SUFISM

Among the different interpretations and approaches to the Islamic revelation, three schools of thought have been particularly influential. In the legal and literal approach to Islam, institutionalized in the corporate group of professional 'ulamá or religious jurist-scholars, the religion of God is understood primarily in terms of legal precepts and juridical commandments. This approach normally takes the literal meaning of the Word of God to be the real meaning and rejects rational speculation and mystical interpretation. The second approach to Islam, institutionalized in philosophical schools and traditions, uses a rational orientation; the real meaning behind the literal text is assumed to be captured through reason and philosophy. Finally, there is the mystical approach to Islam, which has been institutionalized in Sufi orders and rituals. This approach shares the rationalists' belief that the real meanings of the Word are obscure, while it rejects the adequacy of reason to understand those true meanings. For the Sufis it is through love and mystical intuition that the truth of the holy Qur'án and the inner core of reality can be attained.[1]

Of course this basic description represents three ideal types of Islamic discourse. Ideal types, however, as Max Weber argued, are not concrete descriptions of reality but clear and exaggerated categories which may not exist in reality in their pure forms.[2] While the history of Islamic culture has been primarily one of conflict and discord among these three approaches, it is equally true that many Muslim scholars have variously combined elements of these traditions in their cultural and spiritual practice. Similarly, alternative approaches within the three major traditions have created differential tendencies within each category. The basic form of Islamic mysticism, however, has been Sufism.

From its inception, Sufism has been the subject of many controversies, one of which concerns its relation to Islam. Some opponents of Sufism have seen it as a cultural movement intended to undermine Islam's authority and to combat Islamic culture and politics. For them, Sufism has represented a nationalistic movement against Arab domination and Muslim political expansion. They argue that Sufism employed Islamic language and symbols to effectively destroy Islamic ideology from within. Along with many secular nationalistic intellectuals, some of the leading 'ulamá have maintained that Sufism was foreign and un-Islamic.[3]

Contrary to this extremist position, the Sufis normally have defended the absolute commitment of Sufism to Islam and the holy Qur'án, arguing that Sufism is the truth and heart of Islam and the logical embodiment of Islamic principles and ideology. As we shall see, the Sufi approach to the core Islamic principle of the unity of God (tawḥíd) stands at the center of this ideological controversy. While for many opponents of Sufism the Sufi doctrine of the unity of existence (vaḥdatu'l-vujúd) categorically rejects the Qur'ánic principle of the unity of God, for the Sufis it embodies the true and real meaning of this central doctrine of Islam.

Another similar controversy concerns the origin of Sufism. According to one group of writers, Sufism is essentially a product of foreign cultures and borrowings from alien ideologies. For some of these writers, Sufism can be explained by the influence of Buddhism and Hinduism on Muslim cultures. For instance, the Buddhist temple in Balkh is suggested to be a mediating point between oriental mysticism and Islamic Iran and central Asia. According to other writers, Sufism has been largely a product of Greek and Neoplatonic influences, especially the ideas of Plotinus. According to this view, the influential Sufi tradition following Ibnu'l-'Arabí in Muslim Spain and North Africa developed out of the Neoplatonic doctrine of emanation. Still others have pointed to the influence of Christian monasticism on Islamic Sufism and have found direct borrowings from Christian monastic practices in those of Sufi orders. In defense, many Sufis have insisted on the endogenous and autonomous origin of Sufism in Islam and have traced the beginning of Sufism to the Prophet Muḥammad, the Shí'ih Imáms, and prominent early Muslim believers.[4]

Sufi doctrine distinguishes three stages of spiritual progress or three approaches to Islamic revelation. The first stage is that of the law, or sharí'ah. This stage is concerned with the literal meanings of the Qur'án and perceives Islam as a series of legal codes. The next and higher stage is that of the path, or taríqah, which is the stage of mystical learning and development. At this level the initiate follows a Sufi pír (master) and obeys him without question. Gradually the initiate learns about the inner truth of the Qur'án and develops a personal mystical intuition. Finally, there is the stage of truth, or ḥaqíqah, in which the mystic has acquired the ability to perceive the inner core of reality and to understand the esoteric meanings of divine revelation. At this stage, the realm of religious law becomes reduced to a mere instrumental or symbolic expression of the inner, mystic truth. The mystic attains some form of unity with absolute truth and becomes a Perfect Human Being (insán-i-kámil).

Perhaps the most important debate surrounding this triadic

classification centers on the necessity (or irrelevance) of observing religious laws for one who has reached the stage of higher spiritual truth. For many Sufis the realm of sharí'ah or religious law is in tension with the two mystic realms of taríqah and haqíqah. A typical allegorical illustration of the relation between them characterizes the law as a medicine that is necessary to heal the person who is ill but which becomes unnecessary once health has been restored; in fact, observing the law at this stage, it is argued, may cause a new illness. This kind of Sufi position was often expressed in the language of dissimulation out of fear of persecution for its plainly seditious implications, but nevertheless the idea is found among many Sufis and is expressed in many forms.

One important version of the same argument can be found in the frequent claim by many prominent Sufis that the station of Sufi saintliness (viláyah) is superior to the station of prophecy and apostolic legislation. Other Sufis, however, have defended the necessity of observing religious laws in spite of their own instrumental conception of the law. It has to be noted, however, that even among the defenders of observing religious law, the form that observance took was usually different from the ordinary Muslim conception. It was either an obsessively punctilious observance of laws beyond all bounds of moderation, or (for the group called Malámatíyyih) a paradoxical public disregard of the laws for the sake of humility, involving deliberate subjection of oneself to public disapproval as a check against personal vanity and pride.

An issue related to the distinction between the two realms of sharí'ah and haqíqah is the parallel distinction between the outward, literal meanings and the inner, figurative or allegorical meanings of the Qur'án in Shí'ih Islam.[5] For Shí'ih Muslims, interpretation of the Qur'ánic verses is the province of the Imáms, who alone are believed to have access to the true and authentic meanings of the Book. The question concerning the necessity or irrelevance of observing religious laws arises once again in connection with the Shí'ih expectation of the return of the Hidden Imám from occultation, although with an apparent difference of position among Ismá'ílí and Twelver Shí'ihs. For many Ismá'ílís the necessity and binding character of the literal religious laws will cease when the Hidden Imám reappears. His coming will bring access to the inner and real meanings of the Islamic revelation, whereupon there will be no further need for the literal and instrumental laws. That is why many Ismá'ílís view the Imám's return as the time of abrogation of Islamic laws and as the beginning of the age of *ibáḥih* or permission.[6] While normally *ibáḥih* is understood as the elimination of private property, its meaning is much more general, signifying that all laws lose their binding character so that everything becomes permitted. In the technical vocabulary of Islamic law, the realm of *ibáḥih* and *mubáḥ* refers to the class of actions which are religiously indifferent—neither obligatory nor prohibited, neither encouraged nor discouraged. But for the majority of S͟hí'ihs, that is, Twelver S͟hí'ihs, the appearance of the Hidden Imám does not imply the abrogation of Islamic law. Accordingly, they assume that he will maintain and uphold Islamic law.

The earliest form of Sufism can be characterized as primarily an ascetic type. Not yet institutionalized, it was represented by the scattered and personal ascetic practices of certain individuals distinguished by their piety, constant prayer, renunciation of material attachments, and strict observance of religious law. Gradually, however, Sufism became a collective and institutionalized practice characterized by diverse orders with strict membership rules and rituals; one became a Sufi by initiation into an order under the spiritual leadership of a Sufi *pír*. With the decline of Islamic central political authority and the subsequent invasion of Mongol tribes, Sufism became a relatively mass phenomenon with significant social appeal.

Among Sufi schools, the two traditions of philosophical and poetic Sufism have been particularly important. The philosophical mystic tradition developed in the Western parts of the Islamic empires under the influence of Neoplatonic doctrines. The most important and creative representative of this approach was Ibnu'l-'Arabí (d. 1246), considered to be the formulator of the thesis of the unity of existence, or *vaḥdatu'l-vujúd*. Ibnu'l-'Arabí's ideas form an important part of the philosophical, mystical, and literary background of Bahá'u'lláh's mystical writings.

The author of *The Bezels of Wisdom* (*Fuṣúṣu'l-Ḥikam*), Ibnu'l-'Arabí was also a composer of mystical poetry, but his fame lies in his philosophical statements and observations.[7] One of his distinctive characteristics is his formidable command of Arabic and his ability to play with words to derive unusual and surprising meanings from Qur'ánic verses. For instance, in *The Bezels of Wisdom*, Ibnu'l-'Arabí expatiates on the names of the holy book of Islam. In the Qur'án itself, the Book has been given a number of different titles, among which the most familiar are *Qur'án* and *Furqán*. The meaning of *Furqán* is clear. It is derived from the three-letter root *frq* (read: *faraqa*), meaning "he differentiated." *Furqán*, therefore, means the agent or the fact of differentiation. The term *Qur'án* is usually assumed to be a derivative of *qr'* (read: *qara'a*), meaning "he read." Consequently, *Qur'án* is thought to mean "reading," "recitation," or simply "the word." Ibnu'l-'Arabí, however, argues that the term *Qur'án* has a different meaning. He maintains that its root is not *qr'* but *qrn* (read: *qarana*). *Qarana*, however, means "he united or integrated." Ibnu'l-'Arabí argues that *Qur'án* means integration and unity—the exact opposite of *Furqán*, which signifies differentiation and plurality. This etymological argument becomes an exciting defense of his philosophical thesis of the unity of existence—that reality is both one and many. The inner existence or reality of being is nothing but God. At the same time, the realm of plurality and diversity is the realm of the expressions or determinations of that identical existence. These pluralities are in fact illusions which are produced by the limited perspectives of the realm of creation. For Ibnu'l-'Arabí even the name of the Qur'án itself demonstrates and epitomizes that same doctrine: the Word of God is simultaneously *Qur'án* and *Furqán* with the ultimate dominance of *Qur'án*—implying that while reality is both one and many, the true reality is unity.[8]

It should be pointed out that Ibnu'l-'Arabí's derivation of *Qur'án* from the root *qrn* seems to be mistaken. As we will see, the relation of *Qur'án* and *Furqán* is a relation between the Word of God and the Standard of Truth. *Qur'án* is the recitation and Word of God and yet it is the supreme standard (*Furqán*) of the truth of the Manifestation of

God. In other words, it is a text whose justification lies in itself. Nevertheless, Ibnu'l-'Arabí's play with these words is both ingenious and elegant. At times, however, he engages in linguistic games, disregarding the appearance of the text in order to derive from Qur'án the meanings that support his position. For example, in discussing the Qur'ánic accounts of Noah and Moses, he interprets the verses so as to conclude that Pharaoh was closer to the truth than Moses, or that the idolaters were more in accord with the Islamic doctrine of the unity of God than Noah and Abraham.[9]

Aside from any substantive consideration, the type of hermeneutics represented by Ibnu'l-'Arabí in his interpretation of such verses is usually ruled out by Bahá'u'lláh. In one of His tablets (Súratu'sh-Shams, or Tablet of the Sun), Bahá'u'lláh rejects those who emphasize the inner meaning at the expense of the outer meaning as well as those who emphasize the outer meaning at the expense of the inner meaning.[10] Ibnu'l-'Arabí's hermeneutics is clearly one in which esoteric inner meanings are frequently made to oppose the evident outer meanings.

The poetic approach to Islamic Sufism predominates in the love poetry of Persian mysticism. Among the most important representatives of this approach are Saná'í (d. 1131), Farídu'd-Dín 'Attár (d. 1221), and Jalálu'd-Dín Rúmí (d. 1273). 'Attár is particularly significant for the present discussion because Bahá'u'lláh's Seven Valleys draws on one of his mystical poems, The Conference of the Birds (Mantiqu't-Tayr), in which 'Attár delineates seven valleys or stages of spiritual journey. As we will see, Bahá'u'lláh's text is qualitatively different from 'Attár's. However, the mere fact that Bahá'u'lláh has chosen to use 'Attár's terms as vehicles of His revelation is a testimony to the beauty and the spiritual depth of 'Attár's poetry. Other works by 'Attár are also classics of the Sufi tradition. The Láhíjnámih describes his own mystical journey led by the mystic martyr Halláj (d. 923). 'Attár's Memoirs of the Saints (Tadhkiratu'l-Awlíyá') is one of the earliest and foremost examples of Sufi historiography.[11] It follows the typical modes and styles of Islamic medieval historiography in which the most important events are explained in terms of a sudden and seemingly unimportant event or statement without any sensitivity to contextual, psychological, social, or historical analysis.

The other great poet of the "mystic rose garden" is Rúmí. In both the Four Valleys and the Seven Valleys, Bahá'u'lláh frequently quotes passages from Rúmí's poetry to express His points. Rúmí's *Mathnaví* is considered a poetic encyclopedia of Islamic mysticism. Its opening lines present us with a basic conception of Sufi love metaphysics expressed in exquisite imagery:

> Listen to the reed how it tells a tale, complaining of separations—
> Saying, "Ever since I was parted from the reed-bed, my lament hath
>   caused man and woman to moan...."
> This noise of the reed is fire, it is not wind: whoso hath not this fire,
>   may he be naught!
> 'Tis the fire of Love that is in the reed, 'tis the fervour of Love that
>   is in the wine....
> Were I joined to the lip of one in accord with me, I too, like the reed,
>   would tell all that may be told....[12]

These few lines, laden with mystical insights and metaphors, depict the human being as a reed which, uprooted from its reed-bed, suffers the agony of separation from its authentic and original home of unity. But only if the reed becomes hollowed and purified from all material attachments can it become the vehicle for the expression of divine love and spiritual mysteries. This, in turn, is possible only when the reed is placed to the lips of the beloved and becomes infused with the warm, loving fire of the beloved one's breath.

The metaphor of the reed occurs frequently in the Bahá'í writings. In Bahá'u'lláh's own poetic mystical work titled Mathnaví, finished shortly after His Riḍván declaration, Bahá'u'lláh applies the same concept in a different way. He states that when from the word *I-ness* or *identity* (*maní*, written with the three letters *mní*) the letter *m* is burned out, the only thing that remains is the word *reed* (pronounced *niy*, and written with the two letters *n* and *í*).[13] The letter *m* stands for the self (the Persian word *man*—written *mn*—meaning "I"). That is, Bahá'u'lláh is saying that if the selfish and limited ego is eliminated from the identity, what remains is the hollow reed which becomes the instrument of divine inspiration and unites with the breath of the Beloved.[14]

One of the most important themes in Sufism is that of the spiritual journey. In discussing the spiritual journey of the mystic toward God, the Sufis have talked of stations (*maqámát*) and states (*hálát*). Stations are defined as the stages of the wayfarer's spiritual development. These hierarchical stages are ordered in a linear fashion. After attaining a station one can proceed to the next higher one. Stations are acquired and relatively stable; once a particular station has been reached, there will not usually be regression to a lower one. States, on the other hand, are ephemeral and fleeting experiences of divine inspiration without any linear hierarchical movement from one to another. While the concepts of stations and states are universally discussed in the Sufi tradition, there is not much consensus on the identity, number, and the proper order of these stages.

In the Seven Valleys Bahá'u'lláh delineates seven stages of spiritual development, adapting to His purposes 'Attár's seven stages. However, it should be noted that in spite of the unusual beauty of 'Attár's stages, corresponding to the Sufi stations, this classification scheme is almost universally overlooked in Sufi literature dealing with the stations of spiritual development. Instead, the list of stations given in the classic texts of Sufism is completely different. One can say that by adapting 'Attár's terminology, Bahá'u'lláh has revived interest in 'Attár's magnificent poetry of mystical stations. At the same time, as we shall see, Bahá'u'lláh significantly modifies and redefines 'Attár's categories.

While there is no consensus in Sufism on the identity and order of the stations of mystic progression, it may be useful to outline one typical scheme. According to one tradition, the mystical stations are nine. The first is repentance (*tawbah*), defined by the will's repudiation of immoral actions and tendencies. Abstinence (*vara‘*) from unworthy tendencies constitutes the second station. The third station is fear (*khawf*) of the wrath and displeasure of God. The fourth station is yearning (*rajá*), in which one longs for divine grace. The fifth is patience (*ṣabr*), defined by acceptance of suffering. Destiny (*qadar*) represents the consciousness of one's destiny that is the sixth station. The seventh is decree (*qaḍá*), when one submits to the divine decree. The eighth station is reliance (*tavakkul*), in which the mystic has complete trust in God's providence. The ninth and last station is acceptance and pleasure (*riḍá*), in which one finds absolute peace and inner pleasure in relation to life in general.[15]

Among the most important concepts of Sufism are *dhikr* and *samá'*. *Dhikr* has a variety of meanings, including remembrance, mentioning, and utterance. In Sufi practice, *dhikr* is the remembrance of God through repetitive chanting of various prayers, sacred verses, or words. Sufis are usually expected to engage in this form of prayer almost constantly. In other words, *dhikr* is a form of free prayer in addition to the Islamic obligatory prayers. However, the act of *dhikr* is accompanied by strictly defined rituals, which vary among Sufi orders and include chanting, music, and dance. Some Sufi orders practice specific techniques of *dhikr* in terms of the order of inhalation and exhalation: a segment of the verse is spoken while inhaling, and after a pause the next part is uttered in the process of exhaling. These practices were most likely influenced by oriental mysticism. One of the controversies about the practice of *dhikr* concerns whether it should be performed loudly and publicly (*jalí*) or quietly and privately (*khafí*). Sufi orders take conflicting positions on this question.

In the Bahá'í writings the concept of *dhikr* goes through a major transformation. Some have assumed that because the same term frequently occurs in Bahá'u'lláh's writings, He must therefore be endorsing the Sufi practice of *dhikr*. However, as will become evident in Chapter 3, it is a mistake to equate the term *dhikr* in Bahá'u'lláh's writings with the Sufi ritualistic notion.

The practice of *samá'* is also very significant in Sufi tradition. Although the word means hearing, it implies music, chanting, and even dance. Sufism normally has elevated music to a spiritual dimension as the vehicle of purification and perfection. The positive appreciation of music in most of the Sufi orders is one of Sufism's most important contributions to Islamic culture. Yet one of the reasons many legalistic 'ulamá strenuously opposed Sufism is this very practice of *samá'*. The problem is that many Islamic traditions (*ḥadíth*) appear to prohibit playing and listening to music. However, much ambiguity surrounds this issue. The term *ghiná'* is normally used to denote music and the human chanting voice. But Muslim schools have interpreted the prohibition on *ghiná'* in different ways. Most of the Sufis who have defended *samá'* have argued that the music and singing which are prohibited are only those that have selfish and hedonistic purposes, while singing and music performed in the remembrance of God is not included in the Islamic prohibition.

The question of *ghiná'* is the subject of an early treatise of the Báb, Risálah fi'l-Ghiná', written during His stay in Iṣfahán. At this time the Báb was intentionally ambiguous about His station because the people were not ready even to imagine the possibility of a new Manifestation of God. That would seem to explain why, in this early tablet, the Báb refrains from directly abrogating the general prohibition on *ghiná'*. At the same time, though, He also refuses to engage in the normal legalistic approach to the subject. Instead, He turns the question of *ghiná'* into an occasion to enunciate a fundamental metaphysical principle which He would go on to elaborate more fully in His later writings.

In the traditional legalistic approach, the question is whether music and singing is prohibited by Islamic law or not. In the Sufi approach, the question is what kind of music and singing are prohibited. But instead the Báb asks: What are the metaphysical and motivational bases for approving or disapproving any particular human action? Posing the question in this way, the Báb is using the categories of Shaykh Aḥmad-i-Aḥsá'í to address the general issue.[16] He asserts that if an action is oriented toward God it is acceptable, whereas if it is oriented toward the particular essence or self of the actor it is unacceptable.[17] This principle will become a very important one in the concept of spiritual journey. However, it is important to note that the Báb is making the morality of every action dependent on absolute submission to the unquestionable will of the Manifestation of God—a principle which will become the cornerstone of His later statements in the Persian Bayán. Indirectly, the Báb is turning the question of *ghiná'* into the question of obedience to the will of the Manifestation of God. His refusal to address the issue within traditional Islamic terms itself can be seen as testifying to His complete independence from the confines of traditional Islamic discourse and its problematics. In addition, we have here the essence of a fundamental moral principle that will become emphasized by Bahá'u'lláh: morality is not primarily a matter of mere legalistic codes but of purity of spirit and motive, as well as recognition of the Manifestation of God in each age.

METHODOLOGICAL ISSUES IN READING BAHÁ'U'LLÁH'S MYSTICAL WRITINGS

Before discussing the Four Valleys and the Seven Valleys in more detail, however, it is necessary to address the problem of reductionism in the study of Bahá'u'lláh's mystical writings. This issue directly concerns the nature of the relationship between Bahá'u'lláh's texts and traditional discourses including Sufism. The current reductive approach can be seen as an instance of a more general methodological tendency that has existed in some Bahá'í scholarship. The present approach, when applied to the Four Valleys or the Seven Valleys, tends to regard them as simply another Sufi text expressing a Sufi worldview. Advocates of this interpretation have also claimed to see a radical discontinuity between the early writings of Bahá'u'lláh, with their presumed heavily mystical orientation, and His later writings, which are supposedly of a more legalistic and legislative bent. Some of these readings tend to identify the "real" Bahá'í Faith with the early "mystical" stage of Bahá'u'lláh's revelation and to dismiss the more social, administrative, and legal aspects of His later writings as residual or epiphenomenal elements.

This position seems to rest on two different arguments, one of which backs up the other. The first argument emphasizes the difference of language and content between Bahá'u'lláh's early and later teachings and concludes that there is a radical change in the underlying principles: the writings of the first "mystical" stage are assumed to express Sufi doctrine and to be influenced by traditional Islamic concepts, while the writings of the later "social" stage, on the other hand, are perceived to introduce ideas, supposedly absent from the early writings, such as the oneness of humankind and support for political democracy. In an attempt to find causes to account for the supposed change in Bahá'u'lláh's teachings, various sources of influence by Western political theory and contemporary Middle Eastern reformist movements and thinkers have been proposed.[18]

The theory of a change or reversal in the content of Bahá'u'lláh's teachings depends on another argument that claims to find an absence, or even denial, of prophetic consciousness—awareness of being a Manifestation of God—in the early writings of Bahá'u'lláh. Juan Cole, for instance, has claimed that Bahá'u'lláh did not consider Himself a Manifestation of God until a short time before His declaration in the Riḍván Garden (1863). This particular chronology of Bahá'u'lláh's prophetic "consciousness" is necessary to support the readings of His early writings that find them to be typical "Sufi" discourse with meanings that can be interpreted consistently with the normal Sufi meanings.

The thesis of a reversal in Bahá'u'lláh's social and political ideas will be addressed in more detail in later chapters. Here I will only examine the cogency of the argument about the chronology of Bahá'u'lláh's prophetic consciousness, in order to demonstrate several points about contextualizing Bahá'u'lláh's writings and identifying their problematics.

Prophetic Consciousness in Bahá'u'lláh's Early Writings

It has been suggested by Cole that before the later years of the Baghdad period, Bahá'u'lláh did not consider Himself—and in fact, denied being—a Manifestation of God. This argument is based on Cole's translation and interpretation of a tablet revealed in Baghdad, Ṣaḥífiy-i-Shaṭṭíyyih (Book of the River).[19] Elsewhere I have discussed this tablet and its translation at length and will only briefly review that argument here.[20]

The Book of the River is a short but very complex tablet which responds to a question concerning the evidence for claims to prophetic truth. Bahá'u'lláh declares that the revealed words of the Prophets— not miracles—are the conclusive proof of their truth. To explain the standard by which spiritual truth can be known, Bahá'u'lláh uses the metaphor of the river. The world is the land which is flooded by the surge of this divine river:

> When its waters swell and flood, it rusheth forward and moveth turbulently. Whatever it doeth, it remaineth within its own sovereignty. However much the helpless people cry out from every side—clamoring that a great dam hath been rent asunder, or a barrier obliterated, or houses destroyed, or a palace crushed to ruins—the river payeth them no heed. With the utmost force and compulsion, power and sovereignty, it continueth to rush and flow, touching all places equally. For instance, before the onrush of its power it doth not matter whether a building belongeth to a prince or to a pauper; the effect is the same, unless that building hath unique fortifications. Thus do We create analogies for you that haply ye may be of those who are well assured....[21]

Miracles imply a change in the natural expression of divine revelation:

> Observe, furthermore, that were a mighty person to block this river and control its course by means of his authority and sovereign power, as a consequence how many homes and dwellings would be ruined and how many people would be drowned, even though, at the same time, certain dry lands which had long been suffering from lack of rain would be irrigated, obtain fresh and wondrous life, and appear arrayed in a new and fabulous garment....
>
> Similarly, ponder upon the mysteries of divine decree and destiny. Whatever hath appeared or will appear is like this river. Each thing moveth or reposeth in its proper place. But if something contrary to this natural flow of events is manifested, the order of the world becometh gravely disrupted. Couldst thou but grasp this subtle mystery, which is more hidden than any other mystery, thou wouldst find thyself independent of this and all other questions. It is for this reason that, in every age and century, as He desireth, the Unique Hidden One and the Eternal Essence manifesteth that real River and true Sea and causeth it to flow, adorning it with a new temple and a new vesture. All those structures of vain imaginings and palaces of the ungodly are then swept away and destroyed in its waters. With utmost desire and thirst they drown and perish, lacking even the faintest awareness that they could quaff a draught thereof....

This is especially true if the Eastern Winds begin to blow upon the flood of this heavenly river, which is rushing forth from the North of divine unity. How many exalted souls and possessors of true understanding, how many mighty castles and firm lofty edifices, will be destroyed and perish. By Him Who holdeth the heavens by His might and moveth the oceans by His command! Were it not for fear of the malice hidden in the hearts, I would have assuredly unveiled all the inmost divine analogies and all the subtleties of the heavenly principles with regard to the course of this outward river. Yet, alas, I am disinclined to approach any matter. On account of the intensity of My anguish and sorrow, in these days I am sore tried between the Gog of silence and the Magog of utterance....[22]

This mighty River, Bahá'u'lláh explains, is just and universalistic. It deals with all in the same way. The divines and sovereigns are not singled out for special favors. The differences in response are not a product of injustice but of the differential potentialities of the different recipients. The divine river brings out the hidden tendencies of the different beings and tests all things:

For example, with reference to the same analogy of the flooding river, observe that it floweth forward in one manner and its relationship to all buildings and structures is the same, yet any valley that hath more capacity is able to take in more of it, and any dam whose foundation is weaker is less able to resist it. These differences, therefore, have arisen from the diversity of recipients. In like manner, consider the rays of the Eternal Sun, which shine with the same illumination in the heaven of human hearts, but when reflected in the forms of mirrors, differ by reason of differences among the mirrors themselves. Thus it is that some abide exalted in their essences and high in their endeavors, while others sink into the depths of lethargy and degradation. All things have their rank before God, and all return unto Him....[23]

Bahá'u'lláh concludes the tablet by quoting the first passage of the Arabic Hidden Words:

We shall impart unto thee a single word which We have taken from the essence of the Sacred Books and Scriptures as a token of Our mercy and loving-kindness, that the water of immortality may rain from the clouds of God's unity upon thy reality and the realities of

His servants.... That word is this: "Possess a pure, kindly and radiant heart, that thine may be a sovereignty ancient, imperishable and everlasting." This is a treasure that pertaineth to Heaven.... This is a light that shall never be extinguished, a treasure that perisheth not, a raiment that shall never be outworn, and a revelation that will never be concealed. Through it many will go astray and others will be guided. Render thanks unto God that thou hast become the recipient of this All-Encompassing Word, this celestial melody, and heavenly song....[24]

Cole uses his own translation of this tablet to argue that Bahá'u'lláh did not consider Himself a Manifestation of God at the time He wrote it and that Bahá'u'lláh's "self-conception changed mightily between the early 1850s and the later 1850s."[25] The most important aspect of Cole's argument is based on his translation of the sentence "*Valákin chih gúyam kih hích iqbál bih amrí nadáram*" as "But what shall I say? I make no claim to a Cause."[26] In his commentary on the tablet Cole asserts that Bahá'u'lláh "has no 'iqbal bar amri,' is making no claim to have a divine Cause."[27]

That, however, is a serious mistranslation. What Bahá'u'lláh actually says in the passage is that because He is surrounded by spiteful and malicious hearts, He "is disinclined to approach any matter"—meaning that He has no desire to discuss the issue in detail. There is no ambiguity about it; the expression is a common polite Persian idiom indicating reluctance or disinclination to approach an issue or engage in a task. From the context it is unmistakably clear that the "issue" or "task" (*amr*) Bahá'u'lláh is disinclined to approach is nothing but the act of speech, writing, and exposition of His spiritual knowledge through the metaphor of the river. Just before this statement, in the same paragraph, Bahá'u'lláh claims that He *is* in fact able to unveil "all the inmost divine analogies and all the subtleties of the heavenly principles" solely through the metaphor of the river. It is because of the hatred and malice (which Cole mistranslates as "chains") in the hearts of the people surrounding Him that He does not wish to do so. Consequently, the passage is actually clear evidence for, not against, Bahá'u'lláh's prophetic consciousness at the time He revealed the tablet, and a powerful allusion that He is indeed speaking as the Manifestation of God. This interpretation is corroborated by statements in Bahá'u'lláh's later writings, in which He cites His ability to unveil all spiritual truth through a single metaphor as an indication of His exalted station.[28]

In many of His later writings, Bahá'u'lláh also attests that the hatred in the hearts of the people has prevented Him from revealing tablets or unveiling all spiritual truth. He frequently uses a similar expression to express His disinclination to discuss certain matters: in one of His later tablets, for instance, He remarks that He has discussed the techniques of the alchemical "elixir" only because of the believers' frequent requests, but that "otherwise the Most Exalted Pen has had and continues to have no desire to mention these issues" (*Vaillá Qalam-i-A'lá ... iqbál bih dhikr-i-ín umúr nadáshtih va nadárad*).[29] Here, as in the Book of the River, both the words *iqbál* and *umúr* (plural of *amr*) occur. But if we were to translate the expression in the later tablet in the same way that Cole translates it in the Book of the River, it would give us the self-contradiction: "otherwise the Most Exalted Pen makes no claim to utter these divine Causes." There is no doubt that the later tablet was revealed years after Bahá'u'lláh had publicly declared His station.[30]

The concealed stage of Bahá'u'lláh's revelation had begun in 1852 in the Síyáh-Chál in Tehran. It was not until 1863 that Bahá'u'lláh began to reveal His station to an increasing number of people in any public way. He Himself has testified that His writings during the Baghdad period represented a concealed revelation, like the shining of the sun from behind the clouds.[31] Similarly, in one of His tablets He states that "after the consummation of the year nine," God shone upon all beings through the name Bahá, and that the revelation of God at that time was "manifest and concealed" (*ghayban mashhúdan va záhiran mastúran*), until the time of "respite" was completed, when He revealed what had been veiled.[32] The early stage of His revelation, then, was one of preparing the people for the Most Great Announcement. That very fact implies that His early writings should not be expected to make that announcement in any explicit way.

And yet we can find in the early writings of Bahá'u'lláh unmis-

takable indications of the divine nature of His mission. Also, in the
Baghdad period He had already abrogated some of the laws of the Bábí
dispensation (related to the sword)—a clear indication of His effective
symbolic claim, at that stage, to be the Promised One of the Bayán—
for only the Promised One could annul the former law. And, finally,
there is Bahá'u'lláh's own testimony in His later writings about His
revelation in the Síyáh-Chál and His concealed declaration in the early
Baghdad period.

As Shoghi Effendi has written in *God Passes By*, Bahá'u'lláh's
descriptions of His Síyáh-Chál revelation, in both the tablet to Náṣi-
ri'd-Dín Sháh and the Súratu'l-Haykal, leave no room for doubt as to
His self-conception during this time. In the tablet to the shah,
Bahá'u'lláh writes: "O King! I was but a man like others, asleep upon
My couch, when lo, the breezes of the All-Glorious were wafted over
Me, and taught Me the knowledge of all that hath been. This thing is
not from Me, but from One Who is Almighty and All-Knowing. And
He bade me lift up My voice between earth and heaven, and for this
there befell Me what hath caused the tears of every man of under-
standing to flow" (*Epistle* 39).

One would assume this account to be sufficient in itself, but Cole
has argued that here Bahá'u'lláh is only reporting a spiritual experience
which called Him to reform the Bábí community. It is curious that
such an explicit statement should be considered ambiguous. In it
Bahá'u'lláh speaks of the "breezes of the All-Glorious"—an unmistakable mystical symbol of revelation—and describes His experience
as the instantaneous knowledge of "all that hath been"! Similarly, the
statement in the Súratu'l-Haykal dealing with the same experience
settles the issue.[33] But Cole finds that his reading of Bahá'u'lláh's Book
of the River

> raises the most acute questions about the nature of the 'intimation'
> Baha'u'llah is said to have experienced in the Siyah Chal. If one reads
> the account in Epistle to the Son of the Wolf carefully, it appears that
> it consisted more of ilham or inspiration than of wahy or revelation,
> and that Baha'u'llah began thinking of islah or reform of Babism
> rather than of making any claim of his own.[34]

But in fact Bahá'u'lláh does use the term *wahy* (*vaḥy*) or *revelation*, and not *ilham*, to describe His Síyáh-Chál experience. In a different tablet, giving the same account of the same experience, Bahá'u'lláh remarks that this has already been mentioned in the tablets to the kings—obviously He means the same account of what happened in the Síyáh-Chál. In this tablet, however, He says:

> By God! Verily I was asleep, when lo! the breezes of Revelation [*vaḥy*] bestirred Me. I was silent, and thy Lord, the Almighty, the All-Powerful, caused Me to speak forth. Were it not for His behest I would not have revealed Myself. Verily His Will prevailed over My will and raised Me up to establish a Cause which hath made Me the target of the darts of the infidels. Read what We have revealed to the kings that thou mayest be assured that this Servant speaketh as bidden by the All-Knowing, the All-Informed.[35]

Bahá'u'lláh uses the same concept and the same wording in various writings, including the Kitáb-i-Badí', which was written at the end of the Edirne period—the same period as the revelation of the tablet to the shah of Iran—to discuss His station as the Manifestation of God and the Promised One of the Bayán. These statements clearly show that the description of the experience in the Síyáh-Chál as found in the tablet to the shah unequivocally refers to the inception of Bahá'u'lláh's new revelation.[36] Although it was in the Síyáh-Chál that the Bahá'í revelation was born, even this, as we will see in Chapter 9, was not the first instance in which Bahá'u'lláh experienced some form of mystical communion related to His future mission.[37]

Even Bahá'u'lláh's statements about His resolve, while in the Síyáh-Chál, to "reform" the Bábí community, rather than indicating an implicit continuation of the Bábí dispensation under the law of the Bayán, actually attest to the abrogation of the Bayán and the emergence of a new dispensation of revelation. Describing His experience in the Síyáh-Chál, Bahá'u'lláh writes: "One night in a dream these exalted words were heard on every side: 'Verily, We shall render Thee victorious by Thyself and by Thy pen.'"[38] This statement is extremely important. The divine promise to render Him victorious through His own "self" and through His "pen" is a reference to the fact that the

sole evidence and proof of the Manifestation is His being and His verses. But it also implies the principle of the removal of the sword, which
would be announced by Bahá'u'lláh on the first day of His public
Riḍván declaration, signifying the beginning of a new Era and the
effective abrogation of specific laws of the Qur'án and Bayán.³⁹ We
will return to explore the significance of this idea, as a summary of
Bahá'u'lláh's entire future message. But it is evident that in His statement Bahá'u'lláh is implicitly affirming His station as the new Manifestation of God.

It is interesting that in one of His tablets Bahá'u'lláh extensively
discusses the fact, cited as a secondary argument for His divine revelation, that both Qurratu'l-'Ayn (Ṭáhirih) and Ḥájí Muḥammad-
'Alíy-i-Bárfurúshí (Quddús)—who died in 1852 and 1849, respectively—had recognized His station and His "New Cause" (Amr-i-
Badí'). This is by itself a sufficient indication of Bahá'u'lláh's own consciousness of His station even prior to 1852.⁴⁰ Elsewhere, Bahá'u'lláh
refers to the revelation of a tablet which He sent to the Báb. He
describes the Báb's subsequent longing to attain His presence and the
fact that Bahá'u'lláh hid the truth of His Cause from the people for the
sake of protecting the Báb.⁴¹

In addition to those tablets, Bahá'u'lláh often wrote that He revealed Himself as the Promised One of the Bayán in the year nine and
disclosed His station to a few individuals in the early Baghdad years. In
a tablet to Kamálu'd-Dín Naráqí (the recipient of the Tablet of All
Food), Bahá'u'lláh says that Kamál has attained two great bounties.
The first of these was to be blessed by the encounter with God "in the
year nine" as the Báb had promised in saying, "In the year nine ye shall
attain unto the presence of God." The second bounty was to have
received the divine Word in the Qur'ánic verse concerning "All
Food," which is the "good" promised by the Báb in His assertion, "In
the year nine ye shall attain unto all good."⁴²

Similarly, in His tablet on the Báb's Tablet of Nineteen Temples
(Hayákil-i-Váḥid), Bahá'u'lláh writes:

> Verily, by "nineteen" He [the Báb] intended naught but this preem-
> inent and most exalted Revelation. But the promise made unto you

in the Book concerning "nine," through His assertion "in the year nine ye shall attain unto all good" was fulfilled in that year when the dawning of God's Manifestation was divulged according to a preordained measure. By "nineteen" He meant those appointed years of delay as set forth in the Bayán. At the end of that period the promise was fulfilled, the Promised One appeared unto all creation in His all-embracing sovereignty.[43]

Note that in this passage Bahá'u'lláh mentions His concealed revelation in the year nine as well as the stage of preparation between the years nine and nineteen, followed by the complete unveiling of His station.

Finally, in Epistle to the Son of the Wolf, Bahá'u'lláh writes:

> O Shaykh! ... recite thou these sublime words that have been revealed by My Forerunner—the Primal Point.... "This, verily, is the thing We promised thee, ere the moment We answered thy call. Wait thou until nine will have elapsed from the time of the Bayán. Then exclaim: 'Blessed, therefore, be God, the most excellent of Makers!' Say: This, verily, is an Announcement which none except God hath comprehended. Ye, however, will be unaware on that day." In the year nine this Most Great Revelation arose and shone forth brightly above the horizon of the Will of God. None can deny it save he who is heedless and doubteth. (*Epistle* 142)

As will be explicated further in Chapter 6, in the Kitáb-i-Badí' Bahá'u'lláh discusses the argument put forth by Azal's followers, according to which the Promised One of the Bayán would not appear before the completion and perfection of the dispensation of the Bayán. Bahá'u'lláh affirms that, in fact, according to the Báb's prophecies, that completion would take place in nine years, and this was exactly fulfilled by His own revelation.[44]

In at least two tablets, Bahá'u'lláh demonstrates the fulfillment of Qur'ánic prophecies in His revelation by referring to the verse "Ye shall know of His Announcement after Hín," (*ba'da Hín*), which had been cited by Shaykh Ahmad-i-Ahsá'í, Siyyid Kázim-i-Rashtí, and the Báb in regard to the Promised One. He explains that numerically Hín is sixty-eight, and after sixty-eight is sixty-nine—namely, nine years after the Báb's declaration in 1260 A.H. (1844).[45] That is why, He says, the Báb has spoken of attaining "all good" and the "presence of God" in the year nine.[46]

In a tablet revealed in 1863/64, Bahá'u'lláh describes in detail His revelation in the name of the Báb in 1844 (twenty years before the tablet), the Báb's prophecy of His return in the form of the Promised One in the year nine, and Bahá'u'lláh's own concealment during the Baghdad period until His declaration in the Riḍván Garden. He says that God has sent His Messengers to the people of the world solely for the sake of "this luminous, radiant, and manifest Beauty" who appeared twenty years ago. Although His revelation was the Day of Resurrection, no one recognized Him; hence in many of His Books He gave the promise of His encounter in the year nine. When God fulfilled that promise and revealed His hidden Beauty in the year nine, instead of recognition, swords were drawn against Him "by those who are known by His name." Bahá'u'lláh goes on to tell of the people turning away from Him and His retreat to the wilderness for two years, His return from concealment, and His revelation to them of glimmerings of His Beauty from behind the veils in order to prepare them for the encounter with Him. He says that sometimes He revealed His beauty transparently, while at other times He concealed and veiled Himself "behind seventy million veils" until the time was come and the other promise appeared in the "second nine," and the divine promise of the "year eighty" was consummated. At this time, He says, the irrevocable will of God was to reveal Himself even if no one believed in Him. But when He appeared from behind the veils and revealed the lights of His Countenance even to the extent of less than the tip of a hair, all fainted away and returned to nothingness.[47]

Finally, the early writings of Bahá'u'lláh themselves display clear indications of His own conception of the nature of His mission at that time. Here as well the evidence is overwhelming. For instance, the preface to the Arabic Hidden Words declares:

> This is that which hath descended from the realm of glory, uttered by the tongue of power and might, and revealed unto the Prophets of old. We have taken the inner essence thereof and clothed it in the garment of brevity, as a token of grace unto the righ-

teous, that they may stand faithful unto the Covenant of God, may fulfill in their lives His trust, and in the realm of spirit obtain the gem of divine virtue.

Here Bahá'u'lláh characterizes His text as the "inner essence" of all the divine truth revealed in all the former dispensations. No one could make such a claim except one who is himself a Manifestation of God. And, in fact, the style and tone of language used in the Hidden Words is that of the direct revelation of the Word of God. The same style and tone is evident in other early writings of Bahá'u'lláh including His Rashh-i-'Amá',[48] Tablet of All Food, and Ode of the Dove.

Another unmistakable allusion to Bahá'u'lláh's station as the Promised One of the Bayán can be found in the only statement of the Hidden Words which is quoted in the Kitáb-i-Íqán: "O Son of Man! Many a day hath passed over thee whilst thou hast busied thyself with thy fancies and idle imaginings. How long art thou to slumber on thy bed? Lift up thine head from slumber, for the Sun hath risen to the zenith; haply it may shine upon thee with the light of beauty" (Arabic Hidden Words 62). As will become clarified in Chapter 4 in discussing the Kitáb-i-Íqán, that reference to the rising of the Sun to its *zenith* is an allusion to Bahá'u'lláh's station and to His fulfillment of the Báb's prophecies that describe the advent of the Promised One in those same terms.

In the Seven Valleys, Bahá'u'lláh clearly makes a claim to divine and inspired knowledge in the same way that Muḥammad and the Báb did so. Later Bahá'u'lláh would Himself cite that as evidence of Their station as Manifestations of God. In the Seven Valleys we read: "There is many an utterance of the mystic seers and doctors of former times which I have not mentioned here, since I mislike the copious citation from sayings of the past; for quotation from the words of others proveth acquired learning, *not the divine bestowal.* Even so much as We have quoted here is out of deference to the wont of men and after the manner of the friends" (26; italics added).

A further statement in the Four Valleys discloses Bahá'u'lláh's station implicitly. "Methinks at this moment," Bahá'u'lláh writes, "I catch the fragrance of His garment [literally, "the garment of the letter

Há'"] blowing from the Egypt of Bahá [literally, "the Joseph of
Bahá"]; verily He seemeth near at hand, though men may think Him
far away" (59). This appears to refer to the Báb's very similar statement
in the Kitábu'l-Asmá', in which the Báb calls Himself the herald of the
Joseph of Bahá, who offers the garment of Bahá to the lovers of that
Joseph.[49] Bahá'u'lláh, on the other hand (whose own name is Bahá
and, like Joseph, is envied by his ambitious brother) declares the *near-
ness* of the "Joseph of Bahá" while others "may think him far." In these
and so many other instances in His early writings, Bahá'u'lláh's consciousness of His own station as the Manifestation of God is unmistakable.

The New Logic of Bahá'u'lláh's Early Writings

I will argue that, although there is indeed a difference of language as
well as emphasis between the early and later stages of Bahá'u'lláh's
writings, there is neither a formal nor a substantive break between the
message He taught in those periods. On the contrary, all the major elements of the worldview reflected in the later, "social" writings,
including the Kitáb-i-Aqdas, are already present in His early mystical
writings. As we will see, even the order of some of the early writings
clearly expresses an organic unity between His early mystical teachings
and His later social teachings. If that is indeed true, it implies that the
mystical writings of Bahá'u'lláh are qualitatively different from traditional Sufi discourse. In fact, they will be shown to create a new set of
conceptual problematics in spiritual orientation.

Furthermore, even a glance at the early mystical writings themselves, such as the Four Valleys and the Seven Valleys, clearly shows
that it is precisely the reduction of spiritual truth to a merely mystical
approach, and the attempt to find opposition and contradiction between the realms of reason, law, and mystic love, which are the chief
targets of Bahá'u'lláh's condemnation in His early mystical works. In
other words, Bahá'u'lláh's own early writings themselves refute the
premises behind modern reductive readings of those writings. Indeed,
Bahá'u'lláh was explicitly critical of the Sufis, characterizing their mystical treatises as an idle waste of time: "Shouldst thou behold the mystic

knowledge of the mystics, thou wilt know that, by My Life, all rove distraught in the wilderness of vain imaginations and are drowned in the sea of idle fancies. Should any one, for example, study geometry in this day, such a pursuit is exalted in the sight of God above memorizing all the books written by the mystics inasmuch as the former yieldeth fruit, but the latter doth not"[50]—and their extreme ecstatic practices as fraudulent pretensions:

> Would that those who lay claim to passionate devotion, mystic rapture, ecstasy, attraction, and the like would travel to the Abode of Peace [Baghdad] and visit the Qádiríyyih lodge that haply they might become aware of the truth. O 'Alí! A number of men reside and gather in that place. By My Soul! We observed one of them who threw down his backsides on rock and gravel and against the walls for more than a quarter of an hour, in such a manner that it provoked the fear that he might die. Then he fell in a faint on the ground, remaining unconscious for two hours. And yet they regard these acts as noble and miraculous! God, verily, is clear of them.... Likewise there is a group of people who are called Rifá'í. They, according to their words, step into the fire and strike each other with the sword in moments of rapture, in such wise as to cause the beholder to assume that they have dismembered their bodies. All these are naught but tricks, fraud, and deception devised by them. They are truly in grievous loss.[51]

The methodological approach that I critique here is not without its own history and context. The current approach to the early writings of Bahá'u'lláh is part of a more general persistent methodological tendency in the study of the Bahá'í Faith. The current form tends to define Bahá'í Studies as a subcategory of Middle Eastern or Islamic Studies. In this approach, determining the context of a text involves looking at the topics discussed or terminology used in the particular Bahá'í text and then going back to the traditional or prevalent Middle Eastern and Islamic discourse of the time to locate the "normal" meaning of those terms, concepts, or symbols. Then one comes back and imposes those same meanings on the Bahá'í texts, assuming that one has thereby identified what the texts mean—and has excluded what they could not mean. Not surprisingly, readers employing this method tend to find in Bahá'u'lláh's mystical writings exactly what they come expecting to find there—the ordinary Sufi discourse of a typical Sufi writer.

The advocates of the current academic "Middle Eastern Studies" approach consider themselves the exponents of an objective, scientific perspective on Bahá'í Studies which is opposed to "traditional" Bahá'í Studies. But the logic of this "new" approach is in some ways very similar to the traditional approach that characterized some earlier Iranian Bahá'í scholarship, and it shares a fundamental premise in common. The traditional approach was dominated by Iranian, Islamic, and Middle Eastern cultural perspectives and perceived the Bahá'í Faith through the questions and categories of Islamic discourse. This was, of course, understandable—after all, the Bahá'í Faith emerged in Iran, a Middle Eastern environment where it was inevitable that early understandings of the Bahá'í Faith would be mediated by Islamic and Middle Eastern categories and would not pay attention to the complexity and universality of Bahá'u'lláh's revelation. Additionally, the Faith of Bahá'u'lláh was under constant assault by Muslim leaders, an attack carried out in terms of traditional Islamic textual problematics. For that reason, issues such as the textual proofs of Qur'ánic prophecies, the Shí'ih conceptions of the hidden Twelfth Imám, or the refutation of specific Muslim objections to the writings of the Báb or Bahá'u'lláh became the central priorities and topics that preoccupied and defined Bahá'í scholarship. The price of this historical necessity was at times a limitation and narrowing of Bahá'í scholarship to those types of issues.

The irony is that the current professional academic approach of some writers to Bahá'í Studies is in some ways a continuation of that same limiting premise that looks no farther than the immediate Middle Eastern context to locate the problematics of the Bahá'í texts. Instead, in this more complex but in some ways even more restricted approach, the revelation and message of Bahá'u'lláh is read off in terms of such "causes" as social and cultural conditions of the Middle East, and Bahá'u'lláh's discourse is understood in terms of traditional Islamic and Middle Eastern textual logic.

In contrast, it is the argument of this book that the writings of Bahá'u'lláh represent a conceptual break with those traditional assumptions. Bahá'u'lláh's vision, in other words, initiates a new paradigm, a new model, a new logic of discourse, a new episteme, and a new problematic—to use the terms used in various social theories and philosophies—in approaching reality.

It has become well recognized by now that we cannot understand the meaning of a word or sentence independent from the underlying totality, paradigm, and worldview of the text.[52] Certainly, understanding the historical context, including Islamic and Middle Eastern cultural categories, is essential in understanding the Bahá'í texts. But the historical context and traditional discourse with which Bahá'u'lláh engages in His writings is not *the* context of the text; it is only an aspect of that context, and not even the definitive one. If one insists on reading off the meaning of the terms and symbols in the Bahá'í writings by reference to the traditional Islamic and Middle Eastern discourses, one will distort the complexity of Bahá'u'lláh's discourse, miss its subtlety, and systematically overlook the new meanings it deliberately creates.

The problem of reductive approaches to historical texts has attracted attention in recent decades within various academic fields, including philosophy, history, and literature. As LaCapra writes:

> The attempt to return a thinker to his own times or to place his texts squarely in the past has often served as a mode of abstract categorization that drastically oversimplifies the problem of historical understanding. Indeed, the rhetoric of contextualization has often encouraged narrowly documentary readings in which the text becomes little more than a sign of the time or a straightforward expression of one larger phenomenon or another.[53]

We should not forget that the context is itself not an empirical given but a text which must be constructed by the historian. And, as he points out, "The assertion that a specific context or subset of contexts is especially significant in a given case has to be argued and not simply assumed or surreptitiously built into an explanatory model or framework of analysis."[54]

LaCapra calls attention to the crucial difference between the "documentary" aspect of a text—in other words, the "factual or literal dimensions involving reference to empirical reality and conveying information about it"—and the text's "worklike" aspects, which involve

> dimensions of the text not reducible to the documentary, prominently including the roles of commitment, interpretation, and imagination. The worklike is critical and transformative, for it deconstructs and reconstructs the given, in a sense repeating it but also bringing into the world something that did not exist before in that significant variation, alteration, or transformation. With deceptive simplicity, one might say that while the documentary marks a difference, the worklike makes a difference—one that engages the reader in recreative dialogue with the text and the problems it raises.[55]

LaCapra also reminds us that "a fact is a pertinent fact only with respect to a frame of reference involving questions that we pose to the past, and it is the ability to pose the 'right' questions that distinguishes productive scholarship."[56] Posing the wrong questions arises as a consequence of imposing on the text a frame of reference, categories, and problematics that are alien to its own discourse.

But if the reduction of ordinary texts leads to oversimplified readings of them, reduction or "asking the wrong questions" of the revealed Text leads to far greater distortions. The words of Prophets, above all others, elude and transcend the ordinary and normal; they overturn the status quo, defying conventions and reversing and refashioning normal meanings into new, visionary, and creative ones. Divine revelation is not devoid of social and historical reference. According to Bahá'u'lláh, because revelation is the fundamental means of the advancement of humanity, it must be oriented to the conditions of space and time. Sacred Text and historical context, therefore, interact with one other. However, this sense of interaction and accordance with the conditions of the time is not the same as a simple accordance with the immediate context of revelation or the ideas and ideologies current at the time. In fact, the historical context that defines the mode of revelation is usually the exact opposite of those ideologies to the extent that they conflict with the structural requirements and needs defined by the emerging stage of the evolution of civilization.

But here the methodology of reading is itself strongly determined by subjective beliefs. Whether one believes that the meaning of the Sacred Text can or cannot be reduced to its immediate historical context is partly dependent on one's metaphysical conception of the nature of the Sacred Text. If the text is considered to be divinely revealed, that is, inspired by a higher, superhuman source, its meanings will be regarded as irreducible to existing worldviews and human ideologies. It will be regarded not as the reflection of intellectual movements and civilizations, but as the source that inspires them. If, on the other hand, one excludes revelation as a category of reality, the methodology demands that some empirical cause or explanation must be found to explain the origin of ideas. In other words, by privileging certain contexts and ignoring others, the materialist presupposition in the methodology has surreptitiously built into the framework of analysis both the possible "questions" and the acceptable "answers."

CATEGORIES OF BAHÁ'U'LLÁH'S WORLDVIEW

What then are the categories of Bahá'u'lláh's teachings? It will be argued in this book that the novel paradigm of His message is distinguished by the unity and organic synthesis of at least three fundamental principles—spiritual transcendence, historical consciousness, and global unity. The first principle emphasizes the fundamentally spiritual nature of life in which all reality and human values are defined in relation to the totality of being and the transcendent divine Reality. This spiritual orientation is not simply an individualistic ethical process but also a collective one, an active covenant and dialogue between God and His creation. In this approach, spiritual values and divine revelation are the necessary means of achieving social and cultural well-being and progress.

The emphasis on the fundamentally spiritual and transcendent character of life clearly differentiates the worldview of Bahá'u'lláh's teachings from any materialistic framework. But at the same time His worldview is entirely different from any existing form of religious traditionalism. This becomes obvious when we pay attention to Bahá'u'lláh's historical consciousness, in which the spiritual dimension is inherently linked to the historical dimension of human social life. Bahá'u'lláh emphasizes a dynamic and progressive approach to both material culture and divine revelation, a concept of progress which goes beyond the Enlightenment's static notion and creates a dynamic social theory. To put it in sociological terms, the unity of the two concepts of transcendence and history implies the unity and harmony of a dynamic instrumental and practical/moral rationalization process.[57]

Another fundamental category of Bahá'u'lláh's worldview is that of universal human unity. According to this perspective, the conditions of the present sociohistorical stage of human cultural and spiritual development require the adoption of a global and universal orientation to address the social, political, cultural, economic, moral, and spiritual problems facing humanity. At the center of this orientation is the principle of the oneness of humankind, the pivot and the ultimate aim of Bahá'u'lláh's vision and His dispensation. To understand Bahá'u'lláh's discourse in its own terms and within its own context, one must keep in mind those three premises which constitute its foundations as a conceptual and moral system.

It should also be noted that this same complex set of premises is literally identical with the principles of Bahá'í theology. The fundamental theological principle of the Bahá'í Faith is the concept of manifestation and revelation. This same concept reflects itself in three forms of unity in diversity: the revelation of the absolute unity of God in divers historical Manifestations of God, the underlying unity of those historically changing Manifestations of God and the religions They have founded (as dispensations of one eternal progressively revealed religion of God), and the underlying sacred oneness of the human station in all its physical and cultural differentiation. Here as well, those three principles of divine transcendence and revelation, historical dynamics, and the oneness of humankind are harmonized.

From what has been said, it should be clear that Bahá'u'lláh's writings cannot be adequately understood in terms of worldviews which are fundamentally lacking this majestic problematic. But taking this approach to the writings of Bahá'u'lláh, it can be seen that the historical order of those writings corresponds precisely with the three constitutive parts of His vision and also with the structure of His theology. In Bahá'u'lláh's early writings, exemplified by the Four Valleys and the Seven Valleys, the emphasis is placed on metaphysical and ethical foundations, the spiritual purpose of life, and the mystic or spiritual journey. In the second stage of His writings, exemplified by the Kitáb-i-Íqán, historical consciousness and the principle of progressive revelation are dominant elements. Finally, in the last stage of His writings, the emphasis is put on the social teachings, centering on the principle of the oneness of humankind and its comprehensive global perspective. The revelation, in the Kitáb-i-Aqdas, of laws related to individual life and social institutions belongs to this final stage as well.

And yet, even in the very early mystical writings of the first stage, the totality of this worldview, with each of those elements, is present. In other words, both the principles of historical consciousness and of the oneness of humankind can be found in Bahá'u'lláh's early mystical works, a fact that confounds the attempt to reduce those early writings to mere traditional Sufi discourse. The logic and content of Bahá'u'lláh's Hidden Words provides a definitive example.

The Hidden Words display a logic of ideas which links and affirms the three principles of spiritual journey, historical dynamics, and the oneness of humankind. The Persian Hidden Words begin with the description of the true and authentic habitation of the human soul:

> O YE PEOPLE THAT HAVE MINDS TO KNOW AND EARS TO HEAR!
> The first call of the Beloved is this: O mystic nightingale! Abide not but in the rose garden of the spirit. O messenger of the Solomon of love! Seek thou no shelter except in the Sheba of the well-beloved, and O immortal phoenix! dwell not save on the mount of faithfulness. Therein is thy habitation, if on the wings of thy soul thou soarest to the realm of the infinite and seekest to attain thy goal. (1)

After this mystical, metaphorical beginning, Bahá'u'lláh discourses about various aspects of the soul's journey. But then the text ends with a surprising set of statements, a sequence of pronouncements that emphasize involvement in the concrete world of social relations and

the obligatory character of productive work, economic independence, and rationality:

O MY SERVANTS!
    Ye are the trees of My garden; ye must give forth goodly and
wondrous fruits, that ye yourselves and others may profit therefrom.
Thus it is incumbent on every one to engage in crafts and professions, for therein lies the secret of wealth, O men of understanding!
For results depend upon means, and the grace of God shall be all-
sufficient unto you. Trees that yield no fruit have been and will ever
be for the fire. (80)

He emphasizes this point again: "The basest of men are they that yield
no fruit on earth. Such men are verily counted as among the dead, nay
better are the dead in the sight of God than those idle and worthless
souls" (81).

    Bahá'u'lláh's words here have nothing in common with typical
Sufi discourse—the Sufis have normally either rejected material and
economic involvement in favor of wandering and begging, or accepted work only as an empirical necessity. Yet here Bahá'u'lláh condemns
idleness and dependence and says that an able but unproductive person
is not worthy of life. Bahá'u'lláh has begun His text with a metaphysical conception of the human situation and ends it by translating the
spiritual journey into the dynamics of a socially oriented, responsible,
and moral life. That this commandment is in fact a direct refutation of
some Sufi practices is obvious from a later similar statement in Kalimát-i-Firdawsíyyih (Words of Paradise). There He unequivocally
characterizes what some Sufis deem to be "insight and knowledge" as
"manifest blindness and ignorance." Referring to those "mystics who
bear allegiance to the Faith of Islam" and whose practices lead "to idleness and seclusion," He says: "I swear by God! It lowereth man's station and maketh him swell with pride. Man must bring forth fruit.
One who yieldeth no fruit is, in the words of the Spirit [Jesus], like
unto a fruitless tree, and a fruitless tree is fit but for the fire" (*Tablets*
60). The last statement in the Persian Hidden Words again emphasizes the moral principle of work: "O My Servant! The best of men
are they that earn a livelihood by their calling and spend upon them-

selves and upon their kindred for the love of God, the Lord of all worlds" (82).

A similar logic can be observed in the Arabic Hidden Words. They begin with the preconditions of the spiritual journey, namely purity of heart, immediately followed by a call for justice and fairness as the prime condition for discovering spiritual truth. After describing an ocean of spiritual insights on the path of spiritual progress, toward the end of the Arabic Hidden Words Bahá'u'lláh affirms the principle of the oneness of humanity. As in the Persian Hidden Words, once again the path on the journey to the metaphysical goal leads through the landscape of social relationships and concrete moral actions in the world. And once again, the standard is the principle of human unity:

> O CHILDREN OF MEN!
> Know ye not why We created you all from the same dust? That no one should exalt himself over the other. Ponder at all times in your hearts how ye were created. Since we have created you all from one same substance it is incumbent on you to be even as one soul, to walk with the same feet, eat with the same mouth and dwell in the same land, that from your inmost being, by your deeds and actions, the signs of oneness and the essence of detachment may be made manifest. Such is My counsel to you, O concourse of light! Heed ye this counsel that ye may obtain the fruit of holiness from the tree of wondrous glory. (Arabic Hidden Words 68)

From this brief discussion it should be clear that the underlying principles of the early mystical writings and the later social texts of Bahá'u'lláh are very similar. And in both the Kitáb-i-Aqdas and the Hidden Words there is a consistent logical relationship between mystic love and the observance of laws. In the Kitáb-i-Aqdas Bahá'u'lláh says: "Observe My commandments, for the love of My beauty" (¶ 4), while in the Arabic Hidden Words He had written: "O SON OF MAN! Neglect not My commandments if thou lovest my beauty, and forget not My counsels if thou wouldst attain My good pleasure" (39). The logic and terminology remain exactly the same.

Contrary to the dominant attitude in Sufism, which took mystic love as the stage of truth and as superior to the realm of law, Bahá'u'-

lláh makes the observance of laws dependent on, and the sign of, the attainment of that spiritual love. Love remains the core and motive of individual and social action, while legal codes and institutional and administrative structures are indispensable moments of spiritual truth. Both the early and later writings of Bahá'u'lláh strongly resist reduction either to a mere affirmation of mystic love or a mere code of individual and institutional regulations. On the contrary, it is the unity and inseparability of both which is emphasized.

In fact, the early mystical writings of Bahá'u'lláh explicitly address the issue of the relation between the mystical and the social/legal orientations, which are usually represented in Sufism as conflicting and mutually exclusive. As we will see, it is precisely the message of the Four Valleys that moral/legal, rational, and mystical ways are all valid roads to understanding reality and that, in their perfection, they all reach the same goal. At the same time, while there are differences among these approaches, the most perfect way is neither the legal, nor the rational, nor the mystical way of approaching the truth but the unity and synthesis of them all. The text of the Four Valleys itself contradicts the reading of the early writings of Bahá'u'lláh which finds a radical opposition between His mystical and social teachings.

Furthermore, the logic of the Four Valleys and that of the Kitáb-i-Aqdas show perfect continuity. The beginning of the Kitáb-i-Aqdas is, indeed, a summary of Bahá'í theology and political philosophy. However, we should note that the three principles of knowledge, action, and love take a central place in the conceptual structure of the Kitáb-i-Aqdas. The first duty of human beings is the recognition of the Manifestation of God in each age. But then this knowledge requires both obedience to the commandments of the Manifestation and the will to action. And, once again, the underlying reason for this action should be the love of the Eternal Beauty. The Kitáb-i-Aqdas, in other words, unites the approaches of mind, will, and feeling in a holistic framework in which the logic of knowledge, action, and love are harmonized and integrated—in a way which perfectly corresponds to the central thesis of the Four Valleys.

Finally, it is important to note what Bahá'u'lláh Himself has said

about the relationship of His own discourse to the preexisting traditional discourses. In all the stages of His revelation, Bahá'u'lláh shows
a clear aversion to the interpretation of traditional ideas and the discussion of theological debates. While He does sometimes discuss past
categories in His early writings, He expresses His disinclination for
such subjects, finds them even tiresome, and yet when He does talk
about them, He always endows them with novel and creative meanings.[58] He always notes, particularly in the Kitáb-i-Íqán and Kitáb-i-
Badí', that it is only for the sake of love for the people that He descends
to the discussion of such things. In fact He dislikes the confinement of
His all-embracing, universal, and creative message to the former
debates and controversies that defined Middle Eastern religious and
Sufi discourse. In many of His later writings, however, He simply
refuses to engage in such discussion at all. As will become evident in
the discussion of the Kitáb-i-Íqán, it is in fact only by detachment
from presuppositions, traditional standards, and arbitrary constructs
that the right questions can be asked.

Chapter 2

THE ONTOLOGICAL CIRCLE

THE DIVINE DESIGN OF CREATION can be described schematically as an *arc of descent* and a corresponding *arc of ascent*. The arc of descent comprises the stages of creation, while the arc of ascent delineates the path of return to God. Together these arcs form a "circle" which encompasses all the levels of being and existence. This concept, which may be termed the *ontological circle*, is central to Bahá'u'lláh's mystical discourse. Variations on the ideas of an arc of ascent and descent appear in mystical and philosophical traditions including Neoplatonism, Islamic philosophical traditions, and Sufism. In the writings of Plotinus, for example, the arc of descent consists of four stages of emanation or creation: (1) Absolute One, (2) Intellect, (3) Soul, and (4) Matter. Human beings are located at the end of the fourth stage, Matter, but they potentially contain within themselves all the levels of existence. Through mystical contemplation, the soul is said to be able to ascend to the stage of the Absolute One.[1] This simple and beautiful scheme is further developed in Islamic philosophical and mystical traditions. The Islamic philosophical tradition complicated it by modifying the levels and distinguishing ten different types of intellect (*'aql*) in the conceptualization of the arc of descent. Fárábí's work became the model for that formal and complicated approach.[2] Most of the Sufis also talked about the arcs of descent and ascent, often adopting philosophical categories in their expositions.

This complex metaphor representing the spiritual nature and mission of human life is a basic concept implicit in the Bahá'í writings. In *Some Answered Questions*, for instance, 'Abdu'l-Bahá describes the human condition, located at the end of the arc of descent and the beginning of the arc of ascent, in these terms: "Man is in the highest degree of materiality, and at the beginning of spirituality—that is to say, he is the end of imperfection and the beginning of perfection. He is at the last degree of darkness, and at the beginning of light; that is why it has been said that the condition of man is the end of the night and the beginning of day...."[3]

However, as is apparent in the Bahá'í writings, the notions of the arcs of descent and ascent are relative concepts. Depending on the subject and focus of the particular text, alternative renderings with different stages and degrees of being may be employed. One of the most frequently encountered schemes posits seven stages of creation as the arc of descent and seven stages of spiritual journey as the arc of ascent. The arc of descent, as illustrated in figure 1, can also be understood as the order in which the products of the seven stages of creation appear. In this sense, human beings are located at the apex of the created realm,

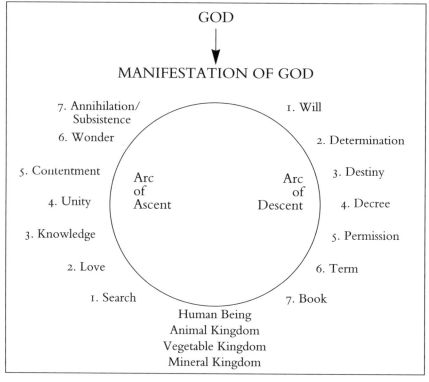

Figure 1. The ontological circle

at the end of the chain consisting of the mineral, vegetable, animal, and human kingdoms. The stages of the arc of descent are often described in the Bahá'í writings as the following: (1) Will (*Mashíyyat*), (2) Determination (*Irádih*), (3) Destiny (*Qadar*), (4) Decree (*Qaḍá*), (5) Permission (*Idhn*), (6) Term (*Ajal*), and (7) Book (*Kitáb*). The seven stages of the arc of ascent are represented by the valleys of the spiritual journey described in Bahá'u'lláh's treatise, the Seven Valleys.

The seven-stage sequence of the arc of descent was first mentioned in an Islamic tradition attributed to the Sixth Imám and is extensively treated in the writings of Shaykh Aḥmad-i-Aḥsá'í and Siyyid Kázim-i-Rashtí.[4] Bahá'u'lláh also discusses these stages,[5] but they are encountered most frequently in the writings of the Báb, where, like every other traditional theological concept, they become redefined and imbued with new meanings.

Above all, one important feature strongly distinguishes the Bahá'í concept of the ontological circle from typical Sufi or Neoplatonic ideas. In the Bahá'í writings, the stations of creation in the arc of descent do not start from the divine Essence itself but from the realm of the divine Will. Likewise, the arc of ascent—or the spiritual journey—terminates not in union with the Essence of God, but in union with the Will of God. Because there can be no direct tie between the transcendent being of God and His contingent creation, the connection between the two takes place through the divine or Primal Will, which, in turn, is the cause of all creation.[6] The Primal Will is also referred to as the Command (*amr*) or Word of God and, as such, refers to the common reality or essence of the Manifestations of God. Because they are the "Vehicle for the transmission of the grace of the Divinity Itself" through which "every man will advance and develop until he attaineth the station at which he can manifest all the potential forces with which his inmost true self hath been endowed" (*Gleanings* 67–68), the goal of the spiritual journey is recognition of, and union with, the will of the Manifestation of God.

Clarification of the relation of the divine Primal Will to the creation may be found in the writings of the Báb on the stages of creation. In His Ṣaḥífiy-i-'Adlíyyih (Book of Justice), He explains that God created the Will from nothing through the causation of the Will itself without any external determination, and created all other beings by the causation of the Will through the seven stages of contingency: Will, Determination, Destiny, Decree, Permission, Term, and Book.[7]

The heart of these seven stages of creation is the union between existence and essence. All created things have both existence and essence. From the point of view of the created entity, existence points toward the Creator and the divine effulgence which is the created entity's source, while essence points toward the entity's self and its thingness. Put another way, existence is a being's active aspect, while essence is its receptive side. The stage of Will affirms the thing's existence, whereas Determination affirms its essence. However, for a thing to "be," existence and essence must interact and unite. Destiny is the stage that designates this interaction and unity. Thus the three stages of Will, Determination, and Destiny mark the fundamental preconditions for any thing to come into being. According to the Báb, the descent and realization of these three stages takes place through the next four stages beginning with Decree, which confirms the previous ones. The details of the creative process then become realized through the final three stages, which represent permission for actualization, determination of duration, and registration of all the details pertaining to the particular being or event.

The active force which affirms all the different stages of creation is the Word of God. All the seven stages represent, in their active mode, differential aspects or activities of the Primal Will. While the active moment is the same Primal Will which appears in different stages in different forms, the receptive aspect represents the inner reality of the product of the activities of the Primal Will.

The stages of creation have also been represented as the act of divine speech. Shaykh Aḥmad-i-Aḥsá'í, in his master theological and doctrinal work Sharḥu'l-Favá'id, explains that the four primary stages of creation refer, in the first place, to different stages of the activity of the Primal Point. Referring to the Qur'ánic statement according to which God created the world by uttering His imperative word, "Be" (kun), Shaykh Aḥmad identifies the four stages as successive stages of

the utterance of the Word of God. This act of speaking, or command-
ing the creation to "be," consists of two stages of inhaling (*istanshaqa*)
and two stages of exhaling (*istantaqa*). The dialectic of inhaling and
exhaling as a metaphorical representation of the act of creation, revelation, and divine command is also mentioned by the Báb, for
instance in His Commentary on the letter Há' (Tafsír-i-Há').[8]

Shaykh Ahmad's allusions to the four stages of the utterance of the
Word may be seen as referring to the four primary stages of the arc of
descent. First, he implies, the air is inhaled into the divine "mouth"
and warmed through the inner heat of the divine Reality. Then it is
exhaled by pushing the divine breath to the fore and externalizing it
in the form of a complete word. Later writings of the Báb, particularly
the Persian Bayán, are filled with alternative metaphors corresponding
to these four stages of creation, which are also different ways of
expressing the unity in diversity of the realm of the Manifestation of
God.

In the Báb's description of the stages of creation, the stage of Will
corresponds to existence. In the writings of both Shaykh Ahmad and
the Báb, the word *shay'* (thing, object) is taken to be derived from the
root *shá'a* meaning "he willed," which is also the root of the word
Mashíyyat (Will). This is very important philosophically and mysti-
cally: the thing or object is actually an event of the Will. The objective
world, then, is conceptualized not as a mechanistic, solid materiality,
but as the expression of spiritual force or energy—an embodiment of
the divine Will. In this connection, we may note Bahá'u'lláh's statement in His Lawh-i-Hikmat (Tablet of Wisdom) that "Nature in its
essence is the embodiment of My Name, the Maker, the Creator....
Nature is God's Will and is its expression in and through the contingent world" (*Tablets* 142).

The accuracy of the representation of Will as existence, and of
Determination as essence can be seen in another statement of the Báb
in Risálah fi'l-Ghiná'. There He explains that the reality of all created
beings depends on two aspects (*jihat*): the existential aspect (*vujúd*),
which signifies the divine effulgence, and the essential aspect (*máhíyyat*),
which signifies servitude and the acceptance of that divine effulgence.

Through the realization of both these aspects, the link of Destiny, which connects the two, becomes manifest. After the appearance of these three stages, the other four are realized, for "the descent of the three is impossible save through the appearance of the four." This, He says, is the reason for the seven stages of causation.[9]

One more point should be emphasized. As the Báb has said, at the first three stages, the possibility exists of alteration, or *badá'*. But once all the four stages have been executed, there is no longer any possibility of alteration. *Badá'* is usually understood as a change in the divine decree, or the nonfulfillment of the divine promise.[10] But in this exposition of the stages of the creative act of the Primal Will, *badá'* refers instead to the flexibility and unconditioned character of the Will and its determination by itself.

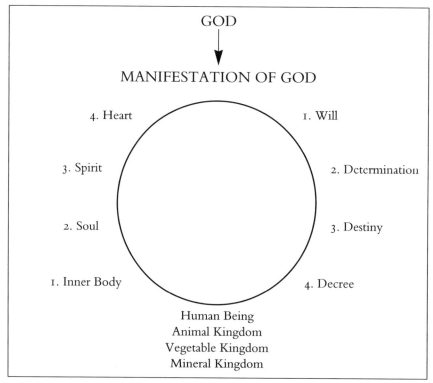

Figure 2. Another representation of the ontological circle

It may be noted that in His writings, particularly the Persian Bayán, the Báb frequently employs another representation of the ontological circle (see figure 2). In this version, the arc of descent is primarily expressed by the four initial stages of creation—will, determination, destiny, and decree—and the arc of ascent by four equivalent stages of spiritual growth. These He identifies as inner or essential body (*jasad-i-dhátí*), soul or self (*nafs*), spirit (*rúḥ*), and heart (*fu'ád*). It should be noted that two of these stages (soul or self, and heart) are identical with two of the valleys in Bahá'u'lláh's Four Valleys. Most importantly, however, in both classifications the ultimate point, namely heart, is the same. Analysis of this version of the ontological circle, however, is beyond the scope of the present discussion.

In the writings of the Báb and Bahá'u'lláh, all these concepts have been subjected to a significant creative redefinition. Most significantly, both the arc of descent and the arc of ascent become historicized. The arc of descent becomes reconceptualized as the creation of a new spiritual civilization through the historical stages of progressive revelation. At the same time, the arc of ascent, or the concept of "return," is defined as the historical unfoldment and renewal of divine revelation and the advent of a new "paradise" in human history. The recognition of the Manifestation of God becomes the center of this historicized arc of ascent. In the context of this Bahá'í theological paradigm, the categories of Destiny, Decree, and *badá'* take on distinctive new meanings. Destiny (or "measure") refers to the particular form of the religion of God which is revealed by the Primal Will (Will) in accordance with the requirements of the time and the level of human development (Determination) by a particular Manifestation of God (Decree).[11] This new meaning of destiny is emphasized by Bahá'u'lláh in His Book of the River:

> Similarly, ponder upon the mysteries of divine decree and destiny. Whatever hath appeared or will appear is like this river. Each thing moveth or reposeth in its proper place. But if something contrary to this natural flow of events is manifested, the order of the world becometh gravely disrupted. Couldst thou but grasp this subtle mystery, which is more hidden than any other mystery, thou

wouldst find thyself independent of this and all other questions. It is for this reason that, in every age and century, as He desireth, the Unique Hidden One and the Eternal Essence manifesteth that true River and real Sea and causeth it to flow, adorning it with a new temple and a new vesture.[12]

Badá', in this case, is nothing less than the change of the ordinances of the religion of God as befits the changing conditions of humanity by the historically progressive Manifestations of God.

The concept of *badá'* is reinterpreted by the Báb in several major but related ways. The first meaning is the change in the divine religion, or the principle of progressive revelation. *Badá'* becomes manifest, the Báb writes in the Persian Bayán, at the time of each revelation of the Primal Will, when all are tested.[13] A second sense of *badá'* is related to the criterion of faith and disbelief. In that sense, the Báb discusses *badá'* as a dialectic of divine justice and mercy. The possession of faith is itself essentially due to divine bounty. One recognizes the true meaning of *badá'* if one realizes that even if a person has worshiped God and has observed all the divine ordinances all one's life, at any moment God can deprive one of faith because of His justice. The fact that such a person continues to be considered among the believers is simply due to divine mercy. Conversely, at any moment a disbeliever may be turned into a letter of paradise and faith through divine mercy, so one should never feel superior on account of possessing faith. In all these cases, faith in divine *badá'* implies the need for a sense of humility, equality, and perpetual self-examination.

The third meaning of *badá'* affirms a fundamental principle of the Persian Bayán. According to the Báb, all previous laws and ordinances are abrogated by the advent of the new Manifestation of God unless reaffirmed by Him. Likewise, the Manifestation can abrogate any of His laws during His lifetime. After the death of the Manifestation, however, there will be no change in His binding laws till the advent of the next Manifestation.[14]

A fourth new meaning of *badá'* found throughout the Persian Bayán is related to the concept of covenant. The essence of this sense of *badá'* can be summarized as follows. According to Islamic traditions, there will be no *badá'* after the completion of the fourth stage, Decree. The Báb explains that the real meaning of this is that one's faith is complete and will not be subject to alteration or negation if one believes in all four supports or pillars of the divine covenant. Decree, here, becomes the symbol of the fourth pillar of the covenant. One's faith is always incomplete and subject to alteration if one has accepted only three levels but has failed to recognize the fourth. In the Bahá'í Faith these four levels of the covenant are God, Bahá'u'lláh, the authorized interpreters of the Faith ('Abdu'l-Bahá and the Guardian), and the Universal House of Justice. The affirmation of divine *badá'*, in this sense, would signify the inseparable unity of all the elements of the divine covenant. Turning away from any part of that covenant constitutes breaking the covenant, which deprives one of faith.

Yet another meaning of *badá'* in the Persian Bayán concerns unconditional divine authority and sovereignty. In fact, the Báb says that acceptance of divine alteration is the highest sign of spiritual maturity because it indicates recognition of the absolute power and unconditioned authority of God. The Word is binding simply because it is uttered by the Manifestation of God, who can pronounce a new decree whenever He wishes and can abrogate previous Scripture or His own previous revelations.[15] Such divine alteration is not due to weakness but to the supreme sovereignty of the Manifestations of God, whose will is not "chained up" by anything else.

In several statements, Bahá'u'lláh refers to Himself as the Divine "Decree." In the Kitáb-i-Aqdas He writes: "God hath made My hidden love the key to the Treasure.... This is, verily, that fixed Decree through which every irrevocable decree hath been established" (¶ 15); and in the Tablet of Visitation He says: "I testify that through Thee the sovereignty of God and His dominion, and the majesty of God and His grandeur, were revealed, and the Day-Stars of ancient splendor have shed their radiance in the heaven of Thine irrevocable decree [*qadá*], and the Beauty of the Unseen hath shone forth above the horizon of creation [*badá'*]."[16] Here *badá'* has been translated by Shoghi Effendi as "creation," apparently indicating the equivalence of *badá'* with the renewal of revelation and spiritual creation.

HISTORICIZING THE SPIRITUAL JOURNEY

At least four fundamental principles distinguish Bahá'u'lláh's writings from previous expressions of mysticism in general and Sufism in particular. They may be considered as constitutive elements of His mystical discourse. First, the principle of absolute divine transcendence indicates that the ultimate end of the spiritual journey is the recognition of the Manifestation of God in each age. Second, the idea of spiritual journey is historicized. The human encounter with the divine Reality takes place in historically specific terms. Third, this manifestation theology also implies harmony, not contradiction, between mysticism and religious law, social teachings, and institutions. And finally, in Bahá'u'lláh's teachings mysticism is inseparably linked to the principle of the unity of humankind as the ultimate goal of Bahá'u'lláh's mission.

Here I will concentrate on the second of these four principles—the application of the principle of historicity in the spiritual journey, or mystical consciousness. Two issues are central to understanding this principle. First, the relation among three of the writings of Bahá'u'lláh—the Seven Valleys, Gems of Mysteries, and the Kitáb-i-Íqán—discloses a complex and holistic view of Bahá'u'lláh's mystical logic. Second, the meaning of "return" in the writings of the Báb and Bahá'u'lláh is the key to the Bahá'í concept of the spiritual journey.

The Gems of Mysteries

The Seven Valleys, the Gems of Mysteries, and the Kitáb-i-Íqán—all revealed during Bahá'u'lláh's stay in Baghdad, constitute a textual triangle and unity. At first that fact may not be obvious. The first impression of the Seven Valleys and the Kitáb-i-Íqán may be that they deal with entirely different topics. The Seven Valleys appears to address the stages of the spiritual journey, while the Kitáb-i-Íqán is concerned with proving the authenticity of the Báb's claim to divine revelation, the progressive character of revelation, the interpretation of prophecies concerning the coming of the Promised One, the allegorical meaning of statements in the holy books of the past, and the like. In other words, the two texts seem entirely dissimilar.

This impression may remain unchallenged until we take into account Bahá'u'lláh's other major work, Javáhiru'l-Asrár (Gems of Mysteries). In the Kitáb-i-Íqán, Bahá'u'lláh refers to Gems of Mysteries and indicates the continuity of its themes with the Kitáb-i-Íqán (25–26). In reading Gems of Mysteries, however, we confront a major bewilderment concerning its form, structure, and content. The full title of the book relates the "Gems of Mysteries" to the highest journeys for those intending to approach God. If this suggests a mystical work about the stages of spiritual search, the first pages of the text will completely surprise the reader: instead of resembling the Seven Valleys, it looks more like the Kitáb-i-Íqán. The text opens with a statement that one must reflect on why all the Messengers of God were rejected in their own time by the believers of the previous religion although they were waiting for their Promised One.[17] Bahá'u'lláh explains that such rejection occurs primarily because people relied on their religious leaders and scholars instead of investigating the new Manifestation of God independently. He quotes allegorical verses from the New Testament concerning the signs of the next revelation and the impossibility of understanding the meanings of such verses without divine interpretation. He then blocks a traditional way to evade the problem by dismissing the specious claim that the existing text of the Gospel is not the original and authentic Bible: if the Word of God had not been authentically present among the people, they would not have been responsible for their failure to recognize the next Manifestation and for deviating from the divine will. To hold them responsible for failure would have been contrary to the justice and mercy of God. After declaring that only those who are inspired and chosen by God can understand the allegorical texts, He offers to explain their meanings.[18]

Clearly such a discussion is fully within the realm of the problematic of the Kitáb-i-Íqán. However, the reader is surprised once again as Bahá'u'lláh then turns to an exposition of the stages of the spiritual journey. The remainder of the text at first seems predictable. Bahá'u'lláh talks of the valleys of search, love, unity, wonder, annihilation in God, and subsistence in God, using the logic and language of the Seven Valleys, although with slight differences in the stages given.[19]

It is evident that Gems of Mysteries cannot be understood either as simply another Seven Valleys or as another Kitáb-i-Íqán. Does Bahá'u'lláh's text then consist of two different topics, beginning with the issues of the Kitáb-i-Íqán and ending with the stages of the Seven Valleys? This easy solution does not work either. The experience of bewilderment continues: in the midst of discussing the stages of the spiritual journey, particularly the stage of unity, suddenly Bahá'u'lláh introduces issues which once again pertain to the topic of the Kitáb-i-Íqán: He interprets the figurative and allegorical meanings of prophecies, proves that neither Muḥammad nor any of the Prophets is the final Manifestation of God, explains the mystery of return and resurrection, corrects misconceptions concerning the Twelfth Imám and the signs of his appearance, and so on.[20] Obviously, this is not a text that deals in different chapters with two different issues. What, then, is the connection between the spiritual journey toward God, on the one hand, and progressive revelation and prophecies concerning the Báb, on the other? Gems of Mysteries makes it clear that it was in fact the first impression of the Seven Valleys and of the Kitáb-i-Íqán, and the assumption, based on that impression, that they have distinct and independent topics, which was not accurate. Both of these texts are, as we shall see, considerably more complex and their subject matter more closely related.

Just how that is so will become more evident in Chapters 4 and 5, but the answer to the apparent paradox should by now be clear. Gems of Mysteries, rather than being an inconsistent text, is the key for understanding Bahá'u'lláh's conceptual revolution in mystical discourse. The subject of the Seven Valleys is the spiritual journey and its stages. The subject of the Kitáb-i-Íqán is progressive revelation and historical consciousness. In Gems of Mysteries these two subjects constitute an organic unity. As I have suggested, it is the interpenetration and the unity of both subjects—historical consciousness and spiritual journey—which distinguishes Bahá'u'lláh's mystical approach from traditional approaches. The traditional Sufi approach conceived of the spiritual journey as a flight from the realm of plurality, change, and history. It is precisely this problematic that Bahá'u'lláh has changed. Because the unknowable Essence of God in its invisibility and transcendence is absolutely inaccessible to human experience, the only way that human beings can approach and experience God is through the experience of the reflection and manifestation of God in the mirrors of the visible realm—the historically specific Manifestations of God. History, therefore, instead of being an obstacle to mystical experience, becomes the only way human beings can approach divine Reality. In this way history is spiritualized and spirit is historicized.

This historical approach to mystical consciousness implies that humanity as a whole also undertakes a spiritual journey, the stages of which are marked by the advent of new Manifestations of God and the appearance of new spiritual civilizations. Because of that fact, the specific form that the process, limits, and dynamics of the individual journey take is conditioned by the spiritual and cultural stage of human society and the revelation of spiritual truth corresponding to that stage. In this respect, the spiritual journey is not identical for all individuals at all stages of human history; the acceptability of any path or form of devotion is dependent on the will of the Manifestation of God and what He reveals.

Having identified the problematic of Gems of Mysteries as the historicization of the spiritual journey, it is possible to understand both the Seven Valleys and the Kitáb-i-Íqán in a new light. This insight, however, is already present explicitly in the Kitáb-i-Íqán. It is there that we find an exposition of the mystical journey's historical aspect. In one well-known passage, Bahá'u'lláh identifies the goal reached by the detached and enlightened "true seeker" as "the City of Certitude." In this, the abode of the "Beloved," the wayfarer

> will discern the wonders of His ancient wisdom, and will perceive all the hidden teachings from the rustling leaves of the Tree—which flourisheth in that City.... The attainment of this City quencheth thirst without water, and kindleth the love of God without fire....
>
> They that valiantly labour in quest of God's will, when once they have renounced all else but Him, will be so attached and

wedded to that City that a moment's separation from it would to them be unthinkable. (*Kitáb-i-Íqán* 197–99)

This "City" is the dispensation of divine revelation in each age: "Once in about a thousand years shall this City be renewed and re-adorned.... In the days of Moses it was the Pentateuch; in the days of Jesus the Gospel; in the days of Muḥammad the Messenger of God the Qur'án; in this day the Bayán; and in the dispensation of Him Whom God will make manifest His own Book...." (199).

Reconceptualizing the Idea of Return

One of the most important ideas in religious and mystical history is the concept of *return*. In the Bahá'í writings, the word *return* is used to express two different but interrelated Arabic terms. One is *raj'ah*, which means the return of a specific person in a future time; the other is *ma'ád*, which is the Day of Resurrection (literally, the time of return). In the Bahá'í definition, these two terms become one and the same concept. The present discussion, however, is directly concerned with the second term, *ma'ád*.

The significance of the concept of return in the early Bábí and Bahá'í periods cannot be overestimated. In fact, debate on the meaning of return was the center of theological and doctrinal discourse in those years, partly due to the importance of that idea in the Shaykhí school. The relevance of the concept to the spiritual journey can be seen by first locating it in terms of Islamic discourse and then examining the transformation that the concept undergoes in the Bahá'í texts.

The fundamental articles of Islamic belief are normally called the Pillars of the Faith. Among Sunní and Shí'ih Muslims the term has slightly different meanings. But three articles of faith are central and essential to all Muslim sects: the unity of God, prophecy, and return. Although the doctrine of return, or the Day of Resurrection, is one of the most important Islamic principles, its precise meaning is subject to extensive controversy. The orthodox and dominant understanding of the doctrine takes it to be a time when history ends and the dead are brought back to life to be judged by divine justice and condemned to eternal hell or rewarded with heaven, according to their merits. The dominant question has centered on whether this resurrection happens to the physical body, to the spirit, or to an inner spiritual or archetypal body (*jasad-i-mithálí* or *jasad-i-dhátí*).

Return may also be interpreted in another way, which is implicit in Islamic literature and is tacitly advocated by some philosophers and particularly by some of the Sufis. According to this interpretation, return is indeed return to God: everything has come from God and returns to God. But the most important meaning of return is not as a distant event at the end of time, but as a description of the process of individual spiritual development or spiritual journey in this life. Suddenly, the thesis of resurrection acquires a mystical meaning. The doctrine of return becomes the arc of ascent and refers to the stages of the mystic wayfarer's journey of return to the divine Origin and Creator.

The relevance of the doctrine of return and resurrection to the concept of spiritual journey becomes evident in this elegant and profound approach. But though the implicit Sufi interpretation of the doctrine of return is very insightful, it still remains within the same underlying problematic of the orthodox Muslim interpretation. Despite the apparent mutual opposition of the Sufi and orthodox views, both assume a fundamental premise in common—the absence of historical consciousness. In the orthodox approach the issue is very clear: return means the end of history. However, in that orthodox interpretation, history has ended long before the Day of Resurrection. The belief that divine revelation is ended, and that consequently Islamic laws and social teachings are unchangeable, has already declared the end of history. The concept of return, in that view, is part of the same ahistorical consciousness. The same paradigm is in fact shared by the Sufis. For them, return is an individual process which is opposed to history and historical change; the mystical journey is assumed to be the same for all people at all times. The only difference is the random differential distribution of mystical capacities. In other words, for the Sufis the idea of return is a flight from history.

Here again, it is at the level of fundamental premises that the Báb and Bahá'u'lláh create novel approaches. In the Bahá'í writings, as we have seen, the doctrine of return becomes the doctrine of mystical and spiritual progress. The doctrine that, in the Islamic interpretation, signified the end of history, becomes transformed into the doctrine of historicity and historical consciousness. Bahá'u'lláh uses the Islamic terms and concepts in a way that means exactly the opposite of the way they were understood in Islamic discourse, thus providing a clear example of why Bahá'u'lláh's discourse cannot be reduced to traditional Islamic assumptions and how the traditional meanings become intentionally changed.

Traditionally, return means going to "heaven" or to "hell." Heaven, however, is now defined as the state of perfection or actualization of the potentialities of beings. As such, paradise is not restricted to human beings but—relatively speaking—is a potentiality of every created nature. The Báb writes:

> No created thing shall ever attain its paradise unless it appeareth in its highest prescribed degree of perfection. For instance, this crystal representeth the paradise of the stone whereof its substance is composed. Likewise there are various stages in the paradise for the crystal itself.... So long as it was stone it was worthless, but if it attaineth the excellence of ruby—a potentiality which is latent in it—how much a carat will it be worth? Consider likewise every created thing.[21]

For human beings, the Báb continues, that state of perfection which constitutes "man's highest station"

> is attained through faith in God in every Dispensation and by acceptance of what hath been revealed by Him, and not through learning; inasmuch as in every nation there are learned men who are versed in diverse sciences. Nor is it attainable through wealth; for it is similarly evident that among the various classes in every nation there are those possessed of riches. Likewise are other transitory things.
>
> True knowledge, therefore, is the knowledge of God, and this is none other than the recognition of His Manifestation in each Dispensation. Nor is there any wealth save in poverty in all save God and sanctity from aught else but Him—a state that can be realized only when demonstrated towards Him Who is the Dayspring of His Revelation.[22]

Like the paradise of other created beings, human paradise or heaven is that state of purification in which the reflection of divine attributes becomes perfectly manifest. The ultimate manifestation of divine attributes is the Manifestation of God. Therefore, heaven for the human soul is the state of acceptance and recognition of the Manifestation of God and conformity to all that He reveals. The principle of progressive revelation becomes the key concept for understanding the idea of heaven and the doctrine of return. The concept of resurrection becomes historical as well. The day of resurrection, instead of being the end of history, represents the end of one historical stage and its corresponding civilization, and the dawning of a new stage of historical development with its new cultural logic and spiritual order.

Although the most important meaning of "return," "resurrection," and "paradise" in such texts as those discussed above is within the context of progressive revelation and in the realm of human history, this does not displace the concept of the moment of accounting and judgment, followed by appropriate recompense, that is experienced by all human souls at the moment of their physical death. In fact, the purpose for which the Prophets and Messengers of God have been sent to humankind "hath been to educate all men, that they may, at the hour of death, ascend, in the utmost purity and sanctity and with absolute detachment, to the throne of the Most High" (*Gleanings* 157–58). Bahá'u'lláh emphasizes that the spiritual journey itself is never ending, and that after death the soul, freed from the limitations of time and space, continues to progress through infinite stages and until it attains the divine presence.[23]

THEOLOGY OF REVELATION AND CRITIQUE OF THE UNITY OF EXISTENCE

Along with the application of historical consciousness to the concept of spiritual journey, an equally important distinguishing feature of Bahá'u'lláh's approach to mysticism, and one which is directly related to the notion of historicity, is Bahá'u'lláh's theology of revelation, according to which the end and the aim of the spiritual journey is not attaining experience or knowledge of the Essence of God but rather the recognition of the revelation of divine attributes in the historically specific Manifestations of God.

In order to point out some of the similarities and differences between Bahá'u'lláh's theology and Sufi ideas, I will briefly review the structure of Sufi philosophical theology. In spite of differences of opinion among Sufi writers, three issues are of central importance, explicitly or implicitly, to almost all of them—the thesis of the unity of existence, the doctrine of determinism, and the concept of the Perfect Human Being.

The fundamental doctrine of Islam, and its first article of faith, is the unity of God (*tawḥíd*). For the Sufis too, this same idea remains the center and foundation of their worldview, and all other Sufi doctrines are reduced to this ultimate principle. However, Sufis understand the unity of God entirely differently from the orthodox Islamic understanding of the unity of God as the rejection of a plurality of gods. For Sufis the unity of God turns into varieties of the doctrine of the unity of existence (*vaḥdatu'l-vujúd*), according to which nothing exists other than God and everything is God. This particular interpretation of the unity of God as the unity of existence is attributed to Ibnu'l-'Arabí, although it is the basic premise of almost all Sufi expressions. The details of this doctrine are contested among the Sufis, as exemplified by the famous debate between the followers of Ibnu'l-'Arabí and the followers of Aḥmad Sirhindí, who argued for the doctrine of the unity of vision (*vaḥdatu'sh-shuhúd*). However, even in this debate the core principle remains identical, which is that the reality of all beings is one and the same, and that reality is God.

The popular pantheistic version of the doctrine is normally expressed through the use of metaphors like snow and water to reconcile the apparent contradiction between the plurality of beings and the unity of reality and to overcome the opposition between the diversity of the contingent world and the unity of God. For the Sufis this difference must be abolished and a synthesis attained. Their solution was to explain plurality as the realm of appearances, and unity as the realm of the inner reality of those appearances. God is likened to water and the world to snow. Snow is actually water with a particular appearance, but the essential reality and existence of snow is the same as that of water. Plurality, in other words, becomes ultimately an illusion. In the writings of Ibnu'l-'Arabí this analogy is accompanied by other expressive descriptions, of which the analogy of numbers is perhaps the most essential. God is defined as One. All plural numbers are created by repetitions of the number one. Ibnu'l-'Arabí argues, however, that all plural numbers are one as well as plural. Their appearance is plurality (two is different from three), but two and three are each one number, so their inner reality is the same as that of one. Therefore, he concludes, plurality is also unity.[24]

The doctrine of the unity of existence is rarely explicated clearly. A pantheistic reading would argue that the reality of things is their existence. We say God "exists" and human beings "exist." In this statement, existence is common to both. Therefore, the reality of all beings is one and the same, and that is their common existence, which is the same as the existence of God. God and the world become one and the same because of the unity of existence. God is pure existence, whereas all beings are God with particular attributes.

The second fundamental theory of philosophical Sufism concerns causation and freedom. These two issues are really one and the same, because the question of human freedom or predestination comes under the general doctrine of causation and agency. To be endowed with freedom of will and action means to possess agency, and that means to be an effective and real cause. But the doctrines of causation and determinism are actually other ways of expressing the unity of existence. This is very predictable, for if only God exists, then only God can be a cause and agent; there is only one cause for every event in the world and that is God, directly. Human beings have no agency in their own right. Their actions are also directly caused by God and everything is predestined. Surprisingly, on this issue most Sufis are in agreement with an extremely orthodox Islamic theological position, that of the Ash'arites. Contrary to their rivals the Mu'tazilites, the Ash'arites rejected the notion of human freedom and agency; for them, there could exist only one cause and that was defined to be God.[25] For both Ash'arites and Sufis, to acknowledge any other pos-

sible cause was equivalent to contradicting the unity of God because
to posit the existence of another agent, such as human beings, sets up
a rival to God.

The Ash'arites, on their part, categorically rejected the Sufi idea of
the unity of existence. According to them, the world is not God and
any assertion of any form of unity of the two contradicts the unity of
God. The Sufis, therefore, were even more extreme than the Ash'arites in their notion of causation. The form of this difference can be
understood by comparing Sufi pantheism to the Ash'arite doctrine of
atomism. Ash'arites defended the theory that the substances of things
are not accompanied by any constant attributes or accidents. They
held that accidents of things, like various qualities, are attached to
things in one moment and cease to exist in the next. These attributes
or accidents, therefore, are directly created at every moment by God.
They come into being and immediately cease to exist even as God
again creates new attributes. While to human beings it appears that
there is continuity in the qualities of things and that natural events are
created by the natural properties of things, in reality, according to the
Ash'arites, all events are directly caused and recreated by God.[26]

The Sufis usually accepted this idea of the impermanent and unreal
character of the attributes of things. But they went one step further,
arguing that the same should be predicated of the substances of things.
In other words, there is no substance independent from the attributes.
Substances are also ephemeral and directly caused and created by God.
But in this analysis, the entire world of creation ceases to exist as such,
becoming modes of divine action and existence.[27]

The third doctrine essential to Sufi philosophical theology is the
idea of the Perfect Human Being. This doctrine is another aspect of
the same underlying principle of the unity of existence. According to
the Sufis, because of the unity of existence, humans are potentially
divine. But as long as they are immersed in the appearance of diversity,
contingency, and plurality, their consciousness will be far removed
from the reality of being. Through the spiritual journey, however,
carried out by means of ecstatic love and mystical intuition, the soul
can transcend the realm of diversity and become aware of the unity of

being. In this journey the mystic can reach such a stage of intuitive love as to become one with Reality and attain the station of sainthood or *viláyah*. Such a person has reached the stage of the Perfect Human Being and is endowed with the knowledge of the invisible and the capacity to work miracles (*karámat*). As we have seen, most Sufis placed sainthood above the station of prophecy and apostolic legislation because the realm of truth was considered higher than the realm of religious law.[28]

The Bahá'í writings contain what are apparently differing estimations of Sufism and its doctrines. Some of the Bahá'í writings employ mystical symbols and discourse, including, as in the Seven Valleys and the Four Valleys, quotations from classics of Sufi literature. At the same time, Bahá'u'lláh strongly criticizes particular Sufi premises, doctrines, and practices. But in fact there is no real contradiction in Bahá'u'lláh's estimation of Sufism. For Bahá'u'lláh, there are many beautiful truths in Islamic mysticism that should be acknowledged and praised, while at the same time, not all the beliefs and practices associated with Sufism are accurate or acceptable. For instance, in the history of Sufism there has frequently been a tendency to underestimate the significance of religious law, to overestimate withdrawal from active social and economic life, to venerate Sufi shaykhs, to emphasize a hierarchy of virtue based upon a hierarchy of knowledge and access to esoteric truth, to defend extremist exercises and practices, and the like. Bahá'u'lláh rejected all those elements of Sufism.[29]

The other problem is the ambiguity in the Sufi writings themselves and in their own articulations of Sufi doctrines. For example, the notion of the unity of existence can be interpreted either as a vulgar pantheism or as the doctrine of revelation. Bahá'u'lláh unvaryingly rejects the former but affirms the latter. This becomes even more evident in specific commentaries Bahá'u'lláh and 'Abdu'l-Bahá wrote on various famous Sufi works. Bahá'u'lláh's explicit rule on the assessment of others' statements is to be sympathetic and open minded in approaching them. Therefore, He tends to emphasize the positive aspects and the acceptable meanings that can be found in those statements.[30] Very often Bahá'u'lláh and 'Abdu'l-Bahá make a distinction

between the popular readings of those statements, which take pantheistic turns, and the original intention of the writer, which is elu-
cidated as the theology of revelation. 'Abdu'l-Bahá's discussion of
Sufism and doctrine of the unity of existence in *Some Answered Questions* is an example of making such distinctions.[31] This evaluative but
equitable approach, constantly sifting the wheat from the chaff, is why,
overall, Bahá'u'lláh's statements about Sufism may superficially appear
to differ. But one should remember, as I have suggested, that it is precisely one of the functions of the early mystical writings of Bahá'u'lláh
to provide a vision of mysticism which rectifies the negative aspects of
Sufism (withdrawal from the world, contradiction with religious law,
veneration of Sufi leaders, and the like) and which becomes an integral
element of a holistic theology and social theory.

The Báb, in many of His writings, also criticizes the thesis of the
unity of existence as understood in its pantheistic form. He argues that
those who advocate it are decisively disproved by the testimony of
existence itself. He points out that such a unity assumes somehow the
reality of both existents, which are then identified as one and the same.
But the Báb affirms that there is only one existence and that is God,
and that nothing else exists at the level of divine existence.[32] The same
principle is emphasized frequently in the writings of Bahá'u'lláh:
nothing else exists at the level of God, God is absolutely transcendent,
and there is no similarity or connection between God and the created
beings. There is no incarnation, immanence, or transformation of God
into the realm of contingency.[33]

In agreement with a long list of Islamic philosophers and Sufis,
including Ṣadru'd-Dín Shírází and Shaykh Aḥmad-i-Aḥsá'í,[34] 'Abdu'l-
Bahá makes a distinction between two types of existence. Existence
can be defined either as a real concrete existence, or as a mental construct which is the universal and general concept of existence. The
latter is something which can be understood by the mind because it is
a general idea and a product of mental abstraction. When we say God
"exists" and humans "exist," we are talking either of a universal concept of existence which is common to both God and humans, or we
are using the term *existence* in two entirely different senses. If we mean

the first possibility, then we are talking of mental and not real existence. The pantheistic understanding of the doctrine of the unity of
existence is a product of conceiving of existence as general, mental,
and common existence. But this, 'Abdu'l-Bahá emphasizes, is obviously false. Therefore, the unity of existence can be true only if by
"existence" we mean real and concrete existence. But real and concrete existence is not a general attribute common to all beings and
God. On the contrary, this means that the Existence of God is one and
unique and that no other existence is similar, let alone identical, to that
Existence. In this sense of "existence," then, only one thing exists and
that is God. All other existences are relative and subsist by the will of
that authentic Existence. All things also exist at their own levels, but
the term *existence*, when applied to the realm of creation, has nothing
in common with the Existence attributed to God. It is simply a product of linguistic limitation and the fact that we can never conceive of
the Existence proper to God that we mistakenly reduce divine Existence to our conception of existence at the level of created reality. It is
precisely this reduction which creates the distorted image of a pantheistic unity of existence.

'Abdu'l-Bahá's argument rejecting the attribution of the general
and mental conception of existence to the Existence of God is as follows. If God's Existence is a general attribute that is equally attribut-
able to all things, in that case the Existence of God becomes an accident or attribute of things. Things become substances (essences)
which have particular attributes, such as existence, and the attributes
become dependent on those substances. But in that case, God becomes the attribute of things and dependent on them. Since God is
pure Existence and this existence is simply an attribute of things, all
contingent beings become more authentic and real than God. That is
obviously false. Therefore, Divine Existence is not the same as the
existence of things, nor can it be predicated of things. Instead of equat-
ing the Existence of God with the existence of contingent created
things, we should affirm the unique, unknowable, and inconceivable
Existence of God, compared to which there is no other existence, and
acknowledge the divine veritable Existence, which is absolutely tran-

scendent, as the source of all reality including the reality of general mental existence.[35] To relate this to the analogy of numbers used by Ibnu'l-'Arabí, although each being, like a number, is *one*, the meaning of this oneness is not the same as the meaning of the term *One* when applied to God.

It is important to note that 'Abdu'l-Bahá's analysis simultaneously refutes two interpretations of the unity of existence. The first one finds existence to be the same in all beings including God. However, a milder version of this theory, which is advocated in the writings of Ṣadru'd-Dín Shírází, maintains that existence is "equivocal" (*mushakkak*)—meaning that although existence is one it has different degrees of intensity. While the existence of all beings is not regarded as the same as the existence of God, the former is defined as similar to the latter. As Shaykh Aḥmad observes, Ṣadru'd-Dín Shírází usually contradicts himself by arguing that the existence of all beings is the same, but the differential intensity is a product of the external accidents added to existence. In this sense, the existence of God and the existence of the world are the same, while the existence of the world is accompanied by external accidents.[36] However, 'Abdu'l-Bahá rejects any similarity between the existence of God and the existence of the created realm. The categories of equivocal existence and sameness of existence apply only to the realm of created things and not to the realm of the unknowable Essence. In other words, common (including equivocal) mental existence is shared among the created beings, while real, unique, and unparalleled Existence applies only to God.[37] This fundamental distinction is already visible in the Bahá'í concept of the arc of descent. In that representation, the existence of the created beings is only an expression and effect of the creative Will of God. It is neither the essence of God nor similar to it.

Bahá'u'lláh's theology, then, is one of absolute transcendence and inaccessibility of God, Who nevertheless reveals Himself through the manifestation of His attributes in the realm of created, contingent existence. Because the created beings, in the realm of plurality and diversity, are expressions and reflections of divine attributes in accordance with their own stations, it is accurate to use the analogy of mirrors reflecting the attributes—never the essence—of the sun, but not the analogy of snow and water (or the sea and its waves), to describe the relation between God and the world. The inner being of every thing is the yearning for recognition of God because everything is a reflection of divine attributes. Because God cannot be known by the contingent beings, the aim of the mystic journey, and the "paradise" of human beings, becomes the knowledge and recognition of the Manifestation of God, Who is the perfect actualization of all divine attributes in each age. That recognition will be identified at the beginning of the Kitáb-i-Aqdas as the first duty incumbent upon all human beings. In the Seven Valleys Bahá'u'lláh asserts the same principle, emphasizing that all references to mystic "knowledge" of God relate only to the Manifestation of God:

> However, let none construe these utterances to be anthropomorphism, nor see in them the descent of the worlds of God into the grades of the creatures.... For God is, in His Essence, holy above ascent and descent, entrance and exit; ... No man hath ever known Him; no soul hath ever found the pathway to His Being. Every mystic knower hath wandered far astray in the valley of the knowledge of Him; every saint hath lost his way in seeking to comprehend His Essence. Sanctified is He above the understanding of the wise; exalted is He above the knowledge of the knowing! ...
>
> Yea, these mentionings that have been made of the grades of knowledge relate to the knowledge of the Manifestations of that Sun of Reality, which casteth Its light upon the Mirrors. (*Seven Valleys* 22–23)

In the theology of revelation, then, we already have the Bahá'í concept of the Perfect Human Being. For Bahá'u'lláh, the exaggerated veneration of Sufi saints and their elevation to the level of Prophets, or even higher, is blasphemy. 'Abdu'l-Bahá has explicated Bahá'u'lláh's position on this question: the Perfect Human Being is none other than the Manifestation of God.[38] Restricting this concept to refer to the station of the Manifestation implies the equality of all ordinary human beings—including the Sufi shaykhs. This is quite the opposite of the typical Sufi construct, which diminishes the authority of the Prophets and Messengers of God, while maintaining the ine-

quality of human beings and a strict hierarchy of spiritual and social status. Bahá'u'lláh, in contrast, equalizes all human beings and affirms the
metaphysical transcendence of the Manifestations of God.

For this reason, the concept of the Perfect Human Being assumes
a new significance in Bahá'í theology and resolves the dilemma of
unity and plurality. To pose it in a dialectical form, God, as absolute
unity and unknowable Essence, is beyond the access of the contingent
plural realm. Humans, however, are confined to that realm of contingency and history. The solution to this antinomy is precisely the
mediating synthesis of the two. In other words, the possibility of spiritual journey depends on the appearance of the invisible at the visible
level. That is the kingdom of revelation, the realm of the Primal Will
as reflected in the form of particular Manifestations of God, who represent the divine Word of God, or *Logos*, at the level of history.[39] Now
it is possible to reinterpret the notion of the unity of existence.
'Abdu'l-Bahá has emphasized that even the Sufi philosophers conceive of reality primarily as the two levels of God and the world. He
asserts, however, that for Bahá'ís there are three fundamental realms or
grades of being, in which the realm of Primal Will—or the Manifestations—is the mediating one between God and creation.[40] The term
Perfect Human Being is also sometimes used in the Bahá'í writings as a
reference to the highest possible limit of spiritual knowledge attainable
by ordinary human beings, but this must be understood relative to the
limitations of the human station, where it is a perfection of those who
are inspired by the Manifestation of God.[41]

Chapter 3
SPIRITUAL JOURNEY IN THE FOUR VALLEYS AND THE SEVEN VALLEYS

THE FOUR VALLEYS and the Seven Valleys are among the earliest writings of Bahá'u'lláh and belong to the early years of His exile to Baghdad. Shoghi Effendi has characterized Bahá'u'lláh's Seven Valleys as "a treatise that may well be regarded as His greatest mystical composition … which He wrote in answer to the questions of Shaykh Muhyi'd-Dín, the Qádí (judge) of Khániqayn, in which He describes the seven stages which the soul of the seeker must needs traverse ere it can attain the object of its existence."[1] The Four Valleys was a shorter epistle written to Shaykh 'Abdu'r-Rahmán-i-Karkúkí.

SPIRITUAL JOURNEY IN THE FOUR VALLEYS

The Four Valleys expresses multiple discourses at the same time. It is a discourse on the mystic journey as well as, among other things, an exposition of an epistemology harmonizing rationalism, mysticism, and revelation; an explication of the station of the Manifestations of God; and an analysis of destiny and of the dialectic of freedom.

The current translation of the Four Valleys and the Seven Valleys, on which translations into other languages have been based, was begun by Ali-Kuli Khan and later revised by his daughter Marzieh Gail. Although they have done an exemplary job of poetically rendering these complex texts as well as identifying the authors of various mystical poems and the source of the various traditions and Qur'ánic verses quoted by Bahá'u'lláh, this translation does not seem to adequately convey the spatial metaphor that is used by Bahá'u'lláh in those works to depict the mystic journey. This metaphor is a crucial aspect of both the Four Valleys and the Seven Valleys, disclosing the structure of both texts—more explicitly so in the case of the Four Valleys. Therefore, in discussing these metaphors I will sometimes suggest (in brackets) a different translation of certain words.

Spatial Metaphor in the Four Valleys

The Four Valleys describes different approaches to truth and different types of truth seekers. Through the systematic development of an extended spatial metaphor, those approaches to truth are placed in a hierarchical order in terms of proximity and remoteness, or externality and internality. After the formal salutations to the addressee, Shaykh 'Abdu'r-Raḥmán, Bahá'u'lláh writes: "O My eminent friend! Those who progress in mystic wayfaring are of four kinds. I shall describe them in brief, that the grades and qualities of each kind may become plain to thee" (*Four Valleys* 49). Bahá'u'lláh then begins to describe the characteristics of the first group of "wayfarers." It should be noted that the headings, "The First Valley," and so on for each of the valleys, have been added in the English translation and are not part of the original Persian text. This is important to keep in mind because the primary object of the Four Valleys is to emphasize the harmony of the three hierarchically connected modes of will, reason, and love as approaches to divine reality. Bahá'u'lláh describes the first group of wayfarers in this way: "If the [wayfarers are among the seekers (*ṭálibán*) of the *ka'bih*] of the Intended One (*Maqṣúd*), this station appertaineth to the self [*nafs*]...." (50).

In this short sentence, we can see, Bahá'u'lláh has used four different aspects of the spatial metaphor, each of which will be developed in the subsequent valleys. The first thing to note is the description of the seeker of truth as a "wayfarer." This evokes remoteness and implies that the seeker has not yet attained any kind of intimate relation with the object of the quest. The second and most important aspect of the metaphor relates to the station of the wayfarer. Those who use the approach based on "self" (*nafs*, which also means soul) are called "seekers." These wayfarers have embarked on a journey toward the beloved one but are still far from the land where the beloved lives. The third aspect of the metaphor concerns the goal of the wayfarer and the location of the beloved. For the first group, the seekers, the aim of the journey is to reach the *ka'bih* of the beloved. This signifies the general mansion in which the beloved is located. However, like a large mansion with many rooms, it includes the entire domicile of the beloved without being coextensive with the beloved herself. The fourth aspect of the metaphor identifies the beloved in terms of the wayfarer's perception of the goal. For this first group, that is, the seekers, the beloved is conceived as the "Intended One" (*Maqṣúd*). Here again, the orientation of the seeker to the beloved is primarily external. The beloved is the object and destination of the journey. All four aspects of the metaphor of the spiritual journey are in complete harmony.

The beauty of Bahá'u'lláh's poetic logic is fully reflected in the description of the four valleys together. Of the second valley Bahá'u'lláh writes: "If the [wayfarers are among the inhabitants (*sákinán*) of the antechamber (*ḥujrih*)] of the Praiseworthy One (*Maḥmúd*), this is the station of ... reason...." (52). This new set of terms is defined precisely in relation to the previous ones. This group of wayfarers takes the rational approach—less remote in its mode of relation to the beloved but still not internal. Although the seeker of truth is still a wayfarer who has not fully reached the goal, progress has been made: the wayfarers are no longer just "seekers" of the beloved one, they are now "inhabitants" of the *ka'bih*, having reached and entered the mansion of the beloved. The place where they reside is the beloved's "antechamber." It is important to remember, however, that this refers to her quarters inside the *ka'bih*, but the reason-based wayfarers have not yet reached the place where the beloved herself is actually to be found. Now, the beloved is described as "the Praiseworthy One," consistent with the other aspects of this valley in relation to the former one. The beloved is no longer merely the vague destination of the traveler; the wayfarer's mode of relation becomes one of focused admiration.

In the third valley, "If the [lovers are among the devoted inmates (*'ákifán*) of the home (*bayt*)] of the Attracting One (*Majdhúb*), no soul may dwell on this Kingly Throne save the [countenance] of love" (54). Obviously the seeker is now in a much closer mode of relation to the absolute Reality that is the object of the spiritual journey. In this approach, based on love and mystical intuition, the seeker of truth is no longer a "wayfarer" but is now termed a "lover." The love-based seeker is now described as among the "devoted inmates" (*'ákifán*) of

the home of the beloved. The term *'ákifán* (inmates) expresses a meaning that perhaps no single English word can adequately capture. An
'ákif, or inmate, differs from an inhabitant in that the latter comes and
goes from the place of residence, but an *'ákif* is permanently secluded
from the world in a particular place of devotion, never leaving the
place of his retreat (*i'tikáf*). Now the seeker is become a lover, and
love, by its very nature, demands that the lover remain near the object
of devotion. The place of permanent settling is now the home (*bayt*)—
the lover has been allowed to enter the very home of the beloved. The
station of love implies the ability to face the beloved one; the mode of
relation to the beloved is now one of attraction, and the beloved is
termed "the Attracting One." This is a relation more intimate than
either the relation to the destination of the journey or to the object of
admiration; it is one in which the seeker actively experiences the
attractive force of the beloved one's beauty.

It is evident that a qualitatively different stage has been reached.
While the distance has decreased through the three successive
stages of self, reason, and love, none of these stages has yet implied an
actual union with the beloved. It is not until the fourth valley that a
qualitative turn in the metaphor occurs. Bahá'u'lláh says: "If the
[attainers of mystic knowledge (*'árifán*) are among the achievers of
union (*váṣilán*) with the countenance (*ṭal'at*)] of the Beloved One
(*Maḥbúb*), this [is the] station [of the throne of the heart and the secret
of maturation]" (57).

It is evident that a qualitatively different stage has been reached.
This station, the approach of the "heart," embraces and unites within
itself all the three previous modes, implying the unity and harmony of
will, reason, and love. It is described as the "secret of maturation" or
fruition of all human potentialities. In this station, the seeker of truth
is described as an "attainer of mystic knowledge," and the station of
the heart-based seeker is now characterized as the "achiever of union
(*váṣilán*) with the countenance of the beloved. *Váṣil* signifies having
attained the goal and being united with it. "Achiever of union"
approximates that notion although it does not adequately express it.
But the object that has been attained is no longer the *ka'bih*, or the
antechamber, or even the home of the beloved. It is the beloved her-

self that the mystic seeker has now attained, and it is with the countenance of the beloved that he is now united. Distance and difference between the lover and the beloved has been obliterated. This is finally reflected in the seeker's mode of relation to the beloved. The object of search is now at last "the Beloved One." In other words, the seeker is beyond admiration and attraction and has now been accepted as her lover. The structure of the Four Valleys is now clearly visible. Not a single word used by Bahá'u'lláh is arbitrary, cosmetic, or unnecessary. His dynamic poetics unveils the beauty of His mystical text.

Although the Four Valleys is concerned with the reflection of divine attributes at the level of ordinary human beings and their spiritual progress, it is the station of the Manifestation that is directly being discussed. This becomes evident in the account given of the different approaches to truth. The first approach is based on self (or soul or will). However, Bahá'u'lláh immediately makes it clear that the ultimate embodiment of this approach in its perfect form is the Manifestation of God. "This station," He says, "appertaineth to the self—but that self which is [the Soul of God that pervadeth all His Laws]" (50). In various tablets Bahá'u'lláh has explained that this Qur'ánic statement regarding the Self or Soul of God refers to the Manifestation of God.[2] Similarly, in His discussion of the second approach, that based on reason, it is evident that this also is primarily a description of the Manifestations: "this is the station of ... reason which is known as the Prophet and the Most Great Pillar" (52). After discussing the approach of love and the high station of that realm, Bahá'u'lláh talks about the valley of the heart and identifies the people of this valley as the representatives of God in the world. Finally, He explains that all these descriptions pertain to the Manifestations of God: "Whatever high proofs and wondrous allusions are recounted herein, [refer to the Letter of Unity and the Point of Unity]" (63). In other words, one may say that the Manifestation of God represents the highest degree of the unity of moral heroism, divine philosophy, and saintly love. This ideal is the model of the spiritual journey for all human beings.

Destiny and the Dialectic of Freedom

We have already seen how in various ways the questions of predestination, divine causation, and determinism are central to Sufi philosophical theology. But the concept of destiny (*qadar*) is particularly relevant to the present discussion because destiny can be seen as the concept central to understanding the Four Valleys. It was noted that, of the four approaches to reality described in the text, the approach based on the heart was qualitatively different from, and superior to, the other three. Bahá'u'lláh tells us that the key to understanding the station of the heart is the mystery of destiny: "[This is the station of destiny (*qadar*) and the foreordained mystery].... The exalted dwellers in this mansion [act,] in the court of rapture, with ... gladness [and joy, as God and the Lord]" (57–61).

Although the nature of destiny is ultimately a mystery that cannot be understood by the human mind, Bahá'u'lláh gives us some clues by devoting much of the rest of the discussion of the fourth valley to what is actually the issue of destiny. He refers to the tradition attributed to Imám 'Alí on the complexity and difficulty of the idea. At the same time, He relates the characteristics of those who have attained the realm of the heart and have understood the mystery of destiny: these people, He tells us, are the representatives of God among humankind. "This is the center of the mystery: 'He doth what He willeth, ordaineth what He pleaseth'" (57). Using the ambiguity of the term *qadar*, which means both destiny and measure or desert, Bahá'u'lláh affirms that these people "on the high seats of justice ... issue their commands, and they send down gifts according to each man's deserving" (61).

In these passages Bahá'u'lláh offers a new meaning for the concept of destiny as the defining feature of the fourth valley. Insight into that mystery can be glimpsed by looking at it in the context of the Bahá'í writings as a whole. First of all, it should be understood that here *destiny* is the same as the third stage of creation in the arc of descent.

The central issue concerning destiny has been the relation between divine and human will and action. Is everything predestined by God so that all human actions are predetermined without any human agency, or do humans have freedom of will and action? Actu-

ally the concept of destiny is even more general. It concerns the relation of the divine will to the creation, as well as the possibility of metaphysical freedom for contingent beings. In approaching the concept of
destiny, therefore, it will be useful to briefly explore the history of the
idea. Of those who have dealt with this issue, two figures particularly
important for our analysis are Ibnu'l-'Arabí and Shaykh Aḥmad-i-
Aḥsá'í.

Ibnu'l-'Arabí wrote extensively on the concept of destiny. For
him, although destiny comes after the divine will in the order of creation, it is actually destiny that determines the divine will and the
divine decree. Destiny, here, becomes the capacities and measures of
things in their archetypal essences. God's will is determined by those
eternal essences. Divine knowledge is seen as dependent on its objects
of knowledge, namely the essences of things or their destiny, and
God's creative will is dictated and determined by their logical requirements. On the other hand, this means that every event is preordained
and that everything happens in accordance with the arbitrary destiny
of things: whatever humans do is part of their predetermined destiny,
and there is no reward or punishment based on freedom of will and
justice. However, a mystic understands that arbitrary reward and punishment are also part of destiny and must be accepted because all things
are foreordained. This concept of destiny calls for a passive attitude of
resignation in the wake of predestination.[3]

Aspects of Ibnu'l-'Arabí's view of destiny are directly criticized in
the writings of Shaykh Aḥmad, the Báb, Bahá'u'lláh, and 'Abdu'l-
Bahá. First of all, Ibnu'l-'Arabí's theory contradicts the principle of the
absolute freedom and transcendence of God. By making divine
knowledge dependent on the archetypal essences, or the objects of
God's knowledge, Ibnu'l-'Arabí has made the essences of contingent
things the determinants and dictators of God's will. As 'Abdu'l-Bahá
has affirmed, however, divine knowledge is unlike human knowledge.[4] Human knowledge requires and depends on the existence of
the objects of knowledge. But God's knowledge does not, which
means that by definition we can have no idea of the nature of divine
knowledge. God's will, in other words, is absolutely free.

Paradoxically, however, Ibnu'l-'Arabí not only violates the principle of divine freedom, he also eliminates the possibility of human freedom through his excessively passive concept of destiny. The concept of destiny in the Bahá'í writings, on the other hand, becomes compatible with the relative freedom of human beings. It is clear that Bahá'u'lláh's concept of the mystery of destiny is not one of passivity and unfreedom. To realize one's destiny is not a mere acceptance of whatever "is"; on the contrary, it is an active movement toward realizing spiritual values in one's own life and developing the potentialities and perfections hidden, like "gems," in the "mine" of one's own being (*Gleanings* 260). The mystery of destiny, then, among other things, precisely implies transcending the opposition between the divine will and the individual will. It represents the actualization of all one's spiritual powers and the maturation of one's potentialities to the degree that one freely chooses spiritual values and the will of God. This is the stage of perfect freedom and moral autonomy, in which human potentialities are actualized in harmony with divine revelation. That is why Bahá'u'lláh defines this valley as both the station of mystery and the secret of maturation. It implies the integration of the approaches based on self, reason, and love.

This gives us a new mystical problematic. First of all, the Four Valleys becomes ultimately an epistemology of harmony among religion, reason, and mystical enlightenment. The Sufi opposition between religious law and spiritual truth is replaced by an ethic of self-actualization, or development of potentialities, encompassing all the various dimensions of human life. Second, the Four Valleys becomes a dialectic of freedom and self-determination. Spiritual journey is conceived as the process of emancipation from unfreedom and enslavement and as the attainment of freedom, self-consciousness, and autonomy.

This dialectic of freedom, however, is the exact opposite of the modern Western conception of freedom and self-realization, rooted in the philosophy of Enlightenment and liberalism, which regards freedom as the elimination and overcoming of any obstacle to the pursuit of human purposes and desires. That concept places spiritual values and divine law in the category of restrictions on freedom rather than freely chosen purposes. It is a freedom *from* rather than freedom *for*.[5] The conception of freedom outlined in the Bahá'í writings is characterized by a level of spiritual development in which the contradiction between the individual will and the divine will is replaced by an active mode of self-perfection, and a resolve to beautify and spiritualize the world. In this view, destiny paradoxically becomes the road to freedom.

This understanding of the concept of destiny and the realm of the heart is already supported in the writings of the Báb. As we have seen in discussing the ontological circle, for the Báb the three stages of Will, Determination, and Destiny represent, respectively, the stations of existence, essence, and the unity of existence and essence. Thus, for human beings true "destiny" is the agreement of their own will—represented by the stage of Determination—with the divine will—represented by the stage of Will.

Similarly, the realm of the heart, as the throne of God and the agreement of the individual will with the divine will, is emphasized in many texts. According to Shaykh Aḥmad, the approach of the heart implies an orientation in which the self has completely turned toward God's will. The realm of the heart is the realm of the perfect annihilation of one's own will in the divine will.[6] In the Kitáb-i-Aqdas Bahá'u'lláh has affirmed the same concept of authentic freedom that we find in the Four Valleys: "True liberty consisteth in man's submission unto My commandments.... The liberty that profiteth you is to be found nowhere except in complete servitude unto God...." (¶ 125).

This acceptance of the divine will as the essence of freedom implies active transformation of the self and the world in order to realize the paradise of every created thing in its own station, a paradise that is its true destiny. In one of His tablets Bahá'u'lláh defines the attainment of true liberty as the station characterized by the realization of His historic moral norm according to which glory is not in loving one's own country but in loving all humankind.[7] Absolute submission to the divine will thus ultimately implies a mode of consciousness and action oriented to realizing the oneness of humankind. That, according to Bahá'u'lláh, is the destiny and true liberty of human beings at the present stage of humanity's collective development.

SPIRITUAL JOURNEY IN THE SEVEN VALLEYS

From the Conference of the Birds to the Seven Valleys

Before considering in more detail some of the subjects discussed in Bahá'u'lláh's Seven Valleys, it is useful to outline briefly 'Aṭṭár's poetic tale of the seven stages of the spiritual journey, *The Conference of the Birds* (*Manṭiqu'ṭ-Ṭayr*). The story begins with an assemblage of birds who converse about their king. They observe that all other creatures have their own king but the birds have lost theirs. The hoopoe (*hudhud*)—according to Islamic tradition the messenger bird of King Solomon and the Queen of Sheba—attempts to gather the birds and prepare them for a quest to find the king of the birds, called the Símurgh (literally "Thirty Birds"), who resides on top of Mount Qáf. But when confronted with the prospect of the actual journey, each of the birds produces an excuse. The nightingale, rhapsodizing about its love for the rose garden, regrets that it cannot join the travelers or it will die from the pain of separation from its beloved. The partridge pleads its need to dig the mines in the mountains in search of treasure; the hawk its attachment to the might and power of the king; the owl its need to find treasure in abandoned places; the sparrow its weakness and inability to endure the long and arduous travel. Each of the birds—symbolizing different social groups, each with its own type of worldly attachment—makes its excuse to stay behind. The hoopoe responds to each bird with stories to show that they are mistaking ephemeral desires for authentic attachment and to stress the necessity of embarking on the journey to find their true beloved, the Símurgh.

Finally, some of the birds are convinced and they begin their journey toward Mount Qáf. To reach their destination they must traverse seven valleys named search, love, knowledge, contentment, unity, wonder, and annihilation in God.[8] Eventually, only thirty of the birds reach Mount Qáf. But when they arrive at the king's court and ask to enter the Símurgh's abode, permission is denied. At last they are allowed to enter and behold the revelation of the Símurgh above

them. They look up and see down. They see themselves—thirty birds
or *símurgh*—in the Símurgh. In this state of confusion, they hear the
Símurgh telling them that he is the mirror in which everyone sees
themselves. If the birds were forty, they would have seen their king as
"forty birds." The birds become annihilated in the revelation of their
king and subsist in their beloved.

'Attár's beautiful story is encapsulated by Bahá'u'lláh in the first
aphorism of the Persian Hidden Words:

> O YE PEOPLE THAT HAVE MINDS TO KNOW AND EARS TO HEAR!
> The first call of the Beloved is this: O mystic nightingale! Abide
> not but in the rose-garden of the spirit. O messenger [*hudhud*] of the
> Solomon of love! Seek thou no shelter except in the Sheba of the
> well-beloved, and O immortal phoenix! dwell not save on the
> mount [*Qáf*] of faithfulness. Therein is thy habitation, if on the
> wings of thy soul thou soarest to the realm of the infinite and seekest
> to attain thy goal.

Although Bahá'u'lláh's Seven Valleys uses 'Attár's categories (which
implies His approval, in general, of 'Attár's poem), Bahá'u'lláh's own
text is based on a new logic of discourse. Some differences between
the two texts are clearly visible. Bahá'u'lláh changes the order of two
of 'Attár's valleys, placing the valley of unity before that of contentment. 'Attár's work is filled with numerous lengthy illustrative tales
refuting the excuses offered by the birds. Stylistically, these stories tend
to overwhelm the unity and continuity of the text. Bahá'u'lláh uses an
economical and beautiful style, with only a few illustrative stories. In
His descriptions of the valleys, He quotes poems and stories from a
number of Sufi authors. 'Attár frequently uses love stories of a man for
another man to symbolize spiritual love. Bahá'u'lláh uses the love
between a man and a woman as an allegory for spiritual, metaphysical,
and cosmic love, consonant with the feminine representation of the
divine in His writings.

A more important difference, however, concerns the content of
the two texts. Bahá'u'lláh uses His modified version of 'Attár's categories to discuss topics and issues that are entirely absent from the latter's work, including spatial/romantic metaphors, theodicy, the

meaning of unity in terms of the Manifestations of God and progressive revelation, the different levels of being and the relativity of these
stages, new conceptions of wonder and the logic of dreams, the harmony of religious law and mystical truth, and the pantheistic interpretation of unity of existence, among others. But the most crucial difference is the fundamental transformation of Sufi symbolism that takes
place, including the historicization of the spiritual journey, the definition of the Manifestation of God as the ultimate destination of the
wayfarer, and the orientation of the spiritual journey toward the unity
of humankind.

Spatial Metaphor in the Seven Valleys

As in the Four Valleys, Bahá'u'lláh uses spatial metaphor to express the
stages of the spiritual journey in the Seven Valleys. The first and most
important of these metaphors is the concept of "steed" [*markab*]. The
description of the valleys opens: "The first is The Valley of Search.
The steed of this valley is patience; without patience the wayfarer on
this journey will reach nowhere and attain no goal" (*Seven Valleys* 4–
5). Similarly, Bahá'u'lláh names the steed of the second valley, the
valley of love: "The steed of this valley is pain; and if there be no pain
this journey will never end" (8).

The reader may be puzzled to find that there is no mention of any
steed in the valleys that follow. However, this is not due to inconsis-
tency or unintentional omission. Rather it is precisely this presence
and absence which provides the clue to the overall structure of the
text. The discussion of the spatial metaphor in the Four Valleys has
made the answer to this puzzle easy. The first two valleys, those of
search and love, imply remoteness from the location of the beloved. As
if in a distant land, the wayfarer requires the assistance of a steed to
traverse the space between himself and the home of the beloved. The
first valley, therefore, implies traveling from a far place until reaching
the gates of the city where the beloved resides. In the second valley,
the valley of love, the wayfarer tries to find the home of the beloved.
The wayfarer's mode of consciousness changes from restless search in
the first valley to enthusiasm and longing in the second. Both "steeds,"

of patience and pain, seem to symbolize the wayfarer's state of alienation, separation, and yearning.

At the end of the second valley it is as if the wayfarer has arrived at the gate of the beloved's house. We can imagine him getting off his steed and walking toward the gate. In the third valley, the valley of knowledge, the wayfarer's "inner eyes will open and he will privily converse with his Beloved; he will set ajar the gate of truth and piety, and shut the doors of vain imaginings" (11).

The valley of knowledge is "the last plane of limitation [taḥdíd]," the intermediate station between the realm of separation and the realm of unity. In the language of the spatial metaphor, this is expressed as the entrance of the wayfarer into the house of the beloved one. The next four valleys represent increasing degrees of intimacy with the beloved. Bahá'u'lláh affirms this romantic logic of space most explicitly in His description of the fourth valley, the valley of unity: "In this station he pierceth the veils of plurality, fleeth from the worlds of the flesh, and ascendeth into the heaven of singleness…. He steppeth into the sanctuary of the Friend, and shareth as an intimate the pavilion of the Loved One. He stretcheth out the hand of truth from the sleeve of the Absolute…." (17–18). At this stage the wayfarer has been taken into the intimate domicile of the beloved. The veils of plurality are cast aside and the lover converses intimately with her. Although Bahá'u'lláh is using romantic metaphors here, He makes it clear that this intimacy has nothing to do with physical and material attachments. That is why the wayfarer "pierceth the veils of plurality, fleeth from the worlds of the flesh." All the debates about the romantic poetry of the Persian Sufi poets become irrelevant here. Bahá'u'lláh always makes it clear that He is talking strictly of spiritual love, a love transcending all earthly desires and limitations.

But as Bahá'u'lláh also makes clear, the fourth valley, the valley of unity, is the beginning of the stage of unity and integration. From now on, the spatial metaphor becomes inherently inadequate because the distance it signified has been closed. After the valley of unity, the spatial metaphor recedes to the background. The next three valleys no longer describe distance and separation but the differential forms of the lover's feelings on being united with the beloved, corresponding to the increasing degree of intimacy. Even words themselves become increasingly inadequate here: "The tongue faileth in describing these three Valleys, and speech falleth short. The pen steppeth not into this region, the ink leaveth only a blot" (30).

The fifth valley is one of contentment and joy. Here, "the traveler witnesseth the beauty of the Friend in everything. Even in fire, he seeth the face of the Beloved. He beholdeth in illusion the secret of reality, and readeth from the attributes the riddle of the Essence. For he hath burnt away the veils with his sighing, and unwrapped the shroudings with a single glance; with piercing sight he gazeth on the new creation; with lucid heart he graspeth subtle verities." The sixth valley is one of wonder, awe, and yet bewilderment and turmoil. In this valley, the wayfarer "seeth the shape of wealth as poverty itself, and the essence of freedom as sheer impotence.... At every moment he beholdeth a wondrous world, a new creation, and goeth from astonishment to astonishment, and is lost in awe at the works of the Lord of Oneness" (31–32).

Finally, the seventh valley "is the dying from self [faná] and the living in God [baqá], the being poor in self and rich in the Desired One." Bahá'u'lláh explicates that "poverty" here means "being poor in the things of the created world, rich in the things of God's world...." (36). In this valley, the image of perfect unity with the beloved is expressed in the blazing out of the lover's being in the fire of love: "For when the true lover and devoted friend reacheth to the presence of the Beloved, the sparkling beauty of the Loved One and the fire of the lover's heart will kindle a blaze and burn away all veils and wrappings. Yea, all he hath, from heart to skin, will be set aflame, so that nothing will remain save the Friend" (36).

The Identity of Unity

The spiritual journey can be seen as the realm of mediation between the two expressions of the Manifestation of God as the origin of human existence (expressed in the arc of descent) and its end (expressed in the arc of ascent). For that reason, the stages of spiritual

journey are the stages of struggle to transcend the fundamental oppositions of visible and invisible, plurality and unity, potentiality and
actuality, finite and infinite. In the first Persian Hidden Word, which
alludes to 'Aṭṭár's poem about the seven valleys, Bahá'u'lláh speaks of
"the realm of the infinite" as the true habitation of the human soul,
which must be regained through that spiritual ascent. In the journey
through the seven valleys the essential human spiritual identity, which
is the highest potentiality of its nature, becomes actualized by transcending diversity and realizing unity in the mirror of the earthly
realm of limitation and opposition. The valleys, in other words, are
stages of overcoming the personality's enslavement in selfish and limited desires, which had been the basis of the identity, and finding its
true nature and identity in a universalistic solidarity with all reality.

The first valley can be conceived as a conscious search for true
identity: the wayfarer thirsts for spiritual growth and searches for spiritual truth in the realm of phenomena. The valley of love may be
understood as the awakening of natural attraction and fervor in the
soul by glimpsing the traces of spiritual truth and oneness within the
diversity of phenomena. The valley of knowledge can be seen as the
stage of the conscious realization of the interconnectedness of all phenomena and events. Here events that once seemed meaningless, pain-
ful, or absurd are disclosed as expressions of teleological order, meaning, and unity. Here the finite is seen as connected with the infinite.

The valley of unity represents the end of the realm of limitation,
opposition, and plurality. In that valley, the wayfarer "looketh on all
things with the eye of oneness, and seeth the brilliant rays of the divine
sun shining from the dawning-point of Essence alike on all created
things, and the lights of singleness reflected over all creation" (18). All
things in the realm of phenomena are now perceived as reflections of
one and the same underlying spiritual reality. All contingent pluralities
are now understood as manifestations of the same divine will, love,
and intellect. The invisible is witnessed in all its visible shadows and
reflections. A sense of universal solidarity and unity with all things
emerges. This stage heralds the birth of a new identity of unity which
must be ripened, expanded, and perfected in the next three stages.

This consciousness of unity must now penetrate the entire being of the wayfarer. Not only the reason, but also the feelings, desires, ethical motivations, and the actual living approach to reality must become transformed in the light of the principle of unity. The next three stages have a systematic relation to one another as different moments of that transformation and consolidation of the identity of unity. In the valley of contentment, the spiritual orientation permeates the wayfarer's will, desire, and feelings, creating a sense of delight and joy. In the valley of wonder, the constraining boundaries of a limited rational consciousness become dissolved by amazement, love, and the creative revelations of the unconscious. Bahá'u'lláh speaks of the mixture of confusion, wonder, ecstasy, bewilderment, and the fusion of ideas and feelings in this stage and uses the example of dreams and the realization of dream revelations in the wakeful state. Here, the identity of unity is accompanied by a profound sense of bewilderment—a constant fusion of ego and non-ego, and a fluid tension between knowledge and ignorance, certainty and doubt, conscious and unconscious.

The last stage of this spiritual journey, the valley of annihilation in God and subsistence in God, represents the apex of the new identity of unity. Here the power of divine love burns away all vestiges of opposition and limitation that belonged to the selfish and limited ego and forges a new identity based on committed, loving, and rational devotion to spiritual values, the will of God, and the essential unity of spiritual reality. Since the Manifestation of God is the supreme reflection and mirror of divine unity that is accessible to human beings, the new spiritual identity implies an engaged spiritual orientation for the individual and a commitment to realizing the kingdom of God in the phenomenal realm of human historical existence.

Relativity of Stages in the Seven Valleys

Although Bahá'u'lláh explores the process of spiritual journey in seven stages in the Seven Valleys, He makes it clear that there is nothing absolute or categorical about this particular seven-stage scheme. He emphasizes this point in three different ways. First, He says that although for most Sufis, including 'Aṭṭár, the stages of spiritual development end with the seventh stage, in His view the seventh valley is only the beginning of the city or valley of *qalb* (heart), which itself has its own stages:[9]

> They who soar in the heaven of singleness and reach to the sea of the Absolute, reckon this city—which is the station of life in God— as the furthermost state of mystic knowers, and the farthest homeland of the lovers. But to this evanescent One of the mystic ocean, this station is the first gate of the heart's citadel, that is, man's first entrance to the city of the heart; and the heart is endowed with four stages, which would be recounted should a kindred soul be found. (41)

Bahá'u'lláh states that these seven stages can never end within the temporal world, and yet with divine assistance they can be traversed in seven steps, or seven breaths, or even one breath. In so saying, Bahá'u'lláh is setting aside the Sufi conception that it is possible to acquire ultimate union with God without the mediation of the Manifestation of God. The seven stages, then, are just the beginning; human beings can progress infinitely in the spiritual journey without ever being able to transcend the inherent limitations of their human nature. Bahá'u'lláh also speaks of the possibility of reaching a stage of mystic unity in the seventh valley which is higher even than the Sufi stages of unity of existence and unity of vision: "In this Valley," He says, "the wayfarer leaveth behind him the stages of the 'oneness of Being [or existence, *vujúd*] and Manifestation [or vision, *shuhúd*],' and reacheth a oneness that is sanctified above these two stations" (39).

There can be no doubt that here again Bahá'u'lláh is affirming His basic principle that both Ibnu'l-'Arabí's concept of the unity of existence and Aḥmad Sirhindí's idea of the unity of vision are inadequate understandings of these spiritual mysteries, and that no human mind and no Sufi doctrine can transcend the limits of the human station. In one of His later tablets Bahá'u'lláh has discussed in more detail the concepts of the unity of existence and unity of vision. There, He writes that appropriate and acceptable meanings of these terms define both as different stages of the concept of the unity of God (*tawḥíd*). The unity of existence (*tawḥíd-i-vujúdí*) refers to the mode of consciousness that finds nothing else existing at the level of divine Existence and affirms the absolute transcendence and ascendancy of God. This is a categorical rejection of any vulgar form of pantheism. The other stage, the unity of vision (*tawḥíd-i-shuhúdí*), refers to recognizing divine attributes in all things and seeing the realm of nature as the mirror of God. Bahá'u'lláh approves both these forms of consciousness.[10]

The relativity of the stages is also expressed in the way Bahá'u'lláh treats the stages themselves, affirming different classifications of the stages of spiritual journey. Bahá'u'lláh divides the Seven Valleys into the two broad categories of differentiation and integration, or limitation and unity. This binary structure, which corresponds to the spatial metaphor in the Seven Valleys, is fundamental to the logic of spiritual journey. But the Seven Valleys is also, in another sense, a discussion of three stages. This will be evident in discussing the passages in the valley of knowledge concerning theodicy. In the description of the fourth valley, Bahá'u'lláh refers to the Sufi literature that classified reality into four levels and talked of four journeys. Bahá'u'lláh here offers a non-absolutistic epistemology according to which different conceptualizations of stages or levels of being correspond to the different stations and perspectives of the observer. However, He notes that these conceptualizations are expressions of particular perspectives, but that there are infinite worlds and various possible classifications: "all the variations which the wayfarer in the stages of his journey beholdeth in the realms of being, proceed from his own vision" (18).

> Although the divine worlds be never ending, yet some refer to them as four: the world of time (*zamán*), which is the one that hath both a beginning and an end; the world of duration (*dahr*), which hath a beginning, but whose end is not revealed; the world of perpetuity (*sarmad*), whose beginning is not to be seen but which is known to have an end; and the world of eternity (*azal*), neither a beginning nor an end of which is visible. Although there are many differing statements as to these points, to recount them in detail would result in weariness. Thus, some have said that the world of perpetuity hath neither beginning nor end, and have named the world of eternity as the invisible, impregnable Empyrean. Others have called these the worlds of the Heavenly Court (*Láhút*), of the Empyrean Heaven

(*Jabarút*), of the Kingdom of the Angels (*Malakút*), and of the mortal
world (*Násút*).

The journeys in the pathway of love are reckoned as four: From
the creatures to the True One; from the True One to the creatures;
from the creatures to the creatures; from the True One to the True
One. (25).

Bahá'u'lláh then remarks that He dislikes "the copious citation from
sayings of the past" (26). It is clear that He does not take any of these
classifications as absolute.[11] They are all accurate—provided that we
do not insist on one to the exclusion of the others. The fivefold classification (*Háhút, Láhút, Jabarút, Malakút,* and *Násút*) discussed in the
Tablet of All Food is only one among many found in the Bahá'í texts.
At the highest level of abstraction, the Bahá'í writings affirm only one
level of existence, and that is God. But reality can also be classified into
the two realms of the invisible (*ghayb*) and the visible (*shuhúd*). Shaykh
Ahmad has written of more than ten alternative classifications of the
levels of being.[12] But if one classification of levels of being is relatively
privileged in the Bahá'í writings, it is without a doubt the three levels
of God, the Manifestations of God, and the created realm.

Much space could be devoted to a discussion of the four levels of
being that Bahá'u'lláh mentions in the valley of unity as there is an
abundance of Islamic literature on the subject. However, given Bahá'-
u'lláh's statements about the relativity of all categories, and His aversion to preoccupation with such explication, a detailed exploration of
the Islamic texts about these categories would have no significant
bearing on Bahá'u'lláh's mystical writings. The logic of Bahá'u'lláh's
discourse makes this silence and absence profoundly expressive and
actively present.

The Seven Valleys and the Problem of Theodicy

As Max Weber has said, all religions have to provide solutions to the
two theological problems of salvation and theodicy (reconciling
God's goodness and the existence of evil).[13] Bahá'u'lláh's discussion of
the seven valleys that comprise the arc of ascent in fact encompasses
both these themes. As stages of the spiritual journey toward the names

and attributes of God, the Seven Valleys addresses the question of salvation. Aspects of this salvation metaphysics have already been discussed. But the Seven Valleys also addresses the question of theodicy. The philosophical problem of theodicy has been concerned with resolving the apparent contradiction posed by the creation of a world of suffering, injustice, and evil by a God who is just and good. However, it is not the philosophical question but the experiential dimension of the problem that is most important. In the Seven Valleys, the stages of the spiritual journey are also the stages of dealing with the problem of suffering.

In all Bahá'u'lláh's mystical writings, the issue of suffering in the path of God is presented as a necessary element of spiritual transformation and growth. The Hidden Words contains many such statements. Many of Baha'u'lláh's major mystical writings, including the Tablet of the Ḥúrí, the Fire Tablet, and the Ode of the Dove are clearly concerned with, among other things, theodicy. These writings frequently represent a dialogue between Bahá'u'lláh speaking as a human being subject to torment and suffering, and Bahá'u'lláh speaking as the Primal Will, the Holy Spirit, and the Manifestation of God. This inner discourse—normally represented through the romantic dialogue between Bahá'u'lláh and the Maid of Heaven—exemplifies the stages and dialectic of creative suffering. At first the lover laments his tormenting conditions and consequent suffering, then the beloved explains that this suffering is part of the quest for the beloved and the attainment of perfection in the world, and finally the problem is resolved by an enthusiastic embrace of creative suffering by the lover. The story of Job and the mystic love poetry of Ibn-i-Fáriḍ, as well as texts from other mystic traditions, also show similar structures.

In the Seven Valleys this process is articulated in discrete stages. The first two valleys, of search and love, constitute the first stage of this theodicy. In both these valleys the wayfarer is beset by afflictions and complains about them. This is because the wayfarer at this stage sees the "beginning" but not the "end." In other words, he perceives only the empirically present difficulties but does not perceive the wisdom and purpose behind the pain. The second stage of theodicy is represented by the valley of knowledge. This is the knowledge of ends. The wayfarer now sees both the beginning and the end and realizes that suffering is not absurd and meaningless, and that it should be borne with steadfastness and patience. To illustrate, Bahá'u'lláh recounts the story of the longing lover who, fleeing the pursuing watchmen, climbs over a wall and thereby comes face to face with his beloved. Finally, in the third stage of theodicy, the beginning and the end become one and the same for the wayfarer. In the highest degrees of this stage, the wayfarer sees neither the beginning nor the end—and even beyond that, sees neither no-beginning nor no-end. Obviously the last and highest stage represents an approach to theodicy characterized by the joyful acceptance of the will of God and the unity of the individual will with the divine will. Bahá'u'lláh comments:

> Now if the lover could have looked ahead, he would have blessed the watchman at the start, and prayed on his behalf, and he would have seen that tyranny as justice; but since the end was veiled to him, he moaned and made his plaint in the beginning. Yet those who journey in the garden land of knowledge, because they see the end in the beginning, see peace in war and friendliness in anger.

> Such is the state of the wayfarers in this Valley; but the people of the Valleys above this see the end and the beginning as one; nay, they see neither beginning nor end, and witness neither "first" nor "last." Nay rather, the denizens of the undying city, who dwell in the green garden land, see not even "neither first nor last"; they fly from all that is first, and repulse all that is last. (15)

The question of theodicy is directly related to the questions of design in nature, progress in human history, the nature of divine providence, and the quality of moral and spiritual action. Usually the denial of divine existence, providence, and justice arises from a belief in the randomness and apparent meaninglessness of events in both nature and history. Such a perspective finds life a set of absurd sufferings and sees no reason for moral and spiritual commitment in the world.

Bahá'u'lláh's approach to theodicy presents a hierarchical solution to these issues. The first three stages of spiritual progress, which are located within the realm of limitation, are still bound by the logic of phenomena pertaining to that realm. The third stage, knowledge, represents a solution to the problem of theodicy in terms of the phenomenal realm: here the meaninglessness of events is replaced by meaningfulness, but this meaningfulness is still in terms of phenomena. The world—both nature and history—is now seen as interconnected and teleological. Because not only the beginning but also the end are now perceived, from this enlarged perspective the gaze of the wayfarer comprehends the grand scheme of order and divine justice in nature and creation and discerns progress and emancipation in the complex course of human history. Even evil becomes apprehended within this perspective which, because it includes the end as well as the beginning, makes it possible to see that, in the end, evil only galvanizes the forces that bring about its defeat. This perspective acknowledges divine providence and finds moral and spiritual action justified in light of its positive consequences in the realm of phenomena.

However, this level is not yet the highest plane of spiritual development. In the realm of unity comprising the last four valleys, a qualitatively new perspective and logic emerges concerning theodicy, the world, and moral action. The world is now perceived in its relation to the invisible divine Reality. The beginning and the end are now one, and increasingly both are liberated from any temporal limitation. Phenomenal consequences are no longer the driving force of moral and spiritual action, which is performed not for any extrinsic reward in this world or the next, but for its own sake. One acts purely for the sake of the love of God. The search for the empirical sign of providence at the level of phenomena (which characterized the stages of limitation) is replaced by consciousness of love, mystery, divine transcendence, and the unity and interconnectedness of all things, which becomes the motivation of moral action and the resolution to the problem of theodicy.

Spiritual Journey as Stages of Moral Development

The themes of both the Seven Valleys and the Four Valleys—theodicy, freedom, and faith—converge on the topic of moral development. A direct account of moral dynamics, however, is to be found in the analysis of self or soul (*nafs*), the first approach to reality mentioned in the Four Valleys. No English word conveys the complexity of the term *nafs*, which means soul, self, and desire. The underlying point is that the human soul is capable of acquiring different characteristics and developing different identities—it can be dominated either by the logic of desire or by spiritual values. That is why the entire process of moral development is presented as stages of "self." In the Four Valleys, Bahá'u'lláh defines the approach of *nafs* in terms of the higher stations of self and not the base self of desire: "On this plane, the self [*nafs*] is not rejected but beloved; it is well-pleasing and not to be shunned. Although at the beginning, this plane is the realm of conflict, yet it endeth in attainment to the throne of splendor" (*Four Valleys* 50).

The discussion of the stages of *nafs* has been a popular topic in Islamic mysticism, and the stages have normally been explicated in the light of Qur'ánic verses. Such a perspective provides a powerful theory of morality and moral development which is not only superior to utilitarian, hedonistic, formalistic, nihilistic, and postmodern–relativistic forms of ethics, but also to complex and insightful theories like Kohlberg's stages of moral development.[14]

Bahá'u'lláh and 'Abdu'l-Bahá have repeatedly talked about the stages of *nafs*.[15] In one of 'Abdu'l-Bahá's tablets, for instance, ten stages of *nafs* are identified: the desiring and aggressive soul (*nafs-i-ammárih*), the blaming soul (*nafs-i-lavvámih*), the inspired soul (*nafs-i-mulhamih*), the well-assured soul (*nafs-i-muṭma'innih*), the pleased soul (*nafs-i-ráḍíyih*), the soul pleasing unto God (*nafs-i-marḍíyyih*), the perfect soul (*nafs-i-kámilih*), the celestial Soul (*nafs-i-malakútíyyih*), the heavenly Soul (*nafs-i-jabarútíyyih*), and the Holy Divine Soul (*nafs-i-láhútíyyih qudsíyyih*).[16] Not all these stages, and definitely not the last one, are within human reach. The present discussion is concerned with the stages of *nafs*, or self, that represent the dynamics of human will. In the beginning, the will is predominantly hedonistic and aggressive. In the next stage, some form of moral values is accepted but without serious transformation of the will. The result is inner conflict, guilt, and struggle against lower impulses. In the stages that follow, moral values become increasingly universalized and spiritualized, and the will becomes transformed, progressively reflecting the divine will. The initial contradiction between moral principles and will is transcended, and increasingly the object of one's desire becomes the will of God. Here again the elimination of contradiction between freedom and obedience to the divine will is the central category of Bahá'u'lláh's concept of self-actualization, self-consciousness, autonomy, and morality.

Two additional points should be emphasized in this connection: first, the fundamental inseparability of law and mystical knowledge; second, the continuity of this principle between Bahá'u'lláh's early mystical writings and His later writings on law. In the Seven Valleys Bahá'u'lláh emphasizes that even the highest degree of mystical knowledge is never above the law. Having mentioned the exalted station that lies beyond both oneness of existence and oneness of vision— the highest stages spoken of by the Sufis—Bahá'u'lláh immediately adds: "In all these journeys the traveler must stray not the breadth of a hair from the 'Law,' for this is indeed the secret of the 'Path' and the fruit of the Tree of 'Truth'; and in all these stages he must cling to the robe of obedience to the commandments, and hold fast to the cord of shunning all forbidden things, that he may be nourished from the cup of the Law and informed of the mysteries of Truth" (39–40). This important concept will be stressed in Bahá'u'lláh's later writings, notably the Kitáb-i-Aqdas, His Book of Laws. In fact, as He states in the Seven Valleys, there is a direct and necessary relation between obedience to the law and the knowledge of mystical Truth.[17] Using a metaphor which will also become important in the Kitáb-i-Aqdas, the law is here described as a "cup" which imparts the knowledge of the spirit to the one who drinks from it.

Spiritual Journey as the Mystery of Sacrifice

The entire structure of the Seven Valleys and the Four Valleys can be understood as the dialectic of negation and affirmation—or death and life, annihilation and subsistence, or effacement (*maḥv*) and sobriety (*ṣaḥv*). This dialectical movement repeats itself in every individual valley and in the relation of the different valleys to each other. For instance, in the valley of search, one must travel away from one's self to be able to travel toward the beloved. Similarly, love implies relinquishing self-love in order to become united with the beloved. Knowledge implies going beyond the immediate suffering in order to attain wisdom. Contentment requires poverty in terms of the world in order to achieve true wealth and independence. Wonder requires negation of one's own categories in order to be exposed to divine reality and truth. And annihilation means nothingness in God as the condition of subsistence in God.

It is through the process of differentiation and integration, movement beyond the self and toward the other, that one achieves a new, more comprehensive and thus more authentic and richer consciousness of reality. This symbolism seems most clearly present in the final stage of the Seven Valleys, which concerns the dialectic of death and life, or annihilation and subsistence. Bahá'u'lláh emphasizes the same point in the need for unity of effacement (or intoxication) and sobriety. This is further developed in the Kitáb-i-Aqdas where the structure of Bahá'í ideal society is presented in terms of the unity of the aesthetic and rational principles. The principle of refinement (liṭáfat) can be seen to correspond to the moment of intoxication, effacement, and annihilation, whereas the principle of rationality, work, and efficiency corresponds to the moment of sobriety. In this way the spiritual journey can also be conceptualized as the dialectics of aesthetic and rational principles.[18]

Finally, another expression of the same principle of negation and affirmation can be found in the concept of the "mystery of sacrifice." As 'Abdu'l-Bahá has explained it, the sacrifice of a seed brings forth a higher life in the form of the tree, which also produces many more seeds. In this sense martyrdom becomes an expression of spiritual advancement.[19]

The Seven Valleys and Recognition of the Manifestation of God

Given that the ultimate aim of spiritual development in Bahá'u'lláh's description of the mystical journey is the recognition of the Manifestation of God, another way to interpret these stages pertains to the process of the individual's recognition of the station of Bahá'u'lláh. In this understanding, the valleys may be represented in the following sequence. At first the wayfarer is looking for answers everywhere (search); then he hears of the new revelation and becomes enthusiastic to investigate it (love). After accepting Bahá'u'lláh as the Manifestation of God (knowledge), he gradually learns about his teachings concerning unity in diversity at different levels of reality and recognizes the oneness of all the Manifestations of God (unity). Having acquired a new spiritual identity and heightened perspective, he experiences contentment, detachment from the world, and confidence in his new identity (contentment).

The next stage is one of bewilderment, wonder, and confusion. This is the stage of deepening and scholarship. By studying his new faith ever more deeply, he realizes new gems and insights that were hidden to him. At the same time he confronts issues that he does not immediately grasp, and which may seem contradictory to his reason or understanding. This stage is, as Bahá'u'lláh testified, a perilous one. Knowledge previously secure is questioned and past confident identities challenged. Like the dream state, this stage is filled with mysteries and insights and yet also with bewilderment and questioning. As in a dream, the identity is fluid and insecure.

This stage opens up two possibilities. One is negative: namely, the individual becomes filled with pride and takes himself and his own categories as the standard to which divine revelation is submitted. He reifies every single judgment of his reason in the form of the myth of total reason. This road is the road of hasty generalizations, disregard of the principles of covenant, and eventual spiritual suicide. The alternate approach is one of patience, humility, faith, and commitment to the divine standard even if there remain questions that one has not yet adequately understood. Such an approach of humility takes the believer to the final stage of annihilation in, and subsistence by, the divine will. Here one recognizes the Words of God with the eye of God and understands their meanings in the light of Bahá'u'lláh's own interpretive principle, namely the principle of covenant. This is the station of the most great steadfastness. It is here that gradually new insights are created, creative solutions are found, and novel identities based on harmony of the individual will and the divine will are developed.

THE METAPHYSICS OF REALITY

Having explored some aspects of Bahá'u'lláh's approach to spiritual journey, several points should be noted concerning the general message of Bahá'u'lláh's mystical texts. The stages of the spiritual journey describe, among other things, the metaphysics—or ontological essence—of reality. All created things, that is, are mirrors of the divine. Therefore the nature of all created things, not only that of human beings, is unfolded through a form of spiritual journey. All beings are embodiments of divine love, long for recognition of God, testify to the unity of God, reflect divine attributes, are bewildered by the divine creative act, and praise God. The essentially spiritual nature of all created things is particularly discussed in Bahá'u'lláh's Book of the River. In refuting rationalist arguments against the possibility of miracles, He explains that "all phenomena, as things endowed with power, are also miracles of God."[20] The miraculous nature of all reality, however, transcends the limits of human reason, which is incapable of comprehending any phenomenon independent from experience and observation. Reason takes for granted all the wonders of natural phenomena, reducing them to necessary truths capable of deduction through rational analysis. In such a mechanistic methodology, the rationalists contrast the "irrationality" of miracles, the existence of God, and the possibility of revelation to the "rational" character of "ordinary" natural events. In the Book of the River, Bahá'u'lláh affirms the necessity of empirical experience for knowledge precisely in order to emphasize the miraculous and divine origin of all reality.

Such a conception of nature challenges the modern mechanistic conception which has "disenchanted" the world, deprived reality of sense and purposiveness, and condemned it to an absurd nihilistic nightmare. Instead, Bahá'u'lláh represents nature as the embodiment of divine love and the mirror of the divine attributes. Human beings, therefore, have an intrinsic affinity and unity with all creatures, but their human consciousness gives them the ability to reflect this metaphysical universal love in their empirical conscious experience as well. The superior conscious faculties of humans thus become the occasion for an attitude of unity, care, love, service, and sacrifice toward life, nature, and humanity.

Reconceptualizing the Idea of Dhikr

The idea of *dhikr* was introduced in Chapter 2 in connection with Sufism. In its general sense, as prayer and remembrance of God, the concept of *dhikr* is approved and strongly emphasized in the writings of Bahá'u'lláh, even while He clearly rejects some of the specific ritualistic practices associated with Sufi *dhikr*.[21] For example, in His ordinances concerning prayer in the Kitáb-i-Aqdas, Bahá'u'lláh prohibits muttering sacred verses in public places (¶ 108) and enjoins moderation even in reading the revealed Word (¶ 149).

The concept of *dhikr* itself becomes fundamentally reinterpreted in the Bahá'í writings. *Dhikr* means both remembrance and utterance. In discussing the ontological circle, it was seen that the four stages of creation—Will, Determination, Destiny, and Decree—are different expressions of the Manifestation of God, which the Báb has identified as different expressions of *dhikr* or "utterance." This *dhikr* is obviously the equivalent of the Word of God, or the creative act of God, which is the realm of the revelation and manifestation of God. The divine command in the form of the word "Be," which brings forth all creation, is precisely the divine *dhikr*.

As to the Word of God and His "Remembrance" in the world, *dhikr* in the Bahá'í writings primarily refers to the Báb and Bahá'u'lláh. For instance, throughout the Báb's Commentary on the Súrih of Joseph (Aḥsanu'l-Qaṣaṣ or Qayyúmu'l-Asmá'), *dhikr* is used as the title of the Báb Himself.[22] In this, the Báb's first revealed scripture, even the term *dhikr* itself is a subtle but unmistakable declaration of His station as a Manifestation of God.

Dhikr as the divine creative Word and revelation finds its mirror in the human *dhikr* or remembrance of God. In this form, *dhikr* takes the character of dialogue with God in the form of prayer. This *dhikr* or praise of God is in fact the essence of created beings. But because no one can adequately praise God because no one can know God, the only way we can remember God in prayer is to mention the self-description of God. _Dhikr_, then, becomes reciting the prayers revealed by the Manifestations of God. Since revelation is progressive, _dhikr_ also becomes a progressive process and presupposes the recognition of the Manifestation of God in each age. In one passage, Bahá'u'lláh simultaneously rejects traditional Sufi practices including _dhikr_ and confirms that the criterion of acceptability for both deeds and worship is the Manifestation of God:

> There hath been, and continueth to be, a number of men in islands who have denied themselves food and water, associate with the beasts of the field, impose upon themselves extreme mortifications, and engage in rituals of a devotional nature [_adhkár_]. And yet not even one among them is remembered by God.... Today the mantle of deeds and the crown of worship are, outwardly and inwardly, this Most Great Remembrance [_Dhikr_]. He is, verily, the Word that decideth between the peoples and reduceth all mountains to dust....[23]

The Bahá'í historical approach to mystical experience is also reflected in the conception of _dhikr_. But this historical consciousness is accompanied by the principle of the oneness of humanity and service to society. That is why the place dedicated to _dhikr_, that is, the Bahá'í House of Worship, or Mashriqu'l-Adhkár (Dawning-place of the Mention of God), as the place of prayer-service is not only open to the followers of all religions, it is also the center of various institutions of social service designed to help the poor and needy, the homeless, the orphans, and the community in general. Once again, the concept of _dhikr_ becomes translated directly into the committed practice of the oneness of humanity. Shoghi Effendi writes of the relationship between the spiritual and social aspects of the Mashriqu'l-Adhkár: "Nothing short of direct and constant interaction between the spiritual forces emanating from this House of Worship centering in the heart of the Mashriqu'l-Adhkár, and the energies consciously displayed by those who administer its affairs in their service to humanity can possibly provide the necessary agency capable of removing the ills that have so long and so grievously afflicted humanity."[24]

It is clear that reducing the word _dhikr_, as it is used in Bahá'u'lláh's writings, to merely Sufi notions and rituals is a distortion ignoring the conceptual revolution undergone by the term in the Bahá'í writings. The highest point of the dialectical journey of _dhikr_ is when the _dhikr_ of human beings, in turn, becomes the occasion for the reciprocal mention (_dhikr_) of the name of the believer by God. In the Kitáb-i-Aqdas Bahá'u'lláh writes: "Happy the days that have been consecrated to the remembrance of God, and blessed the hours which have been spent in praise [_dhikr_] of Him Who is the All-Wise.... Did they but know it, they would renounce their all, that their names may be mentioned [_yudhkaru_, from _dhikr_] before His throne" (¶ 40). And in the Arabic Hidden Words, we read: "Make mention of Me on My earth, that in My heaven I may remember thee, thus shall Mine eyes and thine be solaced" (43).

The Characteristics of Spiritual Knowledge

It is clear that the spiritual knowledge which is the goal of the mystic journey is qualitatively different from prevalent modern notions of knowledge—notably positivistic approaches in which knowledge is a mechanistic product of the interest in control and domination of nature oriented to utilitarian purposes. Some of the characteristics of spiritual knowledge can be summarized as follows. Similar to Plato's concept of knowledge as remembrance of the experience of the spiritual world prior to the descent into the realm of matter,[25] spiritual knowledge is the actualization of the inherent essence and perfections of human beings. Such knowledge is a response to the inner core of existence, and the soul's return to its authentic home. The ultimate interest, so to speak, of this form of knowledge is the realization of the purpose and goal of existence.

Unlike various empirical sciences, this form of knowledge concerns the totality of being and metaphysical reality as well. In spiritual knowledge one attains a sense of unity and sympathy with nature, other humans, and transcendental reality. Spiritual knowledge relates humans to all created things as the mirrors of divine perfection. Such knowledge necessarily becomes inseparable from committed practice and encompassing love. It is a type of knowledge in which art, philosophy, science, religion, and other human faculties are harmonized and oriented toward the spirit of service and love.

In addition to being oriented to the totality of being, this exalted knowledge is also self-reflective and critical in nature (in the Kantian sense of *critique* as a process of self-reflection and self-knowledge).[26] In this way, spiritual knowledge is not a mechanistic reflection of some external phenomenon by the human subject. On the contrary, it is a critical process of self-realization and self-discovery.

Beyond even that, spiritual knowledge is simultaneously a transformative process in which the subject of knowledge, namely the self, is fundamentally changed through the process of knowing. Realization of the self means a structural change in attitudes, goals, values, and priorities. It is a movement away from the logic of enslavement by immediate physical hedonistic and aggressive impulses, and a movement toward actualization of all the self's manifold potentialities. Self-consciousness, consequently, implies freedom and the unity of the individual will with the divine will. The implication of this logic is that the ultimate evidence for the truth of this type of knowledge is the spiritualization of the life and activities of the subject. It is a knowledge that demands expression in a discourse of deeds rather than words.

Such knowledge is universal knowledge in the sense that, with the attainment of knowledge of the self, the wayfarer has also attained knowledge of the totality of reality. This is evident in the notion that the human being is the perfect mirror of the world. Knowledge of the self becomes knowledge of being in general. This self-knowledge is ultimately possible through knowledge of the Manifestation of God, who represents the Perfect Human Being in each particular age. Knowledge of the self through knowledge of the Manifestation of God becomes knowledge of one's own state of perfection or paradise. Finally, this knowledge, by its very nature, becomes a historically specific knowledge—a progressive knowledge in the context of progressive revelation. In Bahá'u'lláh's revelation, the center of that knowledge and the demonstration of its attainment is the principle of the oneness of humankind.

The metaphysics of reality that Bahá'u'lláh expounds in His early mystical writings lays the conceptual and ethical foundations for all His later social teachings. The direct connection between the metaphysical reality of oneness and the ethical orientation of unity that it entails is expressed concisely in the Hidden Words: "Since We have created you all from one same substance it is incumbent on you to be even as one soul, to walk with the same feet, eat with the same mouth and dwell in the same land, that from your inmost being, by your deeds and actions, the signs of oneness and the essence of detachment may be made manifest" (Arabic Hidden Words 68).

Part II

THE CRITIQUE OF SPIRITUAL AND HISTORICAL REASON

Chapter 4

THE KITÁB-I-ÍQÁN:
CONTEXT AND ORDER

THE KITÁB-I-ÍQÁN (The Book of Certitude) is one of the most significant works of Bahá'u'lláh's dispensation. In this text, Bahá'u'lláh
expounds a revolutionary new perspective on theology, hermeneutics, spiritual journey, epistemology, eschatology, and the relation of
society and religion. Its central issue, the doctrine of progressive revelation, is the basis of Bahá'í metaphysics and theology; but much
more than that, it provides new approaches to various questions of epistemology, sociology, political theory, and ethics. In fact, the Kitáb-i-
Íqán addresses a considerable range of issues relevant to traditional and
modern Eastern and Western religious and philosophical discourse.
Although some studies of Bahá'u'lláh's theology have tried to clarify
the connections between Bahá'u'lláh's concept of manifestationhood
(*mazharíyyat*) and Islamic mystical and philosophical traditions, Bahá'-
u'lláh's creative reinterpretation of the concept surpasses the traditional discourse and, as I will argue, offers a resolution to the central antinomies of modern Western philosophy as well. But to be understood,
the Kitáb-i-Íqán must be read in the light of Bahá'u'lláh's global and
historical consciousness and His vision of a New World Order.

In this chapter I will discuss the date and context of the revelation
of the Kitáb-i-Íqán, investigate its relationship to the Bayán, and
explore the order of the Kitáb-i-Íqán. Chapter 5 will be devoted to the
substantive message of the text.

THE DATE AND CONTEXT OF REVELATION

We know that the Kitáb-i-Íqán was revealed by Bahá'u'lláh during the
final years of His stay in Baghdad in response to questions posed by
Ḥájí Mírzá Siyyid Muḥammad, who was an uncle of the Báb. However, the details of both those issues need some clarification. Shoghi

Effendi provides an approximate date for the revelation of the Kitáb-i-Íqán:

> Foremost among the priceless treasures cast forth from the billowing ocean of Bahá'u'lláh's Revelation ranks the Kitáb-i-Íqán (Book of Certitude), revealed, within the space of two days and two nights, in the closing years of that period (1278 A.H.–1862 A.D.). It was written in fulfillment of the prophecy of the Báb, Who had specifically stated that the Promised One would complete the text of the unfinished Persian Bayán, and in reply to the questions addressed to Bahá'u'lláh by the as yet unconverted maternal uncle of the Báb, Ḥájí Mírzá Siyyid Muḥammad, while on a visit, with his brother, Ḥájí Mírzá Ḥasan-'Alí, to Karbilá.[1]

In a discussion of the exact date of the revelation of the Kitáb-i-Íqán, attention has been drawn to a letter dated 17 January 1861 written in Baghdad by Ḥájí Mírzá Siyyid Muḥammad to his son Vakílu'd-Dawlih.[2] In this letter, Ḥájí Mírzá Siyyid Muḥammad describes attaining Bahá'u'lláh's presence. Assuming the accuracy of the date as written, the date of the revelation of the Kitáb-i-Íqán can be determined to be just a few days before the writing of the letter, or mid-January 1861. The letter reads in part:

> If you wonder over our state, praised be God and His grace, on the night of the first of Rajab [12 January 1861] we attained the threshold of the Shrines of the twin Imáms at Káẓimayn…. God willing, the day after next—that is, on the seventh of the month—we will depart this location….
>
> Thank God that one thing I need to write you is that I attained unto the presence of His Holiness Bahá [Bahá'u'lláh], upon Him be God's peace…. He showered us with utmost affection and kindness and asked that we stay for the night, and we remained in His presence. The evident truth is that to be deprived of the blessing of His presence is a mighty and evident loss. May God bestow His grace upon me so that I would everlastingly attain unto the blessing of His presence.[3]

Although it has been concluded from this letter that the Íqán was revealed in early January, the letter clearly indicates that Ḥájí Mírzá Siyyid Muḥammad had returned to Baghdad not earlier than 12 January. Since, according to one of Bahá'u'lláh's own tablets, the uncle attained Bahá'u'lláh's presence at least one day after returning from Kázimayn, and the revelation of the Íqán took place during the second time he visited Bahá'u'lláh (that is, the next day), we may conclude that the revelation of the Íqán must have begun between 14 and 16 January. Although the evidence of the uncle's letter is very significant, it is not categorical proof. Further evidence which identifies the date of his trip can clarify the issue more decisively.

Bahá'u'lláh Himself has set down the story of the revelation of the Kitáb-i-Íqán. In one of His tablets He recounts that one day Siyyid Javád-i-Karbilá'í mentioned the return of the Báb's two uncles from Kázimayn to Baghdad and their intention to depart for Iran. Bahá'-u'lláh asks if Siyyid Javád has proclaimed the Faith to them, to which Siyyid Javád replies in the negative. Bahá'u'lláh then commands Siyyid Javád to go to them and invite them to Bahá'u'lláh's home. The next day, Ḥájí Mírzá Siyyid Muḥammad attains the presence of Bahá'u'lláh, upon which occasion the ocean of divine utterance billows, and at the end Bahá'u'lláh tells him that He does not wish him to be deprived of recognizing the Blessed Tree which has grown in his family. Ḥájí Mírzá Siyyid Muḥammad replies that none of the signs of the Qá'im's appearance, as mentioned for centuries, has been realized, and that he is supposed to come with might, dominion, and miracles. Yet people say that the Qá'im is my nephew; how can I accept that? Bahá'u'lláh permits him to leave, make a list of his questions, and return the following day to receive the answers. The next day Ḥájí Mírzá Siyyid Muḥammad returns, poses his questions, and the Kitáb-i-Íqán is revealed in answer to those questions.[4]

A facsimile of Ḥájí Mírzá Siyyid Muḥammad's questions has been published in *Khándán-i-Afnán* by Muḥammad 'Alí Fayḍí.[5] The questions are organized in four categories: (1) Concerning the day of resurrection and reward and punishment. The Báb has interpreted the day of resurrection as the day of the advent of the Manifestation of God, and yet there is no justice in the world: the oppressors are powerful and the virtuous are persecuted. (2) Concerning the birth of the Qá'im: traditions have reported that he was born a thousand years ago and that he is in occultation. This does not fit the Báb. (3) Concerning the true meaning of the traditions and that they cannot be all equivocal and allegorical. (4) Concerning the dominion of the Qá'im: various traditions have confirmed that the Qá'im would appear with an army with several signs. They do not conform with the Báb's claim.

Bahá'u'lláh classifies these questions in a systematic way and answers them in two parts. Part One deals with the question of interpretation and the meaning of the words of God, as well as the evidence and standard for evaluating the claim of the Manifestation of God. Part Two deals with various specific questions concerning the dominion of the Qá'im, resurrection, and other signs of the Qá'im as reported by various traditions and interpreted by the clergy. In fact, the chaotic sequence of the questions as presented by the Báb's uncle becomes transformed, in the Kitáb-i-Íqán, into an order of presentation that is both systematic and significant.

Both the uncle's questions and Bahá'u'lláh's tablet recounting the story of the revelation of the Kitáb-i-Íqán confirm the accuracy of Shoghi Effendi's statement that Ḥájí Mírzá Siyyid Muḥammad had not yet converted to the Faith. However, this does not mean that he was unsympathetic to his nephew's high spiritual station. In fact, as has been noted, he was one of the Báb's first supporters. But it is entirely inaccurate to conclude from this fact that he believed in the Báb as the Qá'im or as an independent Manifestation of God.

The solution to this apparent paradox is that the Báb revealed His station with wisdom and in a gradual way. Although a careful analysis of all the Báb's writings proves that He was in fact affirming His true station as the Qá'im and an independent Manifestation of God, the appearance of His earlier writings gave the impression that He was claiming to be the Gate to the hidden Imám, the mediator between the people and the Qá'im, and the chosen believer among the believers. In fact, some of those who accepted the Báb as the Gate to the Qá'im failed to recognize Him when, in His later writings, He explicitly disclosed His station as the Qá'im and Manifestation of God.

From the first stages of the Báb's declaration, Ḥájí Mírzá Siyyid Muḥammad had recognized his nephew to be a spiritually exceptional man, a saint, and even the gate to the Qá'im, but before he placed his questions before Bahá'u'lláh, he had not recognized the Báb as either the Qá'im or the Manifestation of God. His questions, and Bahá'u'lláh's description of those questions in the tablet, leave no doubt that, at that time, Ḥájí Mírzá Siyyid Muḥammad was not converted to the Cause of the Báb as the Promised One of Islam. It was for that very reason that Bahá'u'lláh asked Siyyid Javád to proclaim the Faith to him. It was the revelation of the Kitáb-i-Íqán that caused him to reach the state of certitude and led in turn to the complete commitment of the Báb's relatives to His Cause.

It should also be mentioned that the majesty of the Kitáb-i-Íqán was so universally recognized in the Bábí community that, later on, some individuals tried to spread rumors that it had been written by Mírzá Yaḥyá. But considerable evidence within the text attests to the identity of its author. Not only does Bahá'u'lláh conclude with the notation "revealed by the Bá' and the Há'," but within the book itself He refers to both His imprisonment in Tehran's Síyáh-Chál as well as His two-year withdrawal to the mountains of Sulaymáníyyih.[6] Concerning this period of seclusion He writes:

> In the early days of Our arrival in this land, when We discerned the signs of impending events, We decided, ere they happened, to retire. We betook Ourselves to the wilderness, and there, separated and alone, led for two years a life of complete solitude…. By the righteousness of God! Our withdrawal contemplated no return, and Our separation hoped for no reunion. The one object of Our retirement was to avoid becoming a subject of discord among the faithful, a source of disturbance unto Our companions, the means of injury to any soul, or the cause of sorrow to any heart. Beyond these, We cherished no other intention, and apart from them, We had no end in view. And yet, each person schemed after his own desire, and pursued his own idle fancy, until the hour when, from the Mystic Source, there came the summons bidding Us return whence We came. Surrendering Our will to His, We submitted to His injunction. (Kitáb-i-Íqán 250–51)

Bahá'u'lláh's description of His withdrawal to the mountains of Sulaymáníyyih is a typical presentation of a paradoxical structure in

Bahá'u'lláh's identity. This paradox appears in the above paragraph as a tension between Bahá'u'lláh's own desire not to return to Baghdad and the divine decree that He must do so. Failure to give due recognition to the mystical and psychological meanings of this statement has led a few to speculate that the "summons" that led to Bahá'u'lláh's return to Baghdad must have been an external decree. However, the same theme reoccurs in all stages of the writings of Bahá'u'lláh as a description of the basic structure of His self-consciousness. In fact, in one of His later tablets, Bahá'u'lláh says that if it were up to Himself He would never have revealed His identity at all, but whenever He chose silence, the Holy Spirit prompted Him to declare His mission.[7] The point in question becomes even clearer when we recall that (a) in some of His tablets He declares His two-year withdrawal a sufficient proof of His exalted station, and (b) this seclusion from people is repeated in both Edirne and 'Akká, for shorter periods but for the same reason. In all these events, Bahá'u'lláh repeatedly explains, He withdrew so that the fire of hatred and envy might be extinguished in the hearts of His enemies.[8]

One systematic expression of the same fact appears in Bahá'u'lláh's description of His revelation in the Síyáh-Chál. Here Bahá'u'lláh contrasts the stage of silence and sleep with the stage of wakeful speech by the decree of God. In the tablet to the shah of Iran He refers to the same experience in the context of declaring that His claim, His teachings, and His activities are not products of personal desire for power or fame, but obedience to the Call of God. In the Kitáb-i-Badí', Bahá'u'lláh articulates the same point. In all these instances, Bahá'u'lláh is saying that if it were not for the divine decree, He would never have chosen a public leadership role, and that His own personal preference was for meditation and avoidance of fame, leadership, or engagement in situations of conflict. But because of His desire to sacrifice Himself in obedience to the will of God, He would proclaim the Word of God and announce the divine Cause. The same idea occurs in different form in many of Bahá'u'lláh's writings that deal with suffering in the path of God. The Hidden Words is also permeated with the same fundamental message.

As we will explore in more detail later, Bahá'u'lláh turns this dramatic self-consciousness, as a dialectic of suffering and freedom, into a blueprint for humanity's maturity as well. Speaking of the characteristics which would signalize the maturation of humanity, He identifies one of these signs as that condition of society in which desire for power is universally extinguished so that only out of self-sacrifice would a pure soul be willing to assume the burdensome social role of kingship.[9]

VEILED DECLARATION IN THE KITÁB-I-ÍQÁN

Although the Kitáb-i-Íqán is Bahá'u'lláh's apologia demonstrating the truth of the Báb's revelation, it is also a document that reveals in subtle ways the true station of Bahá'u'lláh Himself. Bahá'u'lláh's writings are, in general, self-referential and impart simultaneously a particular knowledge about the Author's exalted station. The reason for this fundamental characteristic of His writings is not hard to discover. As He has frequently attested, the Supreme Object of all knowledge is the Manifestation of God.[10] Consequently, the Manifestation is the true goal and object of any particular discourse of knowledge. While such ordinary specific discourse tells us something about some aspect of reality, it is the recognition of the Manifestation that provides the essence, the totality, and the conditions of the possibility and reality for those particular truths. Thus Bahá'u'lláh's discourse on any topic is ultimately inseparable from discourse on His own station. In fact, the completion and fulfillment of any specific knowledge is the recognition of the Manifestation Himself.

The Kitáb-i-Íqán is no exception to this principle of self-reference in Bahá'u'lláh's writing, and this text contains frequent subtle reference to His station as the Promised One of the Bayán and an independent Manifestation of God. Because the Kitáb-i-Íqán was revealed at the beginning of 1861, before Bahá'u'lláh publicly declared His station in the Garden of Riḍván in April 1863, it would be logical to expect that He would refer to His own station in allusive language. At the same time, those veiled declarations of His station can easily be identified in the text. Here I will briefly discuss a few of them.

One of the simultaneously most hidden and most manifest indications of Bahá'u'lláh's true station can be found in His quotation, in
the Kitáb-i-Íqán, of one of the verses from the Hidden Words. In the
entire book, this is the only passage quoted from the Hidden Words.
The choice is deeply significant. But in order to see why, one has to
be familiar with the language of the Báb's writings. The passage is
introduced thus:

> Behold how the divine Touchstone hath, according to the
> explicit text of the Book, separated and distinguished the true from
> the false. Notwithstanding, they are still oblivious of this truth, and
> in the sleep of heedlessness, are pursuing the vanities of the world,
> and are occupied with thoughts of vain and earthly leadership.
> "O Son of Man! Many a day hath passed over thee whilst thou
> hast busied thyself with thy fancies and idle imaginings. How long
> art thou to slumber on thy bed? Lift up thine head from slumber, for
> the Sun hath risen to the zenith; haply it may shine upon thee with
> the light of beauty." (228)

At first it may seem that this particular Hidden Word has no reference to the advent of "Him Whom God shall make manifest."
However, the exhortation to awaken because the sun has risen is clearly an allusion to the Arabic Bayán, in which the Báb speaks of the
advent of the Promised One as the rising of the Sun to its "zenith"
(*zavál* or noon) as well as the heedlessness of the people, particularly
the Bábí community, by being asleep. In the Arabic Bayán the Báb
writes: "Verily, the Rising of the Sun to its zenith is at hand and yet
do ye not recognize that Day. Do not desire for Him Whose presence
is none other than Mine Own presence that which ye would not wish
for yourselves."[11]

In the Hidden Word quoted above, however, Bahá'u'lláh does
not speak of the Sun as drawing near to its zenith, but announces that
it already has reached its zenith. In other words, in this Hidden Word
itself, and by quoting it in the Kitáb-i-Íqán, Bahá'u'lláh is unmistakably declaring His station as the Promised One of the Bayán. Later, in
the Kitáb-i-Badí' Bahá'u'lláh will discuss the same issue in even more
detail. There He quotes another statement of the Báb: "Verily the

rising of the Sun to its zenith is at hand, and ye are still sleeping!"[12] In the Kitáb-i-Íqán, after quoting the Hidden Word, Bahá'u'lláh adds that His discussion, which forms the context of the quotation, is ultimately related to the appearance of the Promised One of the Bayán.

Another indication of Bahá'u'lláh's station that can be found in the Kitáb-i-Íqán is His identification of Baghdad, where He resided when the Kitáb-i-Íqán was revealed, with the Qur'ánic prophecy concerning the attainment of the presence of God in the Abode of Peace.[13] Bahá'u'lláh writes:

> This wronged One will cite but one of these instances, thus conferring upon mankind, for the sake of God, such bounties as are yet concealed within the treasury of the hidden and sacred Tree, that haply mortal men may not remain deprived of their share of the immortal fruit, and attain to a dewdrop of the waters of everlasting life which, from Baghdád, the "Abode of Peace," are being vouchsafed unto all mankind. (22)

Not only is Bahá'u'lláh describing His words as the "waters of everlasting life which, from Baghdad, the 'Abode of Peace,' are being vouchsafed unto all mankind"—clearly indicating the divine nature of those words—but Bahá'u'lláh declares that everything that has come to pass has been prophesied in the Qur'án, including the exile of the Manifestations and the establishment of the Universal Manifestation in a specially designated land. That land is none other than the "Abode of Peace" mentioned in the Qur'án. The explicitness of this declaration is striking: "Were these people, wholly for the sake of God and with no desire but His good-pleasure, to ponder the verses of the Book in their heart," He says,

> ... they would even recognize in them references unto the departure of the Manifestations of the names and attributes of God from out their native land; to the opposition and disdainful arrogance of government and people; and to the dwelling and establishment of the Universal Manifestation in an appointed and specially designated land. No man, however, can comprehend this except he who is possessed of an understanding heart.
>
> ... He said, and His Word is the truth: "And God calleth to the Abode of Peace; and He guideth whom He will into the right

way."[14] "For them is an Abode of Peace with their Lord! and He shall be their Protector because of their works."[15] This He hath revealed that His grace may encompass the world. Praise be to God, the Lord of all being! (174–75)

One of the clearest expressions of Bahá'u'lláh's authority is His frequent reference to the fact that His words unveil the hidden meanings of all the divine verses, and that the Kitáb-i-Íqán provides the key to unlock all the divine mysteries. These self-referential statements are dispersed throughout the text, and their importance is underscored by the frequent assertion that the hidden meanings of the verses of God are not accessible to anyone except God and His Manifestations:

> It is obvious and manifest that the true meaning of the utterances of the Birds of Eternity is revealed to none except those that manifest the Eternal Being, and the melodies of the Nightingale of Holiness can reach no ear save that of the denizens of the everlasting realm. The Copt of tyranny can never partake of the cup touched by the lips of the Sept of justice, and the Pharaoh of unbelief can never hope to recognize the hand of the Moses of truth. Even as He saith: "None knoweth the meaning thereof except God and them that are well-grounded in knowledge."[16] (17)

Another obvious reference to Bahá'u'lláh's station is the allusion to "Bahá" throughout the Kitáb-i-Íqán. In all the Báb's writings, the Promised One of the Bayán is systematically introduced as "Bahá." Bahá'u'lláh was known among the Bábís by that very name. Another unmistakable reference is at the end of the Kitáb-i-Íqán, where it is written: "Revealed by the Bá' and the Há'" (257). Not only is the identity of the author plainly stated there but the mode of writing of the book is described as revelation (*nuzúl*). There can be no doubt of the intent. Other references confirm that the Íqán itself is a divine revelation imparted to Bahá'u'lláh. For example: "Such are the strains of celestial melody which the immortal Bird of Heaven, warbling upon the Sadrih of Bahá, poureth out upon thee, that, by the permission of God, thou mayest tread the path of divine knowledge and wisdom" (78).

An important related point is the signature "152" found at the end of many of His tablets including the Kitáb-i-Íqán.[17] The reference to

Bahá'u'lláh as 152 is a kind of numeric word code containing many complex allusions to His station. However, two of those meanings can be briefly mentioned here. First, 152 should be read as words rather than as numbers and from right to left. Since in Arabic 2 = *b*, 5 = *h*, and 1 = *á*, when converted to letters 152 is *bhá*, which is of course the word *Bahá*. Second, in both the Arabic and Persian Bayán, the Báb is designated as the reality around whom eight unities revolve.[18] Since in the Bayán a unity (*váḥid*) is equivalent to 19, the Báb (as well as Quddús) would be denoted numerically by 152. Consequently, by the designation 152 Bahá'u'lláh is simultaneously affirming His identity as Bahá and as the return of the Primal Point, the Báb.

A further instance of the veiled declaration of Bahá'u'lláh's station can be found in the texts He chooses in order to demonstrate His hermeneutic principles. It has been noted that Bahá'u'lláh's discussion of the New Testament passage (Matthew 24:29–31) concerning the signs of the coming of Jesus from heaven seems to be an enigmatic choice. After all, Bahá'u'lláh is writing for a Muslim audience to demonstrate the truth of the Báb's station; one might expect Him to use arguments based on the Qur'án and Islamic traditions to make His point. A few commentators have interpreted Bahá'u'lláh's use of the Gospel as the practice of wisdom on the grounds that a radical interpretation of a biblical statement would be less likely to be perceived as threatening than a radical reinterpretation of the Qur'án. However, this reasoning does not seem entirely sound. Certainly, throughout the Íqán Bahá'u'lláh radically reinterprets the most sacred principles and statements of the Qur'án and the Islamic traditions concerning such charged issues as the Day of Resurrection, the Seal of the Prophets, attainment to the presence of God, and the like. And, from the very beginning of the Kitáb-i-Íqán He uncompromisingly refutes the authority of the clergy in understanding of the Sacred Texts. The reason for Bahá'u'lláh's use of the New Testament must be sought in some other direction.

As we know, and as Bahá'u'lláh also notes in the Kitáb-i-Íqán, He had already mentioned the same passage from Matthew in His earlier work in Arabic, Gems of Mysteries.[19] As we have seen, the Kitáb-i-

Íqán is an explication of the themes that are briefly discussed in Gems of Mysteries. Bahá'u'lláh's reference to, and extensive discussion of, the Gospel verses is not paradoxical within the logic of Bahá'u'lláh's own discourse. It is paradoxical only in terms of the prevailing Islamic habits and traditions of discourse that excluded such discussions. It should also be noted that even the writings of the Báb rarely contain explicit reference to the New Testament. Bahá'u'lláh's discussion of those verses is in fact a rejection of tradition and an assertion of the supreme authority of Bahá'u'lláh Himself.

In the context of Bahá'u'lláh's own logic, such a choice is perfectly understandable. Bahá'u'lláh is explicating His epistemological and methodological principle according to which the standard interpretations of the traditions used by Ḥájí Mírzá Siyyid Muḥammad as a measure to judge the authenticity of the claim of the Báb must be put aside. To demonstrate this, Bahá'u'lláh refers to the fact that in all the divine dispensations people objected to the Manifestation of God whom they were waiting for, on the basis of the literal interpretation of the statements in their holy books. In this context, quoting statements from the Bible makes complete sense. Christians were also expecting the appearance of the Promised One, but they rejected the Prophet Muḥammad because they did not understand the true meaning of the words of God. The arguments put forth by the Báb's uncle, in other words, are of exactly the same type as the objections Christians once made against Muḥammad.

Bahá'u'lláh's extensive discussion of the particular statement in Matthew indicates another hidden message besides the universality of His own mission: the passage from Matthew is related to the signs expected to accompany the return of Jesus. According to the Islamic traditions accepted by Shí'ih Muslims, Jesus would appear after the appearance of the Qá'im. Islamic traditions also prophesy that after the appearance of the Qá'im, Imám Ḥusayn will return to the world. To readers familiars with those Islamic traditions, Bahá'u'lláh's emphasis on the Matthew verses could be seen as a subtle but powerful allusion to His own station as the return of both Jesus and Imám Ḥusayn.

A further expression of Bahá'u'lláh's authority in the Kitáb-i-Íqán is His refutation of the philosophical basis of Shí'ih clerical power in contrast to His own authority. The discussion of this issue takes the form of a rejection of the Uṣúlí school of Shí'ih jurisprudence. In the nineteenth century, Shí'ih Islam was divided between the Akhbárí and Uṣúlí schools of thought, with the Uṣúlís increasingly the dominant party. The Uṣúlí school emphasized the concept of *ẓann*, which means conjecture, fancy, guess, and doubt. It argued for the legitimacy and necessity of reason in deducing religious laws. However, the Uṣúlí emphasis on reason was a hierarchical concept in which the masses of believers were defined as ignorant and irrational, while the reason of the mujtahids and the divines was binding on the masses. The Uṣúlí school made it a religious duty of each Shí'ih Muslim to take one of the divines as an object of imitation and follow his decrees. This was a clear move in the direction of expanding the degree and extent of the Shí'ih clergy's power in society.

The Akhbárí school rejected the category of *ẓann* and argued that humanly derived rational deductions based on conjecture cannot be binding. It is significant, we should note, that the Uṣúlí school justified conjecture in terms of the doctrine of occultation. Since the Twelfth Imám—with whom interpretive authority was believed to rest—was hidden, a substitute for *'ilm*, or knowledge, was argued to be necessary and binding until his reappearance. That substitute was the scholar's *ẓann*, or conjecture (fancy).

However, in the Kitáb-i-Íqán, Bahá'u'lláh directly refutes that Uṣúlí claim to authority, and He does so based on its own criteria of validity. He declares that no *ẓann*, or idle fancy, can be binding precisely because the portal to knowledge has now been opened. He affirms the presence of knowledge and argues that in such circumstances, clinging to fancy and conjecture becomes irrelevant. Obviously, the first reference of this portal of knowledge is the Primal Point, the Báb. But because the Báb was no longer present in the world—and given the absence of any other binding authority after Him because of the absence of any institution of vicegerency in His dispensation—the period when the Kitáb-i-Íqán was revealed would have been expected to be understood as a time of "conjecture" and

not of "knowledge." By defining the Kitáb-i-Íqán itself as a revelation
of knowledge, Bahá'u'lláh is making a powerful statement implicitly
declaring His station to be that of the new Manifestation of God. He
writes that

> the fingers of divine power have unlocked the portals of the knowl-
> edge of God, and the light of divine knowledge and heavenly grace
> hath illumined and inspired the essence of all created things, in such
> wise that in each and every thing a door of knowledge hath been
> opened, and within every atom traces of the sun hath been made
> manifest. And yet, in spite of all these manifold revelations of divine
> knowledge, which have encompassed the world, they still vainly
> imagine the door of knowledge to be closed, and the showers of
> mercy to be stilled. Clinging unto idle fancy, they have strayed far
> from the 'Urvatu'l-Vuthqá of divine knowledge. (Kitáb-i-Íqán 29–30)

It is important to note the contrast between this statement of Bahá'-
u'lláh about the nature and authority of His own knowledge and statements of Siyyid Kázim-i-Rashtí about the status of knowledge and
conjecture in the latter's time (that is, prior to the advent of the Báb).
Siyyid Kázim, whom Bahá'u'lláh designated in the Kitáb-i-Íqán as one
of the perfect human beings, defended the Uṣúlí school and wrote
extensively against Akhbárí ideas. Although both Shaykh Aḥmad-i-
Aḥsá'í and Siyyid Kázim claimed access to mystical knowledge beyond
ordinary rational acquisition, Siyyid Kázim still maintained that the
ultimate justification of authority in their time was only conjecture
(ẓann).[20]

THE KITÁB-I-ÍQÁN AND THE BAYÁN

Shoghi Effendi has characterized the Kitáb-i-Íqán as the completion of
the Bayán. Without this statement, it would have been virtually impossible to see the connection between the Bayán and the Kitáb-i-
Íqán, and yet, a careful analysis of both texts demonstrates the statement's validity.

At the beginning of both the Persian Bayán and the Arabic Bayán,
the order of the text is stated to be in accordance with *Kullu Shay'* or
"All Things." In numerical terms *Kullu Shay'* is equal to 19 "unities"
(*váḥids*), each unity consisting of 19 elements, totaling 361. This is the

organizing number of the Báb's dispensation. The first Unity, or *Váḥid*, was the Báb Himself together with His first disciples, the eighteen Letters of the Living. The Bábí calendar was organized in nineteen months of nineteen days. At the beginning of the Arabic Bayán the Báb writes that this Bayán is His Proof for all things and that He has arranged the chapters of this Faith according to the number of *Kullu Shay'* (361), like that of the year; there is one gate (chapter) for each day so that all things shall reach their most exalted paradise.[21] In the first chapter of the Persian Bayán He refers to the inception of the creation of All Things (that is, the Bayán), and that God has organized the creation of All Things in accordance with the number of All Things, so that all things, through the remembrance of All Things, shall attain perfection within all things for the advent of the next Resurrection.[22]

For the Bayán to be in accordance with "All Things," it should have 19 *váḥid*s (unities) of 19 *báb*s (chapters or gates), or 361 chapters in all. However, one of the most puzzling features of both the Persian Bayán and the Arabic Bayán is that both are unfinished texts. The Persian Bayán ends in the middle of the ninth unity, and the Arabic Bayán ends with eleven unities. This means that at least eight unities must be revealed to complete it. Because the purpose of the Bayán is to direct the people to recognize the Promised One (whom the Báb even refers to as the true author of the Bayán itself[23]), one can easily see that the intentional incompleteness of the Mother Book of the Báb's dispensation must be oriented to the same purpose. In fact, this is a powerful and graphic indication that the revelation of the Báb is both essentially and temporally inseparable from that of Him Whom God shall make manifest. The incompleteness of the Bayán eloquently attests to the fact that the religion of the Bayán was not to be like other typical religions with a long time span in which the details of its laws and commandments were to be institutionalized. While the "completion" of any religion is the advent of the next Manifestation, in the case of the dispensation of the Bayán, this is true in a special and literal sense of the term. Not only the spirit but also the letter of the Bayán itself would be completed through the revelation of the Promised One.

The fact of the Bayán's incompleteness, together with the non-binding character of any other writing until the coming of Him Whom God shall make manifest, leaves no doubt about the central message: just as the exaltation of the Cause of the Bayán is dependent on the exaltation of the Cause of the Promised One, the completion of both the letter and the spirit of the Bayán is dependent on the revelation of Bahá'u'lláh.[24] The incompleteness of the Bayán also indicates that the next Manifestation must reveal Himself imminently through "all things"—that is, in nineteen years.

Although all the writings of Bahá'u'lláh constitute the completion of the Bayán, this is specifically true of the Kitáb-i-Íqán. The close relation between the Bayán and the Kitáb-i-Íqán is evident in the striking resemblance between the texts of the two books themselves. The first notable point of similarity is their structure. All the chapters of the Persian Bayán have a common form, beginning with a short paragraph in Arabic summarizing the chapter followed by a long and elaborate explication in Persian. The structure of the Kitáb-i-Íqán is the same: its two major parts each begin with a summary paragraph in Arabic followed by a long discussion and demonstration in Persian. It seems evident that Bahá'u'lláh has chosen this arrangement intentionally to convey a particular veiled message.

Another similarity is the two texts' structure of discourse. In the Persian Bayán, each discussion ends with a statement concerning the "fruit" or purpose of that chapter. Throughout the Persian Bayán the purpose or fruit of each law, each analysis, each theological discussion is stated to be the recognition of the Promised One at the time of His revelation. This unusual feature of the Persian Bayán is unprecedented in the history of Sacred Scriptures. The very form of the Bayán indicates the imminent appearance of the next revelation and the organic unity of the two dispensations. The Kitáb-i-Íqán follows the same pattern. Both parts of the Íqán end with statements indicating that the purpose of the chapter has been to dispel whatsoever may cause people to turn away from the Promised One of the Bayán.[25]

The close relation between the Kitáb-i-Íqán and the Bayán is expressed in many other ways as well. One of these is the basic resemblance between the two terms and their spiritual connotations. The term *Íqán* means certitude, as the synthesis of faith with true knowledge and insight; the term *Bayán* was also intended to express the same basic meaning. According to the Qur'án, the creation of *Bayán* follows that of *Qur'án*.[26] Both *Qur'án* and *Bayán* literally refer to the Word of God. *Qur'án* is the recitation of the Word of God and *Bayán* is the exposition and interpretation of it. *Bayán* implies not only the affirmation of the Word of God but also the exposition and true understanding of that Word. In the writings of both Shaykh Aḥmad-i-Aḥsá'í and Siyyid Káẓim-i-Rashtí the word *Bayán* has been extensively discussed. One of Shaykh Aḥmad's most frequent discussions is his commentary on an Islamic tradition that explains the hierarchy of spiritual stations. The first of these stations is that of *Bayán*, interpreted as the revelation of the Primal Will and the knowledge of God.[27] One of the Báb's early writings, Ṣaḥífiy-i-'Adlíyyih (Book of Justice), also explicates the same tradition. The Báb's discussion of the true meaning of *Bayán* at that early stage of His revelation is one of the most important affirmations of His station in His early writings.

Some of the complex symbolism and implications of Bahá'u'lláh's signature in the form of 152 at the end of the Kitáb-i-Íqán have already been discussed. Another important implication of the number 152 in this context is most likely a reference to the remaining unities of the text of the Bayán which were to be revealed by the Promised One. Eight unities remained unrevealed in the Arabic Bayán (and more than eight in the Persian Bayán). These 8 unities of the Arabic Bayán, with their 19 chapters, add up to 152. In other words, 152 may also imply the completion of the text of the Bayán, and the spiritual truth that is yet to be revealed in the next, but temporally continuous, revelation.

Given the unfinished character of the Bayán, 152 can also be seen to symbolize the completion of the *dispensation* of the Bayán, which in itself may also be another reference to the concept of the Remnant of God, denoted in various writings of the Báb as the Promised One. Consequently Bahá'u'lláh's signature at the end of the Kitáb-i-Íqán in the form of 152 signifies that Bahá'u'lláh is the return of the Primal

Point, and that the Kitáb-i-Íqán is the completion and fulfillment of
the Bayán.

The fact that the Kitáb-i-Íqán consists of two parts can be seen as
yet another indication of the same message. At first one may think that
this order of the Kitáb-i-Íqán contradicts the previous statements. But
a careful analysis of the Persian Bayán demonstrates that the essence of
"nineteen" is contained within "two." This, in fact, is one of the most
significant principles of the Bayán. An adequate discussion of this point
would require an extensive analysis. But, briefly, for the Báb the Bayán
and its nineteen unities are explications of the nineteen letters of the
first verse of the Qur'án, "In the Name of God, the Most Compassionate, the Most Merciful" (Bismi'lláhi'r-raḥmáni'r-raḥím). According
to various Islamic traditions, all spiritual truth revealed in the Holy
Scriptures is contained within this verse, and all of the truth hidden in
that verse is contained within its first letter, b (bá'), and that b is none
other than "Bahá'u'lláh."[28] It should be noted that not only the entire
Persian Bayán but its concept of "All Things" is an elaboration of the
nineteen letters of that first Qur'ánic verse. But since all that is included in the nineteen unities of the Bayán is present in the letter b, which
is equivalent to two, we can understand why the Kitáb-i-Íqán, as the
fulfillment and completion of the Persian and Arabic Bayán, consists of
two chapters. We also saw that according to the Islamic tradition, the
letter b in the Qur'ánic verse refers to Bahá'u'lláh. It becomes clear that
the Báb has intentionally left the Bayán unfinished so that it would be
realized that Bahá'u'lláh, the Promised One of the Bayán, is the
essence and completion of the entire Bayán, and that it is through Him
that the Bayán must be fulfilled.

THE ORDER OF THE KITÁB-I-ÍQÁN

One of the most important, as yet unexplored, features of the Kitáb-
i-Íqán is its remarkable order. On first reading, it may appear that the
Kitáb-i-Íqán repeats different issues without any particular sequence.
It may also seem that there is no substantive difference between the
issues discussed in the first part and those in the second part. However,
these perceptions are products of insufficient attention to the sub-

stance of the arguments expounded in the Íqán. In fact the book represents an extraordinary sense of order and harmony. But the order and the message of the Kitáb-i-Íqán are inseparable from each other. One can better understand the content of the Kitáb-i-Íqán if one apprehends its formal order, and one can better recognize its order if one pays attention to the actual arguments of the text.

To appreciate the order of the Kitáb-i-Íqán we must keep in mind the questions posed by Ḥájí Mírzá Siyyid Muḥammad. His questions were indeed without any order or logic. Bahá'u'lláh's reordering of those questions, as He addresses them, discloses the key to their solution. He divides the Kitáb-i-Íqán into two parts corresponding to what can be referred to as His foundational/epistemological discourse and His specific/substantive discourse. The first part of the text, the foundational/epistemological discourse, addresses the method of acquiring knowledge about God and recognizing spiritual truth. This discourse is foundational because it establishes the basis or standard by which the Manifestations of God can be recognized and Truth distinguished from error. In this analysis, Bahá'u'lláh is actually talking about the nature of the appropriate questions to ask in the process of the spiritual journey. It is a discourse on discourse and a questioning of the act of questioning. In the most loving and kind manner, and by going to the heart of the foundational issues, Bahá'u'lláh demonstrates that the questions raised by Ḥájí Mírzá Siyyid Muḥammad are all the wrong questions. In the first part of the book, He explains what, instead, are the right questions to ask if one desires to attain knowledge of the Manifestations of God.

Bahá'u'lláh's profound and powerful analysis concentrates on the fact that the questions and objections raised by Ḥájí Mírzá Siyyid Muḥammad are exactly the same questions and objections which were raised in the past against all the other Manifestations of God and that it was because of reliance on those standards and questions that people were deprived of recognizing the Manifestation of God in each age. Bahá'u'lláh's discourse on the art of interpretation of the Sacred Texts is an intrinsic part of this same foundational discourse. In it He offers a vision of hermeneutics which requires that the seeker of truth

discard any understanding of the Scripture that is imposed by the
seeker or the clergy as a standard or limiting condition on the authority
of the new Manifestation of God. It is in this context that Bahá'u'lláh
introduces the passage in Matthew about the signs of the Return that
had been cited by Christians as an objection to Muḥammad's claim.
Bahá'u'lláh uses that passage to show that the true meanings of the
words of God are very different from the assumptions of the divines
and the presuppositions of the people. As we will see, Bahá'u'lláh's
foundational discourse is simultaneously a discourse on hermeneutics,
the meaning of idolatry, justice, the conditions of the spiritual journey,
purification of the heart, the equality of all human beings, the unconditional power of God, the authority of the clergy, the standard of
truth, the authority of the sacred books, the principle of detachment,
and many other themes. I will call the totality of these principles the
principle of "heart," or the "critique of spiritual reason."

While any serious reading of the foundational discourse of the first
part of the Íqán should be categorically convincing and sufficient to
answer the type of questions posed by the Báb's uncle, Bahá'u'lláh
undertakes a substantive analysis of the specific questions as well. This
constitutes the second part of the volume. Throughout this substantive analysis, He reminds the reader of the fundamental answer to all
those questions that were addressed in the foundational discourse. It is
for this reason that the same themes are found throughout the entire
book. At the same time, various questions raised by Ḥájí Mírzá Siyyid
Muḥammad are discussed in the second part in yet another highly significant order.

Bahá'u'lláh summarizes the second part of the Kitáb-i-Íqán as a
discourse on the "sovereignty" of God and His Manifestations. At first
glance this may appear puzzling because Bahá'u'lláh begins by dealing
with the question of the dominion of the Qá'im, which was one of the
stumbling-block issues for the uncle of the Báb. Following the discussion of the dominion of the Manifestations of God, Bahá'u'lláh discusses the topics of life and death, resurrection, return, the Seal of the
Prophets, the authority of the traditions about the Qá'im, and the
prophecies related to him. The reader may find it difficult to see how

these topics can possibly be summarized under the sovereignty of the Manifestation. But in fact all these discussions in the second part of the book emphasize the central principle of the sovereignty of God. This is indeed in accord with the premises of the first part of the Íqán. The unconditional sovereignty of God implies that divine revelation cannot be bound by the limited categories and interpretations of the human mind. So all ordinary presuppositions about the meanings of the words of God and the holy traditions must be discarded, and reliance on such arbitrary human constructions and standards amounts to "chaining up the hand of God" and, in fact, denying divine sovereignty. We will see how directly this principle provides the key for solving various theological and scriptural puzzles of the past.

Bahá'u'lláh also affirms the sovereignty of the Prophets through the fundamental concept of manifestation theology. The Prophets are all Manifestations of the attributes of God. Their very existence is the supreme manifestation of the divine attribute of sovereignty. Therefore, the being of the Prophet is itself absolute sovereign over all things. In this way, Bahá'u'lláh's discussion of manifestation theology becomes part of His general discussion of sovereignty. Consequently, Bahá'u'lláh's discourse in the second part of the Íqán is not simply a discussion of the sovereignty of the Manifestations of God but also an analysis of the representation of divine sovereignty in the world through the Manifestations of God.

The Prophets and Messengers of God are representatives or manifestations of divine attributes including God's sovereignty. Since the Manifestations of God are the mirrors of divine attributes, they are all one and the same, they are all the return of one another, and they are all the first and the last Prophet. In other words, all the major theological and scriptural mysteries of the previous revelations are solved by Bahá'u'lláh's manifestation theology and its progressive, perpetual character. In this way, the Kitáb-i-Íqán becomes both an affirmation of historical reason and the principle of manifestationhood.

In addition, the order in which topics are presented in the second part is also meaningful. First Bahá'u'lláh expounds the dominion of the Qá'im and the Manifestations of God. Since in the Islamic traditions the dominion of the Qá'im was identified with his slaying the unjust and rewarding the virtuous, Bahá'u'lláh turns the discussion on dominion into a discussion of the power over life and death. And since the question of life and death is at the heart of the questions of resurrection and return, Bahá'u'lláh turns that into a discourse on both issues. The discussion of return becomes the discourse on the unity and diversity of the Manifestations of God, which, in a revolutionary way, negates the assumption of the finality of religions and reconceptualizes the Islamic idea of the Seal of the Prophets. In the same context Bahá'u'lláh addresses the topic of attaining the presence of God in terms of the principle of continuous, eternal, and progressive revelation. Finally, Bahá'u'lláh deals with the apparent discrepancy between some of the Islamic traditions and the claim of the Báb, arguing that various traditions have literally prophesied different aspects of the Báb's life and mission as well as the heroic detachment and sacrifice of His followers. The chaotic questions of the Báb's uncle have become transmuted into a meaningfully structured discourse in the Kitáb-i-Íqán.

It is perhaps appropriate to conclude this discussion of the order of the Kitáb-i-Íqán with an analysis of the way Bahá'u'lláh concludes His own text by quoting two verses from the Qur'án. At first the significance of these verses may not be obvious. But they can be seen to summarize the fundamental principles and message of the Kitáb-i-Íqán. Bahá'u'lláh writes:

> We conclude Our argument with His words—exalted is He—
> "And whoso shall withdraw from the remembrance of the Merciful,
> We will chain a Satan unto him, and he shall be his fast companion."
> "And whoso turneth away from My remembrance, truly his shall be a life of misery."[29]
> Thus hath it been revealed aforetime, were ye to comprehend.
> Revealed by the "Bá'" and the "Há'."
> Peace be upon him that inclineth his ear unto the melody of the Mystic Bird calling from the Sadratu'l-Muntahá!
> Glorified be our Lord, the Most High! (257)

These two Qur'ánic verses both concern the concept of the Remembrance of God (_dhikr_) and the necessity of total commitment to it. For the Báb's uncle, who was closely familiar with his nephew's early writings, these passages must have had special significance.

The two quotations convey multiple messages. The first message epitomizes the topic of the first part of the Kitáb-i-Íqán. According to the Qur'án one must turn toward God and the remembrance of God, and turn away from all other things and all other attachments in order to be able to recognize the Manifestation of God. This is the principle of "heart," or detachment. But Bahá'u'lláh uses the two Qur'ánic verses to summarize the second part of the Kitáb-i-Íqán as well. This is expressed through two related allusions. The first is the clear reference to the station of the Báb, Who in His early writings had called Himself "the Remembrance of God." Bahá'u'lláh is reminding Ḥájí Mírzá Siyyid Muḥammad that the advent of the Báb and His claim were prophesied in the Qur'án.

The term *remembrance of God* is also a summary of Bahá'u'lláh's concept of manifestationhood. Remembrance implies the representation in the mind of something that is not present. And yet it is a trace of a reality that, while not directly present, is not completely absent. The remembrance of God, in its ultimate meaning, is, as we have seen, the Manifestation of God, who is the consummate symbol, representation, and reflection of the divine hidden Reality within the realm of creation. God Himself is the sole source of reality, even though He Himself is not directly accessible. The Divine Essence is both perfectly present and perfectly absent. For human beings, therefore, the representation of God takes the form of the Manifestations of God, the mirrors of the divine attributes and the supreme reflection of divine Truth in the realm of created reality.

There is yet another subtle message in Bahá'u'lláh's quoting of those two Qur'ánic verses. The repetition of the idea of the remembrance of God in this concluding passage of the Kitáb-i-Íqán can be considered as a prophetic and concealed assertion of the inseparable organic unity of the two revelations in the form of the Báb and Bahá'u'lláh. The first "remembrance of God" refers to the revelation of the Báb, while the second—"Whoso turneth away from *My* remembrance"[30]—refers to the revelation of Bahá'u'lláh Himself.

Chapter 5
THE KITÁB-I-ÍQÁN:
THEOLOGY REVOLUTIONIZED

IN THE FIRST PART of the Kitáb-i-Íqán, Bahá'u'lláh discusses the conditions of the possibility of spiritual knowledge. To situate His exposition of that subject comparatively in terms of modern philosophy, one may say that if Kantian theory attempted a "critique" of instrumental and scientific reason (as reason's attempt to understand itself), Bahá'u'lláh's Kitáb-i-Íqán simultaneously unfolds a critique of both historical and spiritual reason. The Kantian critique of pure reason tried to identify the categories and structures that make possible our knowledge of nature in the form of mathematics and natural science. Kant argued that we "know" nature through the interaction of universal forms and categories of mind with sensory experience.[1] Kantian theory, however, remained predominantly static and ahistorical. As a result, nineteenth-century Western philosophy and social theory attempted to undertake a critique of historical reason, stressing the historical and dynamic character of reality, society, and culture.

Bahá'u'lláh's concept of progressive revelation, discussed in the second part of the Kitáb-i-Íqán, not only applies the concept of historicity to the realm of human truth and cultural dynamics but also to the realm of religious truth and divine revelation. In doing so, Bahá'u'lláh goes beyond nineteenth-century notions of historicity and transcends the limitations of the major models of historical reason such as those of Hegel, Marx, and Dilthey.

THE CRITIQUE OF SPIRITUAL REASON

Before turning to Bahá'u'lláh's critique of historical reason, we will examine what I have called the critique of spiritual reason. It addresses the fundamental question: How does one attain knowledge of God and recognize the bearers of divine revelation (His Manifestations)?

While obviously this is not a question that has preoccupied modern secular philosophical schools of thought, for a religious person it is the most crucial concern of life. Bahá'u'lláh gives it central importance in all His writings, many of which are devoted to its exposition.

The critique of spiritual reason is foundational because the type of knowledge with which it deals concerns the purpose of creation and the ultimate meaning of human existence. As we have seen, recognition and love of God is made possible at its highest level through the recognition and love of the Manifestations of God, who represent the consummate expression of divine attributes in the realm of creation. But if the core of human existence is the divine covenant and primordial yearning to recognize God, then there is a qualitative difference between our knowledge of the Manifestations of God and any other natural or historical type of knowledge. All other forms of knowledge become secondary and accidental, whereas the knowledge of God is a universal presupposition of all other knowledge and a duty that derives from the innermost core of our nature. This unique, exalted, and fundamental type of knowledge is the subject of the critique of spiritual reason.

This critique, as unfolded in the Kitáb-i-Íqán, addresses the most important human existential concerns and offers solutions to the misunderstandings that withhold people from recognizing the Manifestation of God. The questions posed by the Báb's uncle, and which prevented him from recognizing the Báb's station, for example, are really answered through this foundational discourse in the Íqán, which also unravels many other perplexities expressed by others though not specifically included among the uncle's questions.

Bahá'u'lláh's critique of spiritual reason encompasses a vast range of subjects including the spiritual journey, the nature and method of reason in search of spiritual truth, the standard for judging claims to revelation, the interpretation of Sacred Scripture and prophecy, the unity of God and divine dominion, covenant, human equality, and the authority of the divines and clergy. Although such subjects may at first seem unrelated to each other, they are all integral parts of the same foundational discourse, the critique of spiritual reason or the principle of "heart."

To understand Bahá'u'lláh's discourse on spiritual reason, it is helpful compare it to the ways reason and truth have been conceptualized in Western philosophy, where this topic has been explored more explicitly than in Eastern forms of epistemology. In general, modern discourse on systematic knowledge begins with Descartes' famous discourse on method. He argued that to understand objective reality, reason must doubt everything, casting aside all presuppositions based on tradition. Through such methodical and systematic doubt, it is possible to arrive at truth by believing only that which cannot be doubted. In Cartesian analysis it was the act of doubting which was itself beyond doubt, hence Descartes found the basis of certain knowledge in his famous statement "I think, therefore I am."[2] The Cartesian principle was modified in various ways by the "empiricist" philosophers of the Enlightenment, who rejected any idea that could not be justified through sense perception.[3] Later, phenomenologists like Husserl advocated "bracketing" all conceptions about phenomena, particularly all empirical perceptions, in order to arrive at the essences of things.[4] These three ways of applying methodical doubt are all opposed to each other and all defined themselves in refutation of the previous theory. However, all three forms of epistemology and methodology share one thing in common: they all reduce the agent of knowledge to a mechanistic and discursive reason, while excluding other dimensions of human experience and consciousness. Instrumental reason, defined solely in terms of its capacity to perform logical operations, is held to arrive at certain truth.

Bahá'u'lláh's discourse on method is qualitatively different from all these models. This is partly because He is not concerned with ordinary knowledge of material phenomena but with spiritual knowledge—knowledge of God, of the essence of our own existence, and of the Supreme Reflection of God in the world. Spiritual reason deals with the primordial relation between the reality of human beings and the foundation of all realities. Both the subject and the object of this knowledge are different from the normal subject and object of empirical and rational knowledge. The object of this knowledge is God and the Supreme Revelation of God in the form of the Manifestations of

God. This object is not an aspect of empirical reality accessible to discursive categories of reason. On the contrary, it is the Reality of all realities, the source of all existence, and in fact the condition of the possibility of any being and knowledge whatsoever. More than that, this object of knowledge is absolute beauty, the ultimate attractor and point of adoration of all things.

The subject of spiritual knowledge is more than the normal thinking subject. It is the totality of the capacities and potentialities of the human reality because love of God is the very core and essence of human nature. To approach such knowledge, a qualitatively different method is needed; the subject cannot be content with a merely discursive reason, that is, a reason that simply performs logical operations. Reason must transcend the realm of mere instrumental and logical rationality to encompass all human potentialities and aspects of human consciousness. In this way, it becomes a reflection of the Divine Universal Reason, a harmony of mind, feelings, and will, and a synthesis of human capacity and divine confirmation.

Such a subject, possessed of this exalted and holistic reason, must now engage in methodical doubt by casting aside all preconceptions, all merely conventional human authorities (particularly the interpretive authority of the divines and the clergy), all limiting presuppositions and arbitrary constructs, all personal attachments and inclinations, and all personal or traditional interpretations of the Holy Scriptures. Only such a subject, wholly detached from all save God, is capable of attaining spiritual truth and recognizing the Manifestation of God.

It is for this reason that Bahá'u'lláh devotes such attention to the moral and spiritual preconditions of the spiritual journey, especially the dialectic of detachment and attachment—detachment from all presuppositions, from imitation of others, from reliance on the authority of tradition, from the apparent meanings of the Holy Scriptures, from rituals and symbols, and from selfish desire and pride; and attachment to God, which implies an encompassing love of all created things, humility, selflessness, fairness and justice, and reliance on the standards given by God Himself.

Bahá'u'lláh terms this reason which is detached from all save God the "pure heart." He begins the Kitáb-i-Íqán with this concept and refers to it throughout the book:

> No man shall attain the shores of the ocean of true understanding except he be detached from all that is in heaven and on earth. Sanctify your souls, O ye peoples of the world, that haply ye may attain that station which God hath destined for you and enter thus the tabernacle which, according to the dispensations of Providence, hath been raised in the firmament of the Bayán.
>
> The essence of these words is this: they that tread the path of faith, they that thirst for the wine of certitude, must cleanse themselves of all that is earthly—their ears from idle talk, their minds from vain imaginings, their hearts from worldly affections, their eyes from that which perisheth. They should put their trust in God, and, holding fast unto Him, follow in His way. Then will they be made worthy of the effulgent glories of the sun of divine knowledge and understanding, and become the recipients of a grace that is infinite and unseen, inasmuch as man can never hope to attain unto the knowledge of the All-Glorious, can never quaff from the stream of divine knowledge and wisdom, can never enter the abode of immortality, nor partake of the cup of divine nearness and favour, unless and until he ceases to regard the words and deeds of mortal men as a standard for the true understanding and recognition of God and His Prophets. (3–4)

As we saw in Chapter 3, in discussing the Four Valleys, the "heart" represents the throne of God and the place where all the divine attributes are revealed. It signifies the unity of all human potentialities as well as the unity of the divine will and the individual will. The purification of the heart, therefore, is the indispensable first step on the journey toward spiritual truth:

> But, O my brother, when a true seeker determineth to take the step of search in the path leading to the knowledge of the Ancient of Days, he must, before all else, cleanse and purify his heart, which is the seat of the revelation of the inner mysteries of God, from the obscuring dust of all acquired knowledge, and the allusions of the embodiments of satanic fancy. He must purge his breast, which is the sanctuary of the abiding love of the Beloved, of every defilement,

and sanctify his soul from all that pertaineth to water and clay, from
all shadowy and ephemeral attachments. He must so cleanse his heart
that no remnant of either love or hate may linger therein, lest that
love blindly incline him to error, or that hate repel him away from
the truth. (192)

The pure heart is detached and purified from all limiting, particularistic attachments and presuppositions while at the same time it is
supremely attached to love of God and consequently it is completely
committed to moral values as well as imbued with a universal love for
all beings. The reader of the Kitáb-i-Íqán may be surprised to find that
Bahá'u'lláh makes kindness to animals one of the conditions of the
spiritual journey! But this is precisely an integral expression of this
holistic moral orientation that is the principle of heart. Describing that
moral orientation, as the characteristics of the "true seeker," Bahá'u'-
lláh writes:

> He must never seek to exalt himself above any one, must wash away
> from the tablet of his heart every trace of pride and vainglory, must
> cling unto patience and resignation....
>   That seeker should also regard backbiting as grievous error, and
> keep himself aloof from its dominion, inasmuch as backbiting
> quencheth the light of the heart, and extinguisheth the life of the
> soul. He should be content with little, and be freed from all inor-
> dinate desire. He should treasure the companionship of those that
> have renounced the world, and regard avoidance of boastful and
> worldly people a precious benefit. At the dawn of every day he
> should commune with God.... He should succour the dispossessed,
> and never withhold his favour from the destitute. He should show
> kindness to animals, how much more unto his fellow-man, to him
> who is endowed with the power of utterance. He should not hesitate
> to offer up his life for his Beloved, nor allow the censure of the
> people to turn him away from the Truth. He should not wish for
> others that which he doth not wish for himself, nor promise that
> which he doth not fulfil. With all his heart should the seeker avoid
> fellowship with evil doers, and pray for the remission of their sins. He
> should forgive the sinful, and never despise his low estate, for none
> knoweth what his own end shall be. (193–94)

Expressing the dialectic of negation and affirmation Bahá'u'lláh says:

That seeker must at all times put his trust in God, must renounce the peoples of the earth, detach himself from the world of dust, and cleave unto Him Who is the Lord of Lords.

... Our purpose in revealing these convincing and weighty utterances is to impress upon the seeker that he should regard all else beside God as transient, and count all things save Him, Who is the Object of all adoration, as utter nothingness. (193, 95)

Unlike ordinary knowledge which does not affect the subject in any significant way, the recognition of the Manifestation of God, which is the recognition and experience of absolute beauty, and the fulfillment of the fundamental yearning of human existence, is a knowledge that by its very nature is creative, transformative, and ecstatic. It is a knowledge in which the encounter with the object changes the subject, connecting it to the entirety of reality and disclosing the hidden potentialities of human nature. Self-realization, self-consciousness, and the development of a global and universal consciousness and sentiments are necessary products of such spiritual knowledge. Describing the unusual and creative nature of this type of knowledge, Bahá'u'lláh writes:

Then will the manifold favours and outpouring grace of the holy and everlasting Spirit confer such new life upon the seeker that he will find himself endowed with a new eye, a new ear, a new heart, and a new mind. He will contemplate the manifest signs of the universe, and will penetrate the hidden mysteries of the soul. Gazing with the eye of God, he will perceive within every atom a door that leadeth him to the stations of absolute certitude. He will discover in all things the mysteries of divine Revelation and the evidences of an everlasting manifestation. (196)

He describes the Word of God and divine confirmation as the "elixir" which transforms instantaneously the copper of human nature into gold. Speaking of the dramatic character change undergone by believers in past ages as a result of their encounter with the divine presence in the form of the Manifestation of God, Bahá'u'lláh writes:

... how could they, but for the transformation wrought in their lives, be capable of manifesting such deeds which are contrary to the ways of men and incompatible with their worldly desires?

It is evident that nothing short of this mystic transformation could cause such spirit and behaviour, so utterly unlike their previous habits and manners, to be made manifest in the world of being. For their agitation was turned into peace, their doubt into certitude, their timidity into courage. Such is the potency of the Divine Elixir, which, swift as the twinkling of an eye, transmuteth the souls of men! (156–57)

One of the most important aspects of the critique of spiritual reason is Bahá'u'lláh's discussion of scriptural hermeneutics. The question of method leads directly to the question of meaning because it really concerns the standard that should be used as the measure of revealed truth. As we saw, Ḥájí Mírzá Siyyid Muḥammad had offered several objections to the Báb's claims based on the dominant traditional and current interpretations of Islamic Sacred Texts, and he was inclined to reject his nephew's claim because it apparently conflicted with those assumptions. He had taken the clergy's interpretations of the Holy Scriptures as the standard by which to judge the authenticity of the Báb's revelation. Bahá'u'lláh, however, declares all such traditional interpretations, and the questions based on them, erroneous as standards and contrary to the will of God. In arguing this fundamental point, Bahá'u'lláh emphasizes four main principles.

(1) The hidden and real meanings of the words of God are ultimately accessible only to the Manifestations of God and their appointed interpreters—those on whom They have specifically conferred the authority of interpretation. No ordinary human interpretation or understanding of the Holy Scriptures can legitimately be used as a standard or condition for assessing the claim of the new Manifestation of God.

(2) Although the real meanings of the Sacred Scriptures are ultimately inaccessible to human beings unassisted, all humans do have an inherent capacity to recognize both the Manifestation of God and the words of God. Bahá'u'lláh affirms the epistemic equality of all humans: the true standard and proof of the Manifestations of God is accessible to all people regardless of their degree of technical or philosophical knowledge or their social position and power. In this sense no person

can be dependent on the knowledge or understanding of any other human being, and the interpretations of the clergy, divines, and scholars can hold no privileged position. In fact, all can understand the Sacred Texts as the Word of God and as expressions of the divine will, but no one can claim to understand the totality of the meanings inherent in the words of God except the Manifestations and Their authorized interpreters.

(3) No category or condition constructed by humans can limit divine authority and divine revelation. Just as God cannot be known except through Himself, and through His own self-descriptions and self-revelations, the only legitimate standard to be used in the search for spiritual truth must be the divinely appointed standard. This standard is, first, the being of the Manifestation Himself and, second, His revealed words. That is to say, everything must be judged and defined through the will of the Manifestation of God and the Manifestation through Himself.

Because all created things exist by virtue of reflecting divine attributes, within every soul there is a reflection of God and a trace of the divine Manifestations. Human beings are only able to recognize the Supreme Object of their love and attraction because of the presence of those divine attributes within themselves. However, this primordial capacity and attraction to the divine Beloved becomes actualized only when the heart is purified. In such a situation, humans become as pure mirrors who receive divine illumination and certitude. In the absence of the living presence of the Manifestation of God, His words perform the same function. At the end of the first part of the Kitáb-i-Íqán, Bahá'u'lláh defines a hierarchy of standards, in descending order: to know God by God without seeing anything save God (the stage of spirit), to know God through God while assuming the existence of others (the stage of truth), and to know God through His revealed verses (the stage of testimony):

> It is incumbent upon thee, by the permission of God, to cleanse the eye of thine heart from the things of the world, that thou mayest realize the infinitude of divine knowledge, and mayest behold Truth

so clearly that thou wilt need no proof to demonstrate His reality, nor any evidence to bear witness unto His testimony.

O affectionate seeker! Shouldst thou soar in the holy realm of the spirit, thou wouldst recognize God manifest and exalted above all things, in such wise that thine eyes would behold none else but Him. "God was alone; there was none else besides Him." So lofty is this station that no testimony can bear it witness, neither evidence do justice to its truth. Wert thou to explore the sacred domain of truth, thou wilt find that all things are known only by the light of His recognition, that He hath ever been, and will continue forever to be, known through Himself. And if thou dwellest in the land of testimony, content thyself with that which He, Himself, hath revealed: "Is it not enough for them that We have sent down unto Thee the Book?" This is the testimony which He, Himself, hath ordained; greater proof than this there is none, nor ever will be: "This proof is His Word; His own Self, the testimony of His truth." (91–92)

In the "holy realm of the spirit," divine truth is self-evident; in the "domain of truth" it is recognized that only His knowledge makes other knowledge possible; in the "land of testimony," if a testimony is required, His own is the only valid one.

The dialectic of purification and enlightenment is elaborated by Bahá'u'lláh through a metaphor of vision, expressed as the "eye" or the "gaze" of the wayfarer. All the writings of Bahá'u'lláh, including the Kitáb-i-Íqán, confirm that this appropriate gaze is one and the same. It is variously expressed as (a) the gaze of one's own eyes, (b) the gaze of the heart, and (c) as the gaze of God Himself. Seeing with one's own eyes is the mode of independent investigation of truth based on justice, fairness, impartiality, and universality—and without imitation, reliance on others, prejudices, or superstitions. In this case, to see things with one's own eyes is equivalent to detachment from all arbitrary constructs, worship of traditions, and reification of the letter of the revelation. This principle is articulated in the Arabic Hidden Words:

O SON OF SPIRIT!
The best beloved of all things in My sight is Justice; turn not away therefrom if thou desirest Me, and neglect it not that I may

confide in thee. By its aid thou shalt see with thine own eyes and not through the eyes of others, and shalt know of thine own knowledge and not through the knowledge of thy neighbor. Ponder this in thy heart; how it behoveth thee to be. Verily justice is my gift to thee and the sign of My loving-kindness. Set it then before thine eyes. (2)

To see with the gaze of God implies beholding reality through the categories and standards set by God and His Manifestations. It means refusing to subordinate God to any other authority or condition. It also means acknowledging the sovereignty of God and the unconditional power and authority of His Manifestations. Finally, the eye of the heart provides the mediating link between the self and God. The heart is the focal point of divine reflection and effulgence. To purify the heart, therefore, is to purify the human mirror that receives the divine illumination and confirmation. Here one's own gaze and the divine gaze become one and the same.

In explaining these principles in the Kitáb-i-Íqán, Bahá'u'lláh rejects the thesis of the corruption of the Sacred Texts and the authority of the divines, and affirms a new hermeneutics, or scriptural interpretation, and a new conception of the unity of God. These are all systematic expressions of Bahá'u'lláh's discourse on method.

Bahá'u'lláh began the Kitáb-i-Íqán by reminding the uncle of the Báb and all truth seekers of a paradoxical truth. In every age, although the followers of the previous religion anxiously yearned and prayed for their Promised One to appear, when He did appear, they denied, persecuted, and often martyred Him! In all these cases, people used human standards to judge the truth of the Manifestation of God: "having weighed the testimony of God by the standard of their own knowledge, gleaned from the teachings of the leaders of their faith, and found it at variance with their limited understanding, they arose to perpetrate such unseemly acts" (15). Presuming to possess a definitive understanding of the words of God, and relying on literal readings of Scripture, they made the words of God themselves the pretext to reject the Revealer of those words. Bahá'u'lláh demonstrates that the objections raised against the Báb are the same as those that were raised against other Manifestations of God. He rejects these questions,

standards, and limitations on divine will as illegitimate and contrary to
all the Scriptures.

In the course of explicating this foundational principle, Bahá'u'-
lláh refers in turn to the objections the Jews raised against Jesus on the
basis of the literal interpretation of the Sacred Texts, and to the objections Christians brought against Muḥammad based on the words of the
Gospel. He shows that, in all these cases, when the signs expected to
accompany the advent of the Promised One did not literally happen,
the people failed to recognize the sense in which those signs did come
to pass both symbolically and historically. Bahá'u'lláh affirms that the
sole standard of truth, upheld by all the Manifestations of God including Muḥammad, is the being of the Manifestation Himself and the
revelation of verses. And indeed, this is exactly the same standard that
was used by the Báb to justify His claim.

However, Bahá'u'lláh dismisses the argument, traditionally maintained by Muslims, that the text of the Bible is corrupted and therefore
its words may not have been really part of the Scripture. Bahá'u'lláh
affirms that, on all fundamentals, the Bible has not been corrupted or
changed by the Christians, stating that it would be contrary to divine
justice to define the words of God as the standard of truth and faith and
yet allow those words to be corrupted and therefore nonexistent in
their true form among the people. He explains that, instead, "by corruption of the text is meant that in which all Muslim divines are
engaged today, that is the interpretation of God's holy Book in accordance with their idle imaginings and vain desires" (86); the references
in the Scriptures to distortion or perversion of the text indicate "that
the meaning of the Word of God hath been perverted, not that the
actual words have been effaced" (87).

Bahá'u'lláh rejects the authority of the divines to interpret the
words of God and to impose limits and conditions on the Manifestation of God. This radically egalitarian and democratic principle reflects
itself in many other ways in the Kitáb-i-Íqán. Bahá'u'lláh asserts that
anyone possessed of a pure heart can understand the words of God; yet
none but His appointed interpreters can understand their hidden and
real meanings, and that technical knowledge or acquired learning

without purity of heart and divine confirmation cannot provide true understanding:

> The understanding of His words and the comprehension of the utterances of the Birds of Heaven are in no wise dependent upon human learning. They depend solely upon purity of heart, chastity of soul, and freedom of spirit. This is evidenced by those who, today, though without a single letter of the accepted standards of learning, are occupying the loftiest seats of knowledge; and the garden of their hearts is adorned, through the showers of divine grace, with the roses of wisdom and the tulips of understanding. Well is it with the sincere in heart for their share of the light of a mighty Day! (211)

Bahá'u'lláh denounces the claims of the clergy that the Scriptures are beyond the understanding of ordinary people. It is the selfish desires of the divines that make them insist that only they are capable of comprehending the words of God. This is the basis of their social power, and this is the chief reason why the Manifestations of God have been persecuted throughout human history:

> Heed not the idle contention of those who maintain that the Book and verses thereof can never be a testimony unto the common people, inasmuch as they neither grasp their meaning nor appreciate their value. And yet, the unfailing testimony of God to both the East and the West is none other than the Qur'án. Were it beyond the comprehension of men, how could it have been declared as a universal testimony unto all people? If their contention be true, none would therefore be required, nor would it be necessary for them to know God, inasmuch as the knowledge of the divine Being transcendeth the knowledge of His Book, and the common people would not possess the capacity to comprehend it.
>
> Such contention is utterly fallacious and inadmissible. It is actuated solely by arrogance and pride. Its motive is to lead the people astray from the Riḍván of divine good-pleasure and to tighten the reins of their authority over the people. And yet, in the sight of God, these common people are infinitely superior and exalted above their religious leaders who have turned away from the one true God. (210–11)

Bahá'u'lláh refers to several Islamic traditions about the station of the Qá'im as an independent Manifestation of God and the fact that the

divines are unable to comprehend the truth of the new revelation in
terms of their limited knowledge. He rejects the Uṣúlí justification of its
power in terms of ẓann (doubt, conjecture, fancy), declaring it irrelevant
for understanding the fundamental laws of spiritual truth.[5] Finally,
Bahá'u'lláh refers to yet another tradition which predicts the opposition of the clergy to the Qá'im: "'The religious doctors of that age
shall be the most wicked of the divines beneath the shadow of heav-
en. Out of them hath mischief proceeded, and unto them it shall
return'" (247–48).

A notable example of clerical arrogance and ignorance was Ḥájí
Mírzá Karím Khán-i-Kirmání, who was considered by some to be the
successor of Siyyid Káẓim and was counted among the most knowledgeable and prominent Shí'ih clergy in Iran. Bahá'u'lláh, however,
denounces Karím Khán's claim that erudition in numerous esoteric
sciences is required to understand the mysteries of the sacred Word:

> ... How clear and evident it is to every discerning heart that this so-
> called learning is and hath ever been, rejected by Him Who is the
> one true God.... Whoso desireth to fathom the mystery of this
> "Mi'ráj," and craveth a drop from this ocean, if the mirror of his
> heart be already obscured by the dust of these learnings, he must
> needs cleanse and purify it ere the light of this mystery can be
> reflected therein.
>
> In this day, they that are submerged beneath the ocean of ancient
> Knowledge, and dwell within the ark of divine wisdom, forbid the
> people such idle pursuits. Their shining breasts are, praise be to God,
> sanctified from every trace of such learning, and are exalted above
> such grievous veils. We have consumed this densest of all veils, with
> the fire of the love of the Beloved—the veil referred to in the saying:
> "The most grievous of all veils is the veil of knowledge." Upon its
> ashes, We have reared the tabernacle of divine knowledge. (186–88)

The contrast between Karím Khán's acquired "learning," hypocrisy,
and pride, on the one hand, and Bahá'u'lláh's own divinely inspired,
inherent, mystical knowledge and His authority, on the other, sharply
demonstrates the difference between the authority of the Manifestation and the pretensions of the traditional priesthood.

In this connection, it is also interesting to note that one of the prominent Muslim and Sufi leaders, Ṣafí 'Alíshâh, upon reading the Kitáb-i-Íqán, wrote a critique of Bahá'u'lláh's reference to the Islamic tradition that the characteristics of four Prophets would be gathered together in the Qá'im. This is how Bahá'u'lláh quotes the tradition in the Kitáb-i-Íqán:

> In the "Bihár" it is recorded: "In our Qá'im there shall be four signs from four Prophets, Moses, Jesus, Joseph, and Muḥammad. The sign from Moses, is fear and expectation; from Jesus, that which was spoken of Him; from Joseph, imprisonment and dissimulation; from Muḥammad, the revelation of a Book similar to the Qur'án." Notwithstanding such a conclusive tradition, which in such unmistakable language hath foreshadowed the happenings of the present day, none hath been found to heed its prophecy, and methinks none will do so in the future, except him whom thy Lord willeth. (254)

Ṣafí 'Alíshâh mistakenly assumed that only the first part of Bahá'u'lláh's quotation belonged to the tradition and that the rest was Bahá'u'lláh's own interpretation. He charged that Bahá'u'lláh had arbitrarily interpreted the tradition by listing His own understanding of those common characteristics. Ṣafí 'Alíshâh proposed a different set of signs and common characteristics as the accurate interpretation of the tradition. What Ṣafí 'Alíshâh did not realize was that the portion he disputed was also part of the original text of the holy tradition itself.[6]

In Bahá'u'lláh's approach to hermeneutics technical knowledge and acquired learning of any sort is neither necessary nor sufficient to understand the true meanings of the equivocal statements in the Sacred Texts. Instead, only purification of the heart, divine confirmation, and the guidance of the Manifestations of God and their chosen interpreters can unveil those meanings. This hermeneutics implies two things. First, since no one other than the divine representatives can truly know the meanings of the allegorical and figurative statements, and since no one else knows which of the statements concerning the next revelation is allegorical, no person's understanding of the prophecies describing the signs of the advent of the Promised One can be taken as the standard of judgment to test the new Manifestation of God. Second, since all human beings have the capacity to recognize the words of God, and yet none can know all their meanings, the claim to privilege by the divines and the clergy is fundamentally illegitimate.

Bahá'u'lláh's hermeneutical approach at the same time affirms both the egalitarian principle and the principle of covenant: all people have an equal capacity to recognize the words of God and to understand them through the logic of the pure heart, and yet no one knows all their meanings save those invested with interpretive authority by the Manifestation Himself, through the divine covenant. Therefore, all are free to hold their own understandings of the Sacred Texts provided that they realize that their understanding is limited and can never be binding on others, even while all are under the binding authority of the appointed interpreters.

This hermeneutics rejects dogmatism, literalism, and imitation of the clergy at the same time as it affirms an authoritative source of divinely guided interpretation. But reducing the logic of Bahá'u'lláh's hermeneutics to the first principle without the second contradicts the basic message of the entire Kitáb-i-Íqán. From the fact that many scriptural statements have allegorical and multiple meanings one should not deduce a postmodernist or relativistic hermeneutics in which the meaning of the text is indeterminate and all interpretations are equally valid. It is the basic thesis of the Kitáb-i-Íqán that people have been deprived of recognizing the Manifestations of God precisely because they relied on their own interpretations or those of the clergy and scholars. The Kitáb-i-Íqán is also filled with examples of various interpretations which Bahá'u'lláh declares to be entirely erroneous.

> Those words uttered by the Luminaries of Truth must needs be pondered, and should their significance be not grasped, enlightenment should be sought from the Trustees of the depositories of Knowledge, that these may expound their meaning, and unravel their mystery. For it behooveth no man to interpret the holy words according to his own imperfect understanding, nor, having found them to be contrary to his inclination and desires, to reject and repudiate their truth. For such, today, is the manner of the divines and doctors of the age, who occupy the seats of knowledge and learning, and who have named ignorance knowledge, and called oppression justice. (181–82)

Inasmuch as it hath been clearly shown that only those who are initiated into the divine mysteries can comprehend the melodies uttered by the Bird of Heaven, it is therefore incumbent upon every one to seek enlightenment from the illumined in heart and from the Treasuries of divine mysteries regarding the intricacies of God's Faith and the abstruse allusions in the utterances of the Daysprings of Holiness. Thus will these mysteries be unravelled, not by the aid of acquired learning, but solely through the assistance of God and the outpourings of His grace. "Ask ye, therefore, of them that have the custody of the Scriptures, if ye know it not." (191–92)

(4) Bahá'u'lláh's critique of spiritual reason can best be understood through His radical reinterpretation of the concept of the unity of God. Traditional monotheistic religious discourse has defined the unity of God as a rejection of idol worship. From Noah to Muhammad, this principle has been reiterated in categorical language. In addition to that traditional concept of the unity of God, Bahá'u'lláh implicitly offers a definition of idolatry which refers not only to creating a physical image that is worshiped as God, but also to the act of alienating the appearance of the historically specific Word of God from the dynamic Will of God and turning it into an idol by taking it to be superior to the living and speaking Word of God. For example, He writes:

Gracious God! How far have that people strayed from the way of God! Although the Day of Resurrection was ushered in through the Revelation of Muhammad, although His light and tokens had encompassed the earth and all that is therein, yet that people derided Him, gave themselves up to those idols which the divines of that age, in their vain and idle fancy, had conceived, and deprived themselves of the light of heavenly grace and of the showers of divine mercy. (117)

The supreme authority and the supreme sacred is of course the Will and the Word of God. The authority and binding character of all concepts, symbols, names, rituals, commandments, and laws within a dispensation is derived from that Will as revealed by the Manifestations of God. The Manifestations constitute the Speaking Book, while the scripture is the Silent Book. The authority of the Silent Book is due to the command and utterance of the Speaking Book. If the Manifestation of God abrogates any law of the former scripture, that law immediately loses its binding authority. Bahá'u'lláh thus affirms the radical primacy of the authority of the Speaking Book over the Silent Book.

The absolute unity of God requires recognizing the Will of God beyond particular instances of that Will. But to cleave to the Silent Book in order to repudiate the new, Speaking Book (the Manifestation of God), is to refute the Will of God by appeal to past expressions of that Will. Bahá'u'lláh often describes this as clinging to names while turning away from the Revealer and Lord of those names. In sum, to object to a Manifestation of God on the basis of the appearance of the previous Scripture is in fact to worship an idol and to deny the unity of God. As in all cases of idolatry, what was the means and the sign is turned into the end and the meaning.

TRUE POWER AND SOVEREIGNTY

The second part of the Kitáb-i-Íqán begins with Bahá'u'lláh's summary of the chapter:

> Verily He Who is the Day-star of Truth and Revealer of the Supreme Being holdeth, for all time, undisputed sovereignty over all that is in heaven and on earth, though no man be found on earth to obey Him. He verily is independent of all earthly dominion, though He be utterly destitute. Thus We reveal unto thee the mysteries of the Cause of God, and bestow upon thee the gems of divine wisdom, that haply thou mayest soar on the wings of renunciation to those heights that are veiled from the eyes of men. (97)

The reason Bahá'u'lláh emphasizes the meaning of true sovereignty as the solution to all Hájí Mírzá Siyyid Muhammad's questions is clear. Those questions showed that the Báb's uncle was preoccupied with the assumption that, with the coming of the Qá'im and the day of Judgment, miraculous events displaying the extraordinary power of God would occur. Thus he was concerned with such matters as the resurrection of the dead, the punishment of the wicked in the fire, the victory of the forces of the Promised One over the infidels, and the ascendancy and sovereignty of the Qá'im. Bahá'u'lláh extricates the real issue underlying all those questions and directly addresses it as His central category. He shows that the same objection Ḥájí Mírzá Siyyid Muḥammad has raised concerning the sovereignty of the Báb was raised against all the other Prophets in the past. The Scriptures themselves attest that all the Manifestations of God have always possessed sovereignty in the world; this is not unique to the Qá'im. Similarly, He cites various passages to show that in every revelation the dead have been resurrected and the unbelievers were deprived of life, for, according to the Scriptures, "By the terms 'life' and 'death,' ... is intended the life of faith and the death of unbelief" (114).

Again it becomes evident that the scriptural references to the Qá'im's sovereignty and his power over life and death have allegorical and figurative meanings and are not to be taken literally. The sovereignty of the Qá'im is the same as the sovereignty of Jesus and the Imám Ḥusayn. While they were apparently without any worldly power or dominion, in reality they possessed absolute sovereignty and power over all creation. Referring to the interrogation of Jesus before His crucifixion, Bahá'u'lláh says: "consider how to outward seeming He was devoid of all power except that inner power which was of God and which had encompassed all that is in heaven and on earth" (133). Concerning Imám Ḥusayn, He points out that "if ascendancy and dominion be interpreted to mean earthly supremacy and temporal power," it would be impossible to explain such Qur'ánic verses as: "'And verily Our host shall conquer.' 'Fain would they put out God's light with their mouths: But God hath willed to perfect His light, albeit the infidels abhor it.'[7] 'He is the Dominant, above all things'" (125–26). If such verses were to be interpreted literally, they would contradict the truth:

> For in every age the light of God hath, to outward seeming, been quenched by the peoples of the earth, and the Lamps of God extinguished by them. How then could the ascendancy of the sovereignty of these Lamps be explained? What could the potency of God's will to "perfect His light" signify? As hath already been witnessed, so great was the enmity of the infidels, that none of these divine Luminaries ever found a place for shelter, or tasted of the cup of tran-

quillity. So heavily were they oppressed, that the least of men inflicted upon these Essences of being whatsoever he listed. (127)

He explains that the meaning of "sovereignty" that applies to God's chosen ones is a more complex, subtle, and far-reaching concept. Because the Manifestations represent the Will of God, the Word of God, and all the divine attributes in the realm of creation, the very being of the Manifestations of God is absolute divine sovereignty and dominion: "these illuminated Souls, these beauteous Countenances have, each and every one of them, been endowed with all the attributes of God, such as sovereignty, dominion, and the like, even though to outward seeming they be shorn of all earthly majesty. To every discerning eye this is evident and manifest; it requireth neither proof nor evidence" (104).

The spiritual sovereignty and dominion of the Manifestations of God is demonstrated in the transformation of the lives of those who come under the sway of Their attracting and recreative power:

> Hath it not been witnessed that these same people, ere they were endued with the new and wondrous grace of God, sought through innumerable devices, to ensure the protection of their lives against destruction? Would not a thorn fill them with terror, and the sight of a fox put them to flight? But once having been honoured with God's supreme distinction, and having been vouchsafed His bountiful grace, they would, if they were able, have freely offered up ten thousand lives in His path! Nay, their blessed souls, contemptuous of the cage of their bodies, would yearn for deliverance. A single warrior of that host would face and fight a multitude! And yet, how could they, but for the transformation wrought in their lives, be capable of manifesting such deeds which are contrary to the ways of men and incompatible with their worldly desires?
>
> It is evident that nothing short of this mystic transformation could cause such spirit and behaviour, so utterly unlike their previous habits and manners, to be made manifest in the world of being. For their agitation was turned into peace, their doubt into certitude, their timidity into courage. Such is the potency of the Divine Elixir, which, swift as the twinkling of an eye, transmuteth the souls of men! (156–57)

This sovereignty is the creative Word of God that brings to light the hidden potentialities of beings. It is a sovereignty based not on coercion and fear but on the willing surrender of purified hearts who sacrifice life itself for love of the divine Sovereign. The transformative power of the kingdom of the heart is far superior to the outward semblance of power possessed by kings and their armies:

> Our purpose in setting forth these truths hath been to demonstrate the sovereignty of Him Who is the King of kings. Be fair: Is this sovereignty which, through the utterance of one Word, hath manifested such pervading influence, ascendancy, and awful majesty, is this sovereignty superior, or is the worldly dominion of these kings of the earth who, despite their solicitude for their subjects and their help of the poor, are assured only of an outward and fleeting allegiance, while in the hearts of men they inspire neither affection nor respect? Hath not that sovereignty, through the potency of one word, subdued, quickened, and revitalized the whole world? (123–24)

Bahá'u'lláh defines the true sovereignty of the Manifestations of God at two levels. At the level of creation, the world has come into existence through the Word of God, which is the essence of the Manifestations of God. The existence of all things depends on them since it is through them that all things have been created. This is absolute, unconditional, and essential dominion and sovereignty. This dominion is never alienated from the Manifestations of God because the entire creation would cease to exist if divine grace and effulgence were to stop for one moment: "Nay, all else besides these Manifestations live by the operation of their Will, and move and have their being through the outpourings of their grace" (103).

The second mode of the Manifestations' sovereignty is at the level of revelation. Through each dispensation of revelation, all beings are infused with new potentialities and powers, and a new stage in human spiritual and cultural development is ushered in. The Manifestation of God conquers the hearts of the people, transforms their identity, and initiates a new spiritual Springtime. This is the true meaning of "resurrection."

Although the common expectation is that divine sovereignty
should be manifested in the world through extraordinary displays of
power and miraculous events, Bahá'u'lláh demonstrates that the per-
formance of miracles is never endorsed in the Holy Scriptures as the
standard and evidence of the truth of the Manifestations of God. As
Bahá'u'lláh explains in the Book of the River, this does not mean that
the Manifestations do not perform miracles, but only that miracles are
not in themselves sufficient evidence of manifestationhood.[8] The
Manifestations of God have been rejected when They refused to perform miracles to demonstrate their truth, whereas They themselves
have always asserted that the evidence of Their power and ascendancy
is the revelation of the divine Word. The holy books, therefore, are
the supreme expressions of their revealer's power and dominion.
Bahá'u'lláh identifies those scriptures as the immortal "City":

> That city is none other than the Word of God revealed in every age
> and dispensation. In the days of Moses it was the Pentateuch; in the
> days of Jesus the Gospel; in the days of Muḥammad the Messenger
> of God the Qur'án; in this day the Bayán; and in the dispensation of
> Him Whom God will make manifest His own Book—the Book
> unto which all the Books of former Dispensations must needs be
> referred, the Book which standeth amongst them all transcendent
> and supreme. In these cities spiritual sustenance is bountifully
> provided, and incorruptible delights have been ordained. (199–200)

Those who are purified in heart become the residents of that kingdom.

Bahá'u'lláh's analysis of the meaning of divine sovereignty does
not end with the spiritual nature of this dominion. In the Kitáb-i-Íqán
the category of sovereignty becomes the basis for powerful arguments
for the Báb's claim. Two of these arguments are particularly important. First, Bahá'u'lláh uses the concept of divine power to infer the
principles of his critique of spiritual reason. Absolute divine ascendancy implies that God cannot be known or limited by any human categories, presuppositions, or interpretations. God cannot be known
through anything but God. The sole standard for recognizing the
Manifestations of God is the standard authorized by the Prophets
Themselves. To employ another standard or criterion is to deny divine

sovereignty and dominion. Therefore, even the Muslim clergy's discourse on sovereignty and their insistence on external dominion as the sign of the Qá'im and as the test of his claim is itself just such a denial of divine power and an instance of idolatry.

Bahá'u'lláh's second argument based on divine sovereignty concerns the unconditional power of God to manifest Himself through progressive revelation. He particularly emphasizes this point because the idea of the finality of revelation has always constituted the most serious obstacle to the recognition of the Manifestations of God. Muslims, for example, use the Qur'ánic reference to the Prophet Muḥammad as the "Seal of the Prophets" to insist that God will not send any new Messenger to the world. It is notable that the question of the Seal of the Prophets was not among those explicitly posed by the Báb's uncle. This may mean that he was first trying to investigate the Báb's claim to be the Qá'im. But the Shí'ih interpretation holds that the Qá'im, when he appears, will not be an independent Manifestation of God because the age of prophecy has ended with the Prophet Muḥammad. Possibly the idea that the Báb could be an independent Manifestation of God was so far outside the normal Muslim assumption that Ḥájí Mírzá Siyyid Muḥammad did not even voice it.

Bahá'u'lláh, however, does not allow this unspoken question and objection to go unanswered. He directly addresses the issue. In addition to the specific solution that Bahá'u'lláh offers, He resolves the problem of the title "Seal of the Prophets" through the category of divine sovereignty. To dictate terms to God and refuse to accept the divine command in the form of a new revelation is equivalent to denying divine unconditional power. To take the title "Seal of the Prophets" as a limit to the divine will and action presupposes absolute knowledge of the meanings of the word of God. Since the Qur'án itself testifies that some of the Qur'ánic statements are allegorical, and that the meanings of these equivocal verses are not known to the people, it follows that making the commonly assumed meaning of "the Seal of the Prophets" into the standard by which to judge divine will and revelation would be an affront to unconditional divine sovereignty.

THE RENEWAL OF THEOLOGY:
MANIFESTATION AND PROGRESSION

Manifestation is the central category of Bahá'í theology, cosmology, epistemology, eschatology, ethics, history, and sociology. It is partly for this reason that the Kitáb-i-Íqán, in which Bahá'u'lláh defines the concept of manifestation and progressive revelation, is so central to His revelation. His concept of progressive revelation opens up new horizons in theological and philosophical discourse which go beyond both Eastern and Western conceptions of the sacred and society, transcending and uniting the concerns of both Eastern and Western philosophical categories.

Antinomies of Reason and the Concept of Revelation

In order to examine the relevance of Bahá'u'lláh's concept of manifestation theology to both Eastern and Western philosophical questions, I will begin by comparing the message of the Kitáb-i-Íqán and the fundamental question of Kantian epistemology. The importance of Kantian theory of knowledge for modern Western philosophy and social theory needs no explanation for students of both disciplines. Kant changed the structure and order of philosophical discourse by situating the critique of reason at the center of the pursuit of truth. He argued that before making judgments on the truth of various statements and conceptions about the world, we must first ask questions concerning the structure and limits of the mind itself. The Kantian critique of pure reason came to the conclusion that the mind is not a blank tablet that reflects the impressions derived from experience but an active structure that shapes and forms sensory perceptions, imposing order on the chaotic manifold of representations. In other words, the world as it appears to us is created by the categories and forms of our own mind. Kantian theory suggested that both space and time (the forms of intuition) and the categories of understanding (the categories and laws of logic) are parts of the structure of mind itself and have no basis in the things in themselves. Mathematics and the natural sciences are said to be objective in the sense that they are coherent embodiments of the structures of mind. They are necessarily and universally true for humans only because we have no choice but to see them as we do.[9]

Kantian theory concluded that human knowledge applies only to the realm of appearances, or phenomena, which are products of the mind itself. Beyond the realm of phenomena, however, was the realm of the things in themselves, or noumena. This realm is not knowable by the mind because rational analysis is dependent on the application of the categories of mind to sensory data, which makes them automatically part of the phenomena. In other words, whatever we experience is already constituted as a phenomenon and is no longer the thing in itself. Kantian theory, therefore, left us with an unresolved tension: on the one hand, we long to know the noumena, true reality, the realm of things in their essences, infinity, and the unconditioned. On the other hand, we are confined to the realm of phenomena and deprived of the possibility of knowing the infinite and the unconditioned. Since there is no experience of that invisible realm, the application of the laws of logic to these questions cannot yield an ordered, coherent, and objective conclusion. Reason, in other words, finds itself at an impasse.[10] With regard to the realm of noumena or the things in themselves—that is, on issues related to God, the soul, freedom of will, and the limits of time and space—Kant argued, we can rationally argue both affirmatively and negatively. This paradoxical situation is called the *antinomies of reason*.

But yearning for knowledge of the infinite and of the thing in itself led Kant to try to find solutions to the antinomies of reason. He argued that both in the realm of practical reason—the realm of morality and moral action—and in the realm of art and aesthetics, we can transcend the boundaries of the phenomenal realm and attain a knowledge of the invisible realm of the things in themselves, or the "kingdom of ends."[11] The Kantian dilemma remained the basic concern of modern Western philosophy. As I have discussed elsewhere, both the philosophies of Schopenhauer and Nietzsche were attempts at resolving it.[12] Much of the content of the theories of Hegel, Marx, Durkheim, Weber, Simmel, and Bergson is understandable on the basis of the same ultimate question.

Although the Kantian problem is expressed in terms of its own language, the essence of the question can be seen to concern the same
underlying metaphysical problem that is explained by Bahá'u'lláh's
concept of manifestation. According to the Kitáb-i-Íqán and other
writings of Bahá'u'lláh, the longing for knowledge and love of God is
the essence of human nature and the primordial meaning and purpose
of human existence. However, our knowledge is limited in that we
can only understand things which also belong to the realm of creation
and contingent existence. Our knowledge is conditioned by the limitations of our nature: "To whatever heights the mind of the most
exalted of men may soar, however great the depths which the detached and understanding heart can penetrate, such mind and heart
can never transcend that which is the creature of their own conceptions and the product of their own thoughts" (*Gleanings* 317). Above
all, we have no access to the unknowable Essence of God. Bahá'u'lláh
explains:

> To every discerning and illumined heart it is evident that God,
> the unknowable Essence, the divine Being, is immensely exalted
> beyond every human attribute, such as corporeal existence, ascent
> and descent, egress and regress. Far be it from His glory that human
> tongue should adequately recount His praise, or that human heart
> comprehend His fathomless mystery. He is and hath ever been veiled
> in the ancient eternity of His Essence, and will remain in His Reality
> everlastingly hidden from the sight of men. "No vision taketh in
> Him, but He taketh in all vision; He is the Subtle, the All-Perceiv-
> ing."[13] No tie of direct intercourse can possibly bind Him to His
> creatures. He standeth exalted beyond and above all separation and
> union, all proximity and remoteness. No sign can indicate His
> presence or His absence; inasmuch as by a word of His command
> all that are in heaven and on earth have come to exist, and by His
> wish, which is the Primal Will itself, all have stepped out of utter
> nothingness into the realm of being, the world of the visible.
> (*Kitáb-i-Íqán* 98)

We can see that this addresses the same question posed by the critical philosophy of Kant. On the one hand, the purpose and meaning
of human existence is to attain the presence of God and, on the other,

no knowledge of the invisible "kingdom of ends" is possible for the human mind. Bahá'u'lláh's solution to this ontological and epistemological paradox is the concept of manifestation.

> ... All things, in their inmost reality, testify to the revelation of the names and attributes of God within them. Each according to its capacity, indicateth, and is expressive of, the knowledge of God. So potent and universal is this revelation, that it hath encompassed all things, visible and invisible.... Man, the noblest and most perfect of all created things, excelleth them all in the intensity of this revelation, and is a fuller expression of its glory. And of all men, the most accomplished, the most distinguished and the most excellent are the Manifestations of the Sun of Truth. Nay, all else besides these Manifestations, live by the operation of their Will, and move and have their being through the outpourings of their grace.... These Tabernacles of holiness, these primal Mirrors which reflect the light of unfading glory, are but expressions of Him Who is the Invisible of the Invisibles. By the revelation of these gems of divine virtue all the names and attributes of God, such as knowledge and power, sovereignty and dominion, mercy and wisdom, glory, bounty and grace, are made manifest. (102–3)

Although we cannot have direct access to God, we can recognize God through His manifestations in the realm of creation. But while all beings are manifestations of God as mirrors that reflect His attributes, the perfect manifestation and representation of the realm of invisible Truth in the realm of phenomena is the station held by the Prophets and Messengers of God. It is through Their presence in the visible realm that the invisible is recognized and known. Thus the ultimate solution to the existential quest of humanity is the recognition of the Manifestation of God in each age.

We can begin to understand the significance of the conception of manifestation that is disclosed in the Kitáb-i-Íqán by observing that Bahá'u'lláh applies the term *Manifestation of God* to what was traditionally considered to be the Prophet or Messenger of God. The choice of the term *Manifestation* represents a new, organic, and integrative conception not only of prophecy but of all of reality itself, a conception not contained within the idea of *prophet* or *messenger*.

Rather than being an isolated idea, or a repetition of earlier definitions of manifestation, Bahá'u'lláh's concept of manifestation transforms those earlier ideas and links them to the totality of being, integrating the whole structure of being and history together.

Beyond Asceticism and Mysticism: Manifestation

Bahá'u'lláh's concept of manifestation offers a theological perspective on the relationship of God and the realm of creation that is neither "asceticism" nor "mysticism," in Max Weber's terms. Weber was interested in the question of economic rationalization, and he wanted to know the reasons for the emergence of industrialization, capitalism, and economic growth in Western Europe. In his theory, different religious belief systems lead to different orientations to economic behavior which affect the possibility of and tendency to economic rationalization.

According to Weber, asceticism is in principle a theological orientation according to which God is a transcendental reality outside of the world. In this doctrine, the invisible realm of God is the sacred realm, whereas the material and natural world is one of evil and corruption. This opposition between the realms of spirit and flesh results in a particular relation of the believer to the world. The ascetic believer sees himself as the tool of the divine will. He cannot experience God because of the transcendental character of the divine. Consequently he becomes an instrument in the hand of God in order to realize the will of God in a corrupt and evil world. The consequence of this orientation, according to Weber, is a personality that emphasizes rational discipline and self-control and tries to change, dominate, and transform the world. Weber believed asceticism to be compatible with a rational organization of behavior in methodic and disciplined terms. As a result, he felt, asceticism tends toward economic development, capitalist expansion, and industrialization.

Mysticism, Weber assumed, would lead to the opposite implications of asceticism. According to mysticism, God is immanent in the world so that nature and God become identical realities. The "mystical" believer conceives of himself as the vessel of God, and the immanence of God in the world means that God can be experienced by the individual believer. In this theological orientation, the believer is filled with the ecstasy of divine love and overwhelmed by experiential and emotional elevated states. The goal of life and dominant orientation is to attain harmony and unity with nature rather than its conquest and transformation. For Weber, this implied that mysticism is not compatible with economic rationalization and development.[14]

Weber's theory can also be applied to analyze other issues besides economic development, such as the preservation of the environment. Following that same logic, one can conclude from Weber's theory that asceticism would be incompatible with protecting the environment, while mysticism would correspond to a disposition to preserve nature. In other words, asceticism leads to economic development but destruction of the environment, whereas mysticism ends in economic stagnation but protection of the environment.

Despite Weber's creative insights, his typology of religious meaning systems is incomplete. In fact both asceticism and mysticism are capable of opposite implications. This can be seen clearly in terms of Bahá'í theology, which fits neither of the models given in Weber's typology. Instead, Bahá'í theology, as discussed in the Kitáb-i-Íqán, can be termed the perspective of harmonious transcendence. Such a position is radically different from both Weberian mysticism and asceticism. However, this means that the thesis of the transcendence of God can have implications different from those proposed by Weber's concept of asceticism.

In Bahá'u'lláh's teachings, although God is an absolutely transcendental reality, instead of opposition there is harmony between the divine and the created, natural realms. This fits into neither of Weber's types. It can be argued, therefore, that while the doctrine of the transcendence of opposition (the view that God is outside nature and opposed to it) may tend toward economic growth and destruction of nature, and while the doctrine of the immanence of God in nature can be compatible with a stagnant economy and protection of the environment, the principle of harmonious transcendence is compatible with both respect for nature as well as motivation for progress and development. However, this also implies a radically different definition of development, one that is itself defined in the context of respect for the environment and future generations.[15]

Bahá'u'lláh's concept of manifestation simultaneously implies an ethical orientation to history. History becomes the arena where the divine attributes are unveiled through successive stages of humanity's cultural and spiritual development. In this perspective, because the essence of human nature is none other than the hidden sign of the unity of God, human history in its totality can be seen as the progressive realization and unfoldment of this primordial unity and dignity in the form of social relations, cultural institutions, and spiritual orientations which, in ever more complex and complete ways, express and reflect that characteristic of unity and integration.[16] It is for the same reason that Bahá'u'lláh's later writings conceptualize human history as stages of the realization of unity in diversity. The oneness of humankind, the supreme goal of Bahá'u'lláh's revelation, then becomes understandable as the consummate realization of the inherent sacredness of humans and their nature as manifestations of the attributes of God. As such, the concept of manifestation also becomes an ethical doctrine. In this ethical orientation, not only the fundamental equality of all human beings and wholeness of humankind, but also the sacredness of nature are normative principles. Both principles are integral expressions of Bahá'u'lláh's metaphysics of manifestation.

Bahá'u'lláh's Critique of Historical Reason
Unlike previous theological conceptions, Bahá'u'lláh's vision of manifestation is not a static concept. Bahá'u'lláh completely transforms the traditional idea of manifestation theology, making it a historical and dynamic idea. While the typical Islamic conception of prophecy and revelation maintained the finality of divine revelation, Bahá'u'lláh explains all divine revelation as historically progressive and in accordance with the level of spiritual and social development of humanity. In other words, it is not (as, for example, in Sufi mysticism) through

escape from plurality and history that we can recognize God, but rather it is only through these successive, historically specific, and progressive revelations that the divine Reality makes itself known.

The concept of progressive revelation is directly connected to Bahá'u'lláh's critique of spiritual reason. In Chapter 2, we saw how the idea of spiritual journey goes through a fundamental transformation in the writings of Bahá'u'lláh, and how in Gems of Mysteries Bahá'u'lláh's discussion of the valleys of the personal journey becomes an exposition of humanity's journey through successive divine revelations. This metamorphosis becomes fully explicit in the Kitáb-i-Íqán, in which Bahá'u'lláh identifies the City of God—which is the goal and destiny of the mystic wayfarer—as the new Book that is revealed and renewed by God approximately every thousand years. The critique of spiritual reason and the account of the mystic journey become an affirmation of progressive revelation: it is not just individuals but also humanity as a collectivity which is engaged in a journey of return to God, a journey which advances through the recognition of the Word of God and its successive and progressive unveiling in human history.[17]

The typical critique of historical reason in Western philosophy applied the concept of historicity and historical progression to the realm of economics, society, and culture. These theories rejected the eighteenth-century Enlightenment view that held human nature to be static and unchanging; reduced society and culture to expressions of individual natural characteristics; identified nature as a mechanistic and dead object; saw humans as self-interested and utilitarian entities; and took capitalism and liberalist institutions to be eternally rational, moral, and natural social forms.[18] The advocates of historical reason, in contrast, saw society as a dynamic and organic reality, stressed the historical specificity of cultural practices and institutions, and rejected the utilitarian definition of human beings. Many major schools of nineteenth-century social theory advocated a critique of historical reason which emphasized that dynamic view and insisted on the dependence of human reason and social ideologies on the stage of social and historical development. Human knowledge was defined as a historically specific and socially conditioned phenomenon.[19]

However, this critique of historical reason typically suffered from three major limitations. First, while the followers of various religions usually held to an "end of history" through their belief that their own Prophet's revelation was final—and therefore affirmed a contradiction between a changing/contingent world and an unchangeable/absolute divine Word—those modern philosophers who conceived of history and culture as dynamic phenomena failed to realize the principle of historicity at the level of the revelation of the divine Word or *Logos* itself. For these historicists, the revelation of God is static while the human interpretation and realization of that revelation changes throughout history. Both approaches resulted in an inconsistent perspective which could not escape the consequent tension between a static revelation and a dynamic history.

Second, most of these theories failed to remain truly historical and dynamic because they expected an imminent end to the march of historical dynamics. Utopia was to arrive soon as a decisive resolution to all social problems and conflicts. The positivist theories of Saint-Simon and Auguste Comte, for example, adopted a historical consciousness but then reduced the march of history to the three stages of theological, metaphysical, and scientific thinking. The first two stages were defined as superstitious while the third was to be the final stage of human social development, in which the rule of an impersonal reason and a technocratic class would mark the achievement of freedom, morality, and progress.[20] That form of historical consciousness, however, only elevated empirical science into a new form of the sacred, which was itself intolerant of political democracy as well as any metaphysical and spiritual ways of looking at the world. Similarly, Hegelian and Marxian dialectics of history were supposed to culminate in the Prussian state or the communist mode of production, respectively.[21] The former legitimized the status quo as the end goal of historical progression, while the latter sought a stateless, classless communal society where the elimination of private property would bring an end to scarcity and alienation. Needless to say, any doctrine of the end of history must impose some arbitrary model as society's final and eternal form. But since history and real societies are neither simplistic nor static, the advocates of such notions must eventually resort to fabrications and coercion to hide the discrepancy between the objective dynamic reality and the simplistic and ahistorical categories of their models.

The third major limitation of the Western critique of historical reason derived from its materialism. Reducing religion to a mere sociohistorical construct, the critique of historical reason usually rejected the reality of any spiritual or transcendental dimension in human life or history. As a result, those theories increasingly ended in a relativism and moral nihilism in which all truth and value was equally arbitrary and, ultimately, meaningless. Nietzsche's nihilistic philosophy represents the culmination of this critique of historical reason in Western philosophy.[22]

Against that background, and in sharp contrast to those developments in Western philosophy, the revolutionary and historic character of Bahá'u'lláh's exposition in the Kitáb-i-Íqán becomes apparent. Bahá'u'lláh uses the traditional language and categories of Eastern mystical and Islamic philosophical discourse to articulate a worldview that transcends the contemporary Eastern and Western modes of philosophy and social theory. Like Islamic mystics, Bahá'u'lláh emphasizes the reality of a transcendental realm and the ultimately spiritual nature and meaning of human existence, while, similar to Western social theorists, He emphasizes the historical dynamics of civilization. In the Kitáb-i-Íqán He stresses the historical and dynamic character of human institutions precisely because of the historical and dynamic character of manifestation and revelation. The resulting worldview avoids the problems in the Western critique of historical reason: it does away with the thesis of the end of history by affirming the perpetual and progressive nature of revelation; and, by emphasizing spiritual reality and revelation as real forces of social progress, it imparts both meaning and value to history.

The Pillars of the Faith Historicized

In the context of traditional religious discourse, the doctrine of progressive revelation reinterprets some basic theological principles and

offers solutions to traditional scriptural problems. I will review here
the three fundamental principles of Islam and their reconceptualiza-
tion by Bahá'u'lláh.

According to various schools of Islamic thought, the most important theological articles of faith are the unity of God, prophecy, and
the day of return. However, these ideas are typically defined in ways
that are not very much related to each other, and as static and ahistorical concepts supporting the thesis of the end of history and the
finality of revelation. The unity of God is normally defined as a rejection
of a plurality of gods and of idolatry, and it emphasizes the absoluteness
of divine revelation as opposed to the relativity of historical truth.
Prophecy is understood as the divine act of commissioning Prophets and
Messengers to deliver the unchanging divine word to humanity. This
doctrine maintains that Muḥammad is the last Prophet, the Seal of the
Prophets, and there will be no further divine revelation after Him. The
day of return is understood as a day when all the dead return to life and
are judged in accordance with their deeds and then relegated to heaven
or hell.

In the Kitáb-i-Íqán, the doctrines of the unity of God, prophecy,
and the day of return become linked through the concept of manifestation, and all become evidence of dynamic and progressive divine
revelation and an all-encompassing critique of historical reason. It is
for this reason that reductions of Bahá'u'lláh's concept of manifestationhood to the Islamic or Sufi definitions of the term are so inaccurate. While Bahá'u'lláh uses the language customary to the people
around Him, in His usage of that language He fundamentally redefines
both the terms and their philosophical presuppositions.

The concept of the unity of God becomes in fact a unity in diversity through the principle of manifestation. At the level of the
unknowable Essence nothing else has ever existed or will ever exist,
and it is at the level of divine revelation and effulgence that the realm
of plurality and diversity—that is, the created world—comes into
being. All created beings are a reflection of the divine revelation or
manifestation. In their diversity, all are indications pointing to one
absolutely unknowable transcendental Divinity.

As we have seen, the real meaning of recognizing divine unity is recognizing the unity of the diverse divine revelations. That means not merely recognizing one of those revelations, but recognizing the *unity* of all of them by recognizing the most recent Manifestation of God. Such recognition of the fundamental unity of all existence and the unity of the Manifestations of God becomes the summit and furthest limit of human understanding of divine unity. Both the doctrine of the unity of all the Messengers of God and the doctrine of the oneness of humankind become the supreme reflections of the category of divine unity in the realm of human understanding. We can see that in Bahá'u'lláh's analysis, the principle of the unity of God is not separable from the unity of His Manifestations and the unity of humankind. In other words, these unities are not separable from their diversity: the primordial and eternal unity always reflects itself through diversity and historical dynamics. The concept of the unity of God becomes an affirmation of the progressive and dynamic nature of divine manifestation. What was traditionally seen as the realm of prophecy, then, becomes precisely the realm of divine revelation.

The concept of the unity in diversity of the Manifestations, and the progressive and perpetual nature of revelation, puts the traditional Islamic concept of the Seal of the Prophets into a new light. Since the essence of all Manifestations of God is one and the same, they are all the return of each other. In that sense, while Muḥammad is the last Prophet, He is equally the first prophet. The firstness and lastness of the Prophets is itself a reflection of the Qur'ánic definition of God as the First and the Last. However, this firstness is a beginning without beginning and this lastness is an end without an end. As Bahá'u'lláh writes:

> For this reason, hath the Point of the Bayán ... likened the Manifestations of God unto the sun which, though it rise from the "Beginning that hath no beginning" until the "End that knoweth no end," is none the less the same sun. Now, wert thou to say, that this sun is the former sun, thou speakest the truth; and if thou sayest that this sun is the "return" of that sun, thou also speakest the truth. Likewise, from this statement it is made evident that the term "last" is

applicable to the "first," and the term "first" applicable to the "last";
inasmuch as both the "first" and the "last" have risen to proclaim one
and the same Faith.

.... Hath not Muḥammad, Himself, declared: "I am all the
Prophets?" Hath He not said as We have already mentioned: "I am
Adam, Noah, Moses, and Jesus?" Why should Muḥammad, that
immortal Beauty, Who hath said: "I am the first Adam" be incapable
of saying also: "I am the last Adam"? For even as He regarded
Himself to be the "First of the Prophets"—that is Adam—in like
manner, the "Seal of the Prophets" is also applicable unto that
Divine Beauty. It is admittedly obvious that being the "First of the
Prophets," He likewise is their "Seal." (*Kitáb-i-Íqán* 161–62)

In all cases, "finality" is relative to their historical relation to one another.
Now the concept of the Seal of the Prophets takes on a radically different meaning. The essential unity of all the divine Prophets is the
point of reference for the meaning of finality.

As can be seen in that passage, Bahá'u'lláh's concept of manifestation simultaneously solves the traditional problem of "return" as
well. The Manifestations themselves are all the return of one another
despite the difference in their physical, human, or situational characteristics:

As to the matter of names, Muḥammad, Himself, declared: "I am
Jesus." He recognized the truth of the signs, prophecies, and words
of Jesus, and testified that they were all of God. In this sense, neither
the person of Jesus nor His writings hath differed from that of
Muḥammad and of His holy Book, inasmuch as both have cham-
pioned the Cause of God, uttered His praise, and revealed His
commandments. Thus it is that Jesus, Himself, declared: "I go away
and come again unto you." Consider the sun. Were it to say now,
"I am the sun of yesterday," it would speak the truth. And should it,
bearing the sequence of time in mind, claim to be other than that
sun, it still would speak the truth. In like manner, if it be said that all
the days are but one and the same, it is correct and true. And if it be
said, with respect to their particular names and designations, that
they differ, that again is true. For though they are the same, yet one
doth recognize in each a separate designation, a specific attribute, a
particular character. (20–21)

Similarly, Bahá'u'lláh explains the verses in the Qur'án which refer to the people living at the time of Muḥammad as the return of the generations living at the time of previous Manifestations of God. In all these cases, it is not the actual persons who are indicated, but their role of affirming or denying the divine Manifestations.

Bahá'u'lláh also resolves the question of the meaning of attainment to the divine presence on the Day of Resurrection. Analyzing the meaning of "attainment" and "divine presence," as these had been interpreted in terms of the Sufi categories of the "most holy outpouring" and the "holy outpouring," Bahá'u'lláh points out the contradictions in traditional interpretations, and it becomes clear that attaining the divine presence means recognition of the Manifestation of God in each age:

> These Prophets and chosen Ones of God are the recipients and revealers of all the unchangeable attributes and names of God.... Whatsoever is applicable to them is in reality applicable to God, Himself, Who is both the Visible and the Invisible. The knowledge of Him, Who is the Origin of all things, and attainment unto Him, are impossible save through knowledge of, and attainment unto, these luminous Beings who proceed from the Sun of Truth. By attaining, therefore, to the presence of these holy Luminaries, the "Presence of God" Himself is attained. (142)

The references in the Qur'án to attaining the presence of God on the Day of Judgment, therefore, can be seen to affirm the doctrine of manifestation as well as the continuity of divine revelation in the future.

The third fundamental principle of Islam is the day of return or the Day of Resurrection. In the ordinary understanding of the Qur'án, this meant literally the end of history. In the Kitáb-i-Íqán, however, "return" refers to the spiritual journey and the return of human beings to God, or the arc of ascent. The day of return occurs when the Manifestation of God appears, and it reoccurs with the advent of each new Manifestation of God. The revolutionary implications of this reinterpretation of the doctrine of return cannot be overemphasized. What was a static, linear view of life and society, culminating in an end of history, becomes reoriented to a dynamic, progressive, and nonlinear concept of historical and social advancement through a sequence of qualitatively new stages of spiritualization, none of which is reducible to the incremental process within the previous stage. Each revelation imparted by successive Manifestations of God initiates a new cycle of birth and rebirth but the cycle itself is recursive. The Kitáb-i-Íqán represents a stage theory of spiritual and cultural development which synthesizes cyclical and linear conceptions of social and cultural dynamics. The terms *life* and *death* then signify spiritual development or spiritual regression. In this way all the three principles of Islam are defined through the concept of manifestation; those concepts, previously isolated, are united in a dynamic and progressive approach to life, culture, society, history, and divine revelation.

Chapter 6
THE KITÁB-I-BADÍ':
THE PROMISE FULFILLED

ALTHOUGH AS YET UNTRANSLATED and infrequently discussed, the Kitáb-i-Badí' (The Wondrous New Book) is one of Bahá'u'lláh's most important writings and should be considered His main apologia. Revealed in Edirne, it refutes the fallacious arguments, distortions, objections, and accusations of Mírzá Mihdíy-i-Rashtí, who was influenced by Siyyid Muḥammad-i-Iṣfahání (the chief opponent of Bahá'u'lláh and partner of Mírzá Yaḥyá). It employs the same logic as that found in the Kitáb-i-Íqán but expresses its arguments more emphatically and in even stronger language.[1] The Kitáb-i-Badí' was revealed in Persian and is considerably longer than the Kitáb-i-Íqán, consisting of 412 pages in its current edition.

The circumstances leading to the revelation of the Kitáb-i-Badí' are discussed both within the text itself and in many other tablets of Bahá'u'lláh. Mírzá Mihdíy-i-Rashtí, appointed by the Iranian ambassador Mushíru'd-Dawlih as Persian judge in Istanbul, was a Bábí who had come under the influence of Siyyid Muḥammad-i-Iṣfahání and had been persuaded to rebel against Bahá'u'lláh. He wrote a short letter to Áqá Muḥammad 'Alíy-i-Tambákúfurúsh-i-Iṣfahání, one of Bahá'u'lláh's devoted companions and servants, arguing against Bahá'u'lláh's claim and denying His authority. But in fact, as Bahá'u'lláh explains in His text, all the ideas in the letter were actually suggested to Mírzá Mihdí by Siyyid Muḥammad. The Kitáb-i-Badí' thus refutes the accusations of Siyyid Muḥammad as they were conveyed by Mírzá Mihdí. Áqá Muḥammad-'Alí brought the letter to Bahá'u'lláh, Who revealed the Kitáb-i-Badí' in three days. The Kitáb-i-Badí' is both Bahá'u'lláh's demonstration of the truth of His own Cause and His most comprehensive analysis and interpretation of the Báb's writings.

In this book, as in the Kitáb-i-Íqán, Bahá'u'lláh responds at two distinct levels to the objections raised against the Manifestation of God—one level is foundational or general, the other substantive or specific. Because Bahá'u'lláh identifies the foundational discourse as His central message as well as the core message of all the revelations, the Kitáb-i-Badí' can be regarded as a key for understanding the other writings of Bahá'u'lláh as well.

INTRODUCTION

The title of the Kitáb-i-Badí' is particularly revealing of the period and the context in which it was revealed. Bahá'u'lláh frequently uses the term *Amr-i-Badí'* (the Wondrous New Cause) or *Amr-i-Abda'* (the Most Wondrous New Cause) to describe His new revelation as separate and distinct from the Bábí dispensation. The title of the Kitáb-i-Badí' implies that it is a New Book announcing and demonstrating the new Cause of Bahá'u'lláh. The entire book is a demonstration of Bahá'u'lláh's claim to be the Promised One of the Bayán, He Whom God shall make manifest. The Kitáb-i-Badí' is also the decisive pronouncement of the "Most Great Separation" between Bahá'u'lláh and Yaḥyá Azal.

The book is one among many writings of Bahá'u'lláh which were revealed at the end of His residence in Edirne, a few months before His exile to 'Akká. Shoghi Effendi dates the writing of the Kitáb-i-Badí' to shortly after the Most Great Separation, in the same time period when the Súriy-i-Mulúk (Súrih of Kings) was also revealed, during Bahá'u'lláh's stay in the house of 'Izzat Áqá.[2] Bahá'u'lláh moved to that house around April 1867, and the Most Great Separation was effected in September of that year. Bahá'u'lláh departed Edirne for 'Akká around August 1868. Hence the Kitáb-i-Badí' must have been revealed in late 1867 or early 1868.

Internal textual evidence confirms that date. The clearest evidence is Bahá'u'lláh's remark that He has been in this land for "nearly five years"; Bahá'u'lláh resided in Edirne about four years and nine months.[3] Other, more indirect evidence can be found in the text as well. For instance, Bahá'u'lláh refers to the fact that He has reared and educated Yaḥyá (who was born around 1830) for forty years.[4]

Bahá'u'lláh also refers to the Most Great Separation,[5] and He often mentions Siyyid Muḥammad's trip to Istanbul to petition the government for stipends, which took place around early 1866. Bahá'u'lláh mentions His twenty years of suffering in the Cause of God—a frequent expression in His writings of the time, referring to twenty years after the beginning of the new and harsher stage of persecution of the Bábís in 1847–48.[6] Finally, Bahá'u'lláh uses the title of *ahl-i-Bahá* (people of Bahá) to distinguish His followers from *ahl-i-Bayán* (people of the Bayán)—a distinction that became the norm in the late Edirne period.[7]

Although the Kitáb-i-Badí' and the Kitáb-i-Íqán have fundamental similarities, the arrangement and style of the two books is quite different. The logic of analysis in the Kitáb-i-Badí' is composed of two levels of discourse, similar to that of the Kitáb-i-Íqán. However, unlike the Kitáb-i-Íqán's division into two parts dealing with the foundational and substantive arguments, the Kitáb-i-Badí' is presented as responses to successively quoted paragraphs of Mírzá Mihdí's letter, and it follows the order of that letter. An important difference between the two works is the language or voice of the text. Bahá'u'lláh writes the Kitáb-i-Íqán in His own name. The first person of the text is Bahá'u'lláh Himself. The Kitáb-i-Badí', in contrast, is revealed in the name of Áqá Muḥammad-i-Iṣfahání, the servant of Bahá'u'lláh who received Mírzá Mihdí's letter, and Bahá'u'lláh refers to Himself in the third person. The language of the Kitáb-i-Badí' becomes more complex in that Bahá'u'lláh sometimes speaks in the role of the Primal Point (because, in essence, They are one and the same) and reveals statements addressed to the Báb's followers, expressing His sadness that they have failed to heed His words and advice and have denied Him (that is, the Báb) in His second manifestation in the person of Bahá'u'lláh.

Another moving stylistic element in the Kitáb-i-Badí' is Bahá'u'lláh's narrative of the lamentations and supplications of Mírzá Yaḥyá's pen, which has been used to write against the Promised One of the Bayán. Bahá'u'lláh explains that the pen of Mihdí is but a shadow of the pen of Yaḥyá and that the latter's pen has secretly escaped from him and attained the presence of Bahá'u'lláh, where it has wept and wailed, confessing its shame, sorrow, bewilderment, and anger at Yaḥyá and its abuse and suffering in the hand of its owner, the arch covenant-breaker. The pen entreats Bahá'u'lláh to command it to act as a fatal weapon against Yaḥyá, and if He does not grant that wish, at least to liberate it from the fingers of Bahá'u'lláh's enemy. It expresses its shame before the community of pens and avows that even if Bahá'-u'lláh forgave its sins, it would continue to be mortified because of its role. It admits its confusion and distress at its fate, a fate that could not be deserved because it knows that it is nonexistent before the divine will, and yet could not be said to be undeserved because it is unable to understand the logic of mysterious divine wisdom. It complains of the fact that other pens have been used to reveal the words of God in the hand of Bahá'u'lláh, while it has been imprisoned in the grip of the enemy of the Cause of God. The pen declares that its gravest concern is that because of its sins the Pen of Glory may cease to reveal divine words, and it implores Bahá'u'lláh to settle its fate and emancipate it from its sorrow, or else make it cease to exist.

The pen continues to recount its life story to Bahá'u'lláh. From the very first days of its existence as a reed, it longed to attain the presence of Bahá'u'lláh and spent its days and nights in a state of yearning. It endured all hardships for the sake of that wish. Then it was cut off and moved from hand to hand and from place to place until it was bought in the market by one of His servants. But when it was placed in that man's hand it sensed the odor of his heedlessness and became saddened but remained silent. The servant carried the pen from land to land until he arrived in the land of Bahá'u'lláh's residence. Joy and delight overtook the pen and it felt itself the king of all kings. It remained in that state of ecstasy till its bearer arrived at a crossroads—one path led to the right and another path to the left. The man chose the left-hand path, and the pen found itself trembling and wailing until at last the servant reached a house exuding the stench of hell and placed the pen in the hand of the tyrant who rose against Bahá'u'lláh.

The pen continues to express its unending sense of shame and implores Bahá'u'lláh to take its life and then to recreate it so that it might expunge the memory of its unhappy past.[8]

MÍRZÁ MIHDÍY-I-RASHTÍ'S ARGUMENT

Mírzá Mihdí's argument can be divided into seven substantive objections.

(1) He contends that Bahá'u'lláh's claim is based on esoteric interpretation of the Báb's writings and that it ignores the explicit and conclusive (*muḥkamát*) aspects of the Bayán. Bahá'u'lláh's entire approach to the Bayán, he charges, is ungrounded in the Bayán, ignoring its real message and reducing it to arbitrary interpretations. However, Mírzá Mihdí insists, the station and titles of Yaḥyá Azal are among the explicit and conclusive aspects of the Bayán.

(2) Mírzá Mihdí argues that Bahá'u'lláh's claim to be the Promised One cannot be true because according to the Bayán, the next Manifestation will not appear before the completion and perfection of the Cause of the Bayán. Just as the Báb could not appear before the completion and maturation of the Tree of the Qur'án, the next Manifestation will only appear after the completion of the Tree of the Bayán. Such completion requires a long period of time and cannot be achieved so quickly. Furthermore, the prophecies of the Qur'án and the Imáms concerning the signs to accompany the advent of the Qá'im are of two parts. One part is related to the beginning of the Báb's Cause. These signs were fulfilled, even though people did not understand them. However, he maintains, the other part is related to the later period of the Báb's Cause. Those signs, he contends, are as yet unfulfilled; therefore the Báb's religion is not yet completed.

(3) Mírzá Mihdí claims that, according to the Bayán, Yaḥyá is the vicegerent of the Báb, who praised him by bestowing on him the highest titles of the names of God. Yaḥyá is particularly designated as the supreme Mirror reflecting God on earth. Bahá'u'lláh's claim about Yaḥyá's ignominy would imply that truth had been changed into falsehood, which is impossible. His claim, therefore, is a logical contradiction.

(4) Mírzá Mihdí contends that Bahá'u'lláh's claim about His own station cannot be true because either He is the return of the Báb or He is subordinate to Him. If He claims to be the return of the Báb, then this cannot be meant as the return of the essence and reality of the Báb

because that would imply the repetition of revelation ("effulgence") (*tikrár-i-tajallí*), which is impossible. Hence it must mean the return of the Báb's attributes. In that case, He must advocate the same Cause that was advocated by the Báb, and not abrogate the laws of the Bayán nor bring a new religion. But if He is subordinate to the Báb, then He must be a member of the Bábí community and under the leadership of Yaḥyá.

(5) The references to "Bahá" in the Bayán, Mírzá Mihdí claims, are general references and do not refer to the person of Bahá who happens to have the same name. Bahá, he maintains, is just a name of God like the other names of God, not a specific reference to the Promised One of the Bayán. Furthermore, he argues, others have claimed to be the Promised One of the Bayán, including Dayyán, Mírzá Ghawghá, Shaykh Ismá'íl, and Ḥájí Mullá Háshim. Therefore, the mere claim is insufficient.

(6) Bahá'u'lláh supports His claim by claiming to reveal divine verses. However, the revelation of verses, Mihdí argues, is inadequate evidence. Anyone, he says, can produce verses. Bahá'u'lláh, he suggests, has been one of the Sufis and has associated with mystics for a long time and has studied the art of writing. If Bahá'u'lláh's claim is true then He must accept to be tested by miracles, and if He succeeds in producing the evidence, then He can be recognized, but only as a Bábí subordinate to Yaḥyá. A sign of the falsehood of Bahá'u'lláh's claim, Mírzá Mihdí asserts, is the fact that only the uneducated believe in Him.

(7) Lastly, Mírzá Mihdí charges that Bahá'u'lláh has been motivated by the desire for power and material comfort; He drinks tea in coffeehouses and attends feasts of fine food. Bahá'u'lláh, Mihdí notes, has denounced Yaḥyá for being fearful and hiding from the people. However, Mihdí insists, this is because Yaḥyá is detached from worldly desires. Furthermore, he offers, that fear was shared by all the Prophets and spiritual personages. All the Prophets were equally afraid of their enemies and avoided danger: Jesus used dissimulation and Muḥammad hid Himself from His enemies. Siyyid Muḥammad, Mihdí argues, traveled to Istanbul not to obtain bread but to seek amnesty for Yaḥyá and himself from the government of Iran.

BAHÁ'U'LLÁH'S FOUNDATIONAL DISCOURSE

Although Bahá'u'lláh has not formally divided the Kitáb-i-Badí' into two parts to differentiate the foundational or methodological and the substantive or specific discourse, He maintains this distinction throughout the text, referring to these two aspects as the "higher" and "lower" approaches. The higher level is the foundational, methodological, or general one, and Bahá'u'lláh considers the assumptions of the lower level to be a kind of descent from the higher level of discourse.[9] As we have seen, this distinction also constitutes the order of the Kitáb-i-Íqán, which begins with the higher level of analysis. According to Bahá'u'lláh, all the objections of Mírzá Mihdíy-i-Rashtí—like all other forms of objection against the Manifestation of God—can be sufficiently refuted by the foundational argument alone. That Bahá'u'lláh descends from the higher level of general principle to engage in substantive arguments refuting specific objections is simply due to His compassion, as well as the spiritual state of His audience.

The foundational discourse of the Kitáb-i-Badí' is identical to the concept of "heart" or sincerity, which is also the same as the methodological principle of the independent investigation of truth. This consists of two imperatives: *independence* and *investigation*. Independence is that condition of the heart in which it is purified from all prejudice, particularistic attachments, and inclinations. As a method of truth-seeking, it is not inclined to imitation of tradition, received interpretation, or other preconceived ideas about how to investigate the truth of the Manifestation of God. These preconceptions lead to using illegitimate standards and asking the wrong questions. Investigation, as method, means the use of the legitimate and appropriate standards designated by God Himself, asking the right questions, and doing so not just with analytical reason alone but with the totality of one's capacities, which are summarized as the understanding of the "heart."

Bahá'u'lláh demonstrates that this foundational and methodological principle is explicit in the writings of the Báb. That is why the objections of the people of the Bayán against Bahá'u'lláh are most surprising and indicate an unprecedented level of ignorance, confusion, vanity, and distortion. Bahá'u'lláh's discussion of the higher meth-

odological and foundational principle is dispersed throughout the
Kitáb-i-Badí', and it is the most frequently repeated issue in the text.
What we have seen as the principle of "heart" in the Kitáb-i-Íqán—
which involves seeing God with one's own eyes, with the eye of the
heart, and with the eye of God—is expressed in the Kitáb-i-Badí' in
such words as these:

> Behold the Cause of thy Lord with thine own eyes and then recog-
> nize Him in thine own soul and spirit, for recognition through
> others will not suffice thee, nor can their denial constitute a proof
> unto thee.[10]

> And it is especially and clearly revealed throughout the Bayán that
> in the day of His revelation one must turn to no one save Him, for
> that Ancient Beauty cannot be recognized except through His own
> eyes, and this is exactly what hath happened. At this moment the
> Primal Point saith that the words thou hast written are a grievous
> transgression and the proofs thou dost adduce arise from the idle
> fancies of the deluded. Verily He Who is the Truth hath appeared
> in His sovereignty! His proof is the revelation of His divine verses,
> and His testimony is the manifestation of His own Self.[11]

> In this Day it is incumbent upon every discerning person to purify
> his heart from all allusions, proofs, and names, and to fix his gaze
> upon naught but Him Who is the Manifestation and whatever hath
> been revealed by Him. This is enjoined upon all in the Bayán.[12]

> For He Himself [the Promised One of the Bayán] is His own proof
> and cannot be recognized through others, as hath been stated at the
> end of the Báb's Tablet, that whosoever would behold the Ancient
> Beauty through any other than His own eye would never recognize
> Him. He [the Báb] saith, exalted be He: "Behold Him with the eyes
> of thy heart and look upon Him with no other than His own eyes.
> For whosoever looketh upon Him with His eyes, will recognize
> Him; otherwise he will be veiled from Him. Shouldst thou seek God
> and desire to attain His Presence, seek thou His Person and gaze
> upon His Beauty."[13]

Refuting the notion that the general rules current among the
people constitute the standard of proof, Bahá'u'lláh says this is an arrogant idea for it concerns a station which God has elevated above all
else; the Manifestation Himself is the standard of God and His balance

by which truth is determined. He likens the use of human standards to a person who takes a piece of worthless stone to the possessor of a treasury of jewels and insists on judging the jewels by the standard of the stone. Such a standard may be able to recognize those of its own rank, but the Self of God transcends that criterion; the divine standard has been and always will be His own Being. The standard Mírzá Mihdí is attempting to use is the same artificial standard, constructed by the scholars and leaders, that was once used against the Báb, and before Him against Muḥammad and Jesus.[14]

BAHÁʼUʼLLÁHʼS SUBSTANTIVE DISCOURSE

Although all seven of Mírzá Mihdíʼs objections against the station of Baháʼuʼlláh are sufficiently and decisively answered by the methodological, foundational (or "higher") discourse, Baháʼuʼlláh descends from that higher level and addresses each of Mírzá Mihdíʼs (and, implicitly, Siyyid Muḥammadʼs and Mírzá Yaḥyáʼs) arguments in detail as well.

Equivocal and Conclusive Elements of the Bayán

Mírzá Mihdí had objected that Baháʼuʼlláhʼs claim was based on esoteric interpretation of the Bayán, emphasizing its equivocal (*mutashábihát*) parts while ignoring its conclusive aspects. Among the most important of these conclusive and explicit parts, he had asserted, was the reference in the Bayán to Yaḥyá Azalʼs titles. Baháʼuʼlláh responds that Mírzá Mihdí does not understand the real meaning of the distinction between equivocal and conclusive verses. He goes on to prove that the exact opposite of Mírzá Mihdíʼs assertion is the case— namely that the most explicit, emphasized, conclusive, and repeated part of the Bayán is precisely that which upholds the unconditional nature of Baháʼuʼlláhʼs evidence and revelation.

Baháʼuʼlláhʼs specific answer to the objection that has been posed is in fact His foundational principle. He quotes many exhortations of the Báb such as: "Let not names shut you out as by a veil from Him Who is their Lord, even the name of Prophet, for such a name is but a creation of His utterance";[15] "Should any one make a statement, and fail to support it by any proof, reject him not";[16] "Suffer not the Bayán and all that hath been revealed therein to withhold you from that Essence of Being and Lord of the visible and invisible";[17] "Beware, beware lest, in the days of His Revelation, the Váhid of the Bayán shut thee not out as by a veil from Him, inasmuch as this Váhid is but a creature in His sight. And beware, beware that the words sent down in the Bayán shut thee not out as by a veil from Him."[18] (Note that the "Váhid" mentioned in the last statement is the Báb Himself and the eighteen Letters of the Living.)

Bahá'u'lláh also quotes the Báb's assertions that "The whole of the Bayán is only a leaf amongst the leaves of His Paradise,"[19] and "Of all the tributes I have paid to Him Who is to come after Me, the greatest is this, My written confession, that no words of Mine can adequately describe Him, nor can any reference to Him in My Book, the Bayán, do justice to His Cause;"[20] while "through this Book, I have covenanted with all created things concerning the Mission of Him Whom Thou shalt make manifest, ere the covenant concerning Mine own Mission had been established."[21]

Because this principle is so central to the Bayán, constituting its heart and essence, all Mírzá Mihdí's objections directly contradict the most conclusive and essential part of the Bayán. It is Mírzá Mihdí who is ignoring the Bayán's conclusive aspect and is making arbitrary and false interpretations. Furthermore, because the Báb often stressed that the real meaning of the words of the Bayán is known to no one except the Promised One, no reference to the Bayán—nor any name or title, whether of Yahyá or of the Letters of the Living, or even of the Báb Himself—can be legitimately used as an evidence to reject Bahá'u'lláh's claim.

In many places in the Kitáb-i-Badí', Bahá'u'lláh mentions a tablet of the Báb which affirms the authoritative and unconditional nature of the revelation of the Promised One. It was addressed to Mullá Báqir, the Letter of the Living, who had asked the Báb about the date and signs of the Promised One's appearance. In this tablet, the Báb strongly criticizes Mullá Báqir for allowing himself to ask such a question. He emphasizes that the station of the Promised One is far higher than any description, reference, or question, and He even writes that if Mullá Báqir were not one of the Letters of the Living, He would have ordained a punishment for him for his impertinence. The Báb explains that the essence of His words is that the Promised One cannot be described or conditioned by anything written by the Báb or by anything revealed in the Bayán. He warns Báqir not to be withheld from recognizing the Promised One by anything in the Bayán, or by any of the greatest scholars of the Bayán, or by any of the Mirrors of the Bayán. The Promised One, He specifies, should be gazed upon only through His own eyes and not through the eyes of anyone else.[22] Referring to this tablet in the Kitáb-i-Badí', Bahá'u'lláh tells us that the real reason the Báb criticized Mullá Báqir and spoke of punishing him was because the Báb wanted to convey to all that the proof of the Promised One would be His own being and that He would not be defined through anything other than Himself.[23]

Although Bahá'u'lláh effectively disproves Mírzá Mihdí's absurd argument by showing how it contradicts the Báb's explicit statements, He does not stop at that point. As Bahá'u'lláh says, Mírzá Mihdí does not understand the real meaning of the Qur'ánic term *conclusive* (*muḥkamát*). He explains that the meaning of a conclusive verse (*áyih*, which also means sign and miracle) is self-evident—it is understandable by itself and its demonstration requires no external evidence or testimony.[24] Then Bahá'u'lláh asks His reader to reflect deeply in order to discover what is truly a conclusive verse. The truly conclusive "Word," Bahá'u'lláh asserts, is nothing other than the *being* of the Manifestation Himself because it is the sign of God that stands in need of no external evidence or definition, while all others are dependent on Him and are defined through Him.[25] It is true that the laws and commandments revealed in the Holy Books are also conclusive, but they hold that status by virtue of coming from the will and command of the Manifestation. That is why Bahá'u'lláh is Himself the conclusive Word of God and all else must be understood through Him.[26] It is for the same reason that the Báb has frequently emphasized that if a Bábí were to observe all the laws of the Bayán and yet fail to recognize the Promised One for less than a moment, all his acts would be rendered null.[27]

But being able to distinguish between the equivocal and conclusive words of the Bayán is itself dependent on understanding the
Bayán, something which is the sole privilege of the Promised One.
However, the entire Bayán is the praise of the Promised One and an
affirmation of the unconditional nature of His revelation. It is the Báb
who always has insisted that no limitation or condition should be
placed on the revelation of the Promised One, and that the only valid
evidence is His own being and His revelation of verses.

Consequently, Mírzá Mihdí's claim concerning Yaḥyá's high titles
is the exact opposite of the Báb's message. It constitutes worship of the
names while turning away from the possessor and revealer of those
names Himself. Bahá'u'lláh's answer to the argument based on
Yaḥyá's names and titles will be examined in the course of discussing
Mírzá Mihdí's third objection. But it should be noted here that, as it
is often stressed in the Kitáb-i-Badí', the Báb has unequivocally stated
that all the exalted names and attributes mentioned in the Bayán are
descriptions of the Promised One and no one else. All the names of
Yaḥyá and of others, then, are really a description of Bahá'u'lláh, and
only in a secondary and subordinate way do they apply to Yaḥyá—
provided that he remains under the shadow of Bahá'u'lláh. In one passage, the Báb writes that any goodly name revealed in the Bayán primarily means Him Whom God shall make manifest, while any evil
name in the Bayán intends primarily the person who, on that Day,
will be a "letter of negation."[28]

Furthermore, according to Bahá'u'lláh, many of the titles addressed to Yaḥyá are not really intended for him. The Báb praised all
His followers with lofty names and titles, intending them as words of
encouragement.[29] In addition, the Báb intended that all beings should
reflect divine attributes and should turn in the direction of divine revelation. Accordingly, He called all His followers by the titles of God,
even addressing many of them, such as Dayyán, as God and the Promised One. His intention in doing so was to concentrate attention on
divine revelation and not on specific persons and their characteristics.[30] In other words, by addressing every one as God, the Báb intended to underscore the equality of all His believers and diminish any par-

ticular significance for any one of them, including Yaḥyá. All are equal
and all are to turn toward the Promised One. That message is also evident in the Báb's discussion of the seven stations (in the case of the Persian Bayán, five stations[31]) of the unity of God which embrace all
beings.[32] But the most crucial element is that all such titles and names
are conditioned upon turning toward the Sun of Truth. Should that
cease to be the case, all titles and names are removed from the person
and return to the Manifestation.

The Completion and Maturation of the Bayán

Mírzá Mihdíy-i-Rashtí's second objection against Bahá'u'lláh concerns the completion and perfection of the Cause of the Bayán.
According to the Báb, no new Manifestation ever appears before the
completion of the previous dispensation. Mírzá Mihdí argues that it is
impossible that the Bayán could attain completion in only nine years:
that is too soon. Although he does not elaborate, he has apparently
assumed that the completion of the Bayán should take some two thousand years, as implied by reference to the advent of the Promised One
in "Mustagháth" (the Time of Invocation, or He Who is invoked).

Once again Bahá'u'lláh delivers His response to this argument
with the voice of authority and majesty. He does not directly address
the question of Mustagháth since it has not been explicitly posed by
Mírzá Mihdí. His arguments, however, are sufficiently general to
resolve that problem as well. We must keep in mind Bahá'u'lláh's two
foundational answers to the question: first, the Báb has warned that no
statement in the Bayán should withhold anyone from recognizing the
Promised One; second, the meaning of the Bayán is only known to
the Promised One Himself, so none can employ any argument based
on the Bayán against Bahá'u'lláh. However, Bahá'u'lláh descends
from the foundational discourse and responds to Mírzá Mihdí's argument about the completion of the Bayán as follows.

(a) The question of completion is itself an argument for Bahá'u'lláh's
claim. In fact, nothing else is needed to confirm the truth of His authority. Bahá'u'lláh quotes various statements in the Bayán demonstrating
that the promised completion of the Bayán took place in the year nine:

Thou hast made mention of the termination of the [Báb's] Dispensation. Hearken unto the utterance of the Revealer of the Bayán, may the realities of all things be a sacrifice unto Him, who stateth explicitly, "Ere nine will have elapsed from the inception of this Cause, the realities of the created things will not be made manifest. All that thou hast as yet seen is but the stage from the moist germ until We clothed it with flesh. Be patient until thou beholdest a new creation. Say: Blessed, therefore, be God, the Most Excellent of Makers! I testify that the difference between the 'Qá'im' and the 'Qayyúm' is the number nine, which marketh the period when sanctified souls were consummated and established in their own stations. That is also the difference between 'A'ẓam' and "Aẓím."' And in another passage He saith, "Observe the difference between 'Qá'im' and 'Qayyúm,' then in the year nine ye shall attain unto all good." Concerning this He further saith: "This, verily, is the thing We promised thee, ere the moment We answered thy call. Wait thou until nine will have elapsed from the time of the Bayán. Then exclaim: 'Blessed, therefore, be God, the most excellent of Makers!'" O thou who claimest to have seeing eyes and to be an upholder of justice and fairness! Open thou thine eyes to behold how a new creation hath come into being since the year nine and say: "Blessed, therefore, be God, the Most Excellent of Creators." And again, "Hallowed be the Lord, the Most Excellent and the Most Wondrous of Creators." Observe how He hath referred to both the maturation of the people of the Bayán and the superiority of the next Revelation through His explicit and unambiguous reference to the difference between "Qá'im" and "Qayyúm" and "A'ẓam" and "'Aẓím." And when the period was consummated and the appointed time ordained by God completed, the Beauty of Nine was revealed with manifest dominion.[33]

This passage contains many important points. First, in the words quoted from the Báb, the Báb affirms—as He does in many other places—that the attainment of the presence of God and of "all good" (both signifying the next revelation in the Báb's terminology) will take place in the year nine. Second, He emphasizes that the completion of the Bayán and of the essences of all beings will be realized in nine years after the revelation of the Báb. Third, He attests to the superiority of the Promised One's revelation over His own by defining Himself as *Qá'im* (Upright) and *'Aẓím* (Great), while identifying the Promised

One as *Qayyúm* (Self-Subsistent) and *A'ẓam* (Most Great). Fourth, even the numerical difference between *A'ẓam* and *'Aẓím* (and also *Qayyúm* and *Qá'im*) is equal to nine. Fifth, the numerical value of the word *Bahá* is also nine.[34] Obviously, any objection against Bahá'u'lláh based on the question of completion demonstrates a complete misunderstanding of the Bayán.

(b) Bahá'u'lláh argues that the completion of the Bayán is solely dependent on the will of God. It is completed the moment God decrees it to be completed. The completion of all things, Bahá'u'lláh states, is dependent on the assertion and approval of the Point of Truth.[35] Furthermore, He asks the reader to reflect on the meaning of the completion of the Bayán. What is it that should become completed? Is it the revealed words of the Bayán? But they are already complete and perfect. Is it the completion of the believers themselves? But the longer the period of the dispensation, the less complete is the faith of the believers. Is it the observance of laws and rituals? But ritualistic acts have normally veiled people from recognizing the Manifestation of God. In short, completion is related to the essence of beings and that is simply contingent on the divine will.[36]

(c) Bahá'u'lláh refers to various statements of the Báb according to which the Promised One possesses unconditional authority to elevate all beings to the station of the Prophet, which is the highest stage of human completion and perfection, by the mere utterance of His unconditional command. For example, He quotes the Báb's statement that were He to make everyone on earth a Prophet, all would be accounted as Prophets in the sight of God.[37]

(d) Furthermore, Bahá'u'lláh gives a philosophical and mystical analysis of the idea of completion. Completion is simply and solely dependent on the will of God because creation is a continuous process. God does not create a being which then continues to exist on its own. On the contrary, everything is at every moment coming into existence and ceasing to exist. Bahá'u'lláh describes this as the continuous reflection of the different names of God, including the names of Life-Giver and Life-Taker. If nothing in the realm of creation is characterized by continuous existence, and everything is always created anew, then perfection or completion is only a matter of the divine act of creation. It is the will of God to bring into existence any being at any moment in any form He desires. Completion is indeed exclusively a matter of the utterance and command of the Manifestation of God.[38]

(e) Another argument Bahá'u'lláh offers is the Báb's testimony that in His (the Báb's) revelation the period of fifty thousand years—the duration of the Day of Judgment—has been consummated in one hour. Bahá'u'lláh affirms that this is true because it was the will of God to complete fifty thousand years in one hour. The same principle applies to the period of completion of the Bayán and the supposed two thousand years of "Mustagháth."[39] In this regard, the only point emphasized by the Bayán is that the Promised One can appear at any time, and that the date of His revelation is not bound by anything except His own will. For instance, Bahá'u'lláh refers to the Báb's statement that none knows the time of the revelation except God; whenever it appears, all must acknowledge the Point of Truth and render thanks unto God.[40]

(f) An important argument Bahá'u'lláh presents is related to the short time in which the Cause of John the Baptist was completed. Bahá'u'lláh reminds His reader that John is described by the Qur'án as an independent Prophet who was preparing the people for the advent of Jesus. John brought new laws and practices, including fasting and baptism, but his Cause was completed in an extremely short time. Furthermore, Bahá'u'lláh points out the striking similarity between the statements of John the Baptist and the Báb, both of whom were heralds of an imminent Manifestation. John said: "Repent ye: for the kingdom of heaven is at hand."[41] And the Báb, referring to the advent of the Promised One, said: "Verily the rising of the Sun to its zenith is at hand, and ye are still sleeping!"[42]

Related to the argument of completion is the further objection of Mírzá Mihdí that although the signs of the beginning of the Qá'im's ministry have been fulfilled (even if the people did not recognize them), the signs concerning its later period remain unfulfilled; therefore, he argues, the age of the Qá'im's Cause is not yet completed. Bahá'u'lláh again demonstrates His majesty through His response, showing that what is assumed to be an objection to His own revelation is actually a proof of its truth. Just as the signs of the beginning of the Qá'im's appearance were fulfilled but people did not recognize them, the other signs have also been fulfilled even though Mírzá Mihdí and others like him have not understood them. Both those signs are equivocal and both need to be interpreted by the Promised One, who alone is capable of understanding their real meanings. Additionally Bahá'u'lláh makes a most interesting point. He reminds His reader that actually the most important sign, frequently mentioned in the holy traditions, regarding the later times of the Qá'im's revelation is none other than the return of Imám Ḥusayn! This was indeed fulfilled through Bahá'u'lláh's own being; His own name is Ḥusayn and He is the return of the Imám as well.[43]

The meaning of Mustagháth is explained in various writings of Bahá'u'lláh, one of which discusses the Báb's Tablet of Nineteen Temples. In this tablet, the Báb had created nineteen "Temples," each consisting of eleven lines symbolizing the word *Huva* (He), a reference to God. Different lines are different manifestations and elaborations of the twenty-eight letters of the Arabic alphabet, their points, and the numbers one through nine. The Báb derives from each line a particular name of God. Each Temple concludes with the name of God derived from the eleventh line. The nineteen Temples are organized in a hierarchical manner, with the names of God in each Temple numerically higher than the names in the preceding ones. The name that appears at the end of the nineteenth Temple, which is the supreme name of God in the realm of numbers, is Huva'l-Mustaghíth. This name, the Báb says, represents the word *Mustagháth* (from which it is derived).[44] Bahá'u'lláh explains that the Primal Point created this structure in order to tell the people of the Bayán that the time of Mustagháth is realized through nineteen years.[45]

Yaḥyá's Names and His Fall

The other major objection of Mírzá Mihdíy-i-Rashtí concerns the attribution of lofty titles to Yaḥyá Azal, particularly the titles of "Mirror" and "Fruit." Additionally, Mírzá Mihdí claims the station of vicegerency for Yaḥyá and argues that Bahá'u'lláh's pronouncement of Yaḥyá's fall implies that truth has turned into falsehood, which is impossible. Responding to these objections. Bahá'u'lláh emphasizes that, according to the Bayán, there is no institution of vicegerency in the dispensation of the Báb.[46] Bahá'u'lláh is probably referring here to the well-known passage in the Persian Bayán establishing that, in this dispensation, there would be no category of vicegerent or lesser prophet.[47] In addition, both the structure and content of the Persian Bayán attest to the exclusive authority of the Primal Point during His dispensation. The Báb has made it most explicit that between the time of His own martyrdom and the appearance of Him Whom God shall make manifest, the words of no other person are binding.[48] Bahá'u'lláh does not explicate these issues because Mírzá Mihdí's letter makes only a passing reference to the question of vicegerency.

Bahá'u'lláh does discuss in detail the issue of Yaḥyá's titles and shows that Yaḥyá's most important title, that of "Mirror," demonstrates the truth of Bahá'u'lláh's claim. To understand this, we should keep in mind the meaning of "mirror." According to the Báb, the Manifestation of God is like the Sun: "His verses are like its rays, and all believers, should they truly believe in Him, are as mirrors wherein the sun is reflected. Their light is thus a mere reflection."[49] The mirror has no light in and of itself, but if it turns toward the Sun of Truth, then a reflection of the names and attributes of the Manifestation appears in the mirror. The mirror is now praised by those same names and attributes. However, this remains valid only as long as the mirror is turned toward the Sun. The moment it turns away, it is divested of all those names and attributes. In the Báb's terminology, the Tree of Light (Paradise) turns into the Tree of Fire (Hell).

The statements of the Báb quoted by Bahá'u'lláh in the Kitáb-i-Badí' make it clear that the Mirrors only have significance as long as they turn toward the Manifestation; that many Mirrors would oppose the Promised One; that regardless of previous titles, all are equal at the time of the next revelation, and the will of the Promised One determines who is high and who is low; that Yaḥyá is not the only "Fruit" of the Tree of the Bayán; that all the others are also validly so regarded as long as they remain part of the Tree of Truth; that some "Fruits" would not recognize the Promised One and would be cut off from the Tree; that no title or name, even the name of "Prophet," should be used as an evidence against the Promised One; and that the real purpose of being a "Mirror" or "Fruit" is simply to recognize the Promised One, otherwise those titles become null and void.

> "O Sun-like Mirrors! Look ye upon the Sun of Truth. Ye, verily, depend upon it, were ye to perceive it. Ye are all as fishes, moving in the waters of the sea, veiling yourselves therefrom, and yet asking what it is on which ye depend."[50]

> "I complain unto thee, O Mirror of My generosity, against all the other Mirrors. All look upon Me through their own colors."[51]

> He—glorified be His mention—resembleth the sun. Were unnumbered mirrors to be placed before it, each would, according to its capacity, reflect the splendour of that sun, and were none to be placed before it, it would still continue to rise and set, and the mirrors alone would be veiled from its light. I, verily, have not fallen short of My duty to admonish that people, and to devise means whereby they may turn towards God, their Lord, and believe in God, their Creator.[52]

> Consecrate Thou, O my God, the whole of this Tree unto Him, that from it may be revealed all the fruits created by God within it for Him through Whom God hath willed to reveal all that He pleaseth. By Thy glory! I have not wished that this Tree should ever bear any branch, leaf, or fruit that would fail to bow down before Him, on the day of His Revelation, or refuse to laud Thee through Him, as beseemeth the glory of His all-glorious Revelation, and the sublimity of His most sublime Concealment. And shouldst Thou behold, O my God, any branch, leaf, or fruit upon Me that hath failed to bow down before Him, on the day of His Revelation, cut it off, O My God, from that Tree, for it is not of Me, nor shall it return unto Me.[53]

The affirmation of Bahá'u'lláh's foundational argument can be detected in all these statements of the Báb. Although the quotations Bahá'u'lláh adduces effectively shatter Mírzá Mihdí's argument that light can never turn into fire (i.e., that Yaḥyá Azal could become evil), Bahá'u'lláh offers additional forceful arguments. He asserts that it has always been a divine rule that light can become turned into fire. He gives the examples of Satan, who was preeminent among the angels but became evil when he turned away from the will of God; Judas Iscariot, who was one of the twelve apostles of Jesus but turned against Him and became divested of his station; and Ismá'íl, the eldest son of the Sixth Imám of Shí'ih Islam.[54]

The case of Ismá'íl is particularly interesting. Ismá'íl was appointed by the Sixth Imám as his successor and vicegerent. But when his actions went against the will of God, his position was taken away from him and was transferred, by the authority of the Imám, to the younger son, Músá, who then became the Seventh Imám. In this case, we see one who is appointed vicegerent and then divested of that title by the same Imám. In Yaḥyá's case, there was no vicegerency to begin with. But even if there were, he could have been divested of it even before the next Manifestation appeared. Of course, with the new revelation, all are divested of any title whatsoever, unless approved by the Promised One Himself. Bahá'u'lláh stresses the same point in frequent references to the Báb's tablet written to Mullá Báqir, in which the Báb says that if He knew that Báqir would not recognize the Promised One, He would negate the attribution of faith to him.[55]

Based on the metaphysical principles discussed in Chapter 2, the Báb and Bahá'u'lláh affirm that the divine names are exclusively the true attributes of the Manifestation of God. Through the revelation of His Cause, those names appear in the "mirror" of the believers who turn toward the Sun of Truth. In metaphysical terms, the mirror is the essence (the receptive aspect, pointing in the direction of the self), and the name is the existence (the active aspect, pointing in the direction of the Primal Will). The attribution of names and titles to the mirror is not due to the essence of the mirror, but rather due to its turning toward the Sun. If the mirror turns away from the Sun, it becomes as a darkened stone and all the names are withdrawn from it. The names return to their true possessor, the Manifestation of God, and the veiled mirror returns to its original darkness, its own essence. That is why Bahá'u'lláh remarks that such persons are true as long as they are under the shadow of God because at that moment no one save God is visible in them, and after they turn away, divine sovereignty remains within its own sovereign realm, while the created being returns to the realm of its own like and form.[56]

This also means that, once again, the real object of all the names and titles mentioned in the Bayán is solely the Promised One, and any title attributed to anyone in the Bábí dispensation must be considered a description of Bahá'u'lláh. All those titles apply only in a secondary and conditional way to other persons. This means that even Yaḥyá's loftiest titles are actually praise of Bahá'u'lláh. The titles only apply to Yaḥyá as long as he is blessed by remaining under the shadow of Bahá'u'lláh. Bahá'u'lláh points out that the Báb has sent tablets to various people which begin with an inscription from God to Him Whom God shall make Manifest—yet those tablets are obviously addressed to someone else. For this reason, Bahá'u'lláh explains, the Báb has said that whatsoever of good names has been revealed in the Bayán first refers to the next Manifestation, and only then does it apply to others, and then solely because of their relation to that Tree of Truth.[57]

In different parts of the Kitáb-i-Badí', as in many of His other writings as well, Bahá'u'lláh unravels a most significant mystery with regard to the title of "Mirror." As we have seen, a mirror has no light of its own. Its titles refer simply to the Sun that it reflects. However, in His tablets, including a tablet addressed to Yaḥyá Azal, the Báb makes this statement: "Verily, I am He that liveth in the Abhá realm of Glory!"[58] In other words, the Báb, Who is the Sun of Truth, will appear in the realm of Abhá (that is, Bahá) after His physical departure from the world. The Báb is telling Yaḥyá and the other Mirrors that Bahá'u'lláh is the Báb's own return, and after the Báb's martyrdom, all the Mirrors must turn toward Bahá'u'lláh.

The significance of this cannot be overestimated. It demonstrates clearly that Yaḥyá's title of Mirror signifies nothing but the truth of Bahá'u'lláh and Yaḥyá's duty to recognize Him. That is why Bahá'-u'lláh writes in the Kitáb-i-Badí': "If the people of the Bayán had the necessary insight, the blessed verse of the Báb 'Verily, I am He that liveth in the Abhá Realm of Glory!' would have been sufficient unto them and unto all that dwell in heaven and on earth."[59]

The Problem of Return

Mírzá Mihdí also objects to Bahá'u'lláh's claim to be the return of the Primal Point. He charges that this claim is a contradiction: it is either a claim to be the return of the essence, which is impossible because there cannot be repetition of revelation ("effulgence"), or it is a claim to be the return of the attributes. If the latter, then Bahá'u'lláh must uphold the laws ordained in the Bayán. But if Bahá'u'lláh is subordinate to the Báb, then He must be under the leadership of Yaḥyá.

Bahá'u'lláh's response discloses the depth of His ocean of knowledge and the shallowness of His opponent's understanding. He explains that Mírzá Mihdí has failed to comprehend either the concept of return or the station of the new revelation. He begins His response by declaring that His station is not one of revelation but the Revealer of revelation.[60] Then He points out that the alleged contradiction would also apply to the Báb, because it is He who has always called Himself the return of the Point of the Qur'án. If Mihdí's argument were correct, then the Báb should not have abrogated the Qur'án because He could be only the return of the attributes of Muḥammad. Similarly, it is the Báb who has called the Promised One the same as the Point of the Bayán. Furthermore, the Báb and all the other Prophets have affirmed the unity of all the Manifestations of God; They are all the return of one another. Bahá'u'lláh tells Mírzá Mihdí that he has not understood anything explained in the Bayán, and that he should read the Kitáb-i-Íqán to understand the meaning of return, the unity of divine revelation, and the different stations of the Manifestations of God. He goes on to say that all the Manifestations are one and the same in terms of the direction of divine revelation. The differences between Them are due to the variations in the capacities and the conditions of the age.[61]

Bahá'u'lláh also refers to the fact that the Báb has described the station of the Promised One as far superior to the Báb's own station. Needless to say, anyone who has read the Bayán is familiar with the exalted station of the Promised One. He is the One Who cannot be defined by the Letters of the Living or the Báb Himself, Who has the absolute authority to reject or accept the entire Bayán as He wishes, and Whom the Báb proudly announces to be His first believer. Mírzá Mihdí's objection is nothing less than an utter rejection of the essence of the Bayán.

While Bahá'u'lláh affirms His own authority to abrogate the Bayán, He emphasizes that He has not yet done so. On the contrary, He upholds the validity of the Bayán and its laws.[62] However, while Bahá'u'lláh does not abrogate the Bayán in general, He always affirms the basic purpose of His revelation, which is the establishment of unity and love among human beings. He also affirms His fundamental principle that His Cause must be rendered victorious through the pen rather than the sword.[63] However, Bahá'u'lláh makes it clear that the station of the Manifestation cannot be measured by whether He abrogates laws of the previous dispensation or not. In fact He reiterates His foundational principle: the hand of God is not chained up and His will is not subject to the limited understandings or rules of any human being.[64]

The Meaning of "Bahá"

Mírzá Mihdí's fifth objection is related to the title of "Bahá." The reference to "Bahá" in the Bayán, he argues, is a general one, like other divine Names, and does not specifically imply the Promised One. In any case, others including Dayyán, Mírzá Ghawghá, Shaykh Ismá'íl, and Hájí Mullá Háshim have also claimed to be Him Whom God shall make manifest.

Bahá'u'lláh's response again breaks down Mihdí's argument like the waves of the ocean erasing a hill of sand. First He argues that the objection is meaningless because Bahá'u'lláh never made the Báb's reference to "Bahá" in His writings the evidence of His authority. Rather, the opposite is the case. Bahá'u'lláh repeats His foundational argument, emphasizing that His verses are His evidence. Then He tells Mírzá Mihdí that the same arguments which prove the Báb's exalted self-descriptions also demonstrate that He, as "Bahá," is the Promised One of the Bayán. Bahá'u'lláh states that it is the names of God that become exalted because of their relation to Bahá'u'lláh, not the other way around. As the Báb has said, all the names of God mentioned in the Bayán refer first to the Promised One, and even Yaḥyá's names are praise of Bahá'u'lláh.[65] However, Bahá'u'lláh "descends" from His foundational discourse to argue that in reality the word *Bahá* in the Bayán is always a reference to Himself as the Promised One. To demonstrate this, He analyzes a few of those references and quotes the following statement from the Arabic Bayán:

> With a like intent did We send down the Qur'án aforetime; yet were ye veiled from apprehending My purpose. He it is around Whom the nights and days have revolved for eight full Váḥids [152], and ye the while, through Him, have been engaged in worship of the one true God, yet remained in ignorance of His career after that which was decreed. Such is the balance of true guidance in the Bayán; take heed, therefore, that ye believe therein. Thus, until the Sun of Bahá shall have dawned: He it is Whom God shall make manifest. If ye conform your actions unto His bidding, then are ye believers, and shall abide eternally in heaven; otherwise shall ye perish.[66]

This is a complex statement with many hidden meanings beyond our comprehension. Prior to these verses, the Báb has said that any goodly name in the Bayán and all the other Holy Books refers to the Promised One of the Bayán, and that the Manifestation of God is the embodiment of the divine names. Therefore, in the above statement the Báb is saying that all the divine names mentioned in the Qur'án and the Bayán refer to the Manifestation of God, who is presently in the form of the Primal Point and who will return as Bahá in the form of the Promised One. It seems that, here, by "He around Whom the nights and days have revolved for eight full Váḥids [152]" is meant the Báb Himself. It is interesting to note that by "152" the Báb means His disciple Quddús, because 152 mirrors are under the shadow of Quddús, and because it was Quddús alone who succeeded in making true pilgrimage around the true Throne of God (that is, the Báb Himself) when he accompanied the Báb to Mecca.[67]

Bahá'u'lláh then cites two other passages from the same chapter in the Arabic Bayán. The first states that the time between the rising and setting of the Sun of Bahá is better in the Book of God than the entire night, that God has created everything for the sake of that Day, and that the purpose of everyone's actions is to attain the presence of God and His pleasure.[68] Bahá'u'lláh explains that one of the meanings of this statement is that during the "night" of the Bayán (the time between the martyrdom of the Báb and the revelation of the Promised One),[69] no one should consider any leader as equal to the Manifestation of God. A few lines later the Báb writes: "Verily, the rising of the Sun to its zenith is at hand yet do ye not recognize that Day. Do not desire for Him Whose presence is none other than Mine Own presence that which ye would not wish for yourselves."[70]

Bahá'u'lláh explains that those statements not only indicate that the name of the Promised One is Bahá but also emphasize both the proximity of His appearance and His sufferings at the hands of the Bábí community. Bahá'u'lláh also explicates a most significant issue: that the references to the next Manifestation in all the previous dispensations have been primarily equivocal and hidden—unlike the references in the Bayán, which explicitly and conclusively identify the revelation of the Promised One. This by itself is a confirmation of His imminent appearance.

Likewise, Bahá'u'lláh cites from the Qayyúmu'l-Asmá' the following:

> Indeed God hath created everywhere around this Gate oceans of divine elixir, tinged crimson with the essence of existence and vitalized through the animating power of the desired fruit; and for them God hath provided Arks of ruby, tender, crimson-colored, wherein none shall sail but the people of Bahá, by the leave of God, the Most Exalted; and verily He is the All-Glorious, the All-Wise. In that Day, eight angels of the world of 'Amá' [invisible Realm] will carry the Throne of God.[71]

Bahá'u'lláh explains the last part of the Báb's mysterious statement. He says that, in the first place, the "Throne of God" is the Cause of God and His revelation; the fact that only eight of the supreme angels will carry the throne is a testimony to the fact that the Word of God is not accepted at first by most people. It is the Trust of God that not all are capable of bearing. At the same time, the Throne of God, Bahá'u'lláh says, refers to the Manifestation Himself, and the eight angels are indicators of His name. Bahá'u'lláh has said that the name *Bahá* is numerically equal to both eight and nine. The reason is that the Arabic word *Bahá'* actually consists of four elements: the letters *b*, *h*, *a*, and the sign *hamzih* (which is pronounced as *a*). Because *hamzih* is not actually a letter, it is sometimes counted as an *a*, and sometimes disregarded. Thus, *Bahá* can be read as either eight or nine. The eight angels of 'Amá', then, refer to the name of Bahá, which refers to the Manifestation. Finally, by the "Throne of God" sometimes is meant the first believer who becomes the first recipient of divine blessings.

Concerning the other part of Mírzá Mihdíy-i-Rashtí's objection that others have also put forward claims, Bahá'u'lláh argues that the four people named really did not make any claim but expressed such sentiments either in moments of mystic ecstasy or in their longing for the appearance of the Promised One. Bahá'u'lláh defends the dignity and sincerity of these people and adds that even if someone were to make a false claim, no one has the right to treat them unkindly. He quotes the Báb, Who often said that no one should object to anyone who might put forth a claim, and He criticizes Yaḥyá, who had called for the murder of these souls. (Dayyán, who repented and recognized Bahá'u'lláh, was martyred on Yaḥyá's orders.) Bahá'u'lláh particularly praises Dayyán and his high spiritual station. According to Bahá'u'lláh, however, the real evidence of a Manifestation of God is the revelation of verses. With respect to that criterion, He remains peerless.

Before discussing the other objection of Mírzá Mihdíy-i-Rashtí, an important historical point should be noted. Mírzá Mihdí's own argument about those who put forward claims actually supports Bahá'-u'lláh's argument about His own claim. The mere fact that in the early Baghdad period many prominent the Bábís claimed to be the Promised One testifies that the leaders of the Bábí community were awaiting the imminent appearance of the Promised One in the year nine. The picture portrayed by Mírzá Mihdí, and later by others, of a Bábí community that did not expect the appearance of the Promised One for some two thousand years, is decisively refuted by this simple historical fact. Various people put forward claims because they were expecting the new revelation at any moment and yet no public declaration had yet been made. Their claims themselves confirm the general expectation that such an event was imminent.

The Evidence of Verses

Mírzá Mihdíy-i-Rashtí had also argued that revealing verses is not a sufficient proof of the authenticity of a claim. At one point he proposes to test Bahá'u'lláh by quickly reading a randomly chosen page of the Qur'án to Him and asking Him to write immediately multiple commentaries about that page. He also alleges that Bahá'u'lláh has been a Sufi mystic and therefore His writings are not the product of revelation. Furthermore, he argues against Bahá'u'lláh by stating that only the uneducated believe in Him.

Bahá'u'lláh's response to this particular objection is actually dispersed throughout the book in the form of His foundational discourse affirming that the revelation of verses is the sole standard of divine truth. Bahá'u'lláh notes the deliberate attempt of the Bábí leaders to reject the entire Bayán by refusing to accept the authority of verses as proof. Bahá'u'lláh argues that divine justice requires that the divine standard must be accessible to all humans, and that the authority of divine verses must be universal. He refers to frequent assertions in the Qur'án and the Bayán that no one save God can reveal verses, that the revelation of verses is the only evidence of the Manifestations, and that it constitutes the proof of the Promised One. Mírzá Mihdí's assertion that anyone can produce verses is tantamount to a rejection of all the Holy Scriptures and Manifestations of God.

Bahá'u'lláh also discusses the inadequacy of miracles as the evidence of divine revelation. Since He had covered this issue in the Kitáb-i-Íqán, He does not discuss it in detail. He refers to the Qur'ánic verses indicating that miracles would not be a sufficient or persuasive evidence. But at the same time, Bahá'u'lláh accepts Mírzá Mihdí's challenge and invites him to come before Him so that He may fulfill his request for proof.[72] Bahá'u'lláh observes that His companions have witnessed extraordinary events in His presence but that He dislikes to engage in miracle talk.[73] The mere fact that a person would ask for miracles is an indication of spiritual ignorance.

Bahá'u'lláh denies He has been a member of mystical societies or the 'ulamá, stating that "He is not accounted, as thou art aware, among the learned or the ascetics, not regarded as one of the mystics or wearers of the turban."[74] He says that He has not studied the divers branches of knowledge and that He could not have learned anything from mystics because in His presence no one has dared to speak. He declares that He has continually been unveiling oceans of spiritual truth, that He has always been subject to hardships and has had no time for study, and that this same objection was raised against the Báb and the other Prophets.[75]

Finally, with regard to the low level of education of most of His believers, Bahá'u'lláh says that this has always been the divine norm, that it demonstrates His Cause rather than refuting it, and that, as the Báb has frequently emphasized, true knowledge is nothing but the recognition of the Manifestation of God—whosoever attains that has attained the essence of knowledge and whosoever has been deprived of that is accounted as ignorant.[76] Bahá'u'lláh also quotes various passages in which the Báb warns His followers not to be withheld from recognizing the Promised One by the scholars of the Bayán and admonishes the Mirrors against arrogance and pride in their titles or their knowledge. Finally, Bahá'u'lláh notes that Mírzá Mihdí's letter exemplifies poor literary style, lack of courtesy, and inability to make logical arguments. In fact, it testifies to Mírzá Mihdí's inability to write a few paragraphs correctly in Persian, and yet such a person dares to object to the low degree of education of Bahá'u'lláh's followers! In short, Bahá'u'lláh affirms His methodological principle: the standard of divine truth is not arbitrary human tests; rather, it is the evidence ordained by God Himself, and that is none other than the revelation of verses.

Before discussing Mírzá Mihdí's final objection, it should be noted that the rejection, by Yaḥyá Azal and his followers, of verses as sufficient proof is in itself sufficient demonstration of their own violation of the most explicit principles of the Bayán. The reason is obvious to anyone who reads the Bayán with fairness: the Báb always conclusively stipulates that verses are the proof of the Promised One, just as they were His own proof. In fact, the Báb had required all Bábís to read a particular chapter of the Persian Bayán (Váḥid 6, chapter 8) at least once every month so that they would not forget the will of God in this regard. And indeed, the basic point of that chapter is that the sole evidence of the Promised One of the Bayán is the revelation of verses. He also emphasizes that no one should object to anyone who makes such claim even if that person does not offer any evidence. The Báb had asked His followers not to object to anyone's claim because He knew that the Promised One was alive and would imminently declare His Cause. Yaḥyá Azal's objection against Baháʾuʾlláh and against the adequacy of verses as proof is exactly the same as the objection the enemies of the Báb had raised against Him. The Báb says that the truth of Muḥammad, the Apostle of God, was proven by verses, and that

> in this Revelation the Lord of the universe hath deigned to bestow His mighty utterances and resplendent signs upon the Point of the Bayán, and hath ordained them as His matchless testimony for all created things. Were all the people that dwell on earth to assemble together, they would be unable to produce a single verse like unto the ones which God hath caused to stream forth from the tongue of the Point of the Bayán.[77]

The Báb goes on to refute the objection to verses as evidence:

> If ye contend that these verses cannot, of themselves, be regarded as a proof, scan the pages of the Qurʾán. If God hath established therein any evidence other than the revealed verses to demonstrate the validity of the prophethood of His Apostle—may the blessings of God rest upon Him—ye may then have your scruples about Him....
> Concerning the sufficiency of the Book as a proof, God hath revealed: "Is it not enough for them that We have sent down unto Thee the Book to be recited to them? In this verily is a mercy and a warning to those who believe."[78] When God hath testified that the Book is a sufficient testimony, as is affirmed in the text, how can one dispute this truth by saying that the Book in itself is not a conclusive proof?[79]

And in an astonishing passage in the Persian Bayán, the Báb describes the objections which would be raised by His own followers against the

Promised One in the day of His revelation and discloses the answer
that the Promised One will make to those objections:

> Methinks I visualize those who would, prompted by their own
> deluded conceptions, write to Him and ask Him questions about
> that which hath been revealed in the Bayán, and He would answer
> them with words not of His Own, but divinely inspired, saying:
> "Verily, verily, I am God; no God is there but Me. I have called into
> being all the created things, I have raised up divine Messengers in the
> past and have sent down Books unto Them. Take heed not to
> worship anyone but God, He Who is My Lord and your Lord. This
> indeed is the undoubted truth. However, alike shall it be to Me; if
> ye believe in Me, ye will provide good for your own souls, and if ye
> believe not in Me, nor in that which God hath revealed unto Me,
> ye will suffer yourselves to be shut out as by a veil. For verily I have
> been independent of you heretofore, and shall remain independent
> hereafter. Therefore it behooveth you, O creatures of God, to help
> your own selves and to believe in the Verses revealed by Me...."[80]

The answer Bahá'u'lláh gives in the Kitáb-i-Badí' to the supporters of
Yaḥyá Azal is identical to the answer that the Báb had prophesied
would be offered by the Promised One.

Worldly Desires

Mírzá Mihdí's last objection takes the form of personal accusations and
lies as he tries simultaneously to defend Yaḥyá's character and to attack
Bahá'u'lláh's. In his defense of Yaḥyá and Siyyid Muḥammad, Mírzá
Mihdí argues that Yaḥyá's fears, hiding, disguises, and dissimulations
are explained by his detachment from the world. Besides, he contends,
all the Prophets—he gives the examples of Jesus and Muḥammad—
have been fearful of their enemies and have hidden themselves from
the people. Similarly, he maintains, Siyyid Muḥammad's trip to Istanbul was not for the sake of greed and in search of monthly stipends but
to request amnesty for himself and for Yaḥyá from the Iranian government. At the same time, he accuses Bahá'u'lláh of being driven by
desire for power and comfort.

In answering these personal accusations, Bahá'u'lláh often refers to
the extreme sorrow of the Primal Point upon observing such distor-

tions and lies uttered by those who associate themselves with Him. Bahá'u'lláh points out that it has always been the practice of the covenant-breakers to accuse the Manifestation and His followers of the very crimes which the covenant-breakers have themselves committed. Bahá'u'lláh is reluctant to engage in such a discussion, but since Mírzá Mihdí and others constantly tell such lies, He is forced to respond. From what Bahá'u'lláh says, we get a clear picture of Yaḥyá as a cowardly yet power-hungry man, obsessed with material and physical desires, in sharp contrast to the courage of the Manifestation of God, Who, although personally inclined to silence, arises to reveal the words of God openly and before the people at the bidding of the divine will, and who welcomes suffering and hardship in the path of God.

Bahá'u'lláh does not allow Mírzá Mihdí to dignify Yaḥyá's cowardly actions by likening them to the actions of the Prophets. Bahá'-u'lláh declares that all the Prophets were characterized by courage, steadfastness against injustice, advocating the Cause of God before the people, and welcoming suffering in the path of God. Mírzá Mihdí's lies against all the Prophets are another expression of the way that the breakers of the divine covenant project their own inclinations and their own character onto the representatives of God, just as they define God in terms of their own fancies and arbitrary constructions. Bahá'-u'lláh affirms that Jesus did teach His Cause publicly and that is why He was martyred, and that Muḥammad constantly endured hardship and cruelty because He openly advocated the Word of God. In addition, Bahá'u'lláh refers to Imám Ḥusayn, who was martyred heroically because he refused to hide from his enemies and rose against their oppression.

Bahá'u'lláh argues that Imám Ḥusayn's martyrdom should not be distorted by the false notion that he did not wish martyrdom and that he did not know that he would be martyred when he undertook his final campaign and moved his army toward Iraq. As Bahá'u'lláh explains, Imám Ḥusayn knew of his coming martyrdom and that is why, on his final visit to the shrine of Muḥammad before his departure, he expressed his desire to be martyred on that journey. Bahá'-

u'lláh refers to Imám Ḥusayn's courageous statement in which he expresses his trust of and desire for God's will, says he knows that his enemy intends his blood, vows never to acknowledge the claim of the Umayyad ruler Yazíd, begs God to hasten the day of his martyrdom, and implores that he might fall upon the dust in thirst.[81]

After quoting Imám Ḥusayn's powerful words, Bahá'u'lláh says that at this moment as well, this Ḥusayn is saying exactly the same thing. Bahá'u'lláh goes on to speak of the courage and sufferings of the Báb and describes the touching story that, on the way to Mákú, when the Báb's followers wanted to free Him, He smiled and said, "The mountains of Ádhirbáyján too have their claims!"[82]

In discussing Yaḥyá's character, Bahá'u'lláh refers to many of Yaḥyá's cruelties and material attachments. He condemns Yaḥyá's brutality and his order to murder innocent people including Dayyán. He also refers to Yaḥyá's "detachment" by mentioning Yaḥyá's letter to his seven "witnesses" in which Yaḥyá orders each of them to send him money and a young virgin.[83] But Bahá'u'lláh is particularly angry at Yaḥyá for violating Fáṭimih, the second wife of the Báb, marrying her temporarily and then sending her to others. Yaḥyá had committed this desecration during Bahá'u'lláh's two-year absence from Baghdad. Bahá'u'lláh explains that, in fact, this is the main cause of His disapproval of Yaḥyá, whose obsessions and base desires did not even respect the sanctity of the holy family of the Báb.[84]

Similarly Bahá'u'lláh expresses His sadness that for the sake of bread and control of monthly stipends, Yaḥyá has sent his wife to the government officials and Siyyid Muḥammad to Istanbul in order to accuse Bahá'u'lláh of denying him material support. Bahá'u'lláh not only condemns their lies and their attachment to material desires, He also expresses regret that their actions have shamed the Bábí and Bahá'í community in the eyes of the Muslim populace and the government officials. As Bahá'u'lláh notes, Siyyid Muḥammad's trip to Istanbul was to seek stipends and spread lies, not to ask for amnesty. Bahá'u'lláh remarks that, first of all, Yaḥyá was never exiled by the Iranian government. It was Bahá'u'lláh who was banished. Yaḥyá followed Bahá'u'lláh from Iran into exile because of his own fear. Therefore any request for amnesty is senseless, particularly given the fact that Yaḥyá has always hidden and lived under false names so no one really knew him. Bahá'u'lláh also comments that if amnesty was the intent, why then did Siyyid Muḥammad submit the petition for a stipend to the government? He notes that, in fact, government officials opened an investigation following Siyyid Muḥammad's petition and accusations in Istanbul and sent Bahá'u'lláh a copy of the petition and the complaints.[85]

Just as Yaḥyá is characterized by cowardice and lust for power, Bahá'u'lláh's life and writings demonstrate the exact opposite. His extraordinary courage is attested by His rise to defend the Cause of God during the time of the Báb and by standing against all its enemies during the Baghdad period; by His actions to educate and reform the Bábí community; by His refusal to contact government officials or to meet with them in Baghdad, Istanbul, and Edirne; by His majestic tablets and addresses to the kings and rulers; and by His willingness to accept suffering in the path of God. In the Kitáb-i-Badí', Bahá'u'lláh testifies to His hardships in Mázandarán, the Síyáh Chál, Baghdad, and in later times. He mentions that many were the days His family had no food except at night and even that was only by borrowing money. He also mentions that there were many times in Baghdad when He had no change of linen and His only shirt had to be washed, dried, and worn. He refers to the dream He had shortly before leaving Baghdad that portended future sufferings and hardships. Bahá'u'lláh testifies to His rise, in the early Baghdad period, to regenerate the Bábí Faith and prevent the Bábís from committing murder, theft, and other crimes.

The Kitáb-i-Badí', like many other tablets of Bahá'u'lláh, illustrates clearly the paradoxical self-consciousness of Bahá'u'lláh which was discussed in Chapter 4. On the one hand, He personally did not wish fame, attention, or power. If it had been solely up to Him as a human being, He would never have declared His mission. However, the will of God has always moved Him and made Him reveal the words of God, proclaim the divine Cause, and openly declare His mission. That is why Bahá'u'lláh often mentions in the Kitáb-i-Badí' the same idea expressed in the tablet to the shah of Iran—that He did not personally set out to reveal the word of God, but the will of God moved Him and bade Him speak, and that this is not from Him but from God. It was for the sake of His love of God and humanity that He accepted all the hardships and sufferings in the path of God. All these sufferings become more poignant when we pay attention to the Báb's statements, confirmed by Bahá'u'lláh, that all creation has been brought into being for the sake of the glorification of the Manifestation of God and His love.

Bahá'u'lláh acknowledges that, during the early Baghdad period, He visited a coffeehouse on the riverbank and that He sometimes drinks tea. He also says that He sometimes honors His followers by accepting their invitations and visiting their homes. However, He explains that His presence at the coffeehouse was because in the early Baghdad period they were refugees without any support or friends in the city. So, for the sake of proclaiming the Faith to the people of the city and attracting support for the Bábís in exile, He went there to meet and talk with the residents of Baghdad. That was one of the reasons why the Bábí community had a positive reputation in Baghdad and the majesty of the new Faith became recognized by prominent people of that city.

However, Bahá'u'lláh rejects the objections of Mírzá Mihdíy-i-Rashtí by calling attention to the fact that drinking tea is one of the seven commandments the Báb had categorically required of all Bábís. Bahá'u'lláh expresses surprise that Mírzá Mihdí has attacked Him for observing an explicit ordinance of the Primal Point. Similarly, He refers to the laws of the Bayán which encourage refinement in all things, living in the best houses with the best furniture, wearing the best clothes, using the best perfumes, eating the best foods, and which allow more than two thousand types of food in feasts organized to honor the Promised One. As Bahá'u'lláh says, the explicit purpose of the Báb in revealing all these laws was to ensure that the eyes of the Promised One would never gaze upon unpleasant things and that He would never become subject to hardship and suffering. Bahá'u'lláh comments on the irony that the Báb has ordered these things for the Promised One and has told the Bábís not to reject Him or harm Him, and yet Mírzá Mihdí uses drinking tea or accepting invitations as arguments to object against Him. Bahá'u'lláh reminds His reader of the refined and luxurious decoration of Imám Ḥusayn's horse when on his last campaign he rode to martyrdom.

It is in this context that Bahá'u'lláh declares that His religion is for unity, fellowship, and communication among people—and that is why He encourages issuing and accepting invitations. He also declares that His religion is not a product of the ascetic practices of a mystic, that He Himself has never been one, and that He does not endorse asceticism. On the contrary, He encourages people to enjoy life in moderation and to assist the poor because they are the trust of God among the people.[86]

CONCLUSION: THE COVENANT OF UNITY

At the end of the Kitáb-i-Badí', Bahá'u'lláh addresses the people of Bahá. He does not wish what happened among the Bábís to happen among His followers. He wants to make certain of two things: that unity and love will not be destroyed, and that people will remain steadfast in the covenant of God. But the two issues are directly related to each other. Bahá'u'lláh declares that the purpose of His Cause is to remove the causes of hatred and disunity and to establish fellowship and love. He calls upon His followers to be united and not to divide into opposing factions. For this reason He expounds the questions of hermeneutics and succession. He affirms that the divine Word is not contradictory. All people can understand the verses of God and yet the meanings of the text are truly accessible only to the Source of revelation. People can understand the words of God enough to be able to recognize their authority, but beyond that, all human understandings are limited. Bahá'u'lláh orders His followers not to be content with their own understandings of the divine words, otherwise the Word of God itself would lead to disunity. The only thing that will safeguard the unity intended by His revelation is for all Bahá'ís to ask the Mine and the Source of divine verses about the meanings they do not understand.[87]

In this apologia, Bahá'u'lláh expounds the twin principles of the unity of humankind and the covenant, not only as the essence of His foundational and methodological discourse but also as His concluding statements addressed to His followers. Although in the Kitáb-i-Badí' He does not specifically mention the station of 'Abdu'l-Bahá as His successor, He clearly says that the authoritative understanding of His words is only accessible through His own appointed channels. These would be disclosed later in the Kitáb-i-Aqdas and His Book of the Covenant. The unity of the Bahá'í Faith, the supreme purpose of Bahá'u'lláh, is only possible if the Bahá'ís themselves realize that their own understanding of the sacred writings is limited and that it is through Bahá'u'lláh's authorized interpreters that access to its meaning, the unity of the believers, and the unity of humankind itself can be guaranteed.[88]

Part III

THE NEW WORLD ORDER

Chapter 7

THE KITÁB-I-AQDAS:
DATE AND CONSTITUTIVE PRINCIPLES

THE KITÁB-I-AQDAS stands as Bahá'u'lláh's most comprehensive, integrative, and holistic writing. Shoghi Effendi characterizes its promulgation as "the most signal act of His ministry." Identifying the Kitáb-i-Aqdas as the fulfillment of biblical prophecy, he describes it as "the principal repository of that Law which the Prophet Isaiah had anticipated, and which the writer of the Apocalypse had described as the '*new heaven*' and the '*new earth*,' as '*the Tabernacle of God*,' as the '*Holy City*,' as the '*Bride*,' the '*New Jerusalem coming down from God*,' this '*Most Holy Book*,' whose provisions must remain inviolate for no less than a thousand years, and whose system will embrace the entire planet...." The Kitáb-i-Aqdas, he goes on to say, "may well be regarded as the brightest emanation of the mind of Bahá'u'lláh, as the Mother Book of His Dispensation, and the Charter of His New World Order."[1]

Despite such categorical statements of the centrality, significance, and the "inviolate" nature of the laws of the Kitáb-i-Aqdas, some have raised questions about the position of the Most Holy Book among the writings of Bahá'u'lláh, suggesting that it should be interpreted in terms of the traditional Sufi categories and approach to law. It has also been suggested that the Aqdas itself is not an internally coherent text, that it is a random presentation of laws and commandments. This chapter will analyze several recent theories and interpretations of the Kitáb-i-Aqdas and will discuss the status of the laws, the date of revelation, the global order, and the thematic constitutive principles of this, Bahá'u'lláh's Most Holy Book.

THE CENTRALITY OF THE KITÁB-I-AQDAS

In *God Passes By*, Shoghi Effendi summarizes Bahá'u'lláh's own references to the significance of the Kitáb-i-Aqdas:

> The laws and ordinances that constitute the major theme of this Book, Bahá'u'lláh, moreover, has specifically characterized as *"the breath of life unto all created things,"* as *"the mightiest stronghold,"* as the *"fruits"* of His *"Tree,"* as *"the highest means for the maintenance of order in the world and the security of its peoples,"* as *"the lamps of His wisdom and loving-providence,"* as *"the sweet-smelling savour of His garment,"* as the *"keys"* of His *"mercy"* to His creatures. *"This Book,"* He Himself testifies, *"is a heaven which We have adorned with the stars of Our commandments and prohibitions."* *"Blessed the man,"* He, moreover, has stated, *"who will read it, and ponder the verses sent down in it by God, the Lord of Power, the Almighty. Say, O men! Take hold of it with the hand of resignation ... By My life! It hath been sent down in a manner that amazeth the minds of men. Verily, it is My weightiest testimony unto all people, and the proof of the All-Merciful unto all who are in heaven and all who are on earth."* And again: *"Blessed the palate that savoureth its sweetness, and the perceiving eye that recognizeth that which is treasured therein, and the understanding heart that comprehendeth its allusions and mysteries. By God! Such is the majesty of what hath been revealed therein, and so tremendous the revelation of its veiled allusions that the loins of utterance shake when attempting their description."* And finally: *"In such a manner hath the Kitáb-i-Aqdas been revealed that it attracteth and embraceth all the divinely appointed Dispensations. Blessed those who peruse it! Blessed those who apprehend it! Blessed those who meditate upon it! Blessed those who ponder its meaning! So vast is its range that it hath encompassed all men ere their recognition of it. Erelong will its sovereign power, its pervasive influence and the greatness of its might be manifested on earth."*[2]

The significance of the Kitáb-i-Aqdas is further confirmed in the statements of Bahá'u'lláh's authorized interpreters, such as the assessment by Shoghi Effendi quoted above, as well by 'Abdu'l-Bahá, notably in His Will and Testament, in which He designates as a foundational principle of the Bahá'í Faith that "Unto the Most Holy Book every one must turn, and all that is not expressly recorded therein must be referred to the Universal House of Justice."

The name of the Kitáb-i-Aqdas—"The Most Holy Book"—itself indicates the position Bahá'u'lláh accords it in relation to other Sacred Writings. In a tablet addressed to Abu'l-Faḍá'il, Bahá'u'lláh says that the revelation that has been dispensed in this Day is like an "Ocean," a "Root," a "Mother Book" in relation to the revelations of the past.[3] Within His revelation, the Kitáb-i-Aqdas has the position of being the "Mother Book" and "The Most Holy Book."

Another title of the Kitáb-i-Aqdas, used in some of the writings of Bahá'u'lláh, is Kitáb-i-Amna'-i-Aqdas, or "The Most Exalted, The Most Holy Book."[4] To understand the significance of this designation, it should be remembered that in the Kitáb-i-Badí' Bahá'u'lláh refers to Himself as "the Most Exalted, the Most Holy Beauty." And elsewhere He uses the term to refer to His revelation: "The purpose of that which hath been sent down from the heaven of the Will of God in this most exalted, this most holy Revelation, is the unity of the world and love and fellowship among its peoples."[5] Bahá'u'lláh thus uses the title "the Most Exalted, the Most Holy" to denote the essential attribute of His revelation, His own being, and His Mother Book. The term is also used by the Báb at the beginning of the Persian Bayán, where He replaces the opening phrase of the Qur'án, "In the Name of God, the Most Compassionate, the Most Merciful," with: "In the Name of God, the Most Exalted, the Most Holy," and declares that all the divine mysteries are present in this phrase.[6] We can see that Bahá'u'lláh's use of the term "the Most Exalted, the Most Holy" in reference to the Aqdas signifies that this Book is the fulfillment of the Báb's promise, that it represents the revelation of divine mysteries and the universal revelation that would be shed upon all created things.

The distinction between the Islamic mystical terms "holy outpouring" (fayḍ-i-muqaddas) and "most holy outpouring" (fayḍ-i-aqdas), as symbols of differential stages of divine revelation (as discussed in the Kitáb-i-Íqán), may also be inferred from the title of the Kitáb-i-Aqdas. Fayḍ-i-muqaddas signifies revelation and manifestation of the divine in the realm of creation, but fayḍ-i-aqdas signifies revelation in the realm of absolute divine unity itself. As such, the adjective aqdas (most holy) means that the Book that bears that name is the fulfillment of that long-awaited universal divine revelation.[7]

The title of the Kitáb-i-Aqdas, the exalted self-description of the text, the frequent reference to it in later writings of Bahá'u'lláh, His norm of indicating the unique significance of a statement by defining it as belonging to the Kitáb-i-Aqdas, the other exalted titles of the text, and the explicit statements of the authorized interpreters of the words of Bahá'u'lláh, all leave no doubt concerning the centrality and the all-encompassing importance of this book within the body of Bahá'u'lláh's writings.

THE BINDING CHARACTER OF THE LAWS

Despite Shoghi Effendi's statement that the provisions of this Book are "inviolate" for the duration of Bahá'u'lláh's dispensation, it has been suggested by some that the laws of the Kitáb-i-Aqdas may not have been intended to be valid and binding for that entire time. This position seems to argue that the following statement in the Kitáb-i-Aqdas demonstrates that Bahá'u'lláh did not take His laws very seriously: "Think not that We have revealed unto you a mere code of laws. Nay, rather, We have unsealed the choice Wine with the fingers of might and power. To this beareth witness that which the Pen of Revelation hath revealed. Meditate upon this, O men of insight!" (¶ 5).

The argument contends that the metaphor of "choice wine" (rahíq-i-makhtúm) is meant to indicate, in coded Sufi fashion, the rejection of laws because wine "is a symbol of violation of God's law and, through Sufi usage, also a symbol of mystical communion with God—spiritual intoxication—before which the law is at best irrelevant."[8] It is also speculated that the laws of the Kitáb-i-Aqdas were not intended as "a Baha'i shari'a which is to last for a thousand years."[9] This argument itself rests on a series of assumptions about the text including the assumption that the Aqdas was "revealed in short pieces over years," and in response to particular situations so that it represents a compilation of random laws that "developed," rather than an intentional and coherently organized whole. It is also argued that because Bahá'u'lláh made changes and supplemented the text, that "the Aqdas was never regarded by Bahá'u'lláh to be fixed or complete." But that inference is then extended one more step, to conclude that the body of laws Bahá'u'lláh set down in the Aqdas itself still need not be regarded as "fixed" but rather should be seen as "flexible" and may continue to be "modified" since the ordinances were not intended as laws in the first place but as examples of general ethical principles.[10]

When Bahá'u'lláh says: "Think not that We have revealed unto you a mere code of laws. Nay, rather, We have unsealed the choice Wine with the fingers of might and power"—this is indeed a rejection of the traditional Islamic-jurisprudential approach to law. However, it is equally a rejection of the Sufi approach to law. Both those approaches regarded the law as a "mere code." The metaphor of "unsealing" the "choice wine," as Bahá'u'lláh uses it, in fact affirms the centrality and significance of His laws. Wine is the symbol of the sensation of freedom and of emancipation from limits.[11] In calling His laws "choice wine," Bahá'u'lláh is arguing that His laws should be understood not as repressive or constraining limits, the way some Sufis understood law, but as the essence of liberation. In other words, from the very beginning of the Kitáb-i-Aqdas Bahá'u'lláh is warning that people should *not* interpret His laws in the way that the Sufis interpreted law. In the Kitáb-i-Aqdas and in many other tablets, He especially criticizes those who diminish the significance of the laws and interpret them in terms of hidden meanings. In a tablet in which He refers to the revelation of the Kitáb-i-Aqdas itself, He gives the following commentary on one of its verses about this subject:

> During these days the laws of God have shone forth from the Dayspring of Divine utterance. God willing, they will be sent on later. The following two blessed verses have been revealed in that Most Exalted, Most Holy Tablet: "Amongst the people is he who seateth himself amid the sandals by the door whilst coveting in his heart the seat of honour. Say: What manner of man art thou, O vain and heedless one, who wouldst appear as other than thou art? And among the people is he who layeth claim to inner knowledge, and still deeper knowledge concealed within this knowledge. Say: Thou speakest false! By God! What thou dost possess is naught but husks which We have left to thee as bones are left to dogs." Observe how

every vain and worthless soul hath caused a narrow gulf to branch
out from the most great Ocean and, prompted by idle imaginings
and corrupt desires, hath provoked divisions amongst the people of
Islam through evil scheming and deceptions.[12]

In an even more explicit passage, He writes:

Islam with all its mighty strength was utterly weakened by the
actions of those bearing its name. As thou hast seen in the past, and
observest at present, some people who call themselves dervishes
have falsely interpreted all the Divine laws and commandments. If
they were told that obligatory prayer is one of the fundamental laws
of God, they would reply that obligatory prayer is the same as
prayer and inasmuch as we were born in a state of prayer, we have
thus already performed the true obligatory prayer. Such hapless
people are deprived of the outward meanings let alone inner significances! The vain imaginings of the heedless have been, and continue to be, beyond reckoning. Thus, through their idleness and
sloth they have made faulty interpretations of all the laws of God—
laws which serve as mighty bulwarks for the protection of the
world and its security.[13]

In other writings, Bahá'u'lláh categorically rejects the Sufi approach
to laws. Referring to those who claim to have attained the stage of
mystic ecstasy (*ḥál*), He states

In this day, most of those who have laid claim to this state are
accounted as naught but people of idle talk [*qál*]. All things are held
within the grasp of divine power. Whosoever moveth contrary to
His good pleasure is accounted among the people of idle talk,
immersed though he may be in a sea of ecstasy.... And he who
turneth to God and obeyeth His ordinances is mentioned, in the
beginning and the end, as among the people of rapture. In this day,
rapture pleasing unto God is confessing His unity, professing His
oneness, sanctifying His Essence from any similitude, exalting His
Self above all likeness, acting in accordance with the ordinances of
His book, and avoiding worldly desires, false allusions, and vain
conjectures and interpretations.[14]

The argument that Bahá'u'lláh was endorsing the Sufi attitude to
law, which undermines the law at the expense of a private higher
truth, is incompatible with Bahá'u'lláh's own statements. Within the

text of the Kitáb-i-Aqdas and in other tablets, He stresses the necessity of observing the laws revealed in the Kitáb-i-Aqdas. It is Bahá'u'lláh Himself who stipulates at the beginning of the Kitáb-i-Aqdas that recognition of God itself is unacceptable without the observance of the laws revealed by the Manifestation of God and that

> They whom God hath endued with insight will readily recognize that the precepts laid down by God constitute the highest means for the maintenance of order in the world and the security of its peoples. He that turneth away from them is accounted among the abject and foolish. We, verily, have commanded you to refuse the dictates of your evil passions and corrupt desires, and not to transgress the bounds which the Pen of the Most High hath fixed, for these are the breath of life unto all created things. (¶ 2)

He goes on to say that to break those commandments is to violate the Covenant of God: "They that have violated the Covenant of God by breaking His commandments, and have turned back on their heels, these have erred grievously in the sight of God...." (¶ 2).

In His discussion of liberty in the Kitáb-i-Aqdas, it can be seen that liberty itself is defined in terms of the law:

> True liberty consisteth in man's submission unto My commandments, little as ye know it. Were men to observe that which We have sent down unto them from the Heaven of Revelation, they would, of a certainty, attain unto perfect liberty. Happy is the man that hath apprehended the Purpose of God in whatever He hath revealed from the Heaven of His Will that pervadeth all created things. Say: The liberty that profiteth you is to be found nowhere except in complete servitude unto God, the Eternal Truth. Whoso hath tasted of its sweetness will refuse to barter it for all the dominion of earth and heaven. (¶ 125)

In fact both the position that diminishes the significance of the laws for the sake of higher mystical truth, and the position that would emphasize the laws to the detriment of spiritual principles, are similar approaches to the Kitáb-i-Aqdas. Both reduce it to a one-dimensional legalistic text, a "mere code," and both assume a contradiction or separation between spiritual truth and the realm of revealed law. But it was precisely this logic of dissociating the two that Bahá'u'lláh had rejected in His early mystical texts. In works like the Four Valleys, the Seven Valleys, and the Hidden Words, Bahá'u'lláh replaced that traditional opposition with an epistemology in which reason, will, and love are harmonized. Hence both the legalistic and the Sufi approaches, which opposed the external appearance to the inner intent, and the laws to the hidden mystic truth, were rejected by Bahá'u'lláh at all stages of His revelation. The Kitáb-i-Aqdas begins with a philosophical explication of this epistemology in which recognition of the Manifestation, action in accordance with His laws, and love of His beauty are united in one holistic spiritual logic.

However, because this logic might be misinterpreted by the opponents of law in the name of spiritual inner meaning, Bahá'u'lláh clearly states that no one should mistakenly assume that the Most Holy Book merely reveals laws in the way law has been traditionally understood. Instead He emphasizes that His laws themselves are the "choice wine" unsealed, which confers spiritual insight, liberation, and transcendence. The laws are always inalienable from the mystic truth they symbolize. Contrary to past traditions which separated the two, Bahá'u'lláh declares that it is His intention to create harmony between the appearance and the essence, the manifest and the hidden.[15] Indeed, as we will see, the inextricable unity of mystic truth and its embodiment in the form of law is a structural principle of the Kitáb-i-Aqdas itself.

To better understand the reference to "choice wine" in verse 5, it is necessary to go beyond Sufi categories and refer to the writings of Bahá'u'lláh Himself. When asked about His usage of "choice wine," He explained what He meant in using this metaphor. In one tablet, "choice wine" is a reference to the divine words themselves, the love of divine words, the concealed gems in the words, the means that leads man to his Origin, and the Hands of the Cause who teach the word of God.[16] In another tablet He speaks of "choice wine" as "the most exalted Word," "the most great steadfastness," "the most Exalted Pen," and the revelations of the Pen.[17] In both tablets He defines the "choice wine" in terms of its divine sweet-smelling savor and its effect—namely detachment from all save God, teaching the Cause, and arising to serve the Cause of God.[18] In other tablets, Bahá'u'lláh talks of the "wine" of love, of faith, of revelation, and the like. And in the Aqdas itself, in the very verse preceding the one under discussion, He says that the one who has partaken of the "wine" of fairness will uphold the law: "He who hath drunk the choice wine of fairness from the hands of My bountiful favour will circle around My commandments...." (¶ 4). And of course in the Seven Valleys, Bahá'u'lláh had spoken of the Law as a "cup" that imparts the knowledge of the spirit.

In these various instances, it becomes clear that in referring to His laws as "choice wine," Bahá'u'lláh is emphasizing several points. First is the supreme authority of the Kitáb-i-Aqdas: this is no ordinary legal text written by one of the divines, or the arbitrary deductions of a jurist scholar devoid of any authority. These laws are the Word of God, the revelations and commandments of the Pen of Glory. Moreover, the laws are embodiments of God's love for human beings. They should not be perceived as constraining but as liberating, and should be observed not because of external coercion but "for the love of [His] Beauty." And as the "divine sweet-smelling savor" can be perceived from them, they are the very means through which the love of the Beloved can be experienced. Finally, the laws, as He says in one of His tablets, are the "The most mighty ladder" for ascent to the heaven of divine unity.[19] They are not obstacles to mystic union with the divine but the most direct means of attaining it.

One should also note that the term "choice sealed wine" occurs in the Qur'án as a delight that awaits the righteous in paradise: "Choice sealed wine shall be given to them to quaff."[20] As Suheil Bushrui has pointed out, the Kitáb-i-Aqdas itself represents the fulfillment of that Qur'ánic promise.[21] Recognition of the Manifestation of God constitutes attainment to "paradise," and the laws are the choice wine itself, now "unsealed" in the form of the Kitáb-i-Aqdas. As these precepts, when put into effect, are "the highest means for the maintenance of order in the world and the security of its peoples" (¶ 2), the "lamps of My loving providence," and "the keys of My mercy for My creatures" (¶ 3), the implementation of the laws is intended to bring about the transformation of human civilization into a veritable heaven on earth.

In fact, when we look at the context of the statement about choice
sealed wine in the Kitáb-i-Aqdas, it becomes clear that it is actually the
conclusion of an argument for the necessity, the authority, and the
beneficial and fundamentally spiritual character of the laws. The accuracy of these points becomes clear when we note that Bahá'u'lláh's discussion of the relation of "choice wine" to His laws is immediately
preceded by the following three statements in the same paragraph:
"Say: From My laws the sweet smelling savor of My garment can be
smelled"; "Observe My commandments, for the love of My beauty";
"He who hath drunk the choice wine of fairness from the hands of My
bountiful favour, will circle around My commandments that shine
above the Dayspring of My creation" (¶ 4). All those statements
express the idea of "choice wine" in different ways. However,
Bahá'u'lláh is very clear that He is using the concept of choice wine
only to affirm the binding, loving, liberating, and delightsome character of His laws. It is *after* these three statements that He adds that His
Book and His ordinances are not traditional or arbitrary laws but are
the choice wine, the embodiments of the word, mercy, and love of
God.

The speculation that the laws of the Kitáb-i-Aqdas were not
intended to be valid and binding for the entire period of the Bahá'í dispensation appears to conflict with all the interpretations of the authorized interpreters of the words of Bahá'u'lláh. Moreover, if Bahá'u'lláh
did not intend the laws to be binding for the entire course of His dispensation, surely He would never have empowered the institution of
the House of Justice to legislate only on matters that have not been
explicitly ordained in His Book. In fact Bahá'u'lláh makes it clear that
He has revealed some laws as binding for the entire course of His dispensation but has withheld legislation on other laws, or on their
details, because of the historical specificity of those laws. "It is incumbent upon the Trustees of the House of Justice," He writes, "to take
counsel together regarding those things *which have not outwardly been
revealed in the Book*, and to enforce that which is agreeable to them.
God will verily inspire them with whatsoever He willeth, and He, verily, is the Provider, the Omniscient" (*Tablets* 68; italics added).

Abdu'l-Bahá, in his Will and Testament, emphasizes the principle that the House of Justice has the authority to abrogate its own laws but not what is explicitly ordained by Bahá'u'lláh:

And inasmuch as this House of Justice hath power to enact laws that are not expressly recorded in the Book and bear upon daily transactions, so also it hath power to repeal the same. Thus for example, the House of Justice enacteth today a certain law and enforceth it, and a hundred years hence, circumstances having profoundly changed and the conditions having altered, another House of Justice will then have power, according to the exigencies of the time, to alter that law. This it can do because that law formeth no part of the Divine Explicit Text.[22]

The speculation that the laws of the Kitáb-i-Aqdas could be subject to change within Bahá'u'lláh's dispensation appears to overgeneralize the principle of progressive revelation so much that it negates the binding character of the explicitly revealed laws.[23] But this is the exact opposite of Bahá'u'lláh's conception of progressive revelation and His laws. Naturally, the Manifestation of God has unconditional authority to abrogate or change His own or previous revealed law at any moment. However, if He abrogates some of His laws according to the needs of the time or for any other reason,[24] it does not follow that He has also given permission to the human beings who are bound by those laws to abrogate them at will in accordance with any current social trend, intellectual fad, or arbitrary desire. Nor does the fact that Bahá'u'lláh altered some of His laws (such as His substituting three kinds of obligatory prayers in place of the nine-unit prayer originally designated in verse 6 of the Kitáb-i-Aqdas), imply that He intended all His laws to be nonbinding. On the contrary, it can only imply their binding authority and that those of His laws that He did not change remain absolutely binding.

Taken together, these two aspects—the fixed character of His ordained laws and the ability of the House of Justice to legislate on matters not explicitly mentioned in the text—provide, as Shoghi Effendi has observed, a balance of integrity and flexibility in Bahá'u'lláh's system. Referring to these two features of Bahá'í law, Shoghi

Effendi writes: "Such is the immutability of His revealed Word. Such is the elasticity which characterizes the functions of His appointed ministers. The first preserves the identity of His Faith, and guards the integrity of His law. The second enables it, even as a living organism, to expand and adapt itself to the needs and requirements of an ever-changing society."[25]

The exclusive right to alter or abrogate a revealed law is in fact one of the most important meanings of the concept of the Most Great Infallibility as discussed in the Kitáb-i-Aqdas and emphasized in other tablets. According to this principle, only the Manifestation of God can initiate a dispensation of revelation, which carries the authority to abrogate former scriptural laws as well as any of His own laws. This authority is shared by no one else and is not accountable to any human standard. Bahá'u'lláh explains that:

> the Most Great Infallibility is confined to the One Whose station is immeasurably exalted beyond ordinances or prohibitions and is sanctified from errors and omissions. Indeed He is a Light which is not followed by darkness and a Truth not overtaken by error. Were He to pronounce water to be wine or heaven to be earth or light to be fire, He speaketh the truth and no doubt would there be about it; and unto no one is given the right to question His authority or to say why or wherefore. Whosoever raiseth objections will be numbered with the froward in the Book of God, the Lord of the worlds. "Verily He shall not be asked of His doings but all others shall be asked of their doings." He is come from the invisible heaven, bearing the banner "He doeth whatsoever He willeth" and is accompanied by hosts of power and authority while it is the duty of all besides Him to strictly observe whatever laws and ordinances have been enjoined upon them, and should anyone deviate therefrom, even to the extent of a hair's breadth, his work would be brought to naught. (*Tablets* 108)

THE DATE OF THE REVELATION OF THE KITÁB-I-AQDAS

The argument that the laws of the Kitáb-i-Aqdas were not intended as binding laws is apparently based on certain assumptions about the revelation of the text itself, namely that the Kitáb-i-Aqdas was a kind of compilation consisting "of an initial Tablet of laws which was supplemented over time with verses written in response to questions put to Bahá'u'lláh over a period of three or four years."[26] Therefore, it is necessary to examine in detail the evidence for and against the gradualist thesis of the revelation of the Most Holy Book.

According to Shoghi Effendi, the Kitáb-i-Aqdas was "revealed soon after Bahá'u'lláh had been transferred to the house of 'Údí Khammár (circa 1873)."[27] However, in recent years some authors have suggested that the Kitáb-i-Aqdas was instead revealed intermittently, beginning in Bahá'u'lláh's last year in Edirne or the first year of His arrival in 'Akká. Perhaps the first scholar to suggest a similar thesis was Mírzá Asadu'lláh Fádil-i-Mázandarání, a creative, knowledgeable, and eminent Bahá'í scholar. He proposed the idea that the revelation of the Kitáb-i-Aqdas began in 1868 and was completed in 1871 (1288 A.H.). Fádil argued that the entire text of the Kitáb-i-Aqdas was probably released to the believers of Iran in 1873 (1290 A.H.).[28] His argument rested on Bahá'u'lláh's reference, at the end of the Kitáb-i-Aqdas, to the death of Siyyid Muhammad-i-Isfahání. Since this event took place in 1871, Fádil deduced that the Kitáb-i-Aqdas was completed in that year. He gave two arguments for the release of the entire text of the Kitáb-i-Aqdas in 1873. First, according to one of Bahá'u'lláh's tablets, the whole text was not released for a few years after its revelation. In that tablet, Bahá'u'lláh states that the Kitáb-i-Aqdas was revealed from the heaven of the divine will and was hidden for a few years until some of the faithful from different lands asked questions concerning the divine laws and requested them, whereupon, He says, it was decreed to dispatch the Kitáb-i-Aqdas. Since Fádil assumed that the text was completed in 1871, he reasoned that it must have been sent to Iran a few years later, around 1873.[29]

Fádil's second argument is based on a statement in another tablet, from which he concludes that Bahá'u'lláh released the text of the Kitáb-i-Aqdas in 1873 because that is the year in which that tablet was revealed. The statement he has referred to is crucial to the resolution of this issue, so we will return later to analyze it in more detail. The passage reads:

In recent days the Kitáb-i-Aqdas hath been revealed from the
heaven of holiness. Blessed is the man who will read it and ponder
the verses sent down in it by the omnipotent, self-subsisting Lord.
The reason was this: Over the course of some years, questions
concerning the laws of God were received from divers lands, but
the Supreme Pen did not respond to them; then, in the Land of
Mystery [Edirne], a brief tablet was revealed in the Persian language but was not sent out, and, as directed, it was kept in a safe
place. Till in recent days, once again petitions containing questions
have reached the Most Holy Threshold. Thereupon this wondrous
and sublime Book hath been sent down in the form of Divine
verses. As Áqá J. M. [Jamál-i-Burújirdí], upon him rest the glory
of God, was on a visit here, that which was suitable for release at
present was shared with him; namely, he was permitted to take a
copy. God willing, you will receive the Text and act in accordance
with wisdom.[30]

Some of the suggestions made by Fáḍil have been repeated in
recent years by different authors. While they disagree on details, they
agree that the Kitáb-i-Aqdas was revealed gradually, and that its revelation began in the late Edirne period or the first year of Bahá'u'lláh's
arrival in 'Akká. The most articulate expression of this theory has been
made by Kamran Ekbal, who has argued that the Kitáb-i-Aqdas was
revealed in the course of five or six years, beginning in 1867 or 1868
and ending in 1873 or 1874.[31] He follows the basic model proposed by
Fáḍil-i-Mázandarání but disagrees with the latter concerning the date
of the book's completion, maintaining that while the revelation of the
Kitáb-i-Aqdas began in 1867–68, it was completed around 1873 and
was released to the believers in Iran that same year. His position can be
summarized as follows.

(1) In some of Bahá'u'lláh's tablets He has spoken about the revelation of the Kitáb-i-Aqdas in the "Prison of 'Akká." According to
Ekbal, Bahá'u'lláh uses the term "Prison of 'Akká" exclusively in reference to the barracks, as opposed to the term "Most Great Prison,"
which He uses to refer to the city of 'Akká in general and His residence
within the city after His release from the barracks, in particular.[32] Similarly, in some of His tablets, Bahá'u'lláh talks about the revelation of
the Kitáb-i-Aqdas upon arrival in the prison. Ekbal concludes that the

revelation of the Kitáb-i-Aqdas began in 1868, the first year of Bahá'-u'lláh's arrival at the barracks. (2) Bahá'u'lláh refers to the "Crimson Book" in His Tablet of the World (Lawḥ-i-Dunyá). This, Ekbal feels, is the Kitáb-i-Aqdas. Assuming that the Tablet of the World was revealed at the end of 1870, shortly after Bahá'u'lláh's departure from the barracks, Ekbal infers that the Kitáb-i-Aqdas must have been written before 1870. (3) In a tablet, 'Abdu'l-Bahá has spoken of the revelation of the Kitáb-i-Aqdas as occurring twenty-five years before Bahá'u'lláh's ascension. That gives us the year 1867. In another tablet dated 1898, 'Abdu'l-Bahá mentions the revelation of the Kitáb-i-Aqdas as occurring thirty years previously, which would place the date of revelation of the Aqdas at 1868. (4) Bahá'u'lláh confirmed the delay of the release of the Kitáb-i-Aqdas for a few years. The full text was released around 1873. Therefore, Ekbal concludes, the Kitáb-i-Aqdas must have been revealed a few years earlier but completed in 1873.[33]

However, my reading of Bahá'u'lláh's tablets leads me to quite different conclusions, namely, that: (a) the Kitáb-i-Aqdas was most likely revealed in a few days, not gradually in the course of many years; (b) both the beginning and completion of its revelation took place in the first half of 1873; and (c) the release of the full text of the Kitáb-i-Aqdas took place a few years after 1873. In order to demonstrate these points, it is first necessary to address the above four arguments.

It can easily be seen in Bahá'u'lláh's writings that the term "Prison of 'Akká" does not refer exclusively to the barracks. Both the terms "Prison of 'Akká" and "Most Great Prison" are used to refer to all the stages of Bahá'u'lláh's stay in 'Akká and thus may refer to the barracks or any other place of residence thereafter. Two examples should suffice to demonstrate. In His Tablet of the World, Bahá'u'lláh recounts that during His stay in the "Prison of 'Akká," Siyyid Jamálu'd-Dín Asadábádí (known as "Afghání") who had gone "to the seat of the imperial throne in Persia and succeeded in winning the good graces of some of the nobility by his ingratiating behaviour.... proceeded then to Paris where he published a newspaper entitled 'Urvatu'l-Vuthqá and sent copies thereof to all parts of the world. He also sent a copy to the Prison of 'Akká...." (*Tablets* 94–95).

Siyyid Jamálu'd-Dín began to publish *'Urvatu'l-Vuthqá* from Paris in 1884.[34] Consequently, in this passage, Bahá'u'lláh is referring to His residence around 1885, fifteen years after His release from the barracks, as the "Prison of 'Akká." The second example can be found in the title of a tablet revealed after the Kitáb-i-Aqdas, during the later stages of Bahá'u'lláh's stay in 'Akká. The Tablet of Glad-Tidings (Bishárát) opens: "This is the Call of the All-Glorious which is proclaimed from the Supreme Horizon in the Prison of 'Akká" (*Tablets* 21).

In Bahá'u'lláh's writings, the phrase "upon arrival in the prison" (*dar avval-i-vurúd-i-sijn*), literally meaning in the beginning of arrival in prison, usually refers to the early period—although not necessarily to the first year—of Bahá'u'lláh's imprisonment in 'Akká, including His residence in the city of 'Akká after His release from the barracks (which includes the year 1873). One piece of evidence that by "upon arrival in the prison" Bahá'u'lláh may mean neither the beginning of His stay in the barracks nor the first year of His arrival in 'Akká is His use of the same phrase to describe the date of the death of His son Mírzá Mihdí. In a tablet He writes that upon arrival in the prison Mihdí was sacrificed.[35] But we know that Bahá'u'lláh arrived in 'Akká in August 1868 and that Mírzá Mihdí suffered his fatal accident in June 1870, just a few months before Bahá'u'lláh was released from the barracks.

In one of His tablets Bahá'u'lláh speaks of the revelation of certain verses in the Kitáb-i-Aqdas "upon arrival in the prison."[36] These are the verses dealing with events in the city of Kirmán: "O Land of Káf and Rá! We, verily, behold thee in a state displeasing unto God, and see proceeding from thee that which is inscrutable to anyone save Him, the Omniscient, the All-Informed...." (¶ 164). This verse occurs at the end of the Kitáb-i-Aqdas, not at the beginning, and as Ekbal correctly noted, the last sections of the text were revealed in 1873. It is virtually impossible for the reference to the revelation of the verses about Kirmán "upon arrival in the prison" to mean 1868. If that were the case, then the entire book would have to have been revealed in 1868. Yet, there is another reason why the verse about Kirmán was probably revealed in 1873: it appears long after the verse mentioning Napoleon

III, in which Bahá'u'lláh refers not only to Napoleon's overthrow (in 1870), but also to his death (in January 1873). Therefore, the verse about Kirmán can be dated after January 1873.

The second argument has two parts: one is the identification of the Kitáb-i-Aqdas as "the Crimson Book" in the Tablet of the World; the other is the claim that the Tablet of the World was revealed in 1870. But internal evidence in the Tablet of the World shows that it could not have been revealed earlier than 1891. Fáḍil-i-Mázandarání refers to three events mentioned in the tablet—the martyrdom of Muḥammad Riḍá Iṣfahání (1889), the imprisonment of Amín and 'Alí Akbar (1891), and the martyrdom of the believers in Yazd (1891).[37] In addition, the reference to Siyyid Jamálu'd-Dín in the same tablet, as we have seen, can be dated to 1885. These, as well as other evidence, make it clear that the Tablet of the World was revealed not in 1870 but in 1891.

The other part of the argument holds that in the Tablet of the World the Kitáb-i-Aqdas is referred to as "the Crimson Book." The passage in the Tablet of the World reads:

> Whilst in the Prison of 'Akká, We revealed in the Crimson Book that which is conducive to the advancement of mankind and to the reconstruction of the world. The utterances set forth therein by the Pen of the Lord of creation include the following which constitute the fundamental principles for the administration of the affairs of men: First: It is incumbent upon the ministers of the House of Justice to promote the Lesser Peace.... Fifth: Special regard must be paid to agriculture. (*Tablets* 89–90)

If we examine this statement closely, we can see that while it certainly refers to the principles set forth in the Kitáb-i-Aqdas, it can only be understood as a broader reference to the body of Bahá'u'lláh's teachings. Bahá'u'lláh cites five principles from the "Crimson Book," but all five are written in Persian, whereas the Aqdas is in Arabic. The fifth principle, on the utmost importance of agriculture, is not discussed anywhere in the Kitáb-i-Aqdas. Like "Most Holy Book," the term "Crimson Book" is sometimes a reference to the entire body of Bahá'u'lláh's writings, and sometimes to His Book of the Covenant, as 'Abdu'l-Bahá has testified.[38] Nevertheless, as we will see, there is indeed a direct and unequivocal reference to the Kitáb-i-Aqdas in the Tablet of the World.

The third argument concerns 'Abdu'l-Bahá's two references to the revelation of the Kitáb-i-Aqdas. But these references—of which there are many more than these two—do not indicate an actual date but an approximate period of time in relation to some particular event. In various tablets 'Abdu'l-Bahá has actually given different periods of time; if they were taken literally they would date the Aqdas, alternatively, to 1861, 1862, 1863, and 1871.[39]

In all those instances, it seems that 'Abdu'l-Bahá intended to indicate that the particular issue under discussion was emphasized "a long time ago" by Bahá'u'lláh. His references to "twenty-five years" and "thirty years" should also be understood in the same logic, not as identifying 1867 or 1868 as the exact date. And, by "the Kitáb-i-Aqdas," or "Most Holy Book," 'Abdu'l-Bahá is sometimes indicating the body of teachings revealed by Bahá'u'lláh in general and not necessarily that specific book.

The fourth argument, concerning the delay in the release of the whole text, seems to be inconsistent. When Bahá'u'lláh says that after its revelation its release was delayed for a few years, obviously He is speaking of a delay after the completion of the book's revelation, not after the beginning of its revelation. It would make no sense to speak of a delay in sending a tablet which is not yet completed. However, according to Ekbal himself, the Kitáb-i-Aqdas was completed around 1873. But if it was completed in 1873 and released the same year, then there could not have been a delay for a few years. Either the Kitáb-i-Aqdas was completed a few years earlier, or it was released a few years after 1873.

Fádil's belief that the full text of the Kitáb-i-Aqdas was released around 1873 was based on two assumptions. First, he assumed that the book was completed in 1871, then he added two years for the delay, arriving at the approximate date of 1873. However, his first premise was inaccurate. As I will demonstrate, the text of the Kitáb-i-Aqdas itself refers to events that occurred in 1873. Therefore it could not have been completed before that date. In addition, as Ekbal has also noted, many of Bahá'u'lláh's tablets show that 1873 was the year of its revelation.

Fáḍil's second piece of evidence was based on his understanding of Bahá'u'lláh's statement granting permission to Jamál-i-Burújirdí to copy the Kitáb-i-Aqdas in 1873. However, in this tablet Bahá'u'lláh clearly says that the whole of the Kitáb-i-Aqdas was revealed in that year: "Thereupon this wondrous and sublime Book hath been sent down in the form of Divine verses." Furthermore, the tablet does not say that the full text of the book was released in 1873, the year it was revealed; it confirms that Jamál-i-Burújirdí was given, and permitted to copy, only "that which was suitable for release at present." That means only part of the text was released to him; the full release of the Kitáb-i-Aqdas did not take place in 1873 because Bahá'u'lláh did not yet consider it timely.

In fact we do know the reason why Bahá'u'lláh withheld the full release of the Kitáb-i-Aqdas. In another tablet, dated 1879, He tells us that the revelation of the law of Ḥuqúqu'lláh (the Right of God) was the cause of the delay.[40] Out of compassion, Bahá'u'lláh did not want to expose the believers to an obligation which they might not have been ready for.[41]

In light of these facts, the thesis of the gradual revelation of the Kitáb-i-Aqdas, beginning in 1867–68, seems difficult to sustain. In contrast, much evidence indicates that the revelation of the entire text of the Kitáb-i-Aqdas occurred around the year 1873 in a short period of time. This should not be surprising to anyone familiar with the norm for the revelation of Bahá'u'lláh's writings. Bahá'u'lláh revealed His works with incredible speed in a short period of time—the Kitáb-i-Íqán was revealed in two days, the Kitáb-i-Badí' in three. It would be strangely anomalous that the Mother Book of Bahá'u'lláh should show a complete reversal of the norm, when speed of revelation is often mentioned by the Manifestation as a distinguishing feature of divine revelation. In addition, in His tablets Bahá'u'lláh has frequently spoken of the "revelation" of the Kitáb-i-Aqdas. But He always uses the term in a way that indicates one complete event of revelation. In none of His descriptions of the revelation of the Kitáb-i-Aqdas does He hint at anything like a gradual revelation over the course of five or six years.

Entirely aside from the above considerations, Bahá'u'lláh makes it clear that the Kitáb-i-Aqdas was revealed in full around 1873. If we look at the different tablets of Bahá'u'lláh referring to the revelation of the Kitáb-i-Aqdas, we can clearly distinguish three stages leading to that event. The first stage is the arrival, during the Edirne period, of many petitions from His followers requesting laws. In response to this first set of petitions, at the end of His stay in Edirne, Bahá'u'lláh revealed a short tablet in Persian concerning laws, but He never released that tablet. The second stage was the arrival of further petitions, as Bahá'u'lláh says in His tablet, in "recent days." The third stage is the revelation of the Kitáb-i-Aqdas in Arabic in response to the second set of petitions. We know precisely the point of reference for these "recent days" because the tablet mentioning them is dated 11 July 1873. Note that all the scholars who have studied this issue, including Fáḍil, have agreed that "in recent days" means 1873, and that is why they have assumed that the Kitáb-i-Aqdas was released that year. But apparently they did not note that the tablet says that it was the *revelation* of the Kitáb-i-Aqdas that began in those "recent days." Let us reexamine Bahá'u'lláh's words, paying close attention to the sequence of events:

> In recent days the Kitáb-i-Aqdas hath been revealed from the heaven of holiness. Blessed is the man who will read it and ponder the verses sent down in it by the omnipotent, self-subsisting Lord. The reason was this: Over the course of some years, questions concerning the laws of God were received from divers lands, but the Supreme Pen did not respond to them; then, in the Land of Mystery [Edirne], a brief tablet was revealed in the Persian language but was not sent out, and, as directed, it was kept in a safe place. Till in recent days, once again petitions containing questions have reached the Most Holy Threshold. Thereupon this wondrous and sublime Book hath been sent down in the form of Divine verses. As Áqá J. M., upon him rest the glory of God, was on a visit here, that which was suitable for release at present was shared with him; namely, he was permitted to

take a copy. God willing, you will receive the Text and act in accordance with wisdom.[42]

Given the date of that tablet, when Bahá'u'lláh speaks of the revelation of the Kitáb-i-Aqdas "in recent days," that must mean sometime approximately in the first half of 1873. No reference is made to any gradual or intermittent revelation. The reference to "recent days" is reiterated in the same tablet, in describing the arrival of the second set of petitions. Clearly it was in response to these petitions that the Kitáb-i-Aqdas was revealed in Arabic, unlike the previous tablet which was revealed in Persian in response to the first set of petitions. Since the second set arrived in 1873, the revelation of the Kitáb-i-Aqdas must have begun in 1873 and been completed in a very short period of time.

This sequence of events is confirmed within the Kitáb-i-Aqdas itself:

> Various petitions have come before Our throne from the believers, concerning laws from God, the Lord of the seen and the unseen, the Lord of all worlds. We have, in consequence, revealed this Holy Tablet and arrayed it with the mantle of His Law that haply the people may keep the commandments of their Lord. Similar requests had been made of Us over several previous years but We had, in Our wisdom, withheld Our Pen until, in recent days, letters arrived from a number of the friends, and We have therefore responded, through the power of truth, with that which shall quicken the hearts of men. (¶ 98)

The sequence of events is exactly the same, including reference to the arrival of the second series of petitions and the revelation of the Kitáb-i-Aqdas after their arrival. As we know from the other tablet that the second set of petitions arrived in 1873, we can conclude that the "recent days" mentioned in the Kitáb-i-Aqdas also means 1873. But this reference in the Kitáb-i-Aqdas even more definitely establishes that Bahá'u'lláh "withheld [His] Pen" until those letters arrived. It leaves no doubt that the revelation of the Kitáb-i-Aqdas could not have begun earlier. Moreover, all of the Kitáb-i-Aqdas was revealed in the course of a few days—as can be seen from Bahá'u'lláh's mention

of the revelation (that is, the completion) of the Kitáb-i-Aqdas in
"recent days."

The above analysis is further confirmed when we pay attention to
the fact that the section of the Kitáb-i-Aqdas mentioning the petitions
was revealed after Bahá'u'lláh has referred to events concerning Napoleon III that occurred in 1873. Some have assumed that here Bahá'u'-
lláh is referring only to Napoleon's defeat and overthrow, which happened in 1870. However, He also mentions Napoleon's death, which
took place in January 1873. Bahá'u'lláh not only speaks of Napoleon's
return to "dust"—an unmistakable Arabic figure of speech indicating
death, which is often used by Bahá'u'lláh[43]—but, addressing Kaiser
Wilhelm, He speaks of the fall from the palace to the grave of Napoleon and others like him:

> Say: O King of Berlin! ... Do thou remember the one [Napo-
> leon III] whose power transcended thy power, and whose station
> excelled thy station. Where is he? Whither are gone the things he
> possessed? Take warning, and be not of them that are fast asleep. He
> it was who cast the Tablet of God behind him when We made
> known unto him what the hosts of tyranny had caused Us to suffer.
> Wherefore, disgrace assailed him from all sides, and he went down
> to dust in great loss. Think deeply, O King, concerning him, and
> concerning them who, like unto thee, have conquered cities and
> ruled over men. The All-Merciful brought them down from their
> palaces to their graves. Be warned, be of them who reflect. (¶ 86)

Mention has already been made of Bahá'u'lláh's reference to the
revelation of verse 164 upon arrival in the prison. Now it becomes evident that this phrase can only refer to 1873. In the Ishráqát, Bahá'u'lláh
has also referred to the revelation of verse 48 as taking place "upon Our
arrival in the Prison City."[44] Thus all parts of the text, including the
verses at the beginning as well as at the end, must have been revealed
in the same time period in 1873.

As we have seen, it was because of the revelation of the law of
Ḥuqúqu'lláh that the release of the Aqdas was delayed. However, the
law of Ḥuqúqu'lláh was revealed after the verse mentioning the death
of Napoleon. Consequently, Bahá'u'lláh's reference to the delay in

releasing the Kitáb-i-Aqdas must indicate a period of time which begins in 1873 after the law of Ḥuqúqu'lláh was revealed. This means that even the reference to the delay in releasing the Kitáb-i-Aqdas also supports the argument for the revelation of the entire text in 1873.

In addition to this evidence, at least two statements of Bahá'u'lláh mention the date of revelation of the Kitáb-i-Aqdas as being around 1873. The first statement is the one in the tablet dated 1873, which has already been discussed. In another tablet dated 1874–75 (1292 A.H.), Bahá'u'lláh states: "A year ago, the Most Holy Book was sent down from the heaven of the bounty of the Lord of Names" (*Tablets* 268).

In conclusion, various textual and contextual evidence confirms that Shoghi Effendi's statement concerning the revelation of the Kitáb-i-Aqdas after Bahá'u'lláh's transfer to the house of 'Udí Khammár around 1873 is the only account compatible with Bahá'u'lláh's own statements about the Kitáb-i-Aqdas. We can conclude, therefore, that the Kitáb-i-Aqdas was revealed in 1873, and most likely in the course of a few days.

THE ORDER OF THE KITÁB-I-AQDAS

Another assumption related to the theory we have been examining is the idea that the Kitáb-i-Aqdas does not have any order. This impression may stem from perceiving the Kitáb-i-Aqdas as simply a book of laws and regulations. But, although the Kitáb-i-Aqdas contains the structure of Bahá'u'lláh's laws and ordinances, it is not a merely legalistic text. As the Mother Book of Bahá'u'lláh's dispensation, it integrates and unites all the different aspects of His revelation. This implies an essential continuity between the Kitáb-i-Aqdas and all other previous and later writings of Bahá'u'lláh. Whatever is revealed in the other works of Bahá'u'lláh should be expected to be present in some form in the Kitáb-i-Aqdas as well. Indeed, if we approach the Aqdas from this perspective, rather than as a "mere" book of laws, it is possible to discover just what form that continuity takes.

The specific claim of discontinuity between the early and later writings of Bahá'u'lláh will be examined in detail in Chapters 9 and 10. However, the logic of that theory can also be questioned by an analysis

of the order of the Kitáb-i-Aqdas. I will suggest that the order or organization of the Kitáb-i-Aqdas is an expression of its constitutive principles, and that these are principles that Bahá'u'lláh explicitly advocated in His earlier and later writings alike. In fact, they represent the
essence and totality of the worldview which is contained in His writings, including metaphysical, social, political, spiritual, mystical,
philosophical, epistemological, ethical, and legal teachings. However,
this order is not recognizable if the text is read as a "code" of laws and
commandments. Only if the Kitáb-i-Aqdas is seen for what it is—the
Mother Book of Bahá'u'lláh's revelation and the Charter of His New
World Order—does the representation of laws become understandable as ordered and coherent.

The idea of the so-called lack of order of the Kitáb-i-Aqdas
remains at odds with the logic of Bahá'u'lláh's style of revelation.
Bahá'u'lláh's writings are never chaotic or incoherent. Books like the
Kitáb-i-Íqán or the Tablets to the Kings display the beauty of an
organic and graceful order. The Kitáb-i-Aqdas is no exception. Usually
the assumption of the orderlessness of the Kitáb-i-Aqdas is linked to
assumptions concerning the revelation of the text. Some have assumed
that the Kitáb-i-Aqdas has no order because it was revealed cumula-
tively over five or six years, while others have tried to support the
thesis of gradual revelation by pointing to the assumed lack of order of
the text. John Walbridge has suggested that the Kitáb-i-Aqdas was ini-
tially a complete and ordered short work which was later expanded
through apparently random additions over several years of its revelation. In his view, the initial ordered part ends in verse 17 after
Bahá'u'lláh has discussed the laws concerning fasting.[45] Another com-
mentator, on the other hand, speculates that as a book of law the
Kitáb-i-Aqdas is relatively coherent until verse 97, after which it
"becomes quite choppy and random, and appears to consist of answers
to various questions, revealed in no particular order."[46] Both assume
that the supposed incoherence and lack of systematicity of the text is
due to the long and gradual revelation of the text itself in answer to
various unrelated questions.

In contrast, it seems to me that the order in the second half of the

Kitáb-i-Aqdas is much more obvious than in the first half, while the repetition and explication of previously mentioned laws is equally present in the part preceding verse 97. Furthermore, it is immediately following verse 97 that Bahá'u'lláh writes that He has revealed this Book after receiving the petitions "in recent days" (¶ 98). Since we know that these reached Bahá'u'lláh in 1873, and since all agree that the Aqdas was completed in that year, we can safely say that the entire text following verse 97 must have been written in a brief time. So, even if the second half of the Kitáb-i-Aqdas were orderless, this could not have been due to lengthy and gradual revelation of that part.

Walbridge's theory that the text was later expanded seems based at least partly on the assumption that the following statement in verse 17 indicates the end of the theoretical initial text: "These are the ordinances of God that have been set down in the Books and Tablets by His Most Exalted Pen. Hold ye fast unto His statutes and commandments, and be not of those who, following their idle fancies and vain imaginings, have clung to the standards fixed by their own selves, and cast behind their backs the standards laid down by God." But that seems an improbable reading of the sentence, especially since there is no necessity that the indexical "this" or "these" must point back to indicate material just stated; it can equally point forward, introducing what is about to be said.

It seems obvious that "These are the ordinances of God" cannot signify the end of the present work because Bahá'u'lláh is plainly not talking exclusively about the Kitáb-i-Aqdas alone but about laws "that have been set down in the *Books* and *Tablets*" (italics added). The ordinances set down in the text that is being revealed belong to a larger category of Bahá'u'lláh's revelation as a whole—His "Books and Tablets." In other words, the statement "These are the ordinances of God...." declares the authority of the laws as divinely revealed, rather than signaling the termination of a text.

A distinguishing feature of Bahá'u'lláh's writings which is particularly visible in the Kitáb-i-Aqdas is its self-referentiality. As a text, the Kitáb-i-Aqdas is not only a narrative, exposition, or argument, it is also a book about itself, about its author, about the purposes for which

He has revealed it and the appropriate response expected of the reader. Above all, it is a book about the authority and binding character of its content. In other words, the Kitáb-i-Aqdas is constantly a discourse on its own discourse, a book on the revelation of the book. As we will see, this self-referentiality is one of the constitutive principles of the Kitáb-i-Aqdas. In this respect, the statement in verse 17 is a typical recurrent feature of the book, which is found before verse 17 and after it as Bahá'u'lláh repeatedly invokes the philosophical and metaphysical principles that underlie His discourse of laws.[47]

To talk about the order of a text is to identify its logic. It is to realize what relationship the parts have to one another, that is, why they are presented in this particular sequence, and what meaning is implied by that sequence. If we want to understand the order of the Kitáb-i-Aqdas we must first identify the principles of its logic and see what characteristics define its categories.

We expect a book of laws to be structured according to a classification scheme, a series of hierarchically arranged categories, so that related ordinances are grouped together because they share characteristics of a category. The theory that the Kitáb-i-Aqdas is not systematic or intentionally organized is perhaps the result of (1) expecting it to fit some generic model that is taken as normative, and (2) not seeing the actual connections that link the different laws or issues as they are successively discussed. I suggest there is a structure and that normally the laws mentioned in proximity form a group, are conceptually related to each other, and usually express the same fundamental constitutive principle. In fact, I suggest it is the four constitutive principles that create the thematic structure of the text. Each time a principle is introduced, diverse laws and commandments which are implications and expressions of the principle are mentioned. The Kitáb-i-Aqdas can be seen as a discourse on the metaphysical and spiritual principles which underlie the diverse legal and moral reflections of those principles.

The elaboration of the principles in the form of different clusters of verses is itself nested within another, more general structure. In what follows I will first discuss the general structure of the text and then analyze the constitutive principles.

THE GENERAL STRUCTURE OF THE KITÁB-I-AQDAS

The general framework of the text can be understood in terms of the ontological circle, with its arc of descent and arc of ascent describing the process of creation and of return. Verse 1 begins with reference to the three realms of existence: the unknowable Essence of God, the Manifestations of God, and the created beings. It presupposes the arc of descent and Bahá'u'lláh's metaphysics of being, revelation, and will:

> The first duty prescribed by God for His servants is the recognition of Him Who is the Dayspring of His Revelation and the Fountain of His laws, Who representeth the Godhead in both the Kingdom of His Cause and the world of creation. Whoso achieveth this duty hath attained unto all good; and whoso is deprived thereof hath gone astray, though he be the author of every righteous deed. It behoveth every one who reacheth this most sublime station, this summit of transcendent glory, to observe every ordinance of Him Who is the Desire of the world. These twin duties are inseparable. Neither is acceptable without the other. Thus hath it been decreed by Him Who is the Source of Divine inspiration. (¶ 1)

In this opening statement Bahá'u'lláh identifies the action of recognizing the Manifestation as the attainment of "all good," thereby reaffirming the Báb's statements in the Bayán that the supreme purpose of human existence is recognition of the Manifestation and that the ultimate paradise for human beings is His knowledge and love.

Bahá'u'lláh is in fact speaking about the arc of ascent—the spiritual journey which is the supreme meaning and the purpose for which humans were created. As we saw in Chapter 3, this journey is a process leading to the harmonious holistic unity of all human potentialities. Observance of the divine laws is a necessary element of this arc of ascent. It is inalienable from spiritual principles and mystical truths, hence the emphasis on the "inseparable" nature of the "twin duties." But as we can see in verse 4 ("'Observe My commandments, for the love of My beauty'"), the twin duties themselves are actually part of an inseparable triad of recognition, love, and action. This is the same unified holistic logic of spiritual journey that is found in all Bahá'u'lláh's earlier and later writings. In this respect, the opening verses of the

Kitáb-i-Aqdas restate the basic metaphysics and message of Bahá'u'-
lláh's Four Valleys.

In setting down His laws Bahá'u'lláh begins, in verse 6, with individual acts of worship, namely obligatory prayer and fasting, and
moves on to other expressions of worship of God in the arc of ascent.
But, as we have seen, Bahá'u'lláh's arc of ascent differs from traditional
conceptions in having historical and social dimensions. This arc of
ascent is no longer a purely individualistic journey toward God through
solitary worship and withdrawal from people, work, and society.

At the beginning of the Kitáb-i-Aqdas, the concept of progressive
revelation is concisely reaffirmed: it is implicit in the discussion of recognition as a duty and as a perpetual, recurring phenomenon. It is only
through historical developments and successive Manifestations of God
that the spiritual journey (attainment to all good, to the "most sublime
station"—a phrase which may allude to the mystical stations) becomes
possible. Therefore, to progress along the arc of ascent necessarily
implies recognizing the Manifestation of God for this age, that is,
Bahá'u'lláh, and working toward the creation of the universal spiritual
outlook and global civilization delineated in the Aqdas, its Charter.
The supreme goal of this arc of ascent is the realization of a level of collective social development that Bahá'u'lláh characterizes as the "maturation of humanity." That would explain why the Kitáb-i-Aqdas
begins with the first stage of the human spiritual journey as individual
acts of worship and love of God, and ends with the signs of the collective maturation of humanity. The concept of spiritual journey
which we have seen outlined in Bahá'u'lláh's early mystical texts, with
its levels of unity (the unity of God, the unity of Manifestations, and
the unity of humankind), becomes literally the order of the Kitáb-i-
Aqdas. Clearly this order cannot be compared to any other classification scheme, but it does correspond to the "New Wondrous Order"
or "new World Order" (¶ 181) of Bahá'u'lláh.

It can also be argued that the overall order of the Kitáb-i-Aqdas in
a sense recapitulates the order of the stages of Bahá'u'lláh's revelation.
This is not surprising given the fact that the Kitáb-i-Aqdas is the
"Mother Book" containing the essence and totality of His message. If

we look at the historical sequence of Bahá'u'lláh's writings, we can distinguish three stages. In the first stage, His writings are characterized by a primarily theological and mystical message and tone. Works like the Ode of the Dove, the Hidden Words, the Four Valleys, and the Seven Valleys, which concern the spiritual nature of being and the human love relation with the Creator, are typical of this stage. In the second stage of His writings, Bahá'u'lláh emphasizes the principle of progressive revelation, with its historical approach to religion, revelation and spiritual truth, and the unity of all religions. The Kitáb-i-Íqán, and the Kitáb-i-Badí' are among the major examples of such expositions. In the last stage of Bahá'u'lláh's writings, He sets down in detail the social, spiritual, and administrative principles required to bring that vision into fruition in the world of social reality, with emphasis on the idea of the oneness of humankind. Bahá'u'lláh's various tablets to the leaders of the world and His tablets revealed after the Kitáb-i-Aqdas exemplify this last phase of His revelation. It is noteworthy that in one tablet Bahá'u'lláh refers to these same three stages by describing how the call of His Pen was raised among "mystics, then divines, and then kings."[48]

The chronology of the stages of Bahá'u'lláh's writings, the three metaphysical principles of unity, and the premises of His New World Order can be represented in this sequence as they correlate to the thematic order of the Aqdas:

Chronology of Writings	Unity	Terms	Order of Aqdas
1. Early/Middle Baghdad	1. of God	1. Order	1. Beginning
2. Late Baghdad/Edirne	2. of Manifestations	2. New	2. Middle
3. Late Edirne/'Akká	3. of humanity	3. World	3. End

The thematic development of the Kitáb-i-Aqdas begins with the unity of God and the purpose of human creation. Throughout, the book expresses the principle of progressive revelation by the act of abrogating former laws and revealing new ones, as well as discussion of the principle of covenant, including the unconditional authority of Bahá'u'lláh and the coming of another Manifestation after a thousand years. It ends with the supreme expression of the oneness of humanity in the signs of the coming of age of the human race. At the same time, throughout the whole of the Kitáb-i-Aqdas these ideas are reaffirmed in various ways.

CONSTITUTIVE PRINCIPLES OF THE KITÁB-I-AQDAS

Although the Kitáb-i-Aqdas does not follow a rigid order, if we read the Kitáb-i-Aqdas closely we can find organic, thematic connections among clusters of verses. Each cluster usually expresses a constitutive principle. Because these constitutive principles are interrelated, they repeat themselves and frequently shade into each other. But each time, the new laws or new expositions of previously stated laws are discussed as the embodiment of the corresponding principle. Here I will outline what I find to be the four constitutive principles of the Kitáb-i-Aqdas. The following chapter will examine the local order of the laws corresponding to those principles.

The four constitutive principles of the Kitáb-i-Aqdas, as I see them, are a kind of mysterious code of Bahá'u'lláh's revelation. Three of them are substantive, and one is epistemological/methodological. The three substantive principles of the Kitáb-i-Aqdas are the three substantive principles of His revelation as a whole.[49] To understand the nature of these principles we should begin with Bahá'u'lláh's own announcement of them on the first day of His public declaration in the Garden of Riḍván in 1863. In one of His tablets, Bahá'u'lláh recounts:

> On the first day of His arrival in the garden designated the Riḍván, the Ancient Beauty established Himself upon the Most Great Throne. Thereupon, the Tongue of Glory uttered three blessed verses. First, that in this Revelation the use of the sword is prohibited. Second, that whoso layeth a claim ere the expiration of a thousand years is assuredly in grievous error; by year, a complete year is intended and any interpretation of this matter is forbidden. And third, that the one true God, exalted be His Glory, at that very moment shed the splendours of all His Names upon the whole creation.[50]

These principles are affirmed, expounded, and institutionalized in the Kitáb-i-Aqdas.

(1) *The prohibition or removal of the "sword."* Obviously this is a prohibition on violence and killing, but it soon becomes clear that it should be understood in a much wider and more encompassing way that includes all forms of violence, coercion, oppression, and exploitation of human beings. As such, it implies a larger principle of the dignity and equality of all human beings and the effacing of whatever causes division between them. From the very beginning of His revelation in 1852 in the Síyáh <u>Ch</u>ál, Bahá'u'lláh had described His mission as a call for love, unity, equality, and fellowship among all human beings.

The principle of the removal of the sword represents a radical transformation of the concept of *nuṣrat*, meaning "assisting, proclaiming, serving the Cause of God and rendering it victorious." In Islam, *nuṣrat* was traditionally understood to include coercion, fighting, and war.[51] But Bahá'u'lláh creates an entirely new meaning for the term by rejecting holy war, forbidding the coercion of people to faith, and annulling the denial of rights to nonbelievers. He replaces those traditional meanings of *nuṣrat* with a concept of assisting the Cause of God that is based on nonviolence and communication, for example: "Assist ye the Lord of all creation with works of righteousness, and also through wisdom and utterance" (¶ 73). He prohibits the use of violence against others and repeatedly affirms that "it is better to be killed than kill."[52]

The doctrine of the sacredness and equal rights of all human beings and the call for global unity is the principle of the oneness of humankind, the supreme goal of Bahá'u'lláh's dispensation and primary emphasis of His writings. In Epistle to the Son of the Wolf, one of His last writings and one in which He Himself summarizes His entire revelation, Bahá'u'lláh cites numerous examples of statements made throughout His life that reflect the principle of the removal of the sword. The diversity of these statements illustrates the unity of the principle itself. The prohibition of killing, violence, and religious coercion; the promotion of love, unity, and fellowship among peoples; the call for peace among the nations; the condemnation of militarism and of the proliferation of arms; the assertion of the necessity for education and productive employment; the condemnation of sedition; the assertion of the need for religion and social justice—all these are presented by Bahá'u'lláh as systematic expressions of the same underlying principle of the removal of the sword. This text, represented in the following excerpt, gives us the best direct clue to the order of the Kitáb-i-Aqdas, and to the unity of the apparently diverse laws or ideas.

> One night, in a dream, these exalted words were heard on every side: "Verily, We shall render Thee victorious by Thyself and by Thy Pen...."
>
> And when this Wronged One went forth out of His prison, We journeyed ... to 'Iráq.... After Our arrival, We revealed ... Our verses, and sent them to various parts of the world. We exhorted all men, and particularly this people, through Our wise counsels and loving admonitions, and forbade them to engage in sedition, quarrels, disputes and conflict. As a result of this, and by the grace of God, waywardness and folly were changed into piety and understanding, and weapons converted into instruments of peace....
>
> We shall herewith cite a few passages from Tablets specifically revealed to this people....
>
> "O ye friends of God in His cities and His loved ones in His lands! This Wronged One enjoineth on you honesty and piety. Blessed the city that shineth by their light. Through them man is exalted, and the door of security is unlocked before the face of all creation...."
>
> And in another connection these words were revealed: "We enjoin the servants of God and His handmaidens to be pure and to fear God.... They that spread disorder in the land, and lay hands on the property of others, and enter a house without leave of its owner, We, verily, are clear of them, unless they repent and return unto God, the Ever-Forgiving, the Most Merciful."
>
> And in another connection: "O peoples of the earth! Haste ye to do the pleasure of God, and war ye valiantly, as it behooveth you to war, for the sake of proclaiming His resistless and immovable Cause. We have decreed that war shall be waged in the path of God with the armies of wisdom and utterance, and of a goodly character and praiseworthy deeds...."

And yet again in another connection: "Beware lest ye shed the blood of any one. Unsheathe the sword of your tongue from the scabbard of utterance, for therewith ye can conquer the citadels of men's hearts. We have abolished the law to wage holy war against each other. God's mercy hath, verily, encompassed all created things, if ye do but understand."...

And still again in another connection: "... The fruits of the tree of man have ever been and are goodly deeds and a praiseworthy character. Withhold not these fruits from the heedless. If they be accepted, your end is attained, and the purpose of life achieved. If not, leave them in their pastime of vain disputes. Strive, O people of God, that haply the hearts of the divers kindreds of the earth may, through the waters of your forbearance and loving-kindness, be cleansed and sanctified from animosity and hatred, and be made worthy and befitting recipients of the splendors of the Sun of Truth." ...

In the third Tajallí (effulgence) ... We have mentioned: "Arts, crafts and sciences uplift the world of being, and are conducive to its exaltation. Knowledge is as wings to man's life, and a ladder for his ascent. Its acquisition is incumbent upon everyone. The knowledge of such sciences, however, should be acquired as can profit the peoples of the earth, and not those which begin with words and end with words. Great indeed is the claim of scientists and craftsmen on the peoples of the world. Unto this beareth witness the Mother Book in this conspicuous station." ...

The first word which the Abhá Pen hath revealed and inscribed on the first leaf of Paradise is this: "Verily I say: The fear of God hath ever been a sure defense and a safe stronghold for all the peoples of the world...."

The second word We have recorded on the second leaf of Paradise is the following: "The Pen of the Divine Expounder exhorteth, at this moment, the manifestations of authority and the sources of power, namely the kings and rulers of the earth—may God assist them—and enjoineth them to uphold the cause of religion, and to cleave unto it. Religion is, verily, the chief instrument for the establishment of order in the world, and of tranquillity amongst its peoples...."

The third word we have recorded on the third leaf of Paradise is this: "O son of man! If thine eyes be turned towards mercy, forsake the things that profit thee, and cleave unto that which will profit mankind. And if thine eyes be turned towards justice, choose thou for thy neighbor that which thou choosest for thyself. Humility exalteth man to the heaven of glory and power, whilst pride abaseth him to the depths of wretchedness and degradation....

We pray God—exalted be His glory—and cherish the hope that He may graciously assist the manifestations of affluence and power and the daysprings of sovereignty and glory, the kings of the earth—may God aid them through His strengthening grace—to establish the Lesser Peace.... It is incumbent upon the Sovereigns of the world—may God assist them—unitedly to hold fast unto this Peace, which is the chief instrument for the protection of all mankind.... It is their duty to convene an all-inclusive assembly, which either they themselves or their ministers will attend, and to enforce whatever measures are required to establish unity and concord amongst men. They must put away the weapons of war, and turn to the instruments of universal reconstruction. Should one king rise up against another, all the other kings must arise to deter him. Arms and armaments will, then, be no more needed beyond that which is necessary to insure the internal security of their respective countries. If they attain unto this all-surpassing blessing, the people of each nation will pursue, with tranquillity and contentment, their own occupations, and the groanings and lamentations of most men would be silenced....

... By the righteousness of God! Justice is a powerful force. It is, above all else, the conqueror of the citadels of the hearts and souls of men, and the revealer of the secrets of the world of being, and the standard-bearer of love and bounty....

... This Wronged One hath never had, nor hath He now any desire for leadership. Mine aim hath ever been, and still is, to suppress whatever is the cause of contention amidst the peoples of the earth, and of separation amongst the nations, so that all men may be sanctified from every earthly attachment, and be set free to occupy themselves with their own interests....

Briefly, this Wronged One hath, in the face of all that hath befallen Him at their hands, and all that hath been said of Him, endured patiently, and held His peace, inasmuch as it is Our purpose, through the loving providence of God—exalted be His glory—and His surpassing mercy, to abolish, through the force of Our utterance, all disputes, war, and bloodshed, from the face of the earth. (*Epistle* 21–34)

Here issues that may seem to be unconnected—from the fear of God to collective security—are presented by Bahá'u'lláh as embodiments of His principle of the removal of the sword and as part of assisting the Cause of God. In fact, any perceptive sociological analysis can point out the organic connection among these issues in relation to peace and unity: they are all conditions of creating a just society and advancing order, unity, and peace—replacing force and coercion with construction and justice at all levels of human relations and institutions. These same issues mentioned in the passage above (as well as many others) are also found in the Kitáb-i-Aqdas, where, for instance, Bahá'u'lláh abolishes slavery because of the simultaneous nothingness of all humans relative to God and their sacredness as mirrors of divine attributes. He enjoins His followers to courtesy in all human relations and to consort with all peoples in a spirit of loving-kindness and fellowship. He constantly emphasizes that He intends the elevation of the human station and does not wish to see any human being degraded or debased in front of any other.

(2) *The principle of covenant.* The second principle of Bahá'u'lláh's revelation, and a constitutive principle of the Kitáb-i-Aqdas, is the falsehood of any claim to revelation prior to one thousand years. This of course is the principle of covenant. It may seem strange that Bahá'u'lláh should emphasize this aspect of the covenant on the first day of His revelation, following the principle of the removal of the sword. But in fact, these two principles address different sides of the same issue. The first principle is His vision of unity, love, and the oneness of humankind as the supreme aim of His revelation. The second principle supplies the means to maintain the unity and integrity of His Faith after His ascension and to prevent schism, sectarianism, and religious strife. The two are linked together in 'Abdu'l-Bahá's statement: "It is indubitably clear that the pivot of the oneness of mankind is nothing else but the power of the Covenant."[53]

The categorical rejection of any claim to revelation before the expiration of a thousand years demarcates the minimum period of time during which Bahá'u'lláh's dispensation will be valid and His laws may not be abrogated. This matter not only concerns His covenant with the Manifestation to come, but it is directly relevant to the covenant of the Báb with regard to Bahá'u'lláh, as well as the covenant of Bahá'u'lláh with regard to His successor after His ascension. The statement that there will be no new Manifestation before a thousand years signifies the fulfillment of the Báb's covenant: it establishes that the Promised One of the Bayán has appeared in Bahá'u'lláh's own person and no one should accept any other claim to revelation for a considerable time.[54]

The same statement, however, also concerns Bahá'u'lláh's covenant with regard to His own successors, and therefore it has implications for the station and authority of 'Abdu'l-Bahá, Shoghi Effendi, and the Universal House of Justice. This becomes much clearer when we look at the context of the statement as reinforced in many of Bahá'u'lláh's tablets including the Kitáb-i-Badí' and the Kitáb-i-Aqdas. Both those texts show that a primary intention of Bahá'u'lláh in establishing this principle was to safeguard the station of 'Abdu'l-Bahá against the covenant-breakers after Bahá'u'lláh's passing. More specifically, the statement directly blocks the claims of His son Muhammad-'Alí.

In the Kitáb-i-Badí', Bahá'u'lláh introduces this topic with a plea for virtue, holiness, assistance, unity, and righteous conduct, including what might be called the virtue of humility in interpretation:

> We fain would hope that, by the grace of God, in this Spiritual Springtime all may attire themselves with the robe of human virtues and replace outmoded and tattered clothes with the new raiment of holiness. May all arise to promote the Cause of God with the utmost power and to the extent of their ability. The People of Bahá ought to be as wings for one another for all to soar in this spiritual atmosphere and in the holy and luminous space, speak naught save what hath been ordained by God, walk not except in the path of His good pleasure, utter not a word unless by the leave of God, and be not content with their own understanding of the meanings of the words of God, inasmuch as none but God knoweth the true meaning of His words.[55]

He then strongly condemns the claim made by persons in Qazvín who had attributed the station of Manifestation of God to Muhammad-'Alí and says: "Such utterances are unpleasing to God for they provoke dissension and disunity in the Cause of God.... Speak of that which we have commanded you and not of the dictates of your evil passions and corrupt desires."[56]

During the Edirne period, the individuals in question had received letters from Muḥammad-'Alí in which he used extremely exalted adjectives for himself and claimed to reveal verses of God, similar to the way Bahá'u'lláh did. Some of these persons had interpreted certain statements of Bahá'u'lláh, including the phrase "Valley of Nabíl," as referring to Muḥammad-'Alí. Since "Nabíl" is numerically equal to "Muḥammad," they saw this as signifying that Muḥammad-'Alí would be the next Manifestation of God, Bahá'u'lláh's successor and co-equal.

One reason for this misinterpretation was that when Muḥammad-'Alí was a child (around 1859), Bahá'u'lláh had caused him to speak the verses of God. Bahá'u'lláh explains that this incident demonstrated no particular authority for Muḥammad-'Alí; instead, it demonstrated Bahá'u'lláh's own authority as the Manifestation of God: "'Verily We endowed him with eloquent speech when he was six years old as a testimony to this Great, this Most Mighty Announcement. God gave him the power of utterance as a proof for the truth of His Cause.' Those who have spoken such words are unaware of the greatness of this Cause. For, verily, should He wish to enable all things to speak forth, He assuredly is empowered to do so, and He is potent over all things."[57]

It is in response to this controversy that Bahá'u'lláh rejects those interpretations, rejects any particular station for Muḥammad-'Alí, emphasizes that Muḥammad-'Alí has no authority because there will be no revelation before the expiration of a thousand years, and prohibits reliance on the interpretations of the individual believers. In the same part of the Kitáb-i-Badí', He writes:

> Ere the lapse of one thousand, no one will appear save the One Who hath been made manifest. Thus the decree was revealed at the beginning of this Revelation, were ye of them that comprehend. Soon will God raise up Guides for this Cause Who speak forth as bidden by Him, turn at all times towards Him, and move not save by His leave…. Whoso putteth forth a claim ere the expiration of one

thousand hath lied against God, for such a claim would subvert the
authority of the Cause, and thus the Temple of His Primal Will
would not mount the Throne of Majesty and Grandeur. In the
beginning of this Supreme Revelation verses were sent down
concerning this matter, some of which are revealed in certain
Tablets. Look into them that ye may become steadfast in the Cause
and be of those who repent. Likewise, it is evident that by the Valley
of Nabíl, mentioned in the Tablets, is always intended this Most
Great Revelation. This valley is naught but that sacred land which
is created above the heavens, and none is able to enter it save the
people of Bahá. By God, they are the people of the valley of Nabíl,
the valley of grandeur, the valley of independence, and the valley of
splendour.... Others do not abide in that valley, and are lost in the
deserts of evil passion and corrupt desire.... Be united in such wise
that none may perceive the loathsome smell of disunity among you.
By reason of your unity the Cause of God shall be victorious among
the people.... We hope that all may gather round the all-embracing
Word of God, engage in His praise and glorification, manifest
complete detachment, and be ablaze with the fire of divine love in
such wise as to enkindle all the people and cause them to turn to
God. Whatever is not understood from the Holy Writings should be
referred to the Wellspring of Divine Revelation and its Source. The
purpose is to prevent disunity among His friends concerning the
meaning of the Words of God, and make them realize that the
Words of God are all revealed from a Single Source, and all return
unto Him.[58]

In another tablet revealed in response to that controversy, Bahá'-
u'lláh rejects Muḥammad-'Alí's claim to revelation, states that he "is
but one of My servants.... Should he for a moment pass out from
under the shadow of the Cause, he surely shall be brought to naught,"
and mentions the extraordinary station of one of His sons.[59] Later, in
His Book of the Covenant, He would state that this high station
belongs to 'Abdu'l-Bahá, that Muḥammad-'Alí is subordinate to him,
and that all must turn toward 'Abdu'l-Bahá.[60]

The principle of covenant embraces many topics including the
authority and succession after Bahá'u'lláh's passing, the interpretation
of scripture, the administrative order of Bahá'u'lláh, the institution of
the Universal House of Justice, and its final authority in all matters of

conflict and disagreement among Bahá'u'lláh's followers. Diverse expressions of this principle repeatedly appear as clusters of verses in the Kitáb-i-Aqdas.

(3) *The universal revelation.* The third principle is the revelation of all the names and attributes of God upon all beings on the first day of Riḍván. The complexity of meanings contained within this principle is beyond our present understanding. However, we can catch glimpses of this mysterious idea. Bahá'u'lláh has written that "This is the Day, O my Lord, which Thou didst announce unto all mankind as the Day whereon Thou wouldst reveal Thy Self, and shed Thy radiance, and shine brightly over all Thy creatures."[61] Speaking of the First Day of Riḍván, He has said: "Rejoice with exceeding gladness, O people of Bahá, as ye call to remembrance the Day of supreme felicity, the Day whereon the Tongue of the Ancient of Days hath spoken, as He departed from His House, proceeding to the Spot from which He shed upon the whole of creation the splendors of His name, the All-Merciful" (*Gleanings* 35). And elsewhere He explains that

> It is evident that every age in which a Manifestation of God hath lived is divinely ordained, and may, in a sense, be characterized as God's appointed Day. This Day, however, is unique, and is to be distinguished from those that have preceded it.... The Prophetic Cycle hath, verily, ended. The Eternal Truth is now come. He hath lifted up the Ensign of Power, and is now shedding upon the world the unclouded splendor of His Revelation. (*Gleanings* 60).

The implications of this all-embracing revelation can be glimpsed in this passage:

> Forget the world of creation, O Pen, and turn thou towards the face of thy Lord, the Lord of all names. Adorn, then, the world with the ornament of the favors of thy Lord, the King of everlasting days. For We perceive the fragrance of the Day whereon He Who is the Desire of all nations hath shed upon the kingdoms of the unseen and of the seen the splendor of the light of His most excellent names, and enveloped them with the radiance of the luminaries of His most gracious favors—favors which none can reckon except Him, Who is the omnipotent Protector of the entire creation.

Look not upon the creatures of God except with the eye of kindliness and of mercy, for Our loving providence hath pervaded all created things, and Our grace encompassed the earth and the heavens. (*Gleanings* 32–33)

The first implication of this principle is the significance of the present age as a result of such a universal revelation. Although each Manifestation's Day is in one sense the "Day of God," so that the "wonders of His boundless grace" have always "pervaded the whole of creation" (*Gleanings* 62), Bahá'u'lláh declares that in this Day, God has revealed Himself to all beings through a supreme and all-embracing revelation by which all created things have become endued with an unprecedented capacity.

While all creatures are recipients of this universal revelation, it is particularly bestowed upon humanity: through it all human beings have been recreated and all have become mirrors of divine attributes in qualitatively new ways. While humans, who are created in the "image" of God, have always been mirrors of God in the essence of their beings, the reality of social and cultural conditions prevented the full realization of that sacred beauty in the form of social and spiritual institutions. But with the first day of Riḍván all that has changed. Now, the Kitáb-i-Aqdas declares, all must be looked upon as the manifestations of the divine attributes and mirrors of God. The age of exploitation and domination of humans by one another is over. The world is destined to become the mirror of the divine kingdom. The metaphor of *Riḍván* is particularly significant here: Riḍván is simultaneously the name of the Garden of Paradise and the state of divine pleasure. In other words, human culture is to become transformed into a paradise through Bahá'u'lláh's revelation in the Riḍván Garden.

A further implication of the third principle is the unity and equality of humankind, a principle intended to become institutionalized in a united, egalitarian world order, of which democratic and consultative institutions are natural expressions. Like the removal of the sword and the covenant, the principle of universal revelation is directly related to the oneness of humankind.

Another implication of the universal revelation of all the names and attributes of God is that all humans should become manifestations of beauty and purity. This aesthetic element, a crucial idea in the Kitáb-i-Aqdas, is expressed through the concept of "refinement." The original term, *liṭáfat*, means a combination of purity, cleanliness, beauty, grace, art, and aesthetic orientation. It is a complex concept integrating the moral and the physical through the mediation of beauty. The world is to become the mirror of heaven, a work of art, a symbol and reflection of the divine presence, the Supreme Beauty. "Refinement" is one of the most frequent terms in the Kitáb-i-Aqdas, and many of the laws of the Kitáb-i-Aqdas systematically reflect this principle.

The mediating role of aesthetics and art between the material and the spiritual is often mentioned in the Bahá'í writings. 'Abdu'l-Bahá has used the same term in speaking of both physical cleanliness and music, saying that although they are physical and material, they exert great influence in the spiritual domain.[62] In other words, purification and beautification are to be simultaneously material and spiritual, physical and moral. The function of art and of refinement is to unite the physical with the spiritual and to make the kingdom of creation the mirror of the kingdom of God.

Schiller, in his book *On the Aesthetic Education of Mankind*, expresses a similar perspective. For him, aesthetic education was the solution to the dilemma of society. While the philosophers of the Enlightenment tried to create altruistic public morality by emphasizing the freedom of utilitarian, rational, and self-interested individuals, Schiller argued that the movement from self-interest to public interest is not automatic. It requires a mediation, and this mediation is aesthetic cultivation and education. According to Schiller, aesthetic sensibility emphasizes disinterested interest in beauty and prepares individuals for selfless public morality.[63] While for Schiller aesthetic cultivation is the main means of social and cultural betterment, for Bahá'u'lláh it is one important means which should be used in harmony with spiritual, moral, and rational cultivation, combined with the creation of suitable social institutions.

A further implication of the principle of the universal revelation is a new attitude toward nature—one of reverence, respect, protection, and harmony. Already we can discern Bahá'u'lláh's concept of true modernity and true freedom in His third principle. The release of this new creative power into the world of creation will vitalize and advance the realm of science, material culture, and instrumental rationalization. But it also implies the moral imperative of a new attitude that considers all beings as sacred and as mirrors of God. Consequently, it calls for both instrumental and moral types of development and rationalization, harmonizing an advancing civilization with a fragile and sacred nature. Development, for Bahá'u'lláh, is defined not just by an increase in physical productivity but also by improvement in the moral realm. We will see later that His concept of the maturation of humanity is part of the same perspective.

The third principle is also an expression of the idea of the unveiling of the "Most Great Name of God" on the first day of Riḍván. Many Islamic traditions point to "Bahá" as the Most Great Name of God which contains and reveals all other names.[64] The first day of Riḍván was the occasion on which Bahá'u'lláh revealed Himself through His name "Bahá." There is a close connection between the meanings of "Bahá"—including light, beauty, and grandeur—and the principle of refinement.

(4) *The principle of heart*. In addition to the three principles that were declared on the first day of Riḍván, the fourth is Bahá'u'lláh's epistemological and methodological principle, which I have referred to as the principle of heart. This principle is actually present in the first, namely, the removal of the sword. Both the removal of the sword and the principle of heart can be seen in Bahá'u'lláh's description of His experience of revelation in the Síyáh-Chál: "One night, in a dream, these exalted words were heard on every side: 'Verily, We shall render Thee victorious by Thyself and by Thy Pen....'" In addition to abrogating the sword, this is implicitly a statement about the evidence and standard of the recognition of the Manifestation of God—which as we have seen is the Manifestation ("Thyself") and His words ("Thy Pen").

Although the principle of heart has already been discussed in connection with the Kitáb-i-Íqán and the Kitáb-i-Badí', it is necessary to approach it here in a slightly different way. All the writings of Bahá'u'lláh contain various forms of this foundational and epistemological principle, which is the core of the Kitáb-i-Aqdas's self-referential character and of Bahá'u'lláh's apologia.

Although a few of His works, such as the Kitáb-i-Íqán and Kitáb-i-Badí', are directly in the form of apologia, almost all Bahá'u'lláh's writings contain a declaration and defense of the authority of the text and its revealer. This is particularly true of the Kitáb-i-Aqdas, a significant part of which is addressed to the Bábí leaders, proclaiming that Bahá'u'lláh is the Promised One of the Bayán, as well as to the religious leaders and divines, demonstrating the authority of the Book, and to the kings and rulers of the world, summoning them to recognize His authority. These addresses are more explicit in the second half of the Kitáb-i-Aqdas, but the same principle is found throughout the text. He asserts that His words are the Word of God, which is the source of all authority, truth, and proof, and that the truth of the propositions asserted in His texts should be understood primarily in terms of the authority of their revealer, namely, God.

An important purpose of the identification of the Silent Book and the Speaking Book, as frequently found in the Kitáb-i-Aqdas and other writings, concerns the station of the Manifestation and the way His text is to be understood. To say that Bahá'u'lláh is the Speaking Book is to say that the true meaning of the text is the Manifestation Himself, and that the true meanings are only known to Him and to those whom He authorizes. Unlike the work of a "genius," the Manifestation is not an unconscious vehicle for a universal truth unknown to the author himself.[65] That is why the philosophical hermeneutics of Gadamer and the postmodernists, which assert the autonomy of the text from the author, do not apply to the words of the Manifestations.[66] In Epistle to the Son of the Wolf Bahá'u'lláh quotes an Islamic tradition, "'Give heed unto the Bayán (Exposition) and the Ma'ání (Significances),'" which is explained: "'As to the Bayán, it consisteth in thy recognition of God—glorified be He—as the One Who hath no equal, and in thy adoration of Him, and in thy refusal to join partners with Him. As to the Ma'ání, We are its meaning, and its side, and its hand, and its tongue, and its cause, and its command, and its knowledge, and its right.'" (*Epistle* 113).[67]

In this hermeneutics, the authentic meanings of the Sacred Text are determined by the conscious intention of its Author. No other reader of the text can produce a meaning which is true yet which was not intended by the Author. Obviously, this is not so with regard to ordinary texts. The work of a genius often contains insights and meanings that are not known to the author himself, and which can be discovered or created by insightful readers. Bahá'u'lláh, however, affirms that His words should not be approached like any other text.

The station of the Manifestation of God as the Word of God also implies the unconstrained authority of the Manifestation over the Silent Book, the revealed Scripture, because the Scripture itself derives its authority from the Will and Word of God. For this reason neither the Silent Book nor limited human understandings of that text can be used to judge the claim of the new Manifestation; nor can the Word of God be judged in terms of the linguistic and grammatical rules current among the people. The evidence and standard that is accessible to all and is not conditioned on social position, esoteric knowledge, or linguistic expertise is, as we have seen, His being and His verses. In that immediate, direct, and total encounter with the Manifestation—or, in His absence, with His words—all human beings can recognize the truth—provided they possess a pure heart purged of all presuppositions and bias. This state of heart is possessed by the one who sees with the eye of God Himself—through the evidence that God decrees—as well as the eye of the heart, which is the "throne of God"; and one's own eyes, that is, with justice and fairness.

However, because no one can claim complete and perfect knowledge of the meanings contained in the revealed Word, all must turn to the Manifestation and the covenant of interpretive authority He has established. This fourth constitutive principle of the Kitáb-i-Aqdas is simultaneously the principle of justice, as mentioned in the third Arabic Hidden Word; the principle of the purification of the heart, mentioned in all Bahá'u'lláh's writings; the principle of beholding

God through God's eyes; the principle of the verses as sole evidence of manifestationhood; the principle of covenant; the democratic principle; the principle of rejection of clerical authority; and the principle of steadfastness.

In many of His writings Bahá'u'lláh emphasizes steadfastness as a concept of such importance that, as He writes, "The first and foremost duty prescribed unto men, next to the recognition of Him Who is the Eternal Truth, is the duty of steadfastness in His Cause" (*Gleanings* 290). At the beginning of the Kitáb-i-Aqdas, however, we find no direct mention of steadfastness. But steadfastness can be seen as the same as the recognition of the Manifestation of God; it refers to the continuity of that recognition and certitude, not merely commitment but commitment maintained. This principle is also organically connected to other concepts which have already been mentioned; in one of His tablets Bahá'u'lláh discloses that the supreme means of attaining steadfastness is the same as gazing upon God with the eye of God or the eye of the heart, or one's own eye.[68] The core of this idea is the warning against limiting God's absolute authority and His decrees by applying human standards and presuppositions, which is also the principle of the Most Great Infallibility of the Manifestations of God.

The four constitutive principles of the Kitáb-i-Aqdas all center around the idea of the oneness of humankind; at the same time, each principle emphasizes a distinct aspect of Bahá'u'lláh's message. The removal of the sword concerns the relation of humans to one another (the unity of humankind). The principle of covenant details the relation between humans and the institutions and guidance that will ensure that unity. The principle of universal revelation supplies the metaphysical justification for the principle of unity and outlines the relation of humans to nature and culture. Finally, the principle of heart elaborates the relation of humans to God and His Manifestations. Little wonder, then, that these principles together form the central message of the Mother Book of Bahá'u'lláh's dispensation.

Chapter 8

FROM THE ORDER OF THE BOOK
TO THE NEW ORDER

I HAVE SUGGESTED that the four principles that give global thematic
structure and coherence to the Kitáb-i-Aqdas are (1) the removal of
the sword, (2) the principle of covenant, (3) the universal revelation,
and (4) the principle of heart. In this chapter I will examine some ways
in which those principles can be seen to be expressed in the Most Holy
Book in related groupings of verses, with a set of consecutive laws usually expressing the same principle. No attempt is made here to present
a definitive analysis of the order of the Kitáb-i-Aqdas. Instead it is
simply an initial and tentative attempt to explore some of the conceptual relations between the verses that can be discerned when the
text is approached in this way, that is, on the premise that it is an intentional and coherent discourse whose order is defined by its own logic
and its own categories. The final section of the chapter investigates the
relation between the order of the text and Bahá'u'lláh's New World
Order through a discussion of the illuminating interaction of statements in the Kitáb-i-Aqdas and the Persian Bayán.

VERSES 1 THROUGH 34

The Twin and Inseparable Duties

At the beginning of the Kitáb-i-Aqdas, before ordaining any law,
Bahá'u'lláh sets forth the metaphysical principles of His revelation, the
location of laws in the definition of faith, and the basic principles on
which order and society are based. He begins with the recognition of
the Manifestation as the primal duty incumbent upon human beings,
a recognition that must be accompanied by "observance of every ordinance" He has set down (¶ 1). In this concise and clear statement,
Bahá'u'lláh resolves the controversy between different schools of reli-

gious thought concerning the nature of faith in God and the relationship of faith, works or law, and salvation. For some schools of thought,
being an authentic Muslim, Christian, or follower of any other religion has been defined as witnessing through the heart (that is, through
the act of inner recognition and faith). For others it has been defined
as witnessing through the tongue, that is, by public utterance of belief.
For yet others, it has been defined as witnessing through the hands and
feet (*arkán*), that is, by works and deeds in accordance with the laws
and teachings. Some have posited a combination of these criteria.[1]

In emphasizing the primacy of recognition, Bahá'u'lláh affirms the
"heart"—inner recognition and faith—but He immediately makes
this inseparable from the works of "hands and feet"—action in accordance with the laws. At the same time, He stresses the significance of
assisting the Cause of God through utterance and the pen, in the form
of the promotion and teaching of the Cause of God. Together, these
imply witnessing through one's entire being. As He writes in another
tablet, it is the duty of human beings to harmonize the essence and the
appearance, and to arise to elevate the station of humankind.[2]

The inseparability of the twin duties is itself a fundamental principle, a fact which is sometimes ignored by interpreting the opening
passage of the Kitáb-i-Aqdas in ways that lessen or negate the significance either of recognizing the Manifestation or obeying His law.
The latter type of interpretation was discussed in Chapter 7 in connection with the concept of the law as "choice wine." If what is
revealed in the Aqdas is "wine," that argument says, then the laws of
the Aqdas do not have binding character. In some attempts to analyze
Bahá'u'lláh's teachings in terms of received theological categories,
especially those of postmodernist pluralism, the importance of recognition also becomes reduced to an insignificant idea. If all revelations
are equally valid, that argument says, recognition of any Manifestation
of God is sufficient. However, because that same argument implicitly
makes it acceptable to reject some Manifestations of God, it directly
contradicts Bahá'u'lláh's principle of the *unity* of all the revelations.

Furthermore, if such deductions were accurate, one might wonder why Bahá'u'lláh begins His Most Holy Book with an explicit

statement of the twin duties of recognition of the Manifestation and action in accordance with His command. Aside from the completely explicit character of the statement in the Aqdas, all the Bahá'í writings appear to give support to the reading of the statement of the Kitáb-i-Aqdas that takes it as meaning what it says rather than the opposite. As we have seen, it is precisely because of both the validity as well as the unity of all religions that recognition of the new Manifestation is a central principle of Bahá'í metaphysics and theology and is the foundation of Bahá'u'lláh's revelation.

The principle that the acceptability of all beliefs and the goodness of all actions are dependent on the recognition of the Manifestation of God is also established in all the writings of the Báb. In one of the first and foundational statements of the Persian Bayán, the Báb stipulates that even the profession of the unity of God—the most important article of faith in the Qur'án—is valid only if one recognizes the Báb and, after the Báb, Him Whom God shall make manifest, but that without such recognition the profession of faith itself is null and void.[3]

These statements are based on the four theological premises that (1) all the Manifestations are the return of one another; (2) the revelation of the Word of God is progressive and is unfolded to humanity in greater measure through successive revelations because of the development of human capabilities to receive it; (3) the purpose and fruit of each dispensation is the next revelation; and (4) with the inception of a new divine revelation, the eternal covenant is renewed: all, whether believers or unbelievers, become equal, and acceptance or rejection of that covenant through the recognition or repudiation of the new Manifestation becomes the criterion of belief and disbelief in God.[4] The beginning of the Kitáb-i-Aqdas is based on the same premises.

The Meaning of 'Irfán

It should also be noted that the term "recognition" ('irfán) of the Manifestation, as used at the beginning of the Aqdas, is not a generalized mystical knowledge that has no direct or necessary connection to the recognition of the new Manifestation of God. Aside from the fact that the entirety of the writings of the Báb and Bahá'u'lláh testify to the impossibility of any knowledge of God without the mediation of the Manifestation of God, Bahá'u'lláh has directly addressed this specific issue. In one of His tablets, He contrasts true *'irfán* to superficial and nominal (*lafẓíyyih*) *'irfán*: the latter is the idea of *'irfán* current among the mystics, while the former is the recognition of Bahá'u'lláh and devotion to His Cause. He explains that all mystical forms of *'irfán* are acceptable provided they are accompanied by the recognition of Bahá'u'lláh in this age, while none are acceptable without it.[5]

Shoghi Effendi's translation of *'irfán* as "recognition" implies two principles inherent in Bahá'u'lláh's theology: first, human mystical knowledge of the Unknowable Essence is impossible and it is only the revelation of God in the realm of the Manifestations which is the object of human knowledge or experience. Therefore, the first duty of human beings is to discover and acknowledge the station of the new Manifestation of God. Second, this spiritual knowledge is an act of recognition, a remembrance of God, a recollection of the primordial day in which God entered into a covenant with His creation,[6] a return to the true human habitation in the realm of infinity, and the reaffirmation of authentic human nature, which is nothing but the reflection of divine attributes and knowledge.

These issues are also discussed in a tablet addressed to Abu'l-Faḍá'il, who asked Bahá'u'lláh to answer some puzzling intellectual questions posed by the Zoroastrian leader Mánikjí Ṣáḥib, including whether one religion is superior to others and whether all should accept the same religion or whether faith in any religion is equally sufficient and acceptable. In His answer, Bahá'u'lláh affirms the validity of all the revelations while emphasizing the categorical and binding character of recognition of the new Manifestation. He states the following principles: (1) references to the superiority of the Sacred Scriptures apply to the relation of those Scriptures to the ones before them. In other words, the recognition of the new Scripture and the new revelation is imperative and necessary; (2) the unity of all the religions and all the Manifestations of God means that one must recognize all of them, and that turning away from the new Manifestation is turning away from them all; (3) paradise is indeed the condition of recognizing the Manifestation for the age; (4) whenever a Manifestation appears, all must recognize Him, turn toward Him, and observe His new laws and ordinances.[7]

The same theme is emphasized in most powerful terms in the Kitáb-i-Aqdas itself, where Bahá'u'lláh writes:

> Let none, in this Day, hold fast to aught save that which hath been manifested in this Revelation. Such is the decree of God, aforetime and hereafter—a decree wherewith the Scriptures of the Messengers of old have been adorned. Such is the admonition of the Lord, aforetime and hereafter—an admonition wherewith the preamble to the Book of Life hath been embellished, did ye but perceive it. Such is the commandment of the Lord, aforetime and hereafter. (¶ 138)

In this passage Bahá'u'lláh also makes repeated reference to the fact that the authority of the latest revelation is a foundational premise of all of the Sacred Scriptures of the past and is the basis of the primordial covenant between God and humanity.

The fact that Bahá'u'lláh's concept of the recognition ('*irfán*) of the Manifestation should not be reduced to the Sufi conception of the term (as hidden, inner or "gnostic" knowledge) is obvious from many of the statements of Bahá'u'lláh Himself, which warn against such reduction:

> Say! O thou who art occupied with idle imaginings! Verily the hidden and the hidden of the hidden, and the hidden that God hath infinitely sanctified above both the hidden and the manifest, all circle around this Manifest One Who doth proclaim in the midmost heart of the world this sovereign truth: Verily, the Most Great Name, the Lord of all nations, and the Ancient King hath been made manifest.... Fear ye God O people and obey not the fancies of those who follow their evil desires and who are engaged in plots with malicious devices in the kingdom of creation.[8]

A similar statement in Tajallíyát (Effulgences) leaves no doubt about the meaning of recognition or action in the first verse of the Kitáb-i-Aqdas: "The first Tajallí" or effulgence, Bahá'u'lláh writes, "is the knowledge of God," which "can in no wise be attained save by recognizing Him Who is the Bearer of the Most Great Name. He is, in truth, the Speaker on Sinai Who is now seated upon the throne of Revelation...." He goes on to state that "Attainment unto the Divine Presence can be realized solely by attaining His presence" and that "True belief in God and recognition of Him cannot be complete save by acceptance of that which He hath revealed and by observance of whatsoever hath been decreed by Him and set down in the Book by the Pen of Glory" (*Tablets* 50).

In the Kitáb-i-Aqdas, following the statement of the twin duties, Bahá'u'lláh speaks of the significance, necessity, and function of laws for the individual and society. He describes the divine precepts as the "highest means for the maintenance of order in the world and the security of its peoples" (¶ 2). He adds that observance of His laws is an organic and inseparable aspect of the divine covenant and warns against neglecting the laws by following passion and desire. Bahá'-u'lláh uses the metaphor of the choice wine to emphasize that instead of being constraints, obstacles to love, and barriers to union with God, the laws are the means of liberation, spiritual growth, and union with the Beloved. The traditional contradiction between law and mystical love is resolved; the primary motivation for observing His laws should be "the love of My beauty" (¶ 4). In the same verse, He also emphasizes that adherence to His laws is a prime means of promoting His Cause and assisting God.

After this concise summary of the fundamentals of Bahá'í metaphysics and social theory, Bahá'u'lláh begins to set down the laws. The harmony of faith in God and observance of His commands is realized in the act of worship which praises the glory of God. Since obligatory prayer and fasting are the "sun and the moon" (*Kitáb-i-Íqán* 38–39) of the heaven of revelation, they are the first laws to be set down as acts of worship. But in reality, these acts of worship are the means of remembrance of God through His Manifestation. Consequently, both the direction toward which one turns to recite the obligatory prayer (the *qiblih*), as well as the number of units of the prayer itself, are symbols of Bahá'u'lláh. The number of prayer units is nine, equal to "Bahá." While Bahá'u'lláh later replaced that nine-unit obligatory prayer with the more convenient prayer in three options, the basic content of the prayer remains the same: it is an affirmation of Bahá as the Manifestation of God.

At the end of the section on obligatory prayer, Bahá'u'lláh reminds the reader that this is the Word of God, that it is the supreme favor and bounty of God, that He Himself, as the Manifestation of God, constitutes the ultimate limit of all human understanding, remembrance, and prayer. He emphasizes that He is the "key" to the hidden "Treasure," and the "Source of Revelation." Bahá'u'lláh continues to describe His exalted station by defining Himself as the "fixed Decree through which every irrevocable decree hath been established" (¶ 15). Here He is also alluding to the Báb's prophecy in which Imám Ḥusayn is identified as the "fixed Decree" and representative of the Most Great Name.[9]

The period of fasting also becomes a reference to the Most Great Name of God. The days of fasting are assigned to a location between the Days of God (Ayyám-i-Há or Intercalary Days), representing the Manifestation of God, and the first day of the new year, Naw-Rúz. As is explained later (in verse 111), Naw-Rúz is the day of Bahá. In the Persian Bayán the Báb had designated the first day of the year as the day of the Promised One of the Bayán, calling it the day of Bahá in the month of Bahá.[10] Fasting, then, begins with Bahá (the Days of Há) and ends with Bahá, and it takes place in nineteen days—a symbol of the period of the preparation of humanity for the universal revelation at Riḍván. In fact, Bahá'u'lláh's law of fasting also may be seen as a symbolic reenactment of the cosmic stages of spiritual creation in His dispensation. The days of God (Ayyám-i-Há) can represent the revelation of the Báb because the word *Báb* is numerically equal to five, which is also the value of the letter *há'*. The days of fasting represent the nineteen years of the period of preparation, which is followed by the revelation of Bahá'u'lláh on the day of Bahá.

At this point in the Kitáb-i-Aqdas, it may seem that the order of the text has been disrupted because the discussion of fasting is followed by the ordinance of the daily recitation of the Most Great Name (Alláh-u-Abhá), the prohibition of murder, adultery, backbiting, and calumny, and then a lengthy exposition of the law of inheritance. Subsequent laws relate to the House of Justice, the construction of houses of worship throughout the lands, pilgrimage to the Sacred House, engaging in occupations, and the prohibition of the kissing of hands and confession of sins.

Instead of assuming that this is a random listing of unrelated laws, it may be seen that these laws have meaningful connections, and it is the perception of a lack of coherence that is deceptive. The daily remembrance and recitation of the Most Great Name is directly related to the practice of worship, with additional emphases. First, in this dispensation the recognition and remembrance of God are conditioned on the recognition and remembrance of Bahá'u'lláh, Who is the Most Great Name of God. Second, this act of worship must be carried out with a pure motivation, for the sake of God.

One of the multiple symbolic meanings of the number ninety-five in the writings of the Báb is a meaning that concerns the motivation with which the commandments of God are to be observed. As the Báb writes in the Persian Bayán, ninety-five stands for the word *lillah* (which is numerically equivalent to ninety-five), which means "for God." The Báb explains that His purpose in establishing a maximum dowry of ninety-five *mithqáls* is to focus the attention upon that which is the basis of the legitimacy of marriage, which is none other than the word *lillah*, so that in the day of the revelation of Him Whom God shall make manifest, the people will not turn away from Him;[11] "For God" is only realized when action is for the sake of the new Manifestation of God. Ninety-five, standing for *lillah*, then, becomes a symbol of sincerity and purity of heart as well as the doctrine of progressive revelation.

Next we read "Ye have been forbidden to commit murder or adultery, or to engage in backbiting or calumny; shun ye, then, what hath been prohibited in the holy Books and Tablets" (¶ 19). It becomes evident here that Bahá'u'lláh is referring to these particular laws as already established "in the holy Books and Tablets," so they are

FROM THE ORDER OF THE BOOK

being concisely reconfirmed without further explanation. These laws are of course some of the most familiar laws reiterated in all the Holy Books of the former dispensations. In the Tajallíyát, revealed after the Kitáb-i-Aqdas, Bahá'u'lláh has explicitly identified Himself as "the Speaker on Sinai Who is now seated upon the throne of Revelation." In fact, verse 19 recapitulates commandments revealed to Moses by the Speaker on Sinai and first set down on the original "tablets" of stone. Although it is not the purpose here to engage in a comparison of the Kitáb-i-Aqdas with the Holy Books and laws of previous revelations, it may just be noted that the order of the Kitáb-i-Aqdas has general resemblances to the logic of revelation of the Mosaic laws. The latter, significantly called the "Book of the Covenant," begin with the establishment of the covenant of God and recognition of His unity through statements about the unity of God and condemnation of idolatry, followed by laws of worship and behavior, including the specification of punishments.

Such resemblance itself testifies to the fact that the Manifestations of God are essentially one and the same and, as Bahá'u'lláh has said in the Kitáb-i-Íqán, "they one and all summon the people of the earth to acknowledge the Unity of God, and herald unto them the Kawthar of an infinite grace and bounty.... If thou wilt observe with discriminating eyes, thou wilt behold them all abiding in the same tabernacle, soaring in the same heaven, seated upon the same throne, uttering the same speech, and proclaiming the same Faith" (152–54).

At the same time, however, they are "exponents of a new Cause and the Bearers of a new Message." The familiar commandments, then, take on expanded meanings as they become newly articulated in the context of Bahá'u'lláh's own universal revelation. If we look at the laws of verse 19 as expressions of the constitutive principles of the Kitáb-i-Aqdas, we can see that what is common among all the acts prohibited in this verse is the violation of the sanctity and dignity of the human being: murder, adultery, and backbiting involve treating human beings as inferior or as objects. The essence of these laws, in other words, is the sacredness of all humans as mirrors of the attributes of God, and the unity and equality of all people. The supreme aim of

Bahá'u'lláh's dispensation is the attainment of a stage of social development in which humans realize their true station and therefore treat one another as mirrors of the divine. It can also be seen ultimately as the universal fulfillment of the purpose and goal of those divine laws as revealed in the past. In fact, the themes of the Aqdas themselves are distantly anticipated and predicted in those Books, where for example the restatement of the commandments in Leviticus begins: "And the Lord spake unto Moses, saying, Speak unto all the congregation of the children of Israel, and say unto them, Ye shall be holy: for I the Lord your God am holy."[12]

In many of His writings Bahá'u'lláh has confirmed that in this day, the realization of the unity of God is inseparable from the realization of the unity of humankind.[13] Following the affirmation of the unity of God and His Manifestations in the acts of obligatory prayer and fasting, Bahá'u'lláh confirms that the worship of God and recognition of His oneness is not complete without action which brings the essential reflection of divine unity into human relations.

The next law to be set down is the law of inheritance. I will return to discuss this subject in detail and to argue that its meaning is predominantly symbolic, expressing the fulfillment, in the coming of Bahá'u'lláh, of the Báb's prophecies concerning the revelation of the Most Great Name. That symbolic significance would also explain why this particular law with all its detailed numerical structure occurs at the beginning of the Kitáb-i-Aqdas.

Following the discussion (through the symbolism of inheritance numbers) of His station as the Promised One and the Most Great Name, Bahá'u'lláh establishes the institution of the House of Justice. In this discussion, which simultaneously affirms the principle of covenant and sets down the basis of the administrative structure of Bahá'u'lláh's New World Order, one can discern a combination of two principles or pillars of the faith as recognized in Shí'ih Islam—Imamate (the presence of continuous divine guidance) and divine justice. To further emphasize the significance of the House of Justice as the authoritative institution of the Bahá'í community, Bahá'u'lláh specifies the number of the members of the House of Justice as equal to the "number of Bahá"

(¶ 30). In other words, the institution of the House of Justice would represent Bahá and, as He subsequently indicates in verse 42, after the termination of the line of Branches. That the number of the members has primarily symbolic importance is suggested by the fact that He specifies that in practice the members may exceed nine.

The institution of the House of Justice combines and unites within itself the four constitutive principles of the Kitáb-i-Aqdas: it represents the principle of covenant, but it also represents the principle of the oneness of humankind, being democratically elected, based on consultation, and concerned for the collective interests of humanity. It represents the principle of beautification through the symbolism of Bahá, the Ancient Beauty, and it represents the principle of heart through its foundation in justice. The discussion of the House of Justice in the context of the principle of the oneness of humankind is another reflection of the inseparable unity of Bahá'u'lláh's spiritual and administrative principles, and of the organic relation between the idea of the unity of the human race and the unity of the Bahá'í Faith under the guidance of the institutions ordained in His covenant.

The next law decrees the construction of the most beautiful houses of worship dedicated to the remembrance of God—an immediate realization of the principle of worship in the realm of the physical world. It unites the idea of worship with the principle of beautification and refinement. The house of worship, Bahá'u'lláh states, should be constructed "as perfect as is possible in the world of being" (¶ 31) and should be decorated in ways worthy of its dignity as the place devoted to the remembrance of God. This law about houses dedicated to worship is followed by the law concerning pilgrimage to the most sacred houses, those that are the concrete embodiment of the remembrance of the physical presence of the Manifestation. Next, Bahá'u'lláh strongly affirms the necessity of engaging in trades and professions and rejects idleness and dependence on the work of others. Again, this law is discussed near the beginning of the Kitáb-i-Aqdas because of its fundamental significance, which is because in His dispensation Bahá'u'lláh has raised "engagement in such work to the rank of worship of the one true God" (¶ 33).

Bahá'u'lláh Himself has presented this same law as an integral expression of His principle of the removal of the sword: the people are to engage in constructive labor which serves humankind and elevates their own station. At the same time the principle of the oneness of humankind is incompatible with human degradation. Bahá'u'lláh does not want to see anyone reduced to begging from another. Although all are called upon to engage in work in a spirit of service to humanity, the House of Justice is assigned the function of ensuring social justice and the welfare of the poor and the needy. Here we have a movement in which the praise of God takes the form of actions designed to lead toward the emergence of a new culture and society, which ultimately culminates in the coming of age of a humanity that is supremely conscious of its own oneness.

Finally, there are the prohibitions against begging, the kissing of hands, and the confession of sins. These ordinances express the dignity and equality of all human beings. Like begging, the practices of kissing the hands of religious leaders and confessing sins are considered degrading and unworthy of the human station. The ordinances against these practices also implicitly reject the institution of priesthood and express the requirements of refinement. In removing the authority of the clergy, Bahá'u'lláh is emphasizing again the supreme position of the House of Justice. All people are equal and no one has authority over another, while the leadership of the community is vested in a democratically elected consultative institution that is under divine guidance and protection.

All the different statements in this initial section of the Kitáb-i-Aqdas, which to a superficial glance may have seemed unrelated or chaotic, can be seen as a systematic exposition of the idea of worship and the realization of worship in the form of the oneness of humankind, the covenant, remembrance of God, constructive labor, and the equality of all believers. In this section of His text, Bahá'u'lláh has affirmed divine unity, His authority as the Promised One of the Bayán, and the authority of the House of Justice as the administrative institutional structure of the Bahá'í Faith.

Symbolic Meaning of the Law of Inheritance

I have suggested that the meaning and function of the law of inheritance is primarily symbolic. From the very beginning of the discussion of the law of inheritance it is evident that Bahá'u'lláh is referring to the distribution of inheritance as discussed in the Arabic Bayán and especially its logic of numbers. Bahá'u'lláh begins by stating: "We have divided inheritance into seven categories." Here, "We" refers to the Báb and to His law in the tenth váhid of the Arabic Bayán. After describing that law, Bahá'u'lláh states: "Such was the ordinance of My Forerunner, He Who extolleth My Name in the night season and at the break of day. When We heard the clamour of the children as yet unborn, We doubled their share and decreased those of the rest. He, of a truth, hath power to ordain whatsoever He desireth, and He doeth as He pleaseth by virtue of His sovereign might" (¶ 20).

Although Bahá'u'lláh changes the particular distribution that had been fixed in the Bayán, He confirms that the ordinance of the Bayán remains the law of the Kitáb-i-Aqdas because "this is that hidden knowledge which shall never change, since its beginning is with nine, the symbol that betokeneth the concealed and manifest, the inviolable and unapproachably exalted Name" (¶ 29). From this description, it appears that the function of the entire discussion of inheritance is not primarily to establish a particular law of passing on material possessions but to emphasize the symbolic meaning of the numbers themselves. The symbolic significance of the mathematics of inheritance is also evident from a tablet in which Bahá'u'lláh says that the inheritance division number (9) accords with the number which is divisible by all of the first nine numbers (2520).[14] It seems obvious that all these numbers are intended to be vehicles of spiritual symbols.

To understand this symbolism, we must turn to the Arabic Bayán. After discussing the seven categories of the recipients of inheritance and their equivalent numbers, the Báb states:

> Say: Verily God had divided your inheritance on the basis of four categories after the first three. Verily, in the order of letters three precedeth four. That is in accordance with a hidden knowledge in

the Book of God—a Knowledge that shall never change or be replaced. Gaze upon your temples, and then recognize, with certitude, Him Whom God shall make manifest in the Day of resurrection shedding the splendours of God's Revelation upon all letters through the number of Há'.[15]

Bahá'u'lláh has stated distinctly that this hidden and unchangeable knowledge refers to "nine"—a reference to Bahá. At first it may seem that there is a discrepancy between the statement of the Báb and Bahá'u'lláh's interpretation because it appears that the Báb is speaking about seven (three plus four), and not nine. But a careful reading of the text of the Bayán confirms the truth of Bahá'u'lláh's statement.

What the Báb is discussing is in fact a reference to the Most Great Name: throughout the Arabic Bayán's inheritance distribution, seven appears as nine.[16] The Báb identifies this mystery as the unchangeable, eternal hidden knowledge of God, which is a clear reference to the hidden Most Great Name of God. There is also a symbolic allusion to the unity of seven and nine in the names of the Báb and Bahá'u'lláh. The Báb's name, 'Alí Muḥammad, consists of seven Arabic letters; Bahá'u'lláh's name, Ḥusayn 'Alí, has seven Arabic letters as well. Bahá'u'lláh thus is the return of the Báb (seven) in the form of Bahá (nine), the Most Great Name of God.

A further point hidden in the same statement is an allusion to the metaphysics of creation. The distribution of inheritance in seven categories because of the primacy of three in relation to four seems also to allude to the seven stages of creation. As we saw in Chapter 2, the Báb distinguished the first three stages of creation as constituting the major elements of the creative act, which are affirmed and elaborated by the next four stages.[17] In that context, His reference to the distribution of inheritance in terms of seven categories which are constituted by three followed by four would refer to the creative Word of God. The supreme stage of creation is of course the first stage, that of the Primal Will. However, in the distribution structure of the Bayán this first and highest stage, Will, appears as nine. That is, the Primal Will is identified as nine, or Bahá.

The identification of the categories of inheritance with the stages of divine creation implies that inheritance itself is a symbol of divine spiritual creation and the Word of God. Bahá'u'lláh is the Inheritance, the Remnant, and the Gift of God to humanity as well as the One who, according to the eternal Covenant, inherits the Báb's authority as the Manifestation of God. According to the writings of the Báb, the Manifestation is the Lord and possessor of all things in heaven and on earth. Similarly, in mystical interpretations of the concept of inheritance, it is only the Manifestation of God who inherits all beings, and Who is Himself the divine Inheritance and Remnant.

The complex symbolism of the inheritance mathematics can be understood by paying attention to the last part of the Báb's statement in the Arabic Bayán in which He refers to "Him Whom God shall make manifest in the Day of Resurrection shedding the splendours of God's Revelation upon all letters through the number of Há'." Here the Báb relates the inheritance law to the Nineteen Temples, which He has named His second proof (after the revelation of verses). He has stated that all spiritual truth is hidden in these temples, which end with the name of the Promised One as Huva'l-Mustaghíth.[18] Bahá'u'lláh has said that these refer to the maturation and completion of all beings in nineteen years and the revelation of Bahá'u'lláh at Riḍván. The interesting point is that the inheritance numbers correspond exactly to the numbers of the fifth temple (the number of Há').[19] The Báb says that it was the fifth temple that God created first and that the law of inheritance contains within itself all the secrets of divine mysteries.[20] We can see that the inheritance numbers signify the exalted station of Bahá'u'lláh as the Most Great Name, who is symbolized by nine and appears publicly in the year nineteen.[21]

We can see that in the Báb's inheritance formulation everything refers to the Promised One. And the very concept of inheritance itself refers to the Remnant of God and the return of the Báb, as the supreme gift of God to humanity. According to the Báb, since the Manifestation of God is the supreme purpose of creation, whoever is deprived of the recognition of the Manifestation is deprived of the divine inheritance. It is in this symbolic context that, for the Báb, inheritance as a symbolic category applies only to believers.

In several ways, Bahá'u'lláh confirms the symbolic meaning of the Báb's law of inheritance, according to which inheritance applies only to believers, at the same time as He virtually abrogates it as a social law by instituting a new law according to which all people must write a will and distribute their inheritance as they freely choose so that both believers and nonbelievers equally can inherit from the deceased in accordance with the choice of the individual. Structurally it is assured that all will be cared for because the House of Justice is charged with assuring the welfare of all and is directed to expend whatever inheritance shares revert to it "on the orphaned and widowed, and on whatsoever will bring benefit to the generality of the people" (¶ 21).

It is evident that the literal distribution structure set down in the Kitáb-i-Aqdas is not intended to be the social norm because Bahá'u'lláh has made writing of a will both obligatory and completely free. 'Abdu'l-Bahá's interpretations concerning the inheritance law emphasize the obligatory nature of writing a will and distributing one's own property in any way deemed appropriate by the testator. As the Universal House of Justice has observed: "It is worth noting that the Bahá'í laws of inheritance apply only when the individual dies without making a will. Indeed, one of 'Abdu'l-Bahá's Tablets seems to indicate that the very provisions of the Bahá'í law of intestacy are intended as an incentive to individuals not to neglect the duty of making a will early in life."[22]

VERSES 35 THROUGH 42

Verses 35 to 42 primarily concern the covenant by emphasizing the principle of heart. While the preceding verse prohibited the kissing of hands and confession of sins, thereby abrogating practices associated with the priesthood, verses 35 and 36 primarily deal with those who make hypocritical shows of humility and false claims to mystical knowledge that would give them a superior spiritual status. It can also be seen that, in one sense, Bahá'u'lláh is still speaking about worship, but now illegitimate forms of it as well as pretensions to spiritual station and former practices that were symbols of the spiritual authority of the clergy.

Bahá'u'lláh begins by calling upon His followers to "arise to serve the Cause of God" (¶ 35). This service or assistance (*nuṣrat*) to the Cause of God is rendered no longer through the sword but instead through the pen and utterance, pure actions, good character, and unity. The major impediment to the proclamation of the divine Cause has normally been the divines and the leaders of religion, who have been responsible for dividing the Cause of God into sects and have often been preoccupied with worldly attachment to power, prestige, wealth, and the like—forgetting the living essence of religion and emphasizing its empty ritual form. Among the forms of vain imagination are extreme ascetic practices. These become not only displays of superior piety, but glorification of physical self-deprivation or "austerities and mortifications" as a means of gaining mystical enlightenment. Bahá'u'lláh emphasizes that all forms of worship are acceptable if they accord with the will of God as it is revealed by the Manifestation of God. All human actions, including acts of worship, are unacceptable if they are expressions of arbitrary human desires and not oriented to the benefit of all humanity and obedience to the Word of God: "Make not your deeds as snares wherewith to entrap the object of your aspiration, and deprive not yourselves of this Ultimate Objective for which have ever yearned all such as have drawn nigh unto God. Say: The very life of all deeds is My good pleasure, and all things depend upon Mine acceptance" (¶ 36).

Instead of such practices, as Bahá'u'lláh has often said, the true means to attain the Ultimate Objective is a pure heart and action solely for the sake of God. Moderation is also implied here: while asceticism is rejected, detachment from all worldly or selfish desire is required of all.

Bahá'u'lláh next discusses false claims to revelation in the future and enunciates the second constitutive principle of the Kitáb-i-Aqdas: no one may legitimately make a claim to an independent revelation prior to the completion of one full thousand years. As we saw in Chapter 7, this principle has implications for all aspects of the covenant of Bahá'u'lláh and the succession and sources of authority for the duration of His dispensation.

The connection of the verse regarding "a thousand years" and the covenant of Bahá'u'lláh becomes immediately visible in the next verse. Bahá'u'lláh directs His followers not to be dismayed after His ascension but to arise to further His Cause. He speaks of the transitory character of earthly possessions, power, and fame, contrasting these empty forms with what is truly of profit and advantage to people. He singles out those for whom acquired learning becomes a veil that shuts them out from true knowledge: "Among the people is he whose learning hath made him proud, and who hath been debarred thereby from recognizing My Name, the Self-Subsisting; who, when he heareth the tread of sandals following behind him, waxeth greater in his own esteem than Nimrod" (¶ 41). Addressing the concourse of divines He says: "Hear ye not the shrill voice of My Most Exalted Pen? See ye not this Sun that shineth in refulgent splendor above the All-Glorious Horizon? For how long will ye worship the idols of your evil passions? Forsake your vain imaginings, and turn yourselves unto God, your Everlasting Lord."

As we have seen before, the principle of heart is inextricably connected with covenant, authority, and hermeneutics. Bahá'u'lláh's rejection of the priesthood simultaneously implies the universal equality of all believers and the interpretive authority of the Manifestation and His designated representatives. It is within this discussion that Bahá'u'lláh talks of succession and authority. If there are no priests in the Bahá'í Faith, and if all the believers are equal, then after the ascension of Bahá'u'lláh, the Bahá'ís must arise to serve the Cause of God with complete unity in the covenant which clearly defines the structure of authority after Bahá'u'lláh. We have seen that the institution of the House of Justice was identified as the representative of Bahá'u'lláh for the future governance of the community. In verse 42 we witness a very clear explication of the lines of authority in the covenant of Bahá'u'lláh:

> Endowments dedicated to charity revert to God, the Revealer of Signs. None hath the right to dispose of them without leave from Him Who is the Dawning-place of Revelation. After Him, this authority shall pass to the Aghṣán, and after them to the House of

Justice—should it be established in the world by then—that they may use these endowments for the benefit of the Places which have been exalted in this Cause, and for whatsoever hath been enjoined upon them by Him Who is the God of might and power. Otherwise, the endowments shall revert to the people of Bahá who speak not except by His leave and judge not save in accordance with what God hath decreed in this Tablet—lo, they are the champions of victory betwixt heaven and earth—that they may use them in the manner that hath been laid down in the Book by God, the Mighty, the Bountiful.

This passage envisions that direct descendants, the line of Aghsán (Branches), would cease, after which authority would be vested in the Universal House of Justice. In the period during which there would exist no Branch and no Universal House of Justice, leadership was to be placed in the hands of the "people of Bahá who speak not except with His leave." In one of His tablets Bahá'u'lláh has described the Hands of the Cause as "Protectors and Defenders" (*Ḥuffáẓ va Ḥurrás*) of the "House of His Cause":

He hath constructed the house of His Cause by His pervasive will upon the foundation of eloquent speech and the pillar of wisdom, and He hath created for it protectors and defenders who shall preserve it from the faithless and the perverse and those who speak out of ignorance. *They are the ones who shall not overstep what God hath revealed in the Book nor shall they speak except by His leave on the Day of Return.* I testify that they are the hands of His Cause amongst mankind and the lamps of His guidance between heaven and earth. They stand before His door and cast out whosoever is not worthy to enter within the precincts of His court. No God is there save Him, the Supreme Ruler, the Ordainer, the All-Knowing, the All-Wise.[23]

In another tablet, Bahá'u'lláh contrasts the Hands of the Cause with those who speak from their own vain imaginations and desires, meaning without the leave of God.[24] We can see that subsequent events were anticipated in the Kitáb-i-Aqdas and that the period between the death of Shoghi Effendi in 1957 and the election of the Universal House of Justice in 1963, during which the Hands of the Cause led the

Bahá'í community, was in accordance with the provisions of the Most Holy Book.

In short, verses 35 to 42 can be understood as explicating the question of authority and the covenant of Bahá'u'lláh. Rejecting the institution of priesthood and all individual claims to hidden knowledge which would imply authority, Bahá'u'lláh assigns the leadership of the Faith after His passing to the Branches and after the end of the line of Branches to the Universal House of Justice. He has called on His followers to arise to the service of God and guarantees that in both cases His inspiration and protection would continue to be present.

VERSES 43 THROUGH 97

The next sequence of verses, comprising 43 through 73, emphasizes the principle of the removal of the sword by rejecting practices which contradict unity and social advancement—including idleness, theft, murder, discrimination against nonbelievers, the ritual impurity of peoples, adultery, and slavery—and advocating whatever is conducive to unity and social progress: promoting the Cause of God, fellowship with all religions and all peoples, marriage, art, the reconstruction of cities, education of children, and the like. After discussing the ephemeral nature of the world and calling His followers to devotion to spiritual ends, and to purify their property by means of service (the endowments), Bahá'u'lláh asks His followers to respond to situations of affliction with a spirit of moderation, defined as remembrance and reflection on the future. This orientation does not mean withdrawal from the world and economic disengagement. On the contrary, detachment requires both productive labor and respect for the rights of others. Bahá'u'lláh then prohibits both shaving the head and wearing long hair, practices that can be understood, among other things, as symbolizing ascetic disengagement from the world, especially the conspicuous public show of detachment, notably as practiced by the monks and the dervishes who are mentioned in earlier verses. In other religions as well, not cutting the hair—or, alternatively, shaving the head—has served to create conspicuous distinctions among people or to signify membership in holy orders. Bahá'u'lláh abolishes all such external signifiers of distinction.

Bahá'u'lláh then turns to setting down the punishments for theft, admonishing the people to uphold justice in enforcing the law and not to allow compassion to lead to neglect of enforcement but to "do that which hath been bidden you by Him Who is compassionate and merciful." Here He alludes again to the principle that the laws themselves, however severe they may appear, are the essence of mercy. He emphasizes this point by commenting: "We school you with the rod of wisdom and laws, like unto the father who educateth his son, and this for naught but the protection of your own selves and the elevation of your stations" (¶ 45).

Next, linking the principle of removal of the sword to the principle of refinement, Bahá'u'lláh abrogates the past prohibition on the use of silver and gold dishes. As symbols of wealth, both had been interpreted as signs of worldly attachment. Bahá'u'lláh now permits the use of such items and states: "Adopt ye such usages as are most in keeping with refinement. He, verily, desireth to see in you the manners of the inmates of Paradise in His mighty and most sublime Kingdom" (¶ 46). Through refined habits and manners, both worldly engagement and spiritual devotion are linked together.

Such a concept of refinement defined by moderation and purity implies a strong element of maturity. This theme is repeatedly expressed in the Kitáb-i-Aqdas in passages where Bahá'u'lláh permits something that has been prohibited in the past. The abrogation of the former prohibition does not necessarily imply that the behavior is now allowed in any form or for any purpose without limit, but that people are now expected to be mature enough to use self-restraint and avoid excesses.

Next, in verse 47, Bahá'u'lláh reiterates His exclusive station and authority as the one endowed with the Most Great Infallibility, the right to command new laws and prohibit the old. However, committing acts unworthy of the human station is partly an effect of lack of education and of poverty. He enjoins every father to educate his sons and daughters, making dereliction punishable by fine, and for those unable to afford education He places responsibility on the House of Justice, thereby guaranteeing universal education for all children regardless of socioeconomic status.

As another case of attachment to selfish desires and disregard for the well-being of others, adultery is contrary to the principle of the removal of the sword. The prohibition of adultery and its punishment, however, should not be interpreted as a condemnation of sex within the bounds of marriage, nor does it imply hostility toward aesthetic expressions of emotions in music, art, and refinement itself. In verse 51 Bahá'u'lláh abolishes the prohibition on listening to music, something previously perceived by Muslim divines as immoral and corrupting. Properly used within the bounds of moderation and spiritual maturity, music can be a powerful means of spiritualization and exaltation of the human soul.

Bahá'u'lláh next assigns to the "Seat of Justice" the duty of protecting the Faith from "the ravening wolves that have appeared in disguise" (¶ 52) and ordains an additional source of revenue for that institution to fulfill its responsibility to implement social justice and protect the people. Bahá'u'lláh has called on His followers to arise to render His Cause victorious after His ascension. But this assistance to the Cause of God requires the unity of the Faith. In case of differences and disagreements, people are directed to turn to Bahá'u'lláh Himself during His lifetime, and after that to His Book and to the institutions ordained in the Book. Understanding His Book, as He specifies later in the Kitáb-i-Aqdas, is dependent on the interpretations of the Center of His Covenant. Guided by the Sacred Writings and divine inspiration, the House of Justice is to protect the unity of the Faith from the assaults of the "wolves." Rendering the Cause of God victorious, or the principle of the removal of the sword, here becomes inseparable from the principle of covenant.

The next verses (56 through 62) enunciate further requirements of the principle of the removal of the sword and the means of binding people together. Bahá'u'lláh specifies penalties for physical violence in the form of indemnities to the injured party, ordains a monthly feast as a means of binding the hearts together, warns against becoming divided, and calls on the believers to be united as the fingers of a hand or the members of a single body. He allows hunting in moderation. He bids His believers to show kindness to His relatives, while emphasizing that the latter have no rights to the property of others (thus placing them equally with all others in that respect). He prescribes penalties for murder and arson, which were the most extreme expressions of the "sword."

In the next verses (63–71), after warning, in strong terms, against stirring up mischief, Bahá'u'lláh returns to the aspect of the principle that deals not with the destruction of life but its creation. The primary institutions that bind people together are marriage and family. They are the means of the creation of human life, the foundation of unity in the world, and the primary setting for the education of children—all of which can be seen as organically connected and essential precon-ditions of the principle of removal of the sword.

The culmination of the principle of the removal of the sword, dis-cussed at length in previous verses, appears in verses 72 and 73. Having confirmed the institution of marriage as the means of unity and the creation of life, Bahá'u'lláh categorically abolishes the institution of slavery, which implied the commodification of human beings. Since all are servants of God and exemplify His unity, they are all equal and no one should degrade or objectify another. Bahá'u'lláh reaffirms that assisting the Cause of God is to be accomplished through righteous works, moral character, and wisdom and utterance, and not through contention, aggression, and violence. Emphasizing the law not to kill, He says: "Fear God, and lift not the hand of injustice and oppression to destroy what He Himself hath raised up" (¶ 73).

Verses 74 through 77 assert the principle of universal revelation and refinement. In the preceding verses, both slavery and murder were prohibited because all people are manifestations of divine attributes. The presence of the divine attributes is a common link between the principle of the removal of the sword and the principle of universal revelation. Bahá'u'lláh now explicitly abolishes the form-er idea of the impurity of semen as well as the entire concept of essen-tial impurity, or "uncleanness, whereby divers things and peoples have been held to be impure" (¶ 75). He attributes this decree to His uni-versal revelation: "Verily, all created things were immersed in the sea of purification when, on that first day of Riḍván, We shed upon the

whole of creation the splendours of Our most excellent Names and
Our most exalted Attributes. This, verily, is a token of My loving
providence, which hath encompassed all the worlds" (¶ 75). He then
connects this directly to an imperative action: "Consort ye then with the
followers of all religions, and proclaim ye the Cause of your Lord, the
Most Compassionate."

He continues to set down the implications of the principle of purity, cleanliness, and refinement in all affairs of life, including spotless
cleanliness in one's attire, especially in prayer, as well as the use of rose-
water and pure perfume. In addition to being conducive to individual
spirituality and mirroring the attributes of God, the purpose is "that
there may be diffused from you what your Lord, the Incomparable,
the All-Wise, desireth" (¶ 76), thus directly connecting to the previous
exhortation to consort with the followers of all religions and to proclaim the Cause.

In the next verse Bahá'u'lláh abrogates the law of the Bayán which
had prohibited reading any books except those of the Báb's revelation.
The sole purpose of the Báb's revelation had been to direct the attention of all to the recognition of the Promised One and to remove anything that might become an obstacle to His recognition. The Báb's
purpose in setting down such laws was to affirm the absolute sovereignty of the Manifestation of God and His message. Bahá'u'lláh
emphasizes the metaphysical meaning of the Bábí law but abrogates its
social implication. Divine sovereignty is now realized through communication and interaction with members of all religions and all cultures. But even in abrogating the law of the Báb, Bahá'u'lláh's statement also implies the principles of refinement and mature self-control
based on detachment that were implied in other extensions of liberty
for what was formerly prohibited. Now, books shall no longer be
destroyed, but that does not imply that there are no longer any standards: He permits reading of "such sciences as are profitable unto you,
not such as end in idle disputation...." (¶ 77). Bahá'u'lláh opens wide
the door to cultural and technological communication with all peoples, but conditions it on the principles of the oneness of humanity
and covenant: those sciences are valued that are "profitable" to the

welfare of humanity, but not those whose main purpose is to create contention.

Verses 78 through 97 again concern the principle of heart. Bahá'-u'lláh addresses the kings of the world as His vassals, emphasizing His supreme authority as the King of Kings. He summons them to become detached from worldly desires and pride, to forsake tyranny and to be just, and speaks of the blessings that await the king who will arise to aid His Cause. He begins by addressing generally the concourse of rulers, then specifically the leaders of Austria, America, the Ottoman Empire, Germany, Iran, and Khurásán. While He calls on them to assist His Cause and act with justice, and predicts that power will fall to the people, He also forbids His followers to engage in political sedition or rebellion and urges them to direct their attention to the hearts.

Since all property and possessions, like all authority, are ultimately from God, the people's possessions must become a manifestation of spiritual attributes and detachment. One means of effecting this purification is through the institution of Ḥuqúqu'lláh (the nineteen percent tax on excess wealth), as a token of human indebtedness to divine grace.

VERSES 98 THROUGH 116

The second half of the Kitáb-i-Aqdas begins with a discussion of the circumstances of the book's revelation, followed by a direct exposition of the principle of heart. Here we meet in unconcealed and forthright form the foundational principles of the critique of spiritual reason which were expressed years earlier in the Kitáb-i-Íqán and Kitáb-i-Badí'. Turning to the leaders of religion, Bahá'u'lláh appeals to them: "Weigh not the Book of God with such standards and sciences as are current amongst you, for the Book itself is the unerring Balance established amongst men. In this most perfect Balance whatsoever the peoples and kindreds of the earth possess must be weighed, while the measure of its weight should be tested according to its own standard" (¶ 99). Although the divines have longed for the coming of the Promised One and have called upon Him in their prayers, they failed to recognize Him when He appeared—and the same thing is happening once again in this revelation. Bahá'u'lláh emphasizes that the "highest and last end of all learning" is the recognition of the Manifestation of God, who is the "Object of all knowledge" (¶ 102), and yet the divines have allowed their own learning to obstruct and veil them from this, the Source of all knowledge.

In asserting the fulfillment of all the promises of the Books of the past in His own revelation, and in the Kitáb-i-Aqdas itself, Bahá'u'lláh reminds the divines that His words are not derived from acquired knowledge but are the words of God. The divines have created division in the religion of God through distortive interpretations that perverted the meaning of the revealed Word. Bahá'u'lláh excludes from His dispensation such distortion and the resulting schism, setting down a clear rule of hermeneutics: to alter the "evident meaning" of the revealed Word constitutes perversion of the Word of God.

Following this discourse with its statement about hermeneutical forms of perversion, Bahá'u'lláh returns to decree laws which, it can be seen, are all related to each other, forbidding practices that are repugnant or perverse. These ordinances can be seen as reflections of the principle of refinement: all should become the embodiments of purity and beauty in every way, physical as well as moral.

Similarly, sincerity and godliness is the purpose of the next law, which forbids muttering sacred verses in public places; the remembrance of God must take place in a situation and place worthy of God's glory. As this remembrance of God must constitute the ornament of human life, He ordains that everyone must give that remembrance concrete form in a written testament bearing witness to the Oneness of God.

Following this discussion of the remembrance of God, Bahá'u'lláh speaks directly of His universal revelation to all beings at Riḍván. Fixing the most important holy days of the Bahá'í calendar, He names the first of the Most Great Festivals and the "King of Festivals" as the Festival of Riḍván, commemorating "those days whereon the All-Merciful shed upon the whole of creation the effulgent glory of His most excellent Names and His most exalted Attributes" (¶ 110). Including as important festivals the birth of the Báb and the Day of His declaration, Bahá'u'lláh institutionalizes for the duration of His dispensation the commemoration of the inseparable twin revelations. Celebration of the Holy Day consecrated to "this Great Name" (the first day of the month of Bahá) should also take the form of performing charitable deeds, to "show forth thanks to God through actions betokening the Lord's munificence which hath encompassed all the worlds" (¶ 111).

Bahá'u'lláh's universal revelation, however, does not set aside but confirms the use of material means, such as for healing; thus He instructs people to turn to competent physicians when ill. He next absolves the believers of the duty prescribed to them in the Bayán to offer unique and priceless objects to Him Whom God shall make manifest. The praise of God and His unity is instead to be expressed in the Mashriqu'l-Adhkár, particularly at the hour of dawn:

> They who recite the verses of the All-Merciful in the most melodious of tones will perceive in them that with which the sovereignty of earth and heaven can never be compared. From them they will inhale the divine fragrance of My worlds—worlds which today none can discern save those who have been endowed with vision through this sublime, this beauteous Revelation. Say: These verses draw hearts that are pure unto those spiritual worlds that can neither be expressed in words nor intimated by allusion (¶ 116).

All these verses have affirmed the authority of the Kitáb-i-Aqdas and the revelation of the Promised One in the Day of God through Bahá'u'lláh, Whose universal revelation makes possible the achievement of all the latent potentialities of the human spirit and the transformation of the earth into a paradise, in which the outer form mirrors forth the inner essence, all things become refined and beautiful, and all praise the beauty of God in the most melodious and pure forms of remembrance. "Truly," He writes, "We desire to behold you as manifestations of paradise on earth, that there may be diffused from you such fragrance as shall rejoice the hearts of the favored of God" (¶ 106). In the Bayán, the Báb had emphasized the principle of refinement and beauty, directing His followers to become manifestations of cleanliness and beauty so that they would be worthy of the Day of God, when they would attain the Divine Presence, and insisting that their life and death must be a remembrance of and homage to His glory.[25]

Bahá'u'lláh introduces the principle of refinement and beauty by linking the concept of universal revelation on the first day of Riḍván with the melodious remembrance of God in the house of worship. In fact, it appears that Bahá'u'lláh intends to make the remembrance of God in the house of worship at the hour of dawn a symbolic reenactment of the Riḍván experience, an occasion for humanity to participate in receiving the universal revelation of Riḍván.

In other words, by remembering God in the most beautiful, sincere, and dignified way, chanting the verses of God melodiously in the house of worship at dawn, and in the testimony of their own life and death, Bahá'ís will reflect that universal revelation of Riḍván, becoming the embodiments of those divine names and attributes that were shed over the whole of creation. The act of remembrance of God itself becomes a participation in the divine revelation of the Remembrance of God on the first day of Riḍván.

VERSES 117 THROUGH 190

Verses 117 through 125 continue the theme of the remembrance of the Word of God in a new context defined by the unity of the two principles of the removal of the sword and covenant. Bahá'u'lláh commands His followers to promote and assist the Cause of God by mentioning and remembering the words of God among the people. For that purpose He approves learning various languages in order to teach the Faith among the peoples of the earth. However, this assistance must be based on faithfulness to the message of His revelation— "but he whose words conflict with that which hath been sent down in My Holy Tablets is not of Me. Beware lest ye follow any impious pretender" (¶ 117). In addition, this remembrance and assistance must be based upon moral character, upright conduct, and rationality. The mention of God must attract and revive the hearts. This choice wine is incompatible with the consumption of substances that deaden the mind and impair the reason. Rather than imitate the misdeeds of the heedless, it behooves human beings to act "in a manner worthy of the human station" (¶ 119). He goes on to elaborate: "Adorn your heads with the garlands of trustworthiness and fidelity, your hearts with the attire of the fear of God, your tongues with absolute truthfulness, your bodies with the vesture of courtesy. These are in truth seemly adornings unto the temple of man, if ye be of them that reflect" (¶ 120). Both assisting and remembering God require complete obedience and servitude of the believers to the word of God as well as to His laws. This servitude is itself the source and essence of the exaltation of the human station.

This discussion of the promotion of the Cause of God and servitude to God then leads to a discussion of His covenant. After Bahá'-u'lláh's passing, the Bahá'ís are directed to turn to 'Abdu'l-Bahá and follow His guidance. The requirement of speaking in accordance with the words of Bahá'u'lláh is inseparable from the principle of covenant. After the ascension of Bahá'u'lláh, the meaning of servitude to Bahá'u'lláh's words is precisely servitude to 'Abdu'l-Bahá's words.

The subsequent discussion of liberty further elaborates the principle of servitude. Although many assume that the absence of law or of any obstruction to desire is the definition of freedom and that such freedom is the supreme human value, Bahá'u'lláh defines "true liberty" as servitude to God and submission to His commandments (¶ 125). Unlimited liberty leads to degradation and infringing on the dignity of the human station. Here the concept of freedom is defined in terms of the categories of the removal of the sword and covenant.

Verses 126 through 131 again express the principle of universal revelation. Since Bahá'u'lláh has commanded His followers to observe what He has ordained, He now abrogates the Báb's prohibition on asking Him questions, so that all may understand His message and promote the Cause of God by putting that message into effect. This freedom is again conditioned on its use for the right purposes—it is not for "such idle questions as those on which the men of former times were wont to dwell but for that which shall be of profit to you in the Cause of God" (¶ 126).

Speaking of "this Name which overshadoweth the whole of cre-

ation" (¶ 127), He approves the Bábí calendar, which was designed to
make the flow of time a symbol of the divine names, its nineteen
months beginning with and returning to "Bahá." Life and the passage
of time thereby become a constant remembrance of the universal revelation of God, a reflection of divine Beauty, and a manifestation of the
spiritual journey.

Not only the passage of time but also the passage out of this life
must become a manifestation of the divine names. By abrogating some
of the laws of the Bayán related to burial, Bahá'u'lláh places death in
the context of the arc of descent and the arc of ascent: we come from
God and return unto Him. Bahá'u'lláh commands the utmost refinement in the treatment of the body after death, and by restricting trans-
portation of the body beyond an hour from the place of death He prohibits the degrading practice, common among Muslims in those days,
of carrying decomposing corpses by mule from one city to another for
burial in holy shrines. Limitation on travel, however, does not apply
to travel by the living. Bahá'u'lláh removes the restrictions that the
Báb had placed on travel. In these verses, the passage of time, death,
and travel are treated through abrogation of the laws of the Bayán,
affirmation of Bahá'u'lláh's sovereignty, and His desire to see all beings
and their lives reflect the divine names and attributes.

The next sequence of verses, including verses 132 through 141, all
express the principle of heart and concentrate on the principle that the
validity of any law is dependent on its conformity with the will of the
Manifestation of God. He calls on the believers to be the embodiments
of steadfastness by turning their eyes toward Him and holding fast to
what has been set down in His revelation. He warns them not to be
prevented from turning to the Speaking Book by what had previously
been set down in the Silent Book. The true *qiblih* is the Manifestation
of God. He reminds the followers of the Báb that the Báb had exalted
the Cause of the Promised One before His Own.

The next several verses move from the principle of Bahá'u'lláh's
station and authority to the exercise of that authority in setting down
new laws which enact the removal of the sword. He refers to a provision of the Bayán which the Báb had stipulated would "only take

effect after the exaltation of the Cause" (¶ 139) of the Promised One. This law would have prohibited marriage with nonbelievers and made a categorical separation between Bábís and non-Bábís. Bahá'u'lláh now annuls that provision and removes all separation, replacing it with the idea of the oneness of humankind, expressed as the command to "Consort with all religions with amity and concord, that they may inhale from you the sweet fragrance of God" (¶ 144). Bahá'u'lláh discloses that the real reason the Báb imposed certain laws in the Bayán was so that Bahá'u'lláh would "have no need to move in aught but the glorification of His own transcendent Station and His most effulgent Beauty" (¶ 142).

This part of the Kitáb-i-Aqdas unveils the secret of the apparently harsh laws of the Bayán. Although many of the Bayán's laws are embodiments of love and mercy, others, such as the marriage law just mentioned, seem to be reflections of the principle of the sword, making distinctions between believers and nonbelievers and according them differential rights. However, it becomes evident that those laws were never intended by the Báb to be ordinances carried out in society. As He reiterates in the Persian Bayán, the purpose of those laws was to emphasize that all must recognize and believe in the Promised One and that nonrecognition of Him is equal to nonexistence. Here, in the Kitáb-i-Aqdas, Bahá'u'lláh confirms this fact. Those laws were revealed only to emphasize the supreme authority of Bahá'u'lláh, to ensure that the Bábís would all recognize His sovereignty, and, as is easily seen in the case of such laws as the prohibition on asking Him questions,[26] to create conditions that would protect the Promised One from being subjected to the vexation and indignity of impudent and idle questions, challenges, and objections. The Báb wished Him to be free to reveal His verses in a way befitting His unconditional authority and majesty and as He desired. In short, it was not the social application, but the metaphysical import, which was the intention of the Báb's revelation of those harsh laws.

The essence of the new law is explored in the next few verses: fellowship with people of all religions; caution not to fall into the "foolish ignorance" of hatred and prejudice; confirmation of the law not to infringe on the property of others; purification of one's property through payment of *zakát* (a form of alms-tax); prohibition of begging while stressing the duty of engagement in productive work, as well as the responsibility of the House of Justice and the rich to take care of those unable to earn a living; restatement of the prohibition on all forms of contention and conflict, including "acts whereby hearts and souls may be saddened" (¶ 148); and emphasis on the moral golden rule.

Verses 149 through 160 set down different manifestations of the principle of refinement, while the self-referential verses 157 and 158 concern the principle of the heart. Bahá'u'lláh commands His followers to read His writings everyday, accounting it as a requirement of His covenant. However, even prayer and reading of the sacred verses must be imbued with refinement, sincerity, and joy. He rejects the ritualistic approach to the remembrance of God and commands teaching children to recite the tablets "in most melodious tones" in the house of worship. He also applies the aesthetic principle to the furnishings of each believer's home, stating that God desires the refinement of the people and their possessions.

Further expounding the principle of refinement, He decrees laws abolishing a variety of repugnant practices and habits, both physical and social, including uncleanliness and anger. The use of pulpits, which had set apart some believers as literally standing above the rest, is abolished, and He directs His followers to seat themselves while making mention of God "as a mark of honour for the love ye bear for Him and for the Manifestation of His glorious and resplendent Cause" (¶ 154). Gambling, opium, and anything which inflicts harm or induces torpor in the human temple is prohibited. Promise keeping even in the context of responding to social invitations is decreed.

Verses 157 and 158 reaffirm the authority of Bahá'u'lláh and His words, rejecting the legitimacy of the divines by referring to the "mystery of the Great Reversal in the Sign of the Sovereign" (as discussed in the writings of Shaykh Aḥmad), and emphasizing the unconditional authority of the Manifestation of God in His decrees. Bahá'u'lláh says that He has borne injustice so that justice might appear on earth and has accepted abasement that the majesty of God would become manifest among mankind. In the next verses, 159 and 160, the discussion of His sovereignty becomes linked with the previous verses on refinement. Having borne injustice and oppression in order to create the means of unity and peace in the world, He forbids carrying weapons and removes previous restrictions on clothing. Once again, however, the abolishing of restriction calls people to a new level of maturity and moderation: "Let there be naught in your demeanour of which sound and upright minds would disapprove, and make not yourselves the playthings of the ignorant" (¶ 159). The true "adornment" befitting those who assist the Cause of God is "the vesture of seemly conduct and a praiseworthy character." Likewise, He exhorts His followers to promote the development of cities and countries and to "glorify Him therein" in "joyous accents." Parallel to the previous verse about inner and outer "adornment," He makes a similar connection between inner and outer forms of constructive power: "In truth the hearts of men are edified through the power of the tongue, even as houses and cities are built up by the hand and other means" (¶ 160). Affirming the principles of divine efficacy and human freedom, Bahá'u'lláh calls for the reconstruction and beautification of both human hearts and physical space.

Verses 161 through 186 constitute a discourse on the principle of heart. Asserting the absolute authority of the Manifestation of God and His decree as a "fundamental verity," acceptance of which leads to "perfect constancy" and "salvation in both this world and the next" (¶ 163), Bahá'u'lláh then turns to address directly the divines, who have rejected and undermined that authority and have led the people astray. He speaks of three categories of the learned: those divines who turn away from Him, those who nominally accept Him but continue to use their own standards and selfish desires to measure the Book of God, and the "learned in Bahá" who take the Word of God as the supreme balance itself. Discussing the second category of the learned, Bahá'u'lláh links the principle of heart to the principle of covenant. He emphasizes that after His physical absence, no learned Bahá'í is permitted to take personal interpretations of the words of Bahá'u'lláh as authoritative, but all are to turn to 'Abdu'l-Bahá as the authorized interpreter. The criterion distinguishing the divines who nominally identify themselves with the Faith from the truly learned in Bahá, therefore, becomes the commitment to the principle of the covenant.

In this extensive elaboration of the principle of heart, Bahá'u'lláh refers to the various objections raised against Him by the divines, particularly the Bábís, those who use the Book of God as the pretext for repudiating the Lord Himself (¶ 168). He refers to Ḥájí Mírzá Karím Khán-i-Kirmání as an example of a disdainful divine blinded by pride who met his end at the hand of angels of wrath by an act of divine justice; alludes to the future opposition of the Bábí divines from Kirmán; addresses the claim that the Promised One of the Bayán must appear in the distant future; and concludes with His historic statement about His "new World Order" (¶ 181). Bahá'u'lláh stresses the point that His Book is the "infallible Balance ... in which all who are in the heavens and all who are on the earth are weighed, and their fate determined" (¶ 183); warns the learned not to "make it a cause of dissension"; and admonishes and counsels the arch-breaker of the covenant, Yaḥyá Azal, to seek forgiveness and return to God in humility.

Finally, verses 187 through 190 may be seen, in a sense, as the summary and culmination of the Kitáb-i-Aqdas. In them Bahá'u'lláh reaffirms the principle that the purpose of His revelation is that all human beings in all aspects of their personal and collective social life should become "the embodiments of justice and fairness amidst all creation," as exemplified not only in their treatment of other human beings but their treatment of animals, and the creation of a united and harmonious civilization. The latter point, the apex of the discussion, is none other than the principle of the maturation of humanity. In Chapters 9 and 10 we will return to examine some of the implications of the signs Bahá'u'lláh appoints to denote the coming of age of the human race, two of which (universal language and the transmutation of elements) are mentioned at the end of the Kitáb-i-Aqdas.

THE ORDER OF THE BOOK AND THE ORDER OF BAHÁ'U'LLÁH

One of the most significant and fundamental verses of the Kitáb-i-Aqdas is Bahá'u'lláh's statement: "The world's equilibrium hath been upset through the vibrating influence of this most great, this new World Order. Mankind's ordered life hath been revolutionized through the agency of this unique, this wondrous System—the like of which mortal eyes have never witnessed" (¶ 181). The expression Bahá'u'lláh uses in Arabic, "*hádha'n-naẓmi'l-a'ẓam.... hádha'l-badí'*" literally says "this most great order.... this new wondrous [order]," but Shoghi Effendi, in his translation of it, has interpreted the statement as signifying the New World Order of Bahá'u'lláh. I will not discuss here the structure of the New World Order but will concentrate on the complex significance of the statement's location and context in the Kitáb-i-Aqdas itself.

It must be pointed out, however, that prior to Shoghi Effendi's interpretation, the typical understanding of Bahá'u'lláh's statement in the Kitáb-i-Aqdas was completely different. The statement is clearly a reference to this prophecy in the Persian Bayán: "Well is it with him who fixeth his gaze upon the Order of Bahá'u'lláh, and rendereth thanks unto his Lord. For He will assuredly be made manifest. God hath indeed irrevocably ordained it in the Bayán."[27] Since the verse in the Kitáb-i-Aqdas obviously refers to the one in the Persian Bayán, the nature of the "new wondrous order" was understood in terms of the prevalent impressions about the Báb's verse in the Bayán. There the reference to the "Order of Bahá'u'lláh" appears in the context of a discussion about the order of the Bayán (as the body of the Báb's writings) in relation to the order of different modes or styles (*sha'n*) of His revelation. Consequently, when the Báb spoke of the "Order of Bahá'u'lláh" it was assumed to mean nothing other than the order of Bahá'u'lláh's writings.

Based on that assumption, Bahá'u'lláh's statement in the Kitáb-i-Aqdas about a *new* "order" was understood to indicate the order of Bahá'u'lláh's writings in general and the order of the Kitáb-i-Aqdas in particular.[28] Shoghi Effendi's interpretation of this "Order of Bahá'u'-lláh" as Bahá'u'lláh's World Order sheds light on the entire structure

of both the Kitáb-i-Aqdas and the writings of the Báb, making it possible to begin to understand the complexity of the meanings in this significant verse. Shoghi Effendi's interpretation, in fact, is the only one
compatible both with the message of the Persian Bayán and the structure of the Kitáb-i-Aqdas.

The fact that in the Persian Bayán the concept of order refers to
the writings of the Báb is beyond any doubt. Similarly, the fact that the
reference to the "order" of Bahá'u'lláh also applies to the order of the
writings of Bahá'u'lláh and His restructuring of the Bayán is completely obvious. Bahá'u'lláh Himself has said as much.[29] However,
what was not obvious to readers of both texts was the fact that, in both,
the "order" of Bahá'u'lláh is also a reference to the structure of the
covenant and the spiritual and social order of Bahá'u'lláh's dispensation. Both the Persian Bayán and the Kitáb-i-Aqdas attest that the
order of the revealed Book is a mirror of the spiritual and social order
outlined by the Book. This is the essence of the discussion in the Persian Bayán, and it is in this context that we can understand the location
of this verse in the Kitáb-i-Aqdas. That the verse appears toward the
end of the Kitáb-i-Aqdas itself suggests that Bahá'u'lláh is referring
both to the order of the Book that He has just revealed, as well as the
fact that the order of this Book is itself the mirror of His New World
Order, which is the object of His covenant and His dispensation.

Bahá'u'lláh reveals verse 182, referring to the Báb's prophecy concerning the "Order of Bahá'u'lláh" just after refuting the objection
leveled against Him by the Bábís concerning the "school of Him
Whom God shall make manifest" as it is referred to in the Báb's writings. At first it may appear that the two issues are not related to each
other. But in fact the two are part of the same discourse. The entire
passage in the Persian Bayán containing the verse about the Order of
Bahá'u'lláh directly argues that the Promised One must appear shortly
after the Báb's martyrdom. In the chapter of the Persian Bayán in
which the question of order is discussed, the Báb writes:

> It is not permissible to engage in religious acts save those ordained in
> the writings of the Point of the Bayán. For in this Dispensation, the
> writings of the Letters of the Living all proceed directly from the Sun

of Truth Himself. Divine verses [*áyát*] especially pertain to the Point of the Bayán, prayers [*munáját*] pertain to the Messenger of God [Muḥammad], commentaries [*tafásír*] to the Imáms of guidance, and educational discourse [*ṣuvar-i- 'ilmíyyih*] to the Gates. However, all of these proceed from this Ocean so that all people can behold the exalted sublimity of these writings of the Primal Truth. And in the eyes of God and of the Possessors of knowledge, there is nothing more glorious than to have faith, which is the most precious of all things, and all bounties are under its shadow. And from the time of the setting of the Sun [of the Báb] until the Rising of the Sun of Him Whom God shall make manifest, there will be no more binding writings, and the Letters of the Living and all the believers in God and in the Bayán will be under their shadow [the writings of the Point of the Bayán].... Well is it with him who fixeth his gaze upon the Order of Bahá'u'lláh, and rendereth thanks unto his Lord. For He will assuredly be made manifest. God hath indeed irrevocably ordained it in the Bayán.[30]

This passage recapitulates the basic structure of the entire revelation of the Báb, including the four elements of the principle of the covenant in the Islamic dispensation and their transformation into a new logic in the dispensation of the Báb. It eliminates the possibility of any sort of successor or vicegerent, and emphasizes the imminence of the revelation of Bahá'u'lláh after the martyrdom of the Báb. The first thing to note is the centrality of the four categories and their reflection in nineteen unities—the basic structure of the Bayán.

As previously mentioned, the structure of the Bayán reflects the structure of the first phrase of the Qur'án, the meaning of which is compressed within the first letter of the phrase, which is *b*, which in turn signifies Bahá'u'lláh.[31] According to the Báb, the order of the Bayán and the order of His Faith and institutions are reflections of the order of that first Qur'ánic verse.[32] The phrase consists of four words, or nineteen letters. The Báb has said that the entire structure of the Qur'án and of the Islamic dispensation was based on the identity of four and nineteen. The "four" refers to the four pillars of divine unity, the levels of authority in the covenant of the Islamic dispensation. They consist of the affirmation of the unity of God, the prophethood of Muḥammad the Messenger of God, the Imamate of the twelve

Imáms (together with the station of Fáṭimih, the daughter of Muḥam-mad), and the mediation of the four Gates after the disappearance of the Twelfth Imám. These four pillars of the covenant correspond to the four words that begin the Qur'án. However, these four levels of authority and succession, which are inseparable, appear in the form of nineteen sacred figures: the Point of the Qur'án, Muḥammad the Messenger of God, the twelve Imáms with Fáṭimih, and the four Gates. These nineteen beings constitute the first and Primary Unity (Váḥid) of the Islamic dispensation.

That same structure repeats itself in the Báb's dispensation, with the Bayán's new opening phrase: "In the Name of God, the Most Exalted, the Most Holy." Again we have (in Arabic) four words and nineteen letters. The Persian Bayán begins with the subject of the unity of the Manifestations and the reality of "return." The Báb declares that all the nineteen sacred figures of the Islamic dispensation have returned to the world in this new dispensation. The Báb himself, as the Point of the Bayán, is the return of the Point of the Qur'án, and the eighteen Letters of the Living are the return of the other eighteen figures of the Islamic dispensation. Together, the Point of the Bayán and the Letters of the Living constitute the Primary Unity (Váḥid) of the new dispensation.

There is a subtle but significant difference between the Islamic and the Bábí structures of Unity. As was noted, in the Bábí dispensation the Báb is the Point of the Bayán, who is the return of the Point of the Qur'án. The eighteen Letters of the Living are the return of the other eighteen figures of the Islamic Primary Unity, which includes the Prophet Muḥammad. The distinction between the Point of the Qur'án and the Prophet Muḥammad is not repeated in the Bábí dis-pensation. The Báb remains primarily the Point of the Bayán, while His first believer corresponds to the return of the Prophet. The reason for this is the Islamic idea that Muḥammad was not always subject to direct divine revelation, so not all of the statements of the Prophet are considered to be part of the Qur'án. The Qur'án itself corresponded to the Point of the Qur'án, while the other statements and prayers of the Prophet were considered sacred but not the words of God. The

Báb, however, stated in His writings that He is always the Point of the Bayán, that divine revelation is continuous in His utterances, and that all His writings are the words of God.[33] This matter was also emphasized in the early writings of the Báb, as is another categorical declaration of His station as the Manifestation of God.[34]

The Báb also declares that the order of the Bayán is a mirror of this divine order: the Bayán is a mirror of All Things (*Kullu Shay'*), and All Things are products of the Primary Unity. As we saw earlier, All Things is reflected in the structure of the Bayán, the calendar, and the community of the Bayán.[35]

The Báb demonstrates that the entire structure of the Islamic covenant and the totality of the sacred history and institutions of Islam and the Bábí dispensation are condensed in the identity of four and nineteen and unity, as contained in the beginning phrases of the Qur'án and the Bayán. This structure, which is the basis of all the various discussions in the Persian Bayán, is entirely a representation of the station of Bahá'u'lláh and His imminent revelation. To see this clearly, we need to explicate one aspect of the passage of the Persian Bayán quoted above.

According to the Qur'án, heaven has four "rivers"—of pure water, milk, honey, and wine.[36] In His analysis of this Qur'ánic statement the Báb makes it clear that "heaven" is nothing less than the new dispensation of revelation and the "rivers" are different modes of revelation. In the "heaven" or revelation of Islam, the words of God were revealed in four modes, each representing one of the heavenly rivers. The mode of verses (*áyát*) is the mode of direct revelation, when God speaks directly as God. This is the most important mode of revelation and corresponds to the immediate nature of the Primal Will, in which none is seen save God. For that reason, "verses" is used both as a description of this specific mode as well as a description of the totality of the modes of revelation.[37] The Qur'án is revealed in the mode of verses. Another mode is that of prayer (*munáját*). In this mode, the Word is revealed in the form of supplication. As this mode addresses God, it is spoken in the voice of a human being, and the Word of God is revealed indirectly. The mode of commentaries (*tafásír*), including sermons, emphasizes the interpretation of other words of God. Finally, the mode of rational and educational discourse (*ṣuvar-i-ʿilmíyyih*) offers scientific, philosophical, and rational arguments in support of divine truth. In the Paradise of the Bayán, we find five modes of revelation. In addition to the previous four, there is a "Persian" mode, unique to the Bábí dispensation, in which the Word is revealed in Persian, rather than in Arabic.

Returning to the Báb's statement, the four pillars of the covenant correspond to the four modes of revelation: the Point of the Qurʾán reveals verses, the Messenger of God (Muḥammad) reveals prayers, the twelve Imáms reveal commentaries, and the four Gates reveal educational discourse. In the twelve centuries of the Islamic dispensation, the words of God were revealed through these modes of revelation by the pillars of the covenant. However, the dispensation of the Báb introduces a significant change: the levels of authority and covenant that were dispersed throughout twelve centuries in the history of Islam have all returned simultaneously in the first year of the Báb's revelation, in the Letters of the Living. Most of these personages were to be martyred or pass away within a few years after the martyrdom of the Báb Himself.

As we saw, the Báb made this identity of the four levels of covenant with the nineteen figures of His dispensation the primary structure of His revelation and the structure of the Bayán. We can now understand the reason for the Báb's insistence on this model. Unlike the Islamic dispensation, in which there was succession and vicegerency after Muḥammad and the covenant extended for twelve centuries, in the new dispensation there would be no successor, so that the Báb's covenant, which applies to just a few years within His own generation, is solely related to the next Manifestation of God, Who would appear imminently. In addition to the fact that the whole of the Bayán explicitly centers on the Promised One and His imminent appearance, even the form of the Bayán attests to the same fact.

But this fact can become even more visible by going back to the Báb's statement concerning the order of the Bayán and the order of Baháʾuʾlláh. There the Báb states that not only are all the figures of His sacred covenant alive in His own time, but that no one except Himself, and no writing but His own, has any particular authority in His dispensation. He declares that all the modes of revelation that correspond to the Letters of the Living (prayers, commentaries, and educational discourse) are revealed by the Báb Himself—unlike the Islamic dispensation, in which each of the four levels of covenant revealed a particular mode. The Letters of the Living (the return of the eighteen sacred figures) have no particular authority. Finally, the Báb makes it clear that during the time between His own martyrdom and the revelation of the Promised One, no person would have any authority, and no one else's word would be binding. In fact, the Báb's knowledge of the living presence of the Promised One explains why He created such a structure for the Bayán and for His covenant.

We can now begin to appreciate the complexity of Bahá'u'lláh's reference to the prophecy of the Báb concerning the Order of Bahá'u'lláh. In the Persian Bayán, the order of the Bayán is simultaneously the order and structure of authority, covenant, sacred history, and the society which embodies those writings. In fact, the unity and parallelism between the realms of creation (takvín) and revelation (tadvín) is the heart of the Báb's message, for the Primal Will is the cause of both spiritual revelation and the ontic creation. The order of the Bayán was indeed the order of the civilization and sacred institutions of the brief Bábí dispensation. Similarly, by the "Order of Bahá'u'lláh," the Báb is referring simultaneously to the modes of Bahá'u'lláh's revelation, the order of His writings, the order of the Kitáb-i-Aqdas, and the New World Order of Bahá'u'lláh. The New World Order of Bahá'u'lláh, therefore, becomes the actualization of the divine covenant in His new dispensation.

From the other parts of the same chapter of the Persian Bayán, one can see that the reference to the Order of Bahá'u'lláh also signifies the restructuring of the Bayán by Bahá'u'lláh through His abrogation of certain provisions and addition of others. However, looking at the many testimonies of Bahá'u'lláh himself, one can also see that the main feature of this new Order that differentiates it from the Order of the Bayán is the principle of the removal of the sword, or the idea of the

oneness of humankind. In other words, the new Order created by
Bahá'u'lláh is a global order. For this reason, the term *New World Order*
is the only full and complete explication of the "new order" of the
Kitáb-i-Aqdas.

Now it is possible to see why Bahá'u'lláh refers to His New World
Order and the prophecy of the Báb in the midst of a discussion about
the "School of Transcendent Oneness." The Bábís had used the Báb's
reference to this "School" to argue that the Promised One would
appear two thousand years hence and therefore could not be Bahá'-
u'lláh.[38] Bahá'u'lláh explains that the "School" is that of the divine
covenant which He entered before the creation of heaven and earth,
and that it was in this School that the Book of the Bayán and the Book
of Aqdas were revealed. The very prophecy of the Báb concerning the
Order of Bahá'u'lláh is itself a demonstration of the proximity of the
revelation of the Promised One.

Bahá'u'lláh's discussion of the School of Transcendent Oneness is
completely compatible with the logic of the writings of the Báb. In
fact, even the Báb's own reference to the School of Him Whom God
shall make manifest implies the proximity of the revelation of the
Promised One. In the Arabic Bayán, the Báb addresses the Teacher of
His own School, and asks Him not to use any form of physical punishment on Him (the Báb) before He reaches five years of age.[39] Obviously this cannot be meant literally because, at the time when the
Arabic Bayán was revealed, the Báb was not a child but an adult and
a Manifestation of God. His reference to the School of the Promised
One implies that, at the time of the revelation of the tablet, the Promised One as well was already an adult and the source of divine knowledge.

A most interesting dynamic can be seen in the movement from
verse 180 to verse 182. Bahá'u'lláh says: "Whatsoever ye understand
not in the Bayán, ask it of God.... Should He so desire He will
expound for you that which is revealed therein, and disclose to you the
pearls of Divine knowledge and wisdom that lie concealed within the
ocean of its words. He, verily, is supreme over all names...." Next He
announces that "The world's equilibrium hath been upset through the

vibrating influence of this most great, this new World Order. Mankind's ordered life hath been revolutionized through the agency of this unique, this wondrous System...." Here, the new order itself is a force which upsets the established equilibrium, disrupting its previous pattern, even as it institutionalizes a new equilibrium and a new pattern based on a new center of attraction. In the next verse, Bahá'u'lláh directs: "Immerse yourselves in the ocean of *My* words, that ye may unravel its secrets, and discover all the pearls of wisdom that lie hid in its depths" (italics added). The apparent disorder of chaos is shown to be nothing less than the very means by which the structure of order itself becomes established in the eternal cycle of "the changeless Faith of God, eternal in the past, eternal in the future" (¶ 182).

Chapter 9
PHILOSOPHICAL PREMISES
OF THE NEW WORLD ORDER

ALTHOUGH WE FIND intimations and expressions of the features of Bahá'u'lláh's New World Order at all stages of His revelation, it was during the later stage, beginning in 1867 in Edirne, that He explicated its structure and elaborated the ways in which those principles were to be implemented or institutionalized. Throughout this book I have argued for the consistency and continuity of Bahá'u'lláh's underlying spiritual and social principles in all the stages of His writings, and the qualitative novelty and unprecedented character of those principles. That fact particularly applies to Bahá'u'lláh's teachings about order and governance, or what could be termed the social and political philosophy that is implicit or explicit in His writings. Any analysis of those concepts which assumes that they can be understood by fitting them into the available categories or "camps" of Eastern or Western philosophies or movements will fail to comprehend the complexity, richness, and subtlety of Bahá'u'lláh's writings as well as the actual nature of His message.

We find an example of that methodological approach in Juan Cole's *Modernity and the Millennium*. The reading of Bahá'u'lláh's social and political thought which is presented in that book offers two major theses which will be discussed here: (1) that Bahá'u'lláh's early writings reflect a mystical and Sufi orientation without the presence of a democratic political and social theory (representing instead a traditional absolutist and "divine right" theory of order and sovereignty); and (2) due to exposure to Western philosophical ideas during His exile, Bahá'u'lláh changed His views so that His later writings endorse modern liberal theories of political democracy and separation of religion and state (which is also suggested to have a possible Sufi origin).

However, as I will argue, that analysis falls short of an adequate representation of either the early or the later writings of Bahá'u'lláh. Instead of showing discontinuity and change, both the early and later writings affirm the same underlying premises and principles, including the democratic and egalitarian principles. Although the emphasis and context of expression differs, the principles themselves are consistent. Bahá'u'lláh's early writings offer an outlook and approach that is qualitatively different from traditional social and political theories, while His later writings are significantly different from both Enlightenment and subsequent political traditions. Most importantly, the main category of Bahá'u'lláh's social thought is not political democracy: instead, His democratic and egalitarian principles are themselves derived from more fundamental principles of His comprehensive and global vision.

Before examining those issues in detail, it is necessary to refer to some specific problems in the analysis in *Modernity and the Millennium*. There, a particular chronology is attributed to Bahá'u'lláh's writings, which fits the author's thesis of discontinuity and change, but let us examine the evidence on which it is based. Consider this example: "As he indicates in this passage, Bahá'u'lláh's first overt announcement of his commitment to concord between religions came at his Ridvan 1863 declaration."[1]

The passage in question is found in a tablet in which Bahá'u'lláh recounts an unusual spiritual experience He had for twelve days beginning on His birthday, the second of Muḥarram. In the tablet, Bahá'u'lláh testifies that

> This Servant hath no other intention in manifesting and proclaiming this Cause than the salvation of mankind and the extinction of the fire of enmity and hatred.... In the heavenly books, as it is stated by some sects, the burning of books and the killing of people, and the prohibition of unity and fellowship between certain races and classes are mentioned. Unity and fellowship, however, are the greatest means for the advancement of mankind and the development of nations. In the Qur'án and the Bayán even graver are mentioned.[2]

Bahá'u'lláh goes on to say that "When this Wronged One was a child, He read in a book attributed to Mullá Báqir Majlisí ... about the incident of the Banú-Qurayẓah, whereupon He became so grieved and saddened that the Pen is unable to recount it, even though what occurred was the command of God and its sole purpose was to break the backs of the oppressors." The incident concerned the treatment of the defeated Banú-Qurayẓah, a Jewish tribe who had broken their pact with Muḥammad and had joined with His enemies. After a siege lasting twenty-five days, they agreed to accept the judgment of Muḥammad, who asked Saʻd ibn Muʻádh, the chief of the Aws, to decide their punishment. Subsequently, some seven hundred men were beheaded and their women, children, and property distributed to the Muslim army.[3] Bahá'u'lláh goes on to say (speaking of Himself in the third person):

> But upon beholding the ocean of forgiveness and boundless mercy, He used to beseech the One True God, exalted be His glory, in those days to bring about whatsoever would be the cause of love, fellowship, and unity among all the peoples of the earth—until, suddenly, before sunrise (*qabl az ṭulúʻ*) on the second day of the month of His birth, His entire condition and manner of expression and thinking were transformed in a transformation which proclaimed the joyful tidings of heavenly reunion. This experience occurred repeatedly for twelve consecutive days, after which the waves of the sea of utterance became manifest and the effulgences of the orb of assurance shone forth until it culminated in the advent of His Revelation.
>
> Thus hast thou attained unto that which God hath made the source of joy to all mankind and the dawning-place of His tender mercy to all who are in heaven and on earth. From that point forward, We removed through the agency of the Pen of the Most High whatever had been the cause of suffering, affliction, and discord, and set down with a fixed and irrevocable decree that which is the cause of unity and fellowship. None can deny the overflowing bounty of this Revelation, except for such wayward souls as are veiled from the truth and those odious ones who act unjustly upon the earth. The Holy Writings which have been sent down and the Lawḥ-i-Nidá' (Tablet of the Call) testify and bear witness to the truth of My words. Blessed are those who are fair in their judgment, and happy are they who are trustworthy and sincere.[4]

After quoting his own translation of the tablet, Cole writes: "If I am correct, Bahá'u'lláh is here speaking of a twelve-day, private mystical experience he had beginning on his birthday, Muharram 2, 1279/June 30, 1862, in the months before his formal prophetic declaration of April–May 1863...."[5]

This tablet is indeed an important testimony regarding a crucial early event in the history of Bahá'u'lláh's revelation. But it is almost impossible for the statement in question to be a reference to 1862. The tablet makes it clear that this twelve-day mystical experience occurred during Bahá'u'lláh's childhood. He is speaking of the grief he felt in His childhood on contemplating the severity of the law of the sword in previous dispensations and His desire for that severe law to be annulled. It is in that context that He says that suddenly, after reading the book and becoming saddened by it, He had a profound experience which brought him the joyful tidings of "heavenly reunion." The context of the passage and the word "until" (tá ánkih) make it clear that this is not an event occurring forty years later. Bahá'u'lláh's sadness did not continue for forty years but was dispelled by the joyful tidings. Furthermore, Bahá'u'lláh mentions several events that followed the experience: the appearance of the waves of the sea of utterance; the later time of His revelation (that is, in the Síyáh-Chál); the inception of the new dispensation and the fulfillment of the prophecy concerning the attainment of all good in the year nine; and the disclosure, direct and indirect, of His message to some individuals (through His tablets such as the Tablet of All Food), and the removal of what had been the cause of discord and establishment of the basis of unity—in writings such as the Hidden Words revealed during the Baghdad period and subsequently.

It is possible to argue that the events of revelation both in the Síyáh-Chál and in the Riḍván Garden contain strong symbolic resemblances to that original twelve-day childhood experience. The date of the Síyáh-Chál experience coincides with the date of the childhood experience, and the Riḍván declaration, like the childhood experience, also lasted for twelve days. The second of Muḥarram occurred exactly two months after Bahá'u'lláh's imprisonment in the Síyáh-

Chál. In addition it was the second day of the new year, 1269 A.H., which was the beginning of the year nine after the Báb's declaration in 1260. In other words, the night before Bahá'u'lláh's birthday in 1852 was most likely the beginning of the year nine.[6] But it is clear that the event in which "tidings of heavenly reunion" were imparted to Him occurred during Bahá'u'lláh's childhood.

Cole's interpretation of the tablet, which reads that event as referring to a much later date, is partly accountable to several mistakes in translation. He identifies *Qalam-i-A'lá* as the Báb and comes up with: "After the Most High Pen (the Bab), we abrogated all that which was the cause of hardship...."[7] But in fact, what Bahá'u'lláh says is that "From that point forward, We removed through the agency of the Pen of the Most High [that is, Bahá'u'lláh] whatever had been the cause of suffering...." And while Bahá'u'lláh tells us that His experience happened on the second of Muḥarram before sunrise, this becomes translated as "before the Dawning (of my mission)."[8] But it is simply a reference to the time of the day when the event occurred. The meaning of the tablet is further altered by giving: "... when I attained to that which God rendered the source of joy to the worlds"—as if it referred to Bahá'u'lláh's receiving of revelation. But what He actually says is: "Thus hast thou attained unto that which God hath made the source of joy to all mankind"—referring to Bahá'u'lláh's disclosure of His revelation to the addressee. But the fact that "those days" means Bahá'u'lláh's childhood is obvious even from Cole's translation.

From this tablet we can see that at a very early age Bahá'u'lláh desired to see tolerance, reconciliation, and unity among all on earth as well as an end to the law of the sword even in the path of the Cause of God. Although He practiced wisdom and gradual disclosure during the Bábí dispensation, He was obviously committed to the principles of human unity from the very beginning. For an accurate picture of the origins of Bahá'u'lláh's ideas on the unity and harmony of the religions, as well as His other ideas, we cannot overlook what He Himself says of His own awareness of those ideas in His childhood. In another tablet Bahá'u'lláh emphasizes this very point by alluding apparently to this same childhood experience:

O contending peoples and kindreds of the earth! Set your faces towards unity, and let the radiance of its light shine upon you. Gather ye together, and for the sake of God resolve to root out whatever is the source of contention amongst you. Then will the effulgence of the world's great Luminary envelop the whole earth, and its inhabitants become the citizens of one city, and the occupants of one and the same throne. This wronged One hath, *ever since the early days of His life*, cherished none other desire but this, and will continue to entertain no wish except this wish. There can be no doubt whatever that the peoples of the world, of whatever race or religion, derive their inspiration from one heavenly Source, and are the subjects of one God. The difference between the ordinances under which they abide should be attributed to the varying requirements and exigencies of the age in which they were revealed. All of them, except a few which are the outcome of human perversity, were ordained of God, and are a reflection of His Will and Purpose. Arise and, armed with the power of faith, shatter to pieces the gods of your vain imaginings, the sowers of dissension amongst you. Cleave unto that which draweth you together and uniteth you. This, verily, is the most exalted Word which the Mother Book hath sent down and revealed unto you. (*Gleanings* 217–18; italics added.)

This brings us to the second and more important point. In terms of the internal logic and conceptual categories of Bahá'u'lláh's revelation, all the ideas mentioned in the tablet about His childhood experience are a part of the doctrine I have referred to throughout this book as the removal of the sword. We can see that in the tablet about His childhood experience He is talking directly about that idea. As we saw in Chapter 7, that concept contains by implication all the teachings which would later be elaborated and explicated in His writings; it includes the principle of tolerance and accord between the religions, assisting the Cause of God by peaceful means, and the prohibition of all forms of violence and coercion, as well as the principles of human unity, inherent dignity, and rights, and the like. In other words, all the major teachings that we find in Bahá'u'lláh's later writings were already espoused by Him even before He went to Baghdad and were in fact integral parts of His revelation in the Síyáh-Chál.

As Bahá'u'lláh has said many times, throughout the Baghdad

period He wrote tablets exhorting both humanity in general and the Bábí community in particular to forsake their weapons for the moral force of utterance, tolerance, righteousness, and trustworthiness, thus elevating the human station and realizing unity among all human beings.[9] In Epistle to the Son of the Wolf He states that after His arrival in Iraq,

> ... We revealed, as a copious rain, by the aid of God and His Divine Grace and mercy, Our verses, and sent them to various parts of the world. We exhorted all men, and particularly this people, through Our wise counsels and loving admonitions, and forbade them to engage in sedition, quarrels, disputes and conflict. As a result of this, and by the grace of God, waywardness and folly were changed into piety and understanding, and weapons converted into instruments of peace. (22)

The definitive proof of the early presence of the premises underlying the teaching of religious tolerance is found in the Hidden Words, revealed in the middle Baghdad period around 1858, with its enunciation of a new ethics in which all humans are described as sacred, and all are enjoined to refrain from tyranny, sedition, stealing, violence, and the like—which are all expressions of the principle of the removal of the sword and the new meaning of assisting the Cause of God. 'Abdu'l-Bahá has pointed out that the Hidden Words itself contains the ideas of the oneness of humanity, universal peace, the independent investigation of truth, and global ethics.[10]

Bahá'u'lláh Himself testifies in Epistle to the Son of the Wolf that all His writings and His actions were dedicated to realizing the station of the unity of humankind as expressed in the utterance: "Ye are the fruits of one tree, and the leaves of one branch," which He calls a goal that "excelleth all other goals." Then he writes: "At one time We spoke in the language of the Lawgiver; at another in that of the truth-seeker and the mystic, and yet Our supreme purpose and highest wish hath always been to disclose the glory and sublimity of this station" (Epistle 15). That statement provides yet another indication of Bahá'u'lláh's own awareness of the unitary yet multifaceted nature of His mission and the fact that His mystical writings during the Baghdad period, equally with His later writings, were intended to promulgate the principle of the unity of humankind.

In sum, the entire eleven-year Baghdad period was characterized by Bahá'u'lláh's public declaration of the principle of the removal of the sword, a principle which the tablet about His twelve-day experience enables us to date to His childhood. Because that principle implicitly includes within itself Bahá'u'lláh's basic vision and all its aspects, not only must we conclude that it is basically inaccurate to date the "first" proclamation of His "commitment" to the principle of religious concord or tolerance to His Riḍván declaration in 1863, but any late date or external derivation suggested for His other concepts including consultative democratic government, universal peace, and universal auxiliary language must be similarly incorrect.

We now turn to examine several other claims made in *Modernity and the Millennium* and the methodological issues they raise. Cole has argued that Bahá'u'lláh was opposed to representative democracy before His exile to 'Akká but that He changed His mind after being exposed to the ideas of some of the intellectuals also exiled to 'Akká. He also attempts to find links between Bahá'u'lláh's concept of universal auxiliary language and Middle Eastern movements for script reform. Finally, he suggests that some of Bahá'u'lláh's ideas about peace may have a basis in nineteenth-century French thought about international peace, specifically that of Saint-Simon.

We will return to discuss in detail the theory of a change in Bahá'u'lláh's ideas about ideal forms of government. As we will see, once again, there are significant problems in the logic of the argument. What is presented as evidence to support the presence of so-called undemocratic ideas in Bahá'u'lláh's early writings actually occurs in His *later* writings, and what is offered as evidence for democratic ideas in the later ('Akká) writings was actually revealed years *before* the exile to 'Akká.

The attempt to connect Bahá'u'lláh's principle of universal auxiliary language to movements for Persian and Arabic script reform is farfetched. It is true that in the nineteenth century a few Persian and Arab reformers, influenced by an exaggerated attraction to Western ideas, advocated the reform of the Persian and Arabic scripts. Those proposals for language reform were largely motivated by narrow, nationalistic aspirations. Bahá'u'lláh's principle went far beyond such simplistic proposals, to advocate the imperative need for the entire world to adopt a universal auxiliary language—not only as a requirement of an emerging modern world order but also, as He Himself defines it in the Kitáb-i-Aqdas, as a sign of the maturation of humanity. His principle was a basic component of His global worldview rooted in a spiritual and historically progressive framework—and the whole framework was alien to the mostly atheistic, static, and nationalistic concerns of the Middle Eastern script reformers. In fact, Bahá'u'lláh's idea of universal auxiliary language has no logical connection to script reform.

Nor does it have any connection to the numerous projects of "universal language" in previous centuries.[11] Although termed "universal language" projects, they differed in fundamental ways from the concept of a universal auxiliary language as Bahá'u'lláh defines it. Most were attempts at universal alphabets or were logical, mathematical, and a priori languages designed for specific, limited scientific or philosophical purposes. They tended to be based on the empiricist and Enlightenment premise that natural languages distort the understanding of reality, and they represented attempts to construct a signifying system in which the linguistic sign would mirror the reality of things as they are. In that respect they were new versions of the search for a mythic Adamic language which was believed to unveil the essence of things. Bahá'u'lláh's conception has no affinity with these models. He does not reject natural languages as candidates for the universal auxiliary language but praises them and their communicative capacity. In fact, He does not insist on either a natural or an artificial language as the universal auxiliary language but rather on the process by which it is to be chosen.

In the nineteenth century, there was a sudden dramatic rise of interest in the idea of constructing a language to facilitate international communication.[12] But what Umberto Eco calls the "great flood" of projects for created international languages came in the late nineteenth century[13]—in other words, *after* Bahá'u'lláh's announcement of His principle, which as we know from Epistle to the Son of the Wolf, He had talked about in Istanbul in 1863.

A careful examination of Bahá'u'lláh's own discussions of His principle shows what is the significant and powerful element in it that makes it unique and gives a glimpse of why He designates its realization as one of the signs of the maturity of humankind. Bahá'u'lláh writes:

> Among the things which are conducive to unity and concord and will cause the whole earth to be regarded as one country is that the divers languages be reduced to one language and in like manner the scripts used in the world be confined to a single script. It is incumbent upon all nations to appoint some men of understanding and erudition to convene a gathering and through joint consultation choose one language from among the varied existing languages, or create a new one, to be taught to the children in all the schools of the world. (*Tablets* 165–66)

Eco observes that "for some international body (the UN or the European Parliament) to impose a particular IAL [International Auxiliary Language] as a lingua franca (or perhaps, sanction the actual diffusion of one) … *would be a totally unprecedented historical event.*"[14] Bahá'u'lláh's principle is concerned with precisely both those issues: the collective international agreement to legislate such a language and its systematic diffusion through the schools of the world, for the purpose of creating one of the fundamental conditions for global identity.

Eco makes an observation that is extremely significant. The only remaining serious obstacle to international auxiliary language, he says, is that "governments are naturally egotistical; they enact laws for their own benefit, but never for the benefit of all humanity. Even if we were all to agree on the necessity of an IAL, it is hard to imagine the international bodies, which are still striving to arrive at some agreement over the means to save our planet from an ecological catastrophe, being capable of imposing a painless remedy for the open wound of

Babel."[15] In other words, because such a law would mean abandoning the collective egotism of linguistic nationalism, subordinating self-interest, and acting solely for the benefit of all humanity, when the nations join together to enact that law it will be an unmistakable sign that they have reached an unprecedented stage of maturity.

The attempt to link Bahá'u'lláh's vision of peace and global unity to Saint-Simon's political theory is similarly farfetched and underestimates the creativity and uniqueness of Bahá'u'lláh's vision. Like other "secular millenarians," Saint-Simon was influenced by the long tradition of religious expectations of a reign of universal peace and justice.[16] Eugen Weber suggests that some of Saint-Simon's ideas in turn can be traced to religious sources, particularly the medieval Joachim of Fiore (1135–1202). But what Saint-Simon advocated was the unification of Western Europe. Such a call for European unity was part of the agenda of many European theorists, some of whose ideas were much closer to Bahá'u'lláh's. In fact, it was the Romantics (whom Cole perceives to be the opposite of Bahá'u'lláh's so-called liberalism) who passionately emphasized this idea. Friedrich Schlegel and Novalis, for instance, were among its major proponents. But they all conceived of European unity as a return to the aristocratic medieval order with the Pope as the spiritual head of the continent.[17] Saint-Simon himself defends his vision of a united industrial Europe by celebrating the unity of medieval Europe under the rule of the Catholic church and calls for a return to that unity but under the rule of his own new materialistic "church."[18] In fact, if we must trace Bahá'u'lláh's declaration of the oneness of humankind and global peace to a preexisting program for European unity, it would make more sense to locate its origin in the medieval religious European order rather than Saint-Simon's later, atheistic version of the same plan. But neither the medieval pattern, nor the models of Saint-Simon or the German Romantics, corresponds to Bahá'u'lláh's concept and principles for world order.

Saint-Simon's idea of European cooperation was based on the assumption of the superiority of Europeans and the violent subjugation of inferior non-Europeans. For him European unity was a means of strengthening European productive capacity (industrialism) and extending European domination. Furthermore, membership in his European Parliament was to be only for those European countries that had passed through parliamentary regimes and were willing to create a parliament of technocrats and scientists which would serve as the new clergy. Both peace and unity were secondary to his thesis of industrialism. According to that idea, the supreme purpose of all societies was the maximization of production, and industrial/capitalist society would be peaceful because it was in the interests of the chiefs of industries to maintain peace rather than engage in war. Saint-Simon's analysis conveniently ignores the colonial wars and oppression dictated by the economic and material interests of European industrialists.

Saint-Simon, posing his model as superior to the revelation of God to His Prophets, declares his own "mission" in the form of a racist "divine command" to take up arms and impose the materialistic "church of Newton" on the whole world:

> Hear this: Europeans are the children of Abel. Asia and Africa are inhabited by the descendants of Cain. Just observe how bloodthirsty these Africans are. Look at the indolence of the Asians. These impure men gave up their first attempt to raise themselves to the level of my divine providence. Europeans will unite their forces and free their Greek brothers from the domination of the Turks. The founder of the religion will be commander-in-chief of the armies of the faithful. These armies will subject the children of Cain to the religion, and cover the entire earth with defences for the protection of the members of the Councils of Newton....[19]

Little wonder that Saint-Simon identifies Napoleon as the founder of his new "religion."[20] As Cole himself acknowledges, Saint-Simon was not opposed to colonialism. Compare the above words of Saint-Simon with Bahá'u'lláh's call for the removal of the sword, His summons to international unity and peace, and His critique of the materialistic excesses of the European nations.

Although Saint-Simon talked of a "new Christianity," he did not mean any kind of divine revelation. On the contrary, he was elevating empirical science to the level of absolute truth and the sacred. In Saint-

Simon's words: "Jesus was …. inspired for a fine and good cause. But Jesus was ignorant…. It is obvious that Jesus and his commentators had no clear idea of the workings of the universe…. I believe in the necessity of a religion for the maintenance of the social order. I believe that deism is outworn." Until a transition from the inferior form of belief (deism) to the superior form (physicism) was complete, he says, "I believe that there have to be two distinct doctrines: physicism for educated men, and deism for the ignorant."[21]

Saint-Simon recommended the unity of France and England to assure the dominance of the new religion of physicism in the world. In his second prospectus for a new Encyclopedia, he outlines that the scientists of England and France should form an association charged with "organising the positive doctrine, that is, of basing general science, commonly called religion, on observation." This association of "Anglo-French clergy," it was to be declared, "represents God on earth, and … its decisions are divine."[22] All the inhabitants of the world were to fall under the rule of the new scientist-clergy. Saint-Simon says: "The Council of Newton will represent me [God] on earth. It will divide humanity into four divisions: English, French, German, Italian…. the mathematician who receives the most votes will be president."[23]

His Newtonianism or New Christianity called for a new clergy but with all the old clergy's undemocratic authority, which was just to be transferred to the social and natural scientists. In Saint-Simon's technocratic theory of politics, humanity had gone through two superstitious stages of theological/feudal and metaphysical/democratic orientations and was now arriving at the scientific/industrial or positive stage.[24] In this stage, social and political decision making would be based on reason, which for Saint-Simon was not the vote of the public but the technical expertise of the professional scientists (spiritual power) and the chiefs of industry (temporal power).[25] In fact, the positivism of Saint-Simon was opposed to the democratic ideas of the Enlightenment as well.[26] (One has to remember that for French positivists as well as for German Romantics, the "negative theory" was nothing other than the French Enlightenment perspective.)

The contrast of those ideas with the vision and teachings of Bahá'-u'lláh is clear. Bahá'u'lláh harshly criticized the very same modernist glorification of science into a new sacred and uncompromisingly condemned the authoritarian power and arrogance of divines and clergy—old and new varieties alike. It is true that there are some constructive elements in Saint-Simon and that they can also be found in the writings of Bahá'u'lláh. But this is true of virtually all philosophers and theorists past and present. If one compares the writings of Bahá'u'lláh with those of any major social thinker of the nineteenth or twentieth century, it is possible to find significant similarities—and frequently, more than the similarities with Saint-Simon. For example, any serious student of European social theory will find common elements between some of Bahá'u'lláh's ideas and those of Kant, Hegel, Marx, and the Romantics. However, this does not mean that Bahá'u'lláh has borrowed the ideas from them. On the whole, as is evident from the passages quoted above, the dissimilarities between the ideas of Bahá'u'lláh and those of Saint-Simon are basic and at the foundational level and therefore outweigh any similarities, especially when those similarities prove to be only superficial.

Ascribing Bahá'u'lláh's ideas of the oneness of humankind and global peace to the influence of this or that theorist of European unity or script reform ignores the complexity and internal coherence of Bahá'u'lláh's system. His vision of unity was not a shifting, eclectic product of random external influences, nor it was the effect of mere utopian and moral idealism. On the contrary, He saw the world as an essentially spiritual organic unity and He perceived the historic need for a global ethics—not as an expedient practicality, but as the next developmental stage in the collective spiritual journey of humankind. He elaborated in a systematic way all the different requirements of such an organic and fundamental vision, including unity in religion, language, and international political structures; social justice; consultative and democratic governance; and the like. These (along with all the other elements, including His provisions for an administrative order and explicit covenant of authority and succession) are intrinsic, practical implications of His announcement of the Day of God, the universal revelation, and the removal of the sword. They are necessary parts of an authentic vision of world unity—and far from petty and nationalistic concerns with script reform or the limited unity of European imperialism.

One of the major reasons for reductive approaches to His writings is that the uniqueness of the principles of political philosophy that they contain has not always been understood. Therefore, it is necessary to address that issue directly.

PREMISES OF THE CONCEPT OF NEW WORLD ORDER

It is undoubtable that Bahá'u'lláh approves of certain elements that are also found in modern Western political philosophy and systems of government. But at the same time, and even more significantly, He also criticizes and transcends their limitations. A careful study of His writings discloses that they contain a new philosophical basis for political theory and a holistic vision which, without being merely syncretic, incorporates the positive elements of Eastern and Western political philosophy and represents a novel and unprecedented structure that neither the existing categories and discourse of either East or West are capable of describing.

Not only does Bahá'u'lláh create new categories, He makes it clear that His premises are normally different and often opposed to the dominant premises underlying Western liberal political philosophy. Instead of talking in terms of such notions as psychological utilitarianism, atheistic and deistic rationalism, a mechanistic conception of nature, social contract theory, opposition between civil and natural states, moral utilitarianism, and so on, His premises are based upon His multidimensional and spiritual conception of existence and nature, ethics, action determination, and progressive revelation. His categories are also qualitatively different from those of nation-state-centered liberal political philosophy. He discusses His egalitarian logic and His conception of democratic institutions in terms of the categories of the sacredness of all beings, the oneness of humanity, the principle of covenant, the maturation of humanity, and His New World Order.

To understand the Kitáb-i-Aqdas, or any of Bahá'u'lláh's writings, we must see them in terms of Bahá'u'lláh's own categories. A prime expression of those new categories is found in the three terms of the phrase from the Kitáb-i-Aqdas which was discussed in the last chapter: *New World Order*. These terms reflect the inseparable unity of the triad of order, progress, and global orientation in Bahá'u'lláh's spiritual and social vision. Various systems of political philosophy may have emphasized one or another element of this concept in some form, but it is the totality, organic unity, and harmony of these three principles that defines and distinguishes Bahá'u'lláh's vision. In terms of all three concepts, that vision differs from Enlightenment and liberal political philosophy in that it rejects the Enlightenment's rationalistic theory, which recognizes no spiritual or revelational basis for social order, as well as the Enlightenment's static and ahistorical conception of nature, rationality, and values and its confinement of political discourse to the level of the nation-state.

We will examine these three terms in logical sequence. The first term is *Order*. The question of order was the first systematic question of modern Western political theory. The reason is not difficult to understand—the mere fact of social life and organization requires some sort of order regulating the behavior of individuals in that society.[27] No society is possible without order, or in Kantian terminology, order is a fundamental condition of the possibility of society.[28]

The beginning of modern political theory is associated with the writings of Thomas Hobbes in the seventeenth century. According to Hobbes, human beings are naturally selfish, aggressive, and concerned with the pursuit of their interests; in the state of nature they will use any means to get what they want, including stealing or murder. Consequently, in the state of nature there can be no order but rather the perpetual war of each one against everyone else. Such a life is, as he famously called it, nasty, brutish, and short.[29]

Hobbes's solution to the problem of order is rooted in his definition of human nature. Humans are selfish and yet rational. By "rational," Hobbes means that people will try to maximize their pleasure and minimize their costs. In other words, rational people will follow their selfish interests efficiently and effectively. But since human beings are rational, they understand that the state of nature is harmful to them and conflicts with their interests. Therefore, because of their selfishness, humans will decide to cooperate in the social contract, to create laws and institutions of government so that the fear of punishment by a strong and dictatorial state will prevent selfish individuals from committing criminal acts. Order, in this view, is the product of the fear of punishment and coercion.

Hobbesian theory inspired the philosophy of the eighteenth-century Enlightenment. Although the Enlightenment philosophers disagreed with the dictatorial form of the Hobbesian state, they retained the basic principles of Hobbes's theory of order; that is, they continued to believe that order was based on a combination of human rational selfishness and fear of legal punishment.[30] The inadequacy of this rationalistic conception of order became increasingly evident in nineteenth-century sociology and political theory. Modern social and political theory not only upheld the normative and symbolic character of human action and motivation, it also reconceptualized social relations in terms of ideas like solidarity, common bonds, common religion, shared values or culture, legitimacy, and normative integration.[31]

The distinctiveness of Bahá'u'lláh's concept of order stands out against the background of this theoretical problem. In His writings He specifies that effective and just order requires at least four conditions. The first condition is the system of reward and punishment. The second is social justice. Bahá'u'lláh speaks of reward and punishment as the "two pillars" on which "the canopy of world order is upraised" (*Tablets* 126). But they are inseparable from justice, which "traineth the world" (*Tablets* 27). However, a society characterized by high degrees of inequality among social classes is a society in which rewards and punishments are arbitrary and opposed to justice and rights. In His tablets to the kings and rulers of the world, Bahá'u'lláh emphasizes aspects of social justice including the protection of the rights of the poor, the elimination of poverty, and moderation in the distribution of wealth and privileges. Writing to the Ottoman sultan, 'Abdu'l-'Azíz, for example, He tells him to "Overstep not the bounds of moderation," to deal with his ministers and subjects with "undeviating justice, so that none among them may either suffer want, or be pampered with luxuries," and "to rule with equity among men" (*Gleanings* 235–36).

The third condition of social order is communication and fellowship among individual members of society and among different social groups. Bahá'u'lláh's insight on this issue is unique and fresh. The only sociologist who noted the same point was Emile Durkheim, who advocated something similar two decades after Bahá'u'lláh. According to Durkheim, morality and solidarity are not the products of abstract rules. They require intense interaction among individuals. This frequent relationship among the members of society creates solidarity, altruism, mutual bonds, and commitment to universal principles transcending the selfish interests of the individuals.[32]

Bahá'u'lláh prescribes fellowship among people and groups and emphasizes that unity and love are the results of such communication: "They that are endued with sincerity and faithfulness should associate with all the peoples and kindreds of the earth with joy and radiance, inasmuch as consorting with people hath promoted and will continue to promote unity and concord, which in turn are conducive to the maintenance of order in the world and to the regeneration of nations" (*Tablets* 36). So important was this principle that He made it operative at the international level as well, calling for a universal auxiliary language for the purpose of promoting communication and interaction on a global scale and creating a global conception of identity and citizenship.

The fourth and the foremost precondition of effective order in human society, according to Bahá'u'lláh, is the love and fear of God, religious faith, internalized moral values, and love of humanity. This aspect of Bahá'u'lláh's analysis of the problem of order is most directly opposed to the dominant Western—specifically, French—Enlightenment concept of order. For the latter, there is no need for religion or divine guidance in human life because human reason and selfish orientation are thought to guarantee social order.[33] While the predominant Enlightenment theory of order rejected religion and spiritual values, Bahá'u'lláh sees the question of order as evidence of the need for religion and divine revelation in human history. For instance, He writes that although "penalties ... form an effective instrument for the security and protection of men ... dread of penalties maketh people desist only outwardly from committing vile and contemptible deeds, while that which guardeth and restraineth man both outwardly and inwardly hath been and still is the fear of God. It is man's true protector and his spiritual guardian" (*Tablets* 93). Elsewhere He says: "In truth, religion is a radiant light and an impregnable stronghold for the protection and welfare of the peoples of the world, for the fear of God impelleth man to hold fast to that which is good, and shun all evil. Should the lamp of religion be obscured, chaos and confusion will ensue, and the lights of fairness and justice, of tranquility and peace cease to shine" (*Tablets* 125).

But as we have seen, in his various writings Bahá'u'lláh calls on people to observe divine laws and commandments not merely for fear of divine punishment but because of love for the divine beauty. The beginning of the Kitáb-i-Aqdas expresses this vision of order and the social function of divine laws: "The precepts laid down by God," Bahá'u'lláh says, "constitute the highest means for the maintenance of order in the world and the security of its peoples...." It is "by their aid" that "the standards of Victory will be planted upon the highest peaks"; while the basis of order is to "Observe My commandments, for the love of My beauty" (¶ 2–4).

Likewise, in one of His tablets Bahá'u'lláh argues that the highest expression of order is found in an approach to laws and moral precepts in which action is its own reward. In other words, the supreme reward is the delight in the principles and their voluntary observance with a pure heart and sincere intention. Here reward and punishment merges with the motivation of love:

> For every act performed there shall be a recompense according to the estimate of God, and unto this the very ordinances and prohibitions prescribed by the Almighty amply bear witness. For surely if deeds were not rewarded and yielded no fruit, then the Cause of God—exalted is He—would prove futile. Immeasurably high is He exalted above such blasphemies! However, unto them that are rid of all attachments a deed is, verily, its own reward. (*Tablets* 189)

Bahá'u'lláh's concept of order transcends the limitations and one-sidedness of the current sociological debates on the question of order between conservative and radical sociologists using functionalist and conflict theories, respectively. The conflict model argues that extreme inequalities of income and wealth, and the resulting poverty of dis-privileged groups, are the root causes of the failure of rules and order, and that the ultimate cause of order must be justice in society.[34] In con-trast, advocates of functionalist theory argue that the real basis of order is shared values and moral consensus in society. Consequently, they tend to deemphasize the need for social justice and to equate the status quo with justice.[35] Bahá'u'lláh's theory of order is far more complex. It emphasizes the need for spiritual, religious, and moral commitment in society while at the same time it finds social justice to be the first and basic feature of such a spiritual worldview.

Now we can see the meaning of the term *Order* in the concept of New World Order. Bahá'u'lláh is saying that human social order must be based not only on scientific and instrumental rationality but also on social justice, the promotion and strengthening of communication, and divine guidance.

However, Bahá'u'lláh is not content with simply a theory of order. His concept of order is always accompanied by another equally impor-tant idea. He speaks of a *New* order. This term denotes Bahá'u'lláh's concept of historical change and progress. The philosophers of the Enlightenment revolted against traditional religious theories of order in which it had been argued that human social order should remain unchanged because the Will of God was unchangeable. Religion had been used to bolster the status quo and tradition and to oppose his-torical dynamics. Bahá'u'lláh's concept is exactly the opposite. Instead of being static and unchangeable, religion is the cause of the spiritual and social advancement and progress of humanity. The collective pur-pose of the creation of human beings is "to carry forward an ever-advancing civilization" (*Gleanings* 215). Here the doctrine of progres-sive revelation has a direct bearing on the question of social order.[36] The creative Will of God is oriented to humanity's dynamic journey toward an ever-increasing unity and progress.[37] That is why revelation itself is progressive. Social order is based on the revealed Word—the *Logos*. Those same teachings of religion are periodically renewed by a new revelation according to the conditions and needs of humanity in its new stage of development. Bahá'u'lláh likens this process to the diagnosis of a physician:

> The All-Knowing Physician hath His finger on the pulse of mankind. He perceiveth the disease, and prescribeth, in His unerring wisdom, the remedy. Every age hath its own problem, and every soul its particular aspiration. The remedy the world needeth in its present-day afflictions can never be the same as that which the subsequent age may require. Be anxiously concerned with the needs of the age ye live in, and center your deliberations on its exigencies and requirements. (*Gleanings* 213)

But the "needs of the time" to which revelation responds with new laws and teachings are not dictated by the social and cultural status quo but by the developmental goal of maturity and the requirements to enable it to attain the next stage.

As we have seen, in the language of social theory Bahá'u'lláh's dynamic and historical approach to social reality is usually designated by the term *historical consciousness*. The term *New* in the concept of the New World Order can be seen as an expression of historical consciousness. This emphasis on the dynamic character of existence itself, as well as human life, society, culture, and religion, which is integral to all the writings of Bahá'u'lláh, is simultaneously a metaphysical, sociological, and normative principle. It should be noted, however, that Bahá'u'lláh's historical reason is not only opposed to the static conceptions of the Enlightenment and liberal doctrines, it is also opposed to various forms of thesis of the end of history which can be found among most of the advocates of dialectical and dynamic viewpoints as well.

Bahá'u'lláh's vision of a New World Order is even more clearly understandable when we pay attention to the third term, *World*. This third term follows from Bahá'u'lláh's historical consciousness. Society and culture are constantly in a process of change. In the present context, the emerging stage is a global one and—correspondingly—spirituality, culture, and social order must take a global character. It has become indisputable in the twentieth century that issues like environmental pollution, world hunger, nuclear war, and inequality of opportunities and access to resources can only be resolved if all people regard themselves as members of one human community and as an interdependent organic unity. It is for these reasons that Bahá'u'lláh talks about a New *World* Order and has always declared the realization of the oneness of humanity to be the ultimate goal of His revelation. The historic shift in emphasis is reflected in passages such as the following:

> From the heaven of God's Will, and for the purpose of ennobling the world of being and of elevating the minds and souls of men, hath been sent down that which is the most effective instrument for the education of the whole human race. The highest essence and most perfect expression of whatsoever the peoples of old have either said or written hath, through this most potent Revelation, been sent down from the heaven of the Will of the All-Possessing, the Ever-Abiding God. Of old it hath been revealed: "Love of one's country is an element of the Faith of God." The Tongue of Grandeur hath, however, in the day of His manifestation proclaimed: "It is not his to boast who loveth his country, but it is his who loveth the world." Through the power released by these exalted words He hath lent a fresh impulse, and set a new direction, to the birds of men's hearts, and hath obliterated every trace of restriction and limitation from God's holy Book. (*Gleanings* 95–96)

But the global approach, which is the heart of Bahá'u'lláh's concept of the unity of humankind, is much more than a platitude, nor can it be reduced to simply a form of modern Western doctrines of participatory democracy. Bahá'u'lláh is designating and establishing a new unit of analysis—the global level—at which to reconceptualize human spiritual, economic, and political culture and institutions. His perspective intentionally transcends the limited nationalistically oriented discourse of political theory because solutions based on the category of the nation-state are inadequate to meet the needs and moral challenges of a global human society.

The traditions of the Enlightenment and Romanticism were both imprisoned within the category of the nation-state. Although Enlightenment philosophy spoke of equality and democracy, it accepted the nation-state as the largest legitimate unit of analysis. The consequence of this premise was a hypocritical assertion of inalienable rights for all men, while simultaneously legitimizing inequalities among nations. The conservative Romantics revolted against the mechanistic theories of the French Enlightenment and emphasized the moral character of human beings and society, while still glorifying the nondemocratic modern nation-state as the only space of morality and reality. In contrast, Bahá'u'lláh, without abolishing the nation, moves it from the position of centrality to that of a component part within a larger whole and replaces the ethic of nationalism with an ethic of world citizenship.

At the time Bahá'u'lláh wrote His tablets on this subject, Western political and sociological theory was either mechanistic in its out-look—the liberal philosophy—or adopted an organic approach based on the nation-state. The organic theory of the state was advocated by German Romantics like Friedrich and August Schlegel, conservative philosophers like Edmund Burke and de Maistre, nationalistic German Idealists like Fichte, and cultural idealists like Herder.[38] The organic theory of the state continued to influence the political theory of nineteenth-century Western philosophy, even dominating the liberal Spencer's evolutionary theory.[39] Twentieth-century functionalism and sociological realism are also expressions of the same theory. The organic theory of the state posited the exclusive reality of the nation-state as a cultural and political reality which was the only criterion of values and norms. It rejected any possibility of a universal history because only nations were real and they were incommensurable. German Romantics talked of the *Volkgeist*, the Spirit of the Nation, which denied any international, intercultural, or universal values. Militarism and the justification of international violence, exploitation, and dominance were the natural conclusions of this organic theory of the state. The doctrines of the eighteenth-century French Enlightenment and nineteenth-century British liberalism led to the same conclusions by defending an unrestrained economic world system which dominated poor countries and created massive inequalities among nations.

Bahá'u'lláh's organic theory, in contrast, is based on the unity of the planet. Because humanity has become objectively an interconnected organic reality, all human institutions, cultural principles, norms, and conceptions of equality and justice must be raised to the level of the international unit of analysis. Such a move qualitatively transforms all the previous categories of political and religious discourse. Bahá'u'lláh calls the governors of all societies to just such a reorientation of the guiding principles of public policy when He tells them to "Take ye counsel together, and let your concern be only for that which profiteth mankind, and bettereth the condition thereof...." (Gleanings 254), and

> The time must come when the imperative necessity for the holding of a vast, an all-embracing assemblage of men will be universally realized. The rulers and kings of the earth must needs attend it, and, participating in its deliberations, must consider such ways and means as will lay the foundations of the world's Great Peace amongst men. ... Should any king take up arms against another, all should unitedly arise and prevent him. If this be done, the nations of the world will no longer require any armaments, except for the purpose of preserving the security of their realms and of maintaining internal order within their territories." (Tablets 165)

In fact, global structures of government and collective security were the most significant structural developments in the twentieth century.

The following statement embodies several important aspects of this reorientation to global consciousness:

> That one indeed is a man who, today, dedicateth himself to the service of the entire human race. The Great Being saith: Blessed and happy is he that ariseth to promote the best interests of the peoples and kindreds of the earth. In another passage He hath proclaimed: It is not for him to pride himself who loveth his own country, but rather for him who loveth the whole world. The earth is but one country, and mankind its citizens. (Tablets 167)

At least three principles are emphasized here. The first is the new definition of the human being. The worldview and values of a society are dependent on its particular conception of human nature. A consumerist and mechanistic definition of human nature, for example, will lead to selfish and destructive values and culture. A particularistic definition in terms of a specific race, nation, gender, class, religion, or culture may lead to values of separation, hate, and indifference. The conception of human nature that Bahá'u'lláh offers is essentially spiritual, all-encompassing, and service oriented, leading to values of unity in diversity, justice, and altruism.

The second principle is expressed in the statement that "It is not for him to pride himself who loveth his own country, but rather for him who loveth the whole world." In announcing an ethic of world citizenship, the statement also epitomizes the conception of authentic freedom and liberty discussed in the Kitáb-i-Aqdas. That discourse on the nature of "true liberty" has been misunderstood by various writers who have read Bahá'u'lláh's words through various reductive categories and in terms of their own ideological preferences. Ignaz Goldziher, for example, took Bahá'u'lláh's critique of the modern notion of liberty as a rejection of the democratic principle in Western liberalism.[40] On the other hand, Cole, although noting the inadequacy of Goldziher's analysis, interprets that same discussion of liberty in the Kitáb-i-Aqdas as a rejection of libertine doctrines but holds that Bahá'u'lláh's conception of liberty endorses Western liberal political democracy.[41]

Although Cole's rejection of Goldziher's reading is accurate, he in turn does not note the ways in which Bahá'u'lláh's discussion of liberty in the Kitáb-i-Aqdas simultaneously criticizes specific aspects of the Western liberal conception of democracy as well. Specifically, in one tablet Bahá'u'lláh explains that "true liberty" (the same term that is described in the Kitáb-i-Aqdas) will be achieved when humanity has realized that "It is not for him to pride himself who loveth his own country, but rather for him who loveth the whole world."[42] While approving the general idea of democracy, Bahá'u'lláh finds the limited nationalistic scope that defines democracy and political liberty in the

West utterly inadequate. At the collective level, true liberty is realized through the unity of humankind, implying the establishment of global structures characterized by inclusive democratic norms and oriented to the interests of the entire human race, as opposed to the exclusionary and particularistic interests and structures of Western nationalism, colonialism, and militarism.

The third principle emphasized in Bahá'u'lláh's statement is the rejection of the prevalent nation–state-based definition of citizenship with its nationalistic presuppositions and exclusions. "The earth is but one country, and mankind its citizens" is a radical affirmation of world citizenship and consequently of universal human rights, which questions exclusionary entitlements and rights allocated on the basis of the accident of birth.

Now it is possible to have a general sense of the basic philosophical premises of Bahá'u'lláh's vision of the New World Order. It is the totality and unity of the three premises that comprise His message, in sum: (1) the harmony of the spiritual and the material in the context of a just society and a communicative culture; (2) the dynamic and progressive nature of both material and spiritual aspects of culture, corresponding to the needs of the current stage of human development; and (3) the global character dictated by those requirements at the present time.

SOCIOLOGICAL INTERACTIONISM: BEYOND REALISM AND NOMINALISM

At the basis of the system of thought we have been examining is a particular approach to the questions of reality and causation in human history. The question of reality—that is, of what is real—has been and continues to be a fundamental locus of debate in modern social theory. In fact the emergence of an institutionalized discipline called sociology was partly dependent on it.

One important argument legitimating sociology was the doctrine of sociological realism. According to this doctrine, society and social institutions are real entities which are not reducible to the level of the individual members of the society; in other words, society is more than the sum of its individuals.[43] An extreme form of this theory asserted that individuals do not exist, that only society exists and is real. Individuals, this theory insisted, are nothing but shadows of social structure and the product of social relationships.[44] Sociological realism was supported by the majority of sociologists in the nineteenth century.

For those adhering to sociological nominalism, in contrast, society is just a name—a fiction devoid of any reality—while the only real entity is the individual. Social institutions were to be understood and explained in terms of characteristics and laws of human nature.[45] Advocates of sociological nominalism argued that the idea of "society" is a product of linguistic confusion. Since language is limited, we cannot represent aggregates as the sum of all the individuals. So, for the sake of convenience we create aggregate terms, but then the habit of using those terms creates animistic conceptions of collective "entities."[46] Like many debates over binary oppositions in social and political theory, this debate was first launched in the battle between the Enlightenment (nominalism) and Romanticism (realism).[47] Nineteenth- and twentieth-century social theory has continued the same debate in different forms.

Similar to the question of reality was the question of causation, or the logic of determination in society and culture. Obviously, the question of reality was also very important here because if something does not exist it cannot be a real cause. An important part of the debate on causation was the question whether it is the individual personality or the social structure that determines social action. The relative significance of different social institutions has also been a matter of debate in social and political theory, with materialistic doctrines arguing that the economy determines all aspects of social life and historical dynamics, while idealist doctrines located religion, ideology, or symbolic culture as the base of the society.[48] Again, the philosophy of the Enlightenment and Romanticism were at odds on this question.

While the majority of social theories have defended a one-sided and reductive theory of social reality and social causation, Bahá'-u'lláh's writings, from the very beginning, disclose a perspective that is multidimensional and interactionist. In it, both individual and struc-

tural units of analysis are legitimate and necessary; no effective solution
to social problems is possible without simultaneous reform at both levels. Similarly, Bahá'u'lláh's doctrine of progressive revelation and His
historical approach to religion and spiritual culture imply a multidimensional theory of causation. Religious truth and spiritual culture
change in accordance with the degree of development in human society. It is for this reason that the Manifestations of God are described in
the Bahá'í writings through the metaphors of the "physician" and
"educator." The divine medicine changes in accordance with the state
of the patient and the stage of the illness. The divine teacher imparts
His teachings corresponding to the level of development and progress
of the student.

But at the same time, the revealed Word fundamentally affects the
development of that social and cultural reality. Referring back to the
ontological concepts in Bahá'u'lláh's metaphysics, the cause of all creation and the source of all attributes is the Primal Will, which is manifested in the created realm by the Manifestation of God. All aspects of
civilization including arts and technology are a result of the expression
of the Primal Will in the world of creation through the utterance of
the Word, or *Logos*:

> All the wondrous works ye behold in this world have been mani-
> fested through the operation of His supreme and most exalted Will,
> His wondrous and inflexible Purpose. Through the mere revelation
> of the word "Fashioner," issuing forth from His lips and proclaiming
> His attribute to mankind, such power is released as can generate,
> through successive ages, all the manifold arts which the hands of man
> can produce. This, verily, is a certain truth. No sooner is this resplen-
> dent word uttered, than its animating energies, stirring within all
> created things, give birth to the means and instruments whereby
> such arts can be produced and perfected. All the wondrous achieve-
> ments ye now witness are the direct consequences of the Revelation
> of this Name. (*Gleanings* 141–42)

The revelation shed into the world of creation by the Manifestation
of God in each age is responsible for the regeneration of spirit that

inspires a new civilization. This interaction is perpetual and continues indefinitely.

The interactionist concept of causation is confirmed even at the most basic ontological level. While all of created reality is the effulgence of the Primal Will, at the same time, as we saw in the ontological circle of the stages of creation, freedom plays an important role. The second stage of creation, that of Determination (*Irádih*), is characterized by the free choice to receive the divine effulgence. The concrete reality is always an interaction between Will and Determination. Even though all created things are ultimately dependent on God, even at that fundamental level there is always interaction between the divine and the concrete reality (thus both the Báb and Bahá'u'lláh have described the Primal Will and Determination as the "father" and "mother" of all created things).[49]

The most significant aspect of Bahá'u'lláh's system, in addition to the emphasis on the reality and importance of both individual personality and social structure, is the introduction of the global unit of analysis, which is absent from nineteenth-century social and political theory. In fact, the first systematic social and political theory to explicitly address the material aspect of this global level of analysis has been the world system theory developed in the second half of the twentieth century, and that theory, while influential, remains an exception in sociopolitical theory.[50]

In His discussions of various questions, Bahá'u'lláh systematically deals with the various levels of analysis. For instance, in the context of the doctrine of the removal of the sword, He deals with ethical principles that are to be followed by individuals—such as virtuous character, work ethic, and an egalitarian orientation. But He also addresses the institutional structures responsible for social justice as well as patterns of communication and fellowship among different religions, abolishing institutionalized forms of separation and discrimination and specifically denouncing the anti-Semitic policies of modern European states.[51]

And yet He does not stop at this level; He specifies the international structures which are conducive to fellowship and intercultural communication, calling for collective security and consultative patterns of international decision making, as well as universal auxiliary language.

Furthermore, Bahá'u'lláh looks at the interactions of these various levels. International culture and global institutions become powerful means of implementing social justice within national structures. An ethic of love and unity leads to consultative international and inter-cultural communication. A universal auxiliary language empowers individuals to communicate beyond national linguistic boundaries, at the same time as it fosters the sense of global identity and citizenship and the unity that leads to peace. The Kitáb-i-Aqdas deals simultaneously with all these different levels of analysis. Shoghi Effendi has expressed the same truth with regard to the concept of the oneness of humankind:

> Let there be no mistake. The principle of the Oneness of Mankind—the pivot round which all the teachings of Bahá'u'lláh revolve—is no mere outburst of ignorant emotionalism or an expression of vague and pious hope. Its appeal is not to be merely identified with a reawakening of the spirit of brotherhood and goodwill among men, nor does it aim solely at the fostering of harmonious cooperation among individual peoples and nations. Its implications are deeper, its claims greater than any which the Prophets of old were allowed to advance. Its message is applicable not only to the individual, but concerns itself primarily with the nature of those essential relationships that must bind all the states and nations as members of one human family.... It calls for no less than the reconstruction and the demilitarization of the whole civilized world—a world organically unified in all the essential aspects of its life, its political machinery, its spiritual aspiration, its trade and finance, its script and language, and yet infinite in the diversity of the national characteristics of its federated units.
>
> It represents the consummation of human evolution—an evolution that has had its earliest beginnings in the birth of family life, its subsequent development in the achievement of tribal solidarity, leading in turn to the constitution of the city-state, and expanding later into the institution of independent and sovereign nations.

The principle of the Oneness of Mankind, as proclaimed by Bahá'u'lláh, carries with it no more and no less than a solemn assertion that attainment to this final stage in this stupendous evolution is not only necessary but inevitable, that its realization is fast approaching, and that nothing short of a power that is born of God can succeed in establishing it.[52]

Chapter 10

SPIRIT, HISTORY, AND ORDER

THE EVOLUTION OF CIVILIZATION is a major theme of Bahá'u'lláh's vision. Cole, however, finds the "evolutionary" process to be in Bahá'u'lláh's own thought and understanding. He claims that the early writings of Bahá'u'lláh represent a "Hobbesian" absolutism opposed to democratic principles, while Bahá'u'lláh's later writings abandon that position for Western ideas of representative democracy. This judgment is based largely on his reading of certain of Bahá'u'lláh's tablets, particularly those to the Ottoman sultan 'Abdu'l-'Azíz and the shah of Iran, Náṣiri'd-Dín. In those letters Bahá'u'lláh employs the concept of the king as the "shadow of God"—a metaphor also found in traditional Eastern political theory, where it was associated with the doctrine of the absolute sovereignty of the ruler. In some of Bahá'-u'lláh's other writings, such as His letter to Queen Victoria, however, He expresses approval of the combination of monarchy and consultative institutions of government.

Based on his understanding of these and other tablets, Cole concludes that Bahá'u'lláh underwent a radical change of mind, eventually replacing His previous traditional Eastern political theory, the doctrine of the king as the shadow of God, with a Western theory of political democracy. He also asserts that Bahá'u'lláh's concept of sovereignty called for a modern-style separation of religion and state, which he also suggests was influenced by Sufism.[1] In this chapter I will examine the references to democracy and government in Bahá'u'lláh's writings and will argue that instead of discontinuity and change in His doctrines, we find unity and consistency in the message represented in all His works, while the differences are located in the differing contexts in which the individual tablets were written. Moreover, a careful reading of His statements about the relation of religion and government will show that His teachings cannot be accurately captured in any of the standard Western or Eastern concepts of "theocracy," "secularism," or "separation of church and state."

THE KING AS THE SHADOW OF GOD

In many of His tablets revealed in the later stages of His revelation, Bahá'u'lláh explicitly supports the concept of parliamentary democracy. In the Tablet of the World, revealed in 1891, He writes: "The system of government which the British people have adopted in London appeareth to be good, for it is adorned with the light of both kingship and of the consultation of the people" (*Tablets* 93). Before that, in the tablet of Bishárát (Glad Tidings) He had articulated the same idea: "Although a republican form of government profiteth all the peoples of the world, yet the majesty of kingship is one of the signs of God. We do not wish that the countries of the world should remain deprived thereof. If the sagacious combine the two forms into one, great will be their reward in the presence of God" (*Tablets* 28). Even earlier, in 1868, addressing Queen Victoria and members of various parliaments, Bahá'u'lláh had stated:

> "We have been informed that thou hast forbidden the trading in slaves, both men and women. This, verily, is what God hath enjoined in this wondrous Revelation. God hath, truly, destined a reward for thee, because of this....
>
> "We have also heard that thou hast entrusted the reins of counsel into the hands of the representatives of the people. Thou, indeed, hast done well, for thereby the foundations of the edifice of thine affairs will be strengthened, and the hearts of all that are beneath thy shadow, whether high or low, will be tranquilized. It behoveth them, however, to be trustworthy among His servants, and to regard themselves as the representatives of all that dwell on earth. This is what counselleth them, in this Tablet, He Who is the Ruler, the All-Wise. And if any one of them directeth himself towards the Assembly, let him turn his eyes unto the Supreme Horizon, and say: 'O my God! I ask Thee, by Thy most glorious Name, to aid me in that which will cause the affairs of Thy servants to prosper, and Thy cities to flourish. Thou, indeed, hast power over all things!' Blessed is he that entereth the assembly for the sake of God, and judgeth

between men with pure justice. He, indeed, is of the blissful...."
(*Epistle* 60–62)

According to Cole, it was shortly before writing that tablet to Queen Victoria, after Bahá'u'lláh's arrival in 'Akká in 1868–69, that Bahá'u'lláh adopts Western political ideas and advocates parliamentary democracy. He says:

> Baha'u'llah gradually moved away from the Hobbesian position, expressed in the tablet to Nasiru'd-Din Shah of spring 1868, that kings were the shadows of God on earth and ruled by divine right.... By the second half of 1868 or the first half of 1869, he had, in tandem with the Young Ottomans and other reformers, moved to a profound appreciation for British constitutional monarchy, parliamentary rule, and consultative government....[2]

However, it should be noted that this statement is inconsistent with many other assertions in the same book. Cole himself says that Bahá'u'lláh, in the same tablet to Náṣiri'd-Dín Sháh, *reinterpreted* the idea of the "shadow of God," and that Bahá'u'lláh's usage of it represents "a departure from classical Muslim political thought." In contrast to previous authors who "had called the shah the 'shadow of God on earth' to emphasize the ruler's unrestrained sovereignty"—Cole writes—"Baha'u'llah argued that the phrase implied an impartial meting out of justice to all, regardless of their religion, so that it imposed limits on the shah's arbitrariness and his preferential treatment of Muslims. He thus turns the phrase into a constitutional slogan!"[3] But thirty pages later, Cole finds the concept of the "shadow of God" in that same tablet to be evidence of an undemocratic and "Hobbesian" divine-right theory.[4]

The idea of the king as the shadow of God occurs both in the tablet to the sultan and the tablet to the shah—the latter revealed shortly before Bahá'u'lláh's departure from Edirne.[5] Therefore, we can see that the metaphor of the king as the shadow of God was used by Bahá'u'lláh during the entire period of his stay in Edirne. This Cole takes as his main proof that prior to 1869 Bahá'u'lláh did not believe in democratic principles.

Yet, Cole quotes as proof of Bahá'u'lláh's (supposedly later) democratic political theory the Tablet to Salmán, which was also revealed in Edirne. In it Bahá'u'lláh writes:

> The fact that you see some people exhibit delight in worldly power, and pride themselves in earthly eminence is due to their heedlessness.... "One of the signs of the maturity of the world is that no one will accept to bear the weight of kingship. Kingship will remain with none willing to bear alone its weight. That day will be the day whereon wisdom ('aql) will be manifested among mankind. Only in order to proclaim the Cause of God and spread abroad His Faith will anyone be willing to bear this grievous weight. Well is it with him who, for love of God and His Cause, and for the sake of God and for the purpose of proclaiming His Faith, will expose himself unto this great danger, and will accept this toil and trouble." That is why it hath been revealed in the Tablets that it is necessary to pray for such a king and show love unto him.[6]

Cole repeatedly asserts that this passage (in his own translation of it) demonstrates a rejection of political absolutism and a call for parliamentary rule, mass participation in decision making, and political democracy.[7] Not only was this tablet revealed during the Edirne period—the same period as the tablets Cole claims demonstrate approval of absolutism—but the statement that the refusal to bear the weight of kingship is a sign of the maturation of humanity is actually a quotation from some of Bahá'u'lláh's *earlier* tablets. He Himself says so just before quoting the statement in the Tablet to Salmán. We do not know when those earlier tablets were revealed; they could have been revealed during the early Edirne, Istanbul, or even the Baghdad period. One thing, however, is certain: Bahá'u'lláh used the concept of the king as the shadow of God in the tablet to the shah of Iran long *after* He revealed the statement about kingship and the maturation of humanity. Cole goes so far as to suggest that Bahá'u'lláh learned of the idea of political democracy from other prisoners in 'Akká. However, as we have just seen, long before being exiled to 'Akká, Bahá'u'lláh had affirmed the idea of democracy in His discussion of the maturity of humankind.

Cole repeatedly cites the passage, and others similar to it, to claim that Bahá'u'lláh's conception of "reason" ('aql) is similar to, and inspired by, the idea of reason in Enlightenment philosophy. On that basis, Cole objects to Shoghi Effendi's translation of 'aql in the Tablet to Salmán as "wisdom" and argues that because Bahá'u'lláh is using 'aql in the Enlightenment sense, it should be translated as "reason."[8] I will explore that issue in more detail, but it should be noted here that although the statement in the Tablet to Salmán approves the idea of democratic government, it is not a simple endorsement of any existing form of government. It asserts instead a particular ethical orientation as the basis of civic life and governance. In that orientation, the world-view based on the competitive pursuit of self-interest—which the Enlightenment political philosophers held to be the main mechanism of social order—has been replaced by a spiritualized worldview based on unity, non-competitiveness, and altruism. As a result of that fundamental change in values, in the realm of human governance the desire for power and domination will be replaced by interest in service and self-sacrifice.

Such a fundamental change in values is the very attitude that Bahá'u'lláh enjoined His believers to adopt throughout His revelation, including in His very early tablets. That was one of the reasons why, from the early Baghdad period, He called upon the Bábís to become detached from desire for worldly things including wealth and power. It was the purpose for which He decreed the removal of the sword and prohibited sedition and all forms of conflict and political quarrels. Insight into this issue is provided in an early text called Five Treasures (Panj Kanz), dating from the Baghdad period. As recorded by Nabíl-i-Zarandí, Bahá'u'lláh was speaking to some Qájár princes and high officials about His purpose for coming to the world:

> He was engaged in conversation with them and with loving-kindness sought news of their country. In the course of this interview one of the princes made the following remark: "How is it that You speak of spiritual matters to Your friends when they attain Your presence, while to us You talk only about the news of the town and the market?" He was trying to ask: "How could such men who are devoid of learning and discernment be preferable to us?" In answer to him Bahá'u'lláh said:

> "... I will tell you which people are worthy of listening to My utterances and attaining My presence."

He goes on to discuss five "treasures," which are the true precious possessions. The first concerns power and leadership.

> "Suppose that a person is taken to a vast plain, on the right side of which are placed all the glories of this world, its pleasures and comfort, together with a sovereignty which would be everlasting and freed from every affliction and grief. On the left-hand side of this plain are preserved for eternity all the calamities, hardships, pains and immense sufferings. Then suppose that the Holy Spirit appears before this person and addresses him in these words: 'Shouldst thou choose to have all the eternal pleasures that are placed on the right side in preference to the calamities on the left, not the slightest thing would be reduced from thy station in the sight of God. And shouldst thou choose to be afflicted with innumerable sufferings that are placed on the left, not the slightest thing would be added to thy station in the estimation of God, the Almighty, the Unconstrained.'
>
> "If at that moment this person were moved to choose, with the utmost eagerness and enthusiasm, the left hand of abasement rather than the right hand of glory, then he would be worthy to attain My presence and hearken to My exalted words."

In other words, only those who are not interested in political power or worldly glory are worthy of His Cause and His message. Here, in the Baghdad period, He is expressing a form of the idea that would later be expressed in the Tablet to Salmán, for example, as one of the signs of the maturation of humanity. Bahá'u'lláh is telling the government officials that their obsession with political power and glory is a sign of spiritual immaturity and that is why they are unworthy of hearing His celestial discourse, which is oriented to the detached, the pure, and the wise.

The other "treasures" He describes elaborate the same fact in a different way:

> To the same enquirer Bahá'u'lláh further said, "My purpose in coming to this corrupt world where the tyrants and traitors, by their acts of cruelty and oppression, have closed the doors of peace and tranquillity to all mankind, is to establish, through the power of God

and His might, the forces of justice, trust, security and faith. For instance [in the future] should a woman ..., who is unsurpassed in her beauty and adorned with the most exquisite and priceless jewels, travel unveiled and alone, from the east of the world to the west thereof, passing through every land and journeying in all countries, there would be such a standard of justice, trustworthiness and faith on the one hand, and lack of treachery and degradation on the other, that no one would be found who would wish to rob her of her possessions or to cast a treacherous and lustful eye upon her beauteous chastity!...."

Then Bahá'u'lláh affirmed, "Through the power of God I shall transform the peoples of the world into this exalted state and shall open this most great door to the face of all humanity." ...

Concerning the sincerity of motive and purity of deeds, the Tongue of Grandeur [Bahá'u'lláh] addressed them in these words:

"Suppose there is a very rich person whose wealth is enormous and beyond measure. And suppose that gradually and in the course of time he bestows so much of his wealth upon a poor person...that he himself is reduced to absolute poverty while the poor man has turned into a very rich man.... Suppose in his poor and distressed state he reaches a situation in which he incurs some small debt. Being unable to pay it, he is brought to a public square in town where he is humiliated and punished. He is further informed that his release will not be considered until he pays his debt. At this point suppose he sees his friend (who once was poor and as a result of his generosity has become rich). Should the thought flash through his mind that he wishes that in return for all his generosity to him, this friend would now come forward and relieve him of this calamity, immediately all his deeds would become void, he would become deprived of the virtue of contentment and acquiescence, and would be shut away from the virtues of the human spirit.

"The same thing is true of the second man who has become rich (through the generosity of the captive). Should he think in his heart that he is obliged to pay this man's debts, free him from his ordeal, and enable him to live the rest of his life in comfort, because he had earlier shown immeasurable love and kindness towards him, then such a motive leading him to repay his friend's generosity (instead of giving for the sake of humanity) would cause him to be deprived of the chalice of sincerity and would drive him into the world of ignominy.

"The only way acceptable to God would have been for the first man to have based his acts of generosity on humanitarian principles wholly for the sake of God. In the same way, the second rich man should have acted for the sake of God and as a duty to the world of humanity regardless of the events of the past or the future."[9]

In addition to these qualities, the People of Bahá are those who love all human beings and aim at the exaltation of the human station, and they shun the treacherous and the corrupt.

The discussion of the five "treasures" makes a few things clear: first, the statement about the sign of the maturity of humanity in the Tablet to Salmán is indeed a statement of democratic principle but in the context of, and as a direct consequence of, a fundamental transformation of the structure of values that inform public life and civic participation, and the adoption of a spiritual worldview and ethics. This has nothing in common with either the French Enlightenment utilitarian philosophy, which extolled selfishness and competition, or with the instrumental definition of reason. Bahá'u'lláh approaches democracy through his novel concept of consultation. While consultation is democratic, more importantly (and in fact as its precondition), it is a spiritual and moral orientation. That is why in all His statements to the members of the Houses of Justice or to the members of different parliaments, He calls upon them to address the universal interests of humanity in their consultation. He is not speaking of a simple competitive democracy where electors choose representatives who will advance the particularistic self-interests of their group against the interests of other groups. It is an entirely different concept of democracy, based on a spiritual worldview, values, and individual personality structure. The underlying spiritual personality structure leads to a new normative orientation, culminating in a new mode of discourse and policy orientation, which takes a particular structural form. That is the reason why such an exalted state is the sign of maturity and wisdom (and not just of the instrumental "reason") of humanity.[10]

The distinction between a utilitarian motivation for engaging in a political contract—such as a democratic constitution—and a moral and spiritual motivation is central to Bahá'u'lláh's approach to politics.

Cole's confusion of Bahá'u'lláh's concept of the maturation of humanity with the mere appearance of a particular form of constitution is
based on a systematic neglect of this crucial distinction. The difference
is between a legal and a moral approach to politics. In a legal approach,
the motivation for action is not at issue. If the letter of the law is
observed, no legal problem exists. However, not all legal actions are
moral. The morality of an action concerns both the external action
and its inner motivation. A purely self-interested and utilitarian
approach to law is perfectly compatible with democracy. In fact,
democracy can be observed through a purely utilitarian mutual limitation in the exercise of power by individuals who are themselves
power-hungry (that is, in Bahá'u'lláh's terms, immoral).

The addition of moral and spiritual foundations for democratic
laws and constitution represents a qualitatively different, higher stage
of human growth and collective maturation. Bahá'u'lláh's discourse
on democracy in relation to the maturation of humanity is concerned
with precisely such a moral and spiritual approach to politics. The
same distinction is explicitly made by Bahá'u'lláh in His address to the
political leaders of the world, in which He distinguishes between the
"Lesser Peace" and the "Most Great Peace." The former is simply a
utilitarian agreement but lacks the spiritual and moral foundations of
the latter. It is the Most Great Peace that constitutes Bahá'u'lláh's
vision of the ideal peace. As a preliminary step toward that ideal, however, the merely political agreement, even though lacking the requi-
site foundations, is a move in the right direction. Bahá'u'lláh approves
the queen's action to expand representation in government on the
same principle: it is a step in the right direction even though its full
realization will require a moral and spiritual orientation to politics and
to the very notion of power itself—and that is why Bahá'u'lláh immediately engages in unveiling the moral and spiritual requirements in
the same tablet.

Contributing to the confusion is the significant mistranslation
Cole has made in another statement of Bahá'u'lláh concerning the
sign of the maturity of humanity and the advent of wisdom among the
people. This is his translation: "We affirm (*nuṣaddiq*) the appearance of

Reason (al-'aql) among all human beings. Therefore, you will see absolutism (as-sulṭah al-muṭlaqah) discarded upon the dust, nor will any approach it."[11] But in fact, in this passage Bahá'u'lláh does not say that He affirms the arrival of Reason and consequently absolute kingship will be discarded. He is saying that the state of disinterest in absolute power is the sign of the arrival of wisdom among humans, and that He will acknowledge the advent of wisdom among the nations *when* He sees absolute kingship discarded on dust and no one willing to approach it. The accuracy of this is not only evident from the original Arabic (*Inná nuṣaddiqu ẓuhúra'l-'aql bayna'l-milal idh nara's-salṭanata'l-muṭlaqa maṭrúḥatan 'ala't-turáb*), it is also clear from the other statement in the Tablet to Salmán quoted earlier, that when kingship remains with none willing to bear it alone, "'That day will be the day whereon wisdom will be manifested among mankind.'"[12]

Cole has apparently used a copy of the tablet which contains inaccuracies in transcription.[13] However the real problem is that *idh*, meaning "when" (which occurs in both versions of the text), has been translated as "therefore," but "therefore" is *idhan*, not *idh*. This has led to an inaccurate rendering of the entire structure of the sentence.

While the slight differences between the two versions of the text have nothing to do with that mistranslation, it should be noted that the version used by Cole has *tará* (you see) instead of *nará* (We see) as in the more accurate version. The context of the tablet shows that the word used by Bahá'u'lláh there must be *nará*, while *tará* does not make sense conceptually. This tablet discusses the accusation by one of the power-hungry 'ulamá who had charged that Bahá'u'lláh wrote His tablet to the shah of Iran because He Himself desired kingship (*salṭanah*). Bahá'u'lláh, addressing His accuser, says:

> Woe betide thee, O thou who art heedless and estranged from God! Verily, We have commanded the kings to leave it [kingship] behind them and to turn towards God, the Gracious, the Incomparable. We, verily, can confirm the advent of wisdom among the nations when We see that absolute kingship is fallen upon the dust and no one is willing to approach it. Thus hath it been decreed in a Luminous Tablet. Say: Verily, kingship is most contemptible in My sight, although thou, verily, dost regard it as a most exalted station.[14]

Bahá'u'lláh's statement clearly shows that the addressee does crave power and is willing to approach it. Therefore the word in question cannot be "you see" but must be "We see." Furthermore, Bahá'u'lláh says in this tablet that He has already mentioned this idea in His other writings, which indicates that He is reaffirming what He had already revealed in the Tablet to Salmán and elsewhere.

Another important fact which must not be overlooked in any chronology of Bahá'u'lláh's teachings on government is the fact that the metaphor of the king as the shadow of God is also employed in one of His last works, Epistle to the Son of the Wolf, which was revealed in 1891—decades after He had explicitly advocated democratic political institutions. If the concept of the king as the shadow of God designated an absolutist notion that He had discarded, Bahá'u'lláh should not have spoken favorably about the king as the shadow of God at that late date. And in Epistle to the Son of the Wolf, Bahá'u'lláh affirms the principle precisely by quoting the tablet to the shah of Iran! When Bahá'u'lláh is quoting one of His earlier tablets, that always means an affirmation of that same idea. The fact that most of Epistle to the Son of the Wolf consists largely of quotations from His previous tablets strongly indicates that Bahá'u'lláh Himself considered His early statements to express His own teachings exactly as He intended them at the end of His life. He could not have rejected the idea and yet again confirm it in a book which describes the summary and essence of His revelation. It is significant to note how Bahá'u'lláh introduces that particular passage in that work: "We once again refer unto some of the sublime words revealed in the Tablet to His Majesty the Shah, so that thou mayest know of a certainty that whatever hath been mentioned hath come from God.... Of a verity, God hath made thee His shadow amongst men, and the sign of His power unto all that dwell on earth" (*Epistle* 39–40).

It is clear that the meaning of the king as the shadow of God in the last work of Bahá'u'lláh, as in His early works, is that true sovereignty only belongs to God, that kings must make themselves worthy to reflect the divine attribute of sovereignty by ruling with justice and serving the interests of the people, and that power is legitimate only if it is based on the democratic and universalistic norms of divine love and justice.

The choice of Hobbes to describe Bahá'u'lláh's position, at any point, is incongruous. Evidently the comparison was chosen because Hobbes argues for a theory of the state based on absolutism as the only legitimate form of government. But, as we have seen, the interpretation that equates Bahá'u'lláh's statement with absolutism is mistaken. Hobbes's theory with its materialistic, mechanistic, and hedonistic conception of human nature is entirely opposed to Bahá'u'lláh's spiritual conception. Hobbesian theory explains order in terms of efficiency, self-interest, and fear of coercion. In contradistinction to this, Bahá'u'lláh explains order in terms of love of God, internalized morality, sacrificial service, and solidarity with humanity. Hobbes, the moral relativist, reduces human behavior and ethics to physical causes and bases his social contract on self-interest. Bahá'u'lláh grounds values in the divine covenant and the sacred nature of reality as the mirror of God. The differences are fundamental and irreconcilable.

The attribution to Bahá'u'lláh of a traditional "divine right theory" at any stage of His revelation is also inaccurate. Nowhere in His early writings did Bahá'u'lláh ever affirm or imply any of the main tenets of "absolutist" divine right or Hobbesian political theories—particularly the notion that the ruler's authority is absolutely arbitrary and unconstrained by any law or limit. Nor in those early writings did He ever say that kingship was the sole legitimate form of government. In fact, whenever Bahá'u'lláh speaks about kings and their power it is precisely to emphasize that their very station as rulers in God's "shadow" means that they are always bound by the dictates of divine law and justice. But He never says kingship is a necessary form of government, nor in His later writings does He say that all forms of kingship should be discarded. The subject of His concern is not limited to the "question of whether governments rule by divine fiat or by the consent of the ruled"[15]—those categories are not sufficient to explain Bahá'u'lláh's concept of political sovereignty, which is far more complex.

A reading of Bahá'u'lláh's texts on their own terms shows that the expression "shadow of God" means exactly the same thing as another phrase He frequently uses, "kings as the manifestations of divine power." This latter expression takes different forms in various texts but is present at all stages of His writings—including almost all His major tablets revealed long after the tablet to Queen Victoria. Even in the Kitáb-i-'Ahd (Book of the Covenant), one of His last works, Bahá'-u'lláh writes that "Kings are the manifestations of the power, and the daysprings of the might and riches, of God" (*Tablets* 220). Those statements could not intend to justify a notion of absolutism that He discarded in the 'Akká period because they frequently occur in His 'Akká writings as well. But rather than either of those expressions implying any approval of absolutism or traditional divine right theories, both indicate that political authority, whatever the form, is legitimate only if it approximates the divine attributes of universality and justice. Perfect legitimacy, truly reflecting divine universal sovereignty, requires many measures and institutions that include but transcend the present versions of democracy—while on the other hand monarchy is never ruled out, even in the statements about the maturity of humanity. In His writings Bahá'u'lláh both encourages advancements in justice within the existing structures of the time and offers a systematic vision of ideal order and government which is spiritual, universalistic, global, democratic, and based on the divine covenant.

At the same time, Bahá'u'lláh's statement to Queen Victoria, in which He comments positively on representative government, is far from a simplistic endorsement of existing Western political systems and ideologies. What Bahá'u'lláh expounds in that tablet is qualitatively different. First, He combines the Eastern and Western discourse on legitimacy. In modern liberal Western theory, legitimacy is ultimately based on the consent of the governed. If the government officials are elected by the people, their rule is legitimate. However, in traditional Islamic political discourse, legitimacy is based primarily on the moral qualities of the ruler.[16] While Bahá'u'lláh praises Queen Victoria's attempt to expand parliamentary democracy, He emphasizes that this is not sufficient: the elected officials must consider themselves as the trusted ones of God for the people, and must turn to God to assist them in making policies that are beneficial to all. The representatives should also show certain moral and spiritual qualities and commitment to divine laws and principles.

Bahá'u'lláh emphasizes that, in deliberating about their policies, the members of Parliament should see themselves as representatives not only of the British people but of the entire human race, and should consider the interests not merely of the British Empire but of all humankind. In saying so, Bahá'u'lláh is actually indirectly criticizing that political system by implying that it falls short of the ideal and that its nationalistic, militaristic, and colonialist orientation and policies should be replaced by spiritual and global ones. Bahá'u'lláh approves and reinforces the positive advances He discerns, and He prescribes measures for improvement in the context of the existing conditions and variables.

The same principle of diagnosis and prescription applies in the case of the tablets to the sultan and the shah. Bahá'u'lláh employs what for those rulers was a familiar and valid concept of the king as the shadow of God but reinterprets it in the direction of democratic principles. In both their cases, Bahá'u'lláh denounces the corruption of the patrimonial political structure with its semifeudalism, arbitrary power, and exploitation of the people. In these texts Bahá'u'lláh is contrasting the interests of the people with the interests of the officials. In His tablet to the sultan, Bahá'u'lláh condemns the corrupt, immoral ministers, rejecting consultation with them because of their corruption but urging consultation with ministers who are virtuous:

> Beware, O King, that thou gather not around thee such ministers as follow the desires of a corrupt inclination, as have cast behind their backs that which hath been committed into their hands and manifestly betrayed their trust. Be bounteous to others as God hath been bounteous to thee, and abandon not the interests of thy people to the mercy of such ministers as these. Lay not aside the fear of God, and be thou of them that act uprightly. Gather around thee those ministers from whom thou canst perceive the fragrance of faith and of justice, and take thou counsel with them, and choose whatever is best in thy sight, and be of them that act generously. (*Gleanings* 232–33)

This is the same principle He would later emphasize in His tablet to Queen Victoria—the moral qualities of the official. In the tablet to the sultan, Bahá'u'lláh defines the basic task of the ruler to be the protection of the collective interests of the people and the realization of social justice. For Bahá'u'lláh, the realm of political authority and governance must be the realm of altruistic, universal, and public welfare. He tells the sultan not to allow "the abject to rule over and dominate them who are noble and worthy of honor, and suffer not the high-minded to be at the mercy of the contemptible and worthless." For some to possess excessive wealth while others languish in the utmost poverty "ill beseemeth thy sovereignty, and is unworthy of thy rank." He urges him to "strive ... to rule with equity among men, that God may exalt thy name and spread abroad the fame of thy justice in all the world"; warns him not to "aggrandize thy ministers at the expense of thy subjects"; and admonishes:

> Fear the sighs of the poor and of the upright in heart who, at every break of day, bewail their plight, and be unto them a benignant sovereign. They, verily, are thy treasures on earth. It behoveth thee, therefore, to safeguard thy treasures from the assaults of them who wish to rob thee. Inquire into their affairs, and ascertain, every year, nay every month, their condition, and be not of them that are careless of their duty.
>
> Set before thine eyes God's unerring Balance and, as one standing in His Presence, weigh in that Balance thine actions every day, every moment of thy life....
>
> It behoveth every king to be as bountiful as the sun, which fostereth the growth of all beings, and giveth to each its due, whose benefits are not inherent in itself, but are ordained by Him Who is the Most Powerful, the Almighty. The King should be as generous, as liberal in his mercy as the clouds, the outpourings of whose bounty are showered upon every land, by the behest of Him Who is the Supreme Ordainer, the All-Knowing. (*Gleanings* 236–37)

Bahá'u'lláh's objective in these addresses to the rulers of His day is to encourage them through incremental steps in the path toward the ideal model of governance. The steps they need to take differ depending on His diagnosis of their particular level. At the same time, He is completely aware not only of their spiritual condition and level of receptivity and capacity, but of the background of misunderstanding and suspicion on the part of the rulers, particularly the Ottoman sultan and the shah of Iran, about the intentions of the Bábís—and by extension the Bahá'ís—who were suspected of having designs of sedition or revolution. As a result, Bahá'u'lláh does not directly reject the political authority of rulers, but redefines the basis of their own legitimacy in a new way that is conducive to political justice and egalitarian principles. Chief among these categories is the idea of the king as the shadow of God:

> Thou art God's shadow on earth. Strive, therefore, to act in such a manner as befitteth so eminent, so august a station. If thou dost depart from following the things We have caused to descend upon thee and taught thee, thou wilt, assuredly, be derogating from that great and priceless honor. Return, then, and cleave wholly unto God, and cleanse thine heart from the world and all its vanities, and suffer not the love of any stranger to enter and dwell therein. Not until thou dost purify thine heart from every trace of such love can the brightness of the light of God shed its radiance upon it, for to none hath God given more than one heart. (*Gleanings* 237)

But, as evident from this statement and the ones preceding it, which likened the king to the bountiful sun, Bahá'u'lláh is giving a normative meaning to this concept. A king is the *shadow* of God in that a true king faithfully reflects the divine attributes in his exercise of power. That means acting with justice and equity, as a servant of the people who has no interest in personal power or wealth, and refraining from arbitrariness, corruption, and abuse of authority. Naturally, this definition of the doctrine of the king as the shadow of God is not only compatible with the democratic principle but it is the very essence of it. When Bahá'u'lláh counseled the British Parliament that they should all regard themselves as the representatives, trustees, and guardians of all that dwell on earth, this too was the same doctrine of the ruler as the shadow of God.

Considering the climate of suspicion at the time, in view of the attempt on the life of the shah in 1852, it would not have been prudent to advocate democracy directly to the shah and the sultan. To do so would only have led to further brutal persecution of the Bahá'ís in Iran and Ottoman lands. On the contrary, we would expect that Bahá'u'lláh would try to dissipate those rulers' fears and misunderstandings. To read Bahá'u'lláh's writings with the interpretive assumption that He would have used overt democratic terms in His letters if He in fact preferred democratic institutions, and that because He did not do so, He must not have preferred them Himself (or that if He used such terms speaking to a different ruler at a *later* time, that must indicate that Bahá'u'lláh changed His own mind about what was right) ignores the differential parts of the context of the different tablets. It also ignores Bahá'u'lláh's own principles of discourse according to which every utterance should be adapted to the recipient. It was Bahá'u'lláh Himself who wrote not only about this as a principle of wisdom but about the fact that He practiced it in His own revelation:

> Were all the things that lie enshrined within the heart of Bahá, and which the Lord, His God, the Lord of all names, hath taught Him, to be unveiled to mankind, every man on earth would be dumbfounded.
>
> How great the multitude of truths which the garment of words can never contain! How vast the number of such verities as no expression can adequately describe, whose significance can never be unfolded, and to which not even the remotest allusions can be made! How manifold are the truths which must remain unuttered until the appointed time is come! Even as it hath been said: "Not everything that a man knoweth can be disclosed, nor can everything that he can disclose be regarded as timely, nor can every timely utterance be considered as suited to the capacity of those who hear it."
>
> Of these truths some can be disclosed only to the extent of the capacity of the repositories of the light of Our knowledge, and the recipients of Our hidden grace. (*Gleanings* 176)

Even though Bahá'u'lláh did not directly advocate a democratic constitution to these nondemocratic rulers, He redefined the basis of their authority and summoned them to implement justice in their rule. At the same time, He called on all the rulers to recognize His revelation as the embodiment of the model of justice for the future. He urged them to move toward the (political) "Lesser Peace"—a political union based on the rational pursuit of peace by the secular political rulers—even if they would not accept the (spiritual) "Most Great Peace"—a spiritual civilization characterized by the recognition of His revelation and application of His principles to the various human institutions. By Bahá'u'lláh's standard, no political system of the time, including those of Western nations, was truly just. True justice was dependent on the spiritual transformation of society as a whole. Meanwhile, however, Bahá'u'lláh suggested additional immediate, short-run measures for the improvement of existing conditions in contemporary societies. The tablets to Sultan 'Abdu'l-'Azíz and Náṣiri'd-Dín Sháh represent examples of that endeavor.

It should be noted that in the Epistle to the Son of the Wolf, one of His last works, Bahá'u'lláh speaks favorably of both political democracy and the king as the shadow of God. He quotes from the tablet to Queen Victoria (60–63), approving representative government, and from the tablet to the shah, referring to the king as the shadow of God (40), and emphasizes yet again: "Every nation must have a high regard for the position of its sovereign, must be submissive unto him, must carry out his behests, and hold fast his authority. The sovereigns of the earth have been and are the manifestations of the power, the grandeur and the majesty of God" (89). It is thus clear that the notion of the king as the shadow of God cannot be an evidence of nondemocratic preference in Bahá'u'lláh's writings.

DEMOCRATIC PRINCIPLE IN
THE EARLY WRITINGS OF BAHÁ'U'LLÁH

As we saw, in addressing the sultan and the shah Bahá'u'lláh discusses governance and authority as the representation and realization of justice and universal interests. This is the core of the democratic principle, and the various aspects of representative democracy derive from this fundamental idea. Bahá'u'lláh unveils the logical implications of this principle gradually and in accordance with the capacity of the recipient so that His challenging message will not be misunderstood and rejected as threatening. That explains why He speaks openly of representative democracy only when He addresses the queen of England, to whom the idea of a parliament was hardly a radical innovation or a threat to her authority, as it was to the autocratic rulers of Iran and the Ottoman Empire.

In the discussion of the four constitutive principles of the Kitáb-i-Aqdas, we saw that all the democratic principles of Bahá'u'lláh, as well as His concept of covenant and the New World Order, are deduced from those four constitutive principles. Those principles are all explicitly present in the early writings of Bahá'u'lláh revealed long before the tablets to the sultan and the shah. Bahá'u'lláh's approach to democracy was part of a holistic concern that included the sacredness of human beings and consultation as the basis of decision making at all levels of social and political reality including the global level. As is clear from the tablet about His childhood experience, Bahá'u'lláh was aware of this structure from the beginning of His revelation. The democratic sentiment explicit in His concept of the maturation of humanity is implicit in his discussion of the "five treasures" during the Baghdad period. He unveiled these ideas, however, in accordance with the requirements of wisdom in each particular case, and also according to the logic of the progressive revelation of His own mission.

Universal auxiliary language presents another case of that progressive logical unfoldment of Bahá'u'lláh's teachings. It is only in His later writings that He emphasizes this as an explicit imperative and a command. That timing makes perfect sense because the concept of world language, as a prerequisite for the development of an identity of global citizenship, belongs logically to the international orientation and structure of order which Bahá'u'lláh outlines in the later stages of His writings. However, the fact that Bahá'u'lláh did not emphasize this issue in earlier tablets was not because He had not yet thought of the idea. We know this for certain because Bahá'u'lláh Himself, in one of His later writings, recounts a conversation about it with Kamál Páshá, an Ottoman official, which took place in Istanbul in 1863. In that conversation Bahá'u'lláh articulates the identical principle of universal auxiliary language which would have a central place as a law of the Kitáb-i-Aqdas and a sign of the maturation of humanity:

One day, while in Constantinople, Kamál Páshá visited this Wronged One. Our conversation turned upon topics profitable unto man. He said that he had learned several languages. In reply We observed: "You have wasted your life. It beseemeth you and the other officials of the Government to convene a gathering and choose one of the divers languages, and likewise one of the existing scripts, or else to create a new language and a new script to be taught children in schools throughout the world." (*Epistle* 137–38)

Clearly, it was because of the inner logic of the gradual revelation of His mission that He expressed certain precepts in a more explicit way only in His later writings. Furthermore, it would be illogical that at Riḍván 1863 Bahá'u'lláh would announce the universal sacredness of all humans, abolish the causes of division and distinctions, and (in the account described above) affirm the consultative principle of decision making at the international level, calling for a universal auxiliary language as a means of bringing the earth together as one country— and yet at the same time believe in Hobbesian despotism at the level of the nation-state.

One of the most powerful of His early statements on this theme is found in the Arabic Hidden Words, written in 1858, a time when the giants of European political theory were excluding different groups of people from various political and economic rights. John Stuart Mill, the major representative of liberal democratic theory, outlined his argument for excluding the uneducated and working class from the right to vote by defining them as irrational enemies of representative democracy.[17] He suggested either making suffrage dependent on education (which in effect meant property ownership) or counting the vote of the middle class as equal to the vote of several members of the working class. Herbert Spencer, the libertarian philosopher, argued for a brutal Social Darwinism and implied that because intelligence is hereditary, the state should not provide public education or other services that waste scarce resources on the inherently less intelligent poor.[18] We need to remember that at this time in the West, political democracy was still really an aristocracy of the rich which expressed an inegalitarian worldview using the labels of democracy.

Bahá'u'lláh, however, wrote in 1858:

O CHILDREN OF MEN!

Know ye not why We created you all from the same dust? That no one should exalt himself over the other. Ponder at all times in your hearts how ye were created. Since We have created you all from one same substance it is incumbent on you to be even as one soul, to walk with the same feet, eat with the same mouth and dwell in the same land, that from your inmost being, by your deeds and actions, the signs of oneness and the essence of detachment may be made manifest. Such is My counsel to you, O concourse of light! Heed ye this counsel that ye may obtain the fruit of holiness from the tree of wondrous glory. (Arabic Hidden Words 68)

Western political theory has yet to catch up with that egalitarian message.

FROM REASON TO WISDOM

In the Five Treasures Bahá'u'lláh tells us of His intention to create a society in which people not only abstain from dominating others but do not even desire to dominate. This, a constant message of Bahá'-u'lláh, is another expression of His principle of heart. Bahá'u'lláh terms this condition of society the stage of the manifestation of wisdom, or reason. Obviously this "reason" is not the one-dimensional, instrumental, calculative, utilitarian, hedonistic, and selfish reason of the French philosophy of the Enlightenment. It is not a mechanical reason of efficiency and technical manipulation. It is "political" reason in the original, but now vestigial, sense of concern for the universal and collective interests of the polity, which employs the insights of practical reason that Aristotle termed *phronesis* (prudence). As such, Bahá'u'lláh's definition of this moral approach to authority as "reason" is surely aimed at criticizing the one-dimensional modern liberal conception of reason and replacing that notion with a multidimensional concept that unites instrumental reason with moral and spiritual reason. The term *wisdom*, however, precisely emphasizes that complex structure of reason; it implies the unity of reason, virtue, and prudence. Consequently, the translation of the word *'aql* in this context as "wisdom" is more expressive than "reason." It conveys the meaning directly and unambiguously.

Cole, however, has dismissed Shoghi Effendi's translation of *'aql* as "wisdom":

> Compare the translation of this passage in Rabbani, *The Promised Day Is Come*, p. 72, which rather strangely renders *'aql* as "wisdom." Since this word is the precise technical equivalent in Islamic philosophy of *nous*, or intellect, and differs radically in its connotations from *sophia* (Ar. *ḥikmah*), or wisdom, I am at a loss to explain this translation choice. The original, however, does show a certain confluence of Baha'u'llah's thought with Enlightenment ideals, such that the advent of Reason among the citizenry obviates the need for kingship, and it may be that that confluence offended the Romantic and antimodernist sentiments of Baha'is in the 1920s and 1930s.[19]

But, that statement, like the one we examined before, is based on a misunderstanding of Bahá'u'lláh's concept of the maturation of the world. First, however, it is correct that Bahá'u'lláh writes the passage in the Tablet to Salmán partly in reference to the Enlightenment conception of rationalization. But not to endorse it—instead, He is criticizing the Enlightenment notion of reason and is replacing it with one that combines instrumental reason with moral and spiritual reason. This same point is also expounded by 'Abdu'l-Bahá, who described the age of the "advent of the Most Great *'Aql*" as the age in which material civilization is united with spiritual civilization.[20]

Bahá'u'lláh's judgment that humanity cannot be considered mature as long as people seek power and domination is as applicable to representative democracy as it is to absolutist government. According to Bahá'u'lláh's standard, as long as the politicians of democratic countries thirst for power, fame, and wealth, and act to further their self-interest and the interests of their party rather than serving the interests of humanity—morally speaking they are no different from autocratic rulers who demonstrated the same lack of the virtues of leadership. Modern democratic societies, far from being embodiments of a mature humanity, remain dominated by the logic of consumerism, obsession with power, aggressive competition, and divisive partisanship. This insight was the heart of Bahá'u'lláh's criticism of the members of Parliament.

Bahá'u'lláh's concept of the maturation of humanity and the advent of the age of wisdom affirms the democratic principle along

with a universalistic ethical orientation that is embodied in His concept of consultation. Consultation is not a discursive arena of struggle
for power and domination, nor is it a utilitarian enterprise geared
toward hedonistic and material interests. For Bahá'u'lláh consultation
is selfless devotion to truth, to the universal interests of humanity, and
to the will of God. This cannot be achieved by a mere change of political constitution but implies a fundamental spiritual transformation
which brings about global structural and institutional changes. This
sense of maturation and wisdom ('aql) is much more than a matter of
universal suffrage in the nation-state. The centrality of its spiritual
dimension becomes clear when we observe that in one tablet Bahá'-
u'lláh has identified consultation as the means of the advent of reason
(khirad) and defines reason as a heaven whose sun and moon are forbearance and fear of God.[21]

Second, in Islamic discourse the word 'aql is usually not the one-
sided reason of the Enlightenment. It was Islamic philosophy that used
'aql to describe the Word of God, the Primal Will, and divine revelation. This usage of 'aql in Islamic philosophy was much more complex than the Enlightenment's mechanistic and naturalistic conception of reason. One should remember, for example, the famous Islamic tradition, quoted by 'Abdu'l-Bahá at the beginning of *The Secret of
Divine Civilization*, that "The first thing created by God was ['aql],"[22]
or Fárábí's hierarchy of ten stages of 'aql, the lowest of which is the
equivalent of the Holy Spirit and the Creator of the world.[23] The concept of 'aql in Islamic philosophy implied both human and divine reason, and it referred to the divine inspiration and the divine creative act.
It also referred to the divine will, the object of attraction and love.
That is why, for many Muslim philosophers, human beings are only
potentially rational ('aql bi'l-quvvah)—and only if they gain spiritual
knowledge and transcend the level of base and appetitive desires do
they become actually rational ('aql bi'l-fi'l). In other words, 'aql in
Islamic philosophy also involves practical reason, moral orientation,
and spiritual maturity.

Third, even if we assume, hypothetically, that Muslim philosophy
had used 'aql in the sense Cole claims, that of course would not nec-

essarily dictate Bahá'u'lláh's usage of the term. The Manifestation of God, above all, is a force of not only spiritual and cultural but semantic change—and not an imitator or passive transmitter of human conventional meanings.

Fourth, Bahá'u'lláh Himself affirms in many of His tablets that His concept of *'aql* is not confined to the mechanistic definition of individual reason but includes divine inspiration and education. Already in the Four Valleys and the Seven Valleys Bahá'u'lláh had expounded His multidimensional concept of reason. In the Four Valleys, the second valley is the valley of reason or intellect (*'aql*). There He states that the integrative and authentic meaning of reason must include the universal divine reason as well. In other words, unlike the Western, Enlightenment concept, this reason must incorporate spiritual guidance and moral orientation. In the station of reason (*'aql*) "which is known as the Prophet and the Most Great Pillar," He writes:

> Here reason signifieth the divine, universal mind, whose sovereignty enlighteneth all created things—nor doth it refer to every feeble brain; for it is as the wise Saná'í hath written:
>
> "How can feeble reason encompass the Qur'án,
> Or the spider snare a phoenix in her web?
> Wouldst thou that the mind should not entrap thee?
> Teach it the science of the love of God!" (*Four Valleys* 52)

In the Seven Valleys, speaking of the mysterious nature and wisdom of dreams, He writes that "God, the Exalted, hath placed these signs in men, to the end that philosophers may not deny the mysteries of the life beyond nor belittle that which hath been promised them. For some hold to reason and deny whatever the reason comprehendeth not, and yet weak minds can never grasp the matters which we have related, but only the Supreme, Divine Intelligence can comprehend them" (33).

Finally, instead of looking at Greek or Islamic definitions of *'aql*, we need to look directly at Bahá'u'lláh's own explicit discussion of the term. This we can find in the tablet in which Bahá'u'lláh answers the questions posed by Mánikjí Ṣáḥib through Abu'l-Faḍá'il. Mánikjí Ṣáḥib asks whether reason (*'aql*) is sufficient for the discovery of moral values and spiritual truth, and whether one should act on the basis of reason or revelation. Bahá'u'lláh replies that true reason ('aql) is sufficient for understanding moral values and spiritual truth, but He adds that for Him 'aql means true understanding, compatible with revelation. This kind of 'aql, He explains, is not the typical definition of reason. The limited sense of reason leads to misrecognition of moral and spiritual truth. 'Aql, Bahá'u'lláh says, is really the attribute of the Manifestations of God. He explains that by 'aql He means the Universal Divine Reason ('Aql-i-Kullíy-i-Iláhí). Human 'aql is acceptable when it is connected to and educated by divine wisdom, for this is the means by which it becomes enabled to understand moral imperatives and celestial truth. Finally, Bahá'u'lláh says that in the true sense of the term, 'aql is the recognition of the Manifestation of God. He adds that whoever is deprived of that is not rational but ignorant even if he assumes himself to be the possessor of all 'aql.[24] This explanation also makes it clear why in some of His tablets Bahá'u'lláh speaks of the appearance of khirad (the Persian word for 'aql) in the year nine. In His Kalimát-i-Firdawsíyyih, Bahá'u'lláh writes: "Above all else, the greatest gift and the most wondrous blessing hath ever been and will continue to be Wisdom [khirad]. It is man's unfailing Protector.... In the city of justice it is the unrivalled Speaker Who, in the year nine, illumined the world with the joyful tidings of this Revelation" (Tablets 66).

In any case, these tablets leave no doubt about the meaning of 'aql for Bahá'u'lláh, and that it is the exact opposite of the Enlightenment concept of reason. In fact, it may be precisely in order to convey this radical difference that Shoghi Effendi translated 'aql, in relation to the signs of the maturity of humanity, as "wisdom" rather than "reason." He would have been aware that some in the West might read into Bahá'u'lláh's concept of 'aql the Enlightenment concept of reason that was familiar to them. Therefore, knowing the fundamental difference between these concepts, he deliberately translated it as "wisdom." This, however, is the best translation in this specific context anyway. Bahá'u'lláh is not only talking about maturity, He is also talking about phronesis or practical reason and ethical sentiments.

Bahá'u'lláh frequently criticized the deviation from moderation which resulted from the modern Western approach to civilization and freedom.[25] He insisted that the afflictions that beset the "body" of the world cannot be remedied by materialistic and militaristic means. The unity of humanity was the essential prerequisite of any true modernity. In the Tablet of Wisdom, Bahá'u'lláh criticized that infatuation with Western technological rationalization which dismisses spiritual and moral orientation and seeks a civilization based on instrumental rationality.[26] According to Bahá'u'lláh, true political wisdom would recognize the inadequacy of such a destructive and heedless worldview.

In Bahá'u'lláh's vision, the eminently rational society is characterized by the unity and harmonious cooperation of science and religion, technology and spirituality, knowledge and morality. But the Enlightenment's one-sided concept of rationalization had no place for practical, moral, and spiritual rationalization. It has been only in the second half of the twentieth century that sociologists like Habermas have explicitly differentiated two forms of rationalization and have called for development in the communicative, symbolic, interactive, and practical domains of human life.[27] Bahá'u'lláh's concept of rationalization, however, recognizes three distinct kinds of rationalization processes: instrumental, communicative, and spiritual. This becomes more evident when we remember the other signs of the maturation of humanity discussed in Bahá'u'lláh's texts.

BEYOND THEOCRATISM AND SECULARISM

We have seen that, in His discussions of the basis of legitimacy and sovereignty, what Bahá'u'lláh stressed was not the external forms of government but the more foundational level of the norms of divine justice and universal interests based on the oneness of humankind. It is through the implementation of those values that the true attribute of spiritual divine sovereignty becomes manifested in the realm of the world, in the form of sociopolitical order. This means that there is an important relationship between the realm that is the source of those norms and ethical authority—namely, religion—and the place where that ethical authority is exercised—namely, the world.

However, conceptual confusion about Bahá'u'lláh's discussions of this subject, and reading out of context such statements as "earthly sovereignty is of no worth, nor will it ever be, in the eyes of God and His chosen Ones" (*Kitáb-i-Íqán* 124), has led some to conclude that Bahá'u'lláh's writings advocate secularism and the complete separation of religion and state in the modern Western sense. In *Modernity and the Millennium*, Cole offers the fanciful theory that the ideas on political sovereignty that he attributes to Bahá'u'lláh were "probably influenced by the Sufi enthusiasms of his youth."[28] Specifically, the argument is that Bahá'u'lláh borrowed from the tradition of Ni'matu'lláhí Sufi mystics who were called _sháh_ to indicate their sovereignty in the realm of esoteric mystical knowledge as opposed to the sovereignty of the (inferior) social world which they disdained. At the same time, they believed that "the fortunes of the civil state depended in a supernatural manner upon how well the government treated the Sufi master."[29] Based on that model, Cole suggests, Bahá'u'lláh divides sovereignty into separate realms of mystical/spiritual and civil/secular authority. "In the same way" as the Sufis, Cole asserts, "Baha'u'llah viewed his station as implying spiritual sovereignty but not secular power."[30] But everything we have seen about Bahá'u'lláh's rejection of the Sufi ascetic withdrawal from the world, as well as His rejection of all those who make arrogant claims to superior spiritual status because of their position in a mystical order, makes the notion that His concept of political sovereignty is *based* on those ideas most strange.

In fact, in His approach to authority, freedom, and the relation of religion to state, Bahá'u'lláh advocates neither the modern Western conception of a complete separation of church and state—especially its American form—nor the premodern idea of their absolute identity. (The improbability of the Sufi theory needs no further elaboration.) In other words, Bahá'u'lláh's teachings on this question, as reflected in His own writings as well as in the writings of His authorized interpreters, are irreducible to the binary discourse of secularism versus theocratism in either the traditional Muslim or the modern Western contexts. But what is most illogical is the idea that a system of belief that proposes to spiritualize order and governance should totally separate the realm that is the source of spirit from any relation to the order that institutionalizes it.

Harmony of the Political and the Spiritual in Bahá'u'lláh's Writings

Modern Western liberal political philosophy defended a rationalist vision of society in which civil society is completely separate from the realm of collective political life. The state does not interfere in the economy, and is likewise separate from religion. The opposite vision of society is found in the various forms of the collectivist/communist economy as well as the traditional theocratic state defined by its use of state power to enforce the dominance of a particular religion. Bahá'u'lláh's vision transcends such binary oppositions and cannot be captured by any of these or similar political models. With regard to both aspects of civil society—economic enterprise and religious belief and practice—Bahá'u'lláh affirms fundamental rights of freedom. From the very beginning, the removal of the sword was simultaneously a prohibition on infringing on the property of others, as well as on the use of coercion to propagate religion. For Bahá'u'lláh, the rights of believers and nonbelievers are equal in society. His prohibition of holy war and the removal of interdictions on communication, friendship, and marriage with nonbelievers were all part of that same logic.

But as we have seen in the Five Treasures, the standard of ethics that Bahá'u'lláh expects from His followers is much higher than just respect for the rights of others. For example, in the Tablet of the World He writes, referring to an incident when Bahá'ís pleaded for leniency for their persecutors:

> Day and night this Wronged One yieldeth thanks and praise unto the Lord of men, for it is witnessed that the words of counsel and exhortation We uttered have proved effective and that this people hath evinced such character and conduct as are acceptable in Our sight. This is affirmed by virtue of the event which hath truly cheered the eye of the world, and is none other than the intercession of the friends with the high authorities in favour of their enemies. Indeed one's righteous deeds testify to the truth of one's words. (*Tablets* 90–91)

Shoghi Effendi, in interpreting the policy implications of the Bahá'í texts, articulated a strong principle of affirmative action that "If any discrimination is at all to be tolerated, it should be discrimination not against, but rather in favor of the minority, be it racial or otherwise."[31] Likewise, he has explicitly stated that wherever Bahá'ís find themselves in the majority, not only must they not exclude nonbelievers from equal rights but that they must give them priority:

> Unlike the nations and peoples of the earth, be they of the East or of the West, democratic or authoritarian, communist or capitalist, whether belonging to the Old World or the New, who either ignore, trample upon, or extirpate, the racial, religious, or political minorities within the sphere of their jurisdiction, every organized community enlisted under the banner of Bahá'u'lláh should feel it to be its first and inescapable obligation to nurture, encourage, and safeguard every minority belonging to any faith, race, class, or nation within it.[32]

In 1925 he wrote to the Bahá'ís of Iran a clear statement of the attitude Bahá'ís must take toward the rights of nonbelievers:

> ... The mere fact of disaffection, estrangement, or recantation of belief, can in no wise detract from, or otherwise impinge upon, the legitimate civil rights of individuals in a free society, be it to the most insignificant degree. Were the friends to follow other than this course, it would be tantamount to a reversion on their part, in this century of radiance and light, to the ways and standards of a former age: they would reignite in men's breasts the fire of bigotry and blind fanaticism, cut themselves off from the glorious bestowals of this promised Day of God, and impede the full flow of divine assistance in this wondrous age.[33]

We can see that the basic positive spirit of the doctrine of toleration advocated by John Locke is far more strongly affirmed by Bahá'u'lláh and His successors.[34] Not only must the state abstain from using coercion to force citizens to adopt a particular religion, but a state comprising a Bahá'í majority would have an obligation to safeguard minority rights. We can see that this idea is one of the basic implications of the removal of the sword.

However, Bahá'u'lláh's message also cannot be equated with the liberal Western conception of civil society, religion, and state. If Bahá'u'lláh prohibits the use of coercion to enforce His religion, this does not mean that He therefore also accepts the Western—especially the American—idea of complete separation of religion from public life. These realms can be neither completely identical nor absolutely separate. They can be relatively autonomous but they must constitute an organic, cooperative, and interactive unity.

Bahá'u'lláh's analysis of the relation of religion to the collective realm is similar to His analysis of the relation of private enterprise to the state. Contrary to the liberal doctrine of civil society, unbridled capitalism unchecked by collective policy destroys the possibility of political democracy. No true political democracy is possible under conditions of extremes of inequality and consumerist, hedonistic values. Although Bahá'u'lláh affirms the right of private property and sanctifies the product of each person's trade and industry, He also provides for collective policy to ensure equality of opportunity for the poor and the disprivileged. The presence of structural inequalities means that a purely independent civil society would imply systematic exclusion of the poor and minorities from equal access. Consequently, a truly democratic and humanitarian order implies the active harmony, interaction, and mutual cooperation of the civil society and state without destroying their relative autonomy. In fact the history of the modern West has been precisely a movement in this direction. But even in the case of the economy, intervention and imposition from above is neither the optimal nor the normal means of ensuring equality or prosperity. Bahá'u'lláh calls for the true solution of economic problems through completely voluntary spiritual means and institutions such as the Ḥuqúqu'lláh, which are the expression, in the economic realm, of the spiritual transformation of the hearts.

A similar principle is applied in the writings of Bahá'u'lláh to the relation of religion and state. Bahá'u'lláh affirmed the principle of complete freedom of conscience. At the same time, He called for the interaction and cooperation of religious and political authorities. This mutual relationship is based on the fact that the subject of civil society must be committed to the norms of morality, justice, and universal values. In turn, the basis of these norms—especially trustworthiness and truthfulness—is ultimately only religious belief.[35] Such a subject, without whom neither freedom nor civil society is possible, can only be safeguarded through the collective institutionalization of respect for religion and spiritual orientation. In fact, Bahá'u'lláh identifies the typical modern disregard for religion's role as the basis of a just and moral social order to be a complete disaster:

> The Pen of the Most High exhorteth, at this moment, the manifestations of authority and the sources of power, namely the kings, the sovereigns, the presidents, the rulers, the divines and the wise, and enjoineth them to uphold the cause of religion, and to cleave unto it. Religion is verily the chief instrument for the establishment of order in the world and of tranquillity amongst its peoples. The weakening of the pillars of religion hath strengthened the foolish and emboldened them and made them more arrogant. Verily I say: The greater the decline of religion, the more grievous the waywardness of the ungodly. This cannot but lead in the end to chaos and confusion. Hear Me, O men of insight, and be warned, ye who are endued with discernment!" (*Tablets* 63–64)

A further significant expression of the same principle is the fact that Bahá'u'lláh has consistently called on the rulers of the world to rise to promote and assist His Cause. In fact He describes the station of such a ruler in exceptionally exalted ways. In the Kitáb-i-Aqdas Bahá'u'lláh writes:

> How great the blessedness that awaiteth the king who will arise to aid My Cause in My kingdom, who will detach himself from all else but Me! Such a king is numbered with the companions of the Crimson Ark—the Ark which God hath prepared for the people of Bahá. All must glorify his name, must reverence his station, and aid him to unlock the cities with the keys of My Name, the omnipotent Protector of all that inhabit the visible and invisible kingdoms. Such a king is the very eye of mankind, the luminous ornament on the brow of creation, the fountainhead of blessings unto the whole world. Offer up, O people of Bahá, your substance, nay your very lives, for his assistance. (¶ 84)

It is very significant that in the discussion of the signs of the maturation of humanity, the only legitimate reason to be willing to bear the weight of kingship is to assist the Cause of God: "'Well is it with him who, for love of God and His Cause, and for the sake of God and for the purpose of proclaiming His Faith,'" Bahá'u'lláh says, "'will expose himself unto this great danger, and will accept this toil and trouble.'"[36]

Finally, as we saw in Bahá'u'lláh's tablet to Queen Victoria, although parliamentary structure is necessary, it is not sufficient; the other condition, which is indeed necessary for the ideal political system, is that the members of government should ask for divine guidance in their consultations and in their policy making, "in that which will cause the affairs of Thy servants to prosper, and Thy cities to flourish" (*Epistle* 61). Bahá'u'lláh exhorts the rulers of the world in terms such as these:

> Hearken ye, O Rulers of America and the Presidents of the Republics therein, unto that which the Dove is warbling on the Branch of Eternity: "There is none other God but Me, the Ever-Abiding, the Forgiving, the All-Bountiful." Adorn ye the temple of dominion with the ornament of justice and of the fear of God, and its head with the crown of the remembrance of your Lord, the Creator of the heavens. Thus counselleth you He Who is the Dayspring of Names, as bidden by Him Who is the All-Knowing, the All-Wise. (*Kitáb-i-Aqdas* ¶ 88)

The Unity of the Realms of Heart and Earth

Just as the true means of solving economic problems is noncoercive and through a spiritualized orientation that leads to voluntary sharing of one's property with others, similarly the true means of creating the ideal political order is noncoercive and through the spiritualization of the hearts.[37]

In the many expositions of the principles of heart and removal of the sword, Bahá'u'lláh consistently elaborates a series of connected concepts. Let us examine these two examples.

> The one true God, exalted be His glory, hath bestowed the government of the earth upon the kings. To none is given the right

to act in any manner that would run counter to the considered views of them who are in authority. That which He hath reserved for Himself are the cities of men's hearts; and of these the loved ones of Him Who is the Sovereign Truth are, in this Day, as the keys. Please God they may, one and all, be enabled to unlock, through the power of the Most Great Name, the gates of these cities. This is what is meant by aiding the one true God—a theme to which the Pen of Him Who causeth the dawn to break hath referred in all His Books and Tablets.

It behoveth, likewise, the loved ones of God to be forbearing towards their fellow-men, and to be so sanctified and detached from all things, and to evince such sincerity and fairness, that all the peoples of the earth may recognize them as the trustees of God amongst men. (*Gleanings* 241–42)

Know thou that We have annulled the rule of the sword, as an aid to Our Cause, and substituted for it the power born of the utterance of men. Thus have We irrevocably decreed, by virtue of Our grace. Say: O people! Sow not the seeds of discord among men, and refrain from contending with your neighbor, for your Lord hath committed the world and the cities thereof to the care of the kings of the earth, and made them the emblems of His own power, by virtue of the sovereignty He hath chosen to bestow upon them. He hath refused to reserve for Himself any share whatever of this world's dominion.... The things He hath reserved for Himself are the cities of men's hearts, that He may cleanse them from all earthly defilements, and enable them to draw nigh unto the hallowed Spot which the hands of the infidel can never profane. Open, O people, the city of the human heart with the key of your utterance. (*Gleanings* 303–4)

In these and other statements there is a contrast between dominion in the realm of the heart and dominion in the realm of the earth. The former is the sole interest of God and His Manifestation, while the latter has been entrusted to the kings and rulers of the world.

Bahá'u'lláh affirms that He has not revealed His Cause for the sake of wealth and political power or any worldly motive whatsoever but is revealing the word of God for the sake of God. He assures the rulers, for example, "It is not Our wish to lay hands on your kingdoms. Our mission is to seize and possess the hearts of men. Upon them the eyes of Bahá are fastened" (*Gleanings* 212). He emphasizes this point for two

reasons. First, suspicion of the Bábí movement was exploited by political and religious leaders to persecute the Bábí community and
attribute to them base worldly motivations. Despite the fact that
Bahá'u'lláh explicitly prohibited all forms of the "sword" (with the
exception of punishments provided under criminal law) and His message is entirely one of reconciliation, unity, and peace, nevertheless
His religion was viewed as a threat to the power and authority of the
clerical and political establishment. Therefore, He ceaselessly dis-
claimed personal interest in political power, while declaring that He
was only interested in "seizing" the hearts.

The second reason was Bahá'u'lláh's own personal inclinations,
which were always averse to personal fame. He never ceased to
emphasize that He Himself had no desire for leadership but that His
call for spiritual sovereignty was from God and not from Himself.

However, a paradox appears immediately: on the one hand He
emphasizes that He is not interested in earthly dominion, and yet He
constantly adds that the highest form of earthly authority is one which
is devoted to assisting and promoting the Cause of God. In other
words, we have here a dialectical discourse: the realm of earthly
dominion is opposed to the realm of the heart at this moment. As long
as those who govern in the world are motivated by personal power and
material gain, the political realm cannot become the realm of authentic spiritual dominion. Spiritual dominion is in the realm of the heart,
which is entered through selfless, voluntary, and sincere devotion to
the will of God—never through coercion or expediency. That is why
He cannot accept the use of coercion to promote His Faith and why
He is uninterested in any worldly dominion that is "worldly" because
it is motivated by anything other than the spirit. The meaning of
"worldly" or "earthly" in this sense concerns materialistic or self-cen-
tered motivation. The rejection of the "world" is not a literal rejection, like the Sufi rejection, of the world of social and economic relations.

Bahá'u'lláh and His followers, as He often says, are not interested
in earthly dominion, coercion, and power but in the dominion of the
spirit and the kingdom of the heart. The kingdom of the heart becomes

a thesis opposed to the antithesis of the kingdom of the earth. However, Bahá'u'lláh never stops at this point. He immediately affirms a higher synthesis and ideal: the organic unity of the two kingdoms.

This is realized when earthly authority becomes spiritualized, and that occurs when it is voluntarily devoted to the promotion and assistance of the Cause of God, which is the same as the cause of justice and the true collective interests of humanity. It is for this reason that, as in the passage on absolute kingship, Bahá'u'lláh frequently speaks of the king who has no personal interest in earthly dominion, but who accepts it in order to assist the Cause of God. In this synthesis the earthly kingdom ceases to be "earthly" and becomes a reflection of the spiritual kingdom of the heart. The ideal politics is not the irreconcilable opposition of the earthly and divine kingdoms, but a synthesis of the two in a democratic and noncoercive spiritual authority. This is the moment of mutual interaction, harmony, and cooperation between the civil society and the state.

In fact, this structure is nothing less than the outline of Bahá'u'lláh's concept of the maturation of humanity. The ultimate rationalization of the world (the age of wisdom) is envisioned as an age of the spiritualization of the world, in which people are detached from earthly concerns for their own sake and pursue them only for the sake of putting into practice the principles of the kingdom of the heart. In this moral and spiritual culture, the aggressive pursuit of power has been transformed into dedication to altruistic service to humankind.

In Bahá'u'lláh's statements we can see that although coercion is forbidden in the propagation of religion, discourse has been substituted for it, but the greatest influence and power is exercised by the example of righteous deeds and moral character. It is forbidden to struggle to gain political power; therefore all forms of political conflict are prohibited. Not only is it forbidden to use force to seize power, but "sowing seeds of discord" to gain influence and divide people into factions is similarly banned. Bahá'u'lláh affirms the legitimacy of civil governments but has reserved for Himself the "cities of men's hearts," to which His loved ones are the "keys." The keys can unlock the gates of those cities only by the moral force of righteous character and the example of forbearance, detachment, sincerity, fairness—which, once again, is the definition of assisting the Cause of God. This is the non-coercive means by which the authentic ethical authority of those who are truly the "trustees" of the interests of humankind becomes recognized. When Bahá'u'lláh says that He is only interested in possessing the "hearts," He is in fact stating the first of a sequence of transformations that begin with the heart of the individual and ultimately reshape the institutions of human society, culminating in a spiritualized global civilization which represents the "kingdom of God on earth" and is characterized by the Most Great Peace. Such a historical process of the spiritualization of order is the essence of the promise contained in the revelation imparted to Bahá'u'lláh in the Síyáh-Chál: "Verily, We shall render Thee victorious by Thyself and by Thy pen."

NOTES

Author's provisional translations are indicated by the symbol ⋆.

INTRODUCTION

1. Shoghi Effendi, *The Advent of Divine Justice*, 59.
2. See Shoghi Effendi, *God Passes By*.
3. A discussion of this point is beyond the scope of this book. Much work needs to be done to explore the complex, subtle message of the Báb in the context of its relationship to and particularly its conditionality on the Cause of the Promised One. A brief but useful discussion of the issue of the sword in the writings of the Báb can be found in Nusrat'u'lláh Muhammad-Husainí, *The Báb*, 426–30.
4. See Nabíl-i-A'zam, *The Dawn-Breakers*.
5. Here I am using the terms *asceticism* and *mysticism* in Weber's definition. See Max Weber, *Protestant Ethic and the Spirit of Capitalism* and *The Sociology of Religion*, 166–83.
6. For a sociological analysis of this, see Max Weber, *The Sociology of Religion*, 151–222.
7. See Seena Fazel, "Understanding Exclusivist Texts."

PART I

CHAPTER 1 – MYSTICISM AND METHODOLOGY

1. For a general introduction to Sufism, see Annemarie Schimmel, *Mystical Dimensions of Islam*; Reynold A. Nicholson, *The Mystics of Islam*; Michael A. Sells, ed., *Early Islamic Mysticism*; William C. Chittick, *The Self-Disclosure of God*; Muhammad Iqbal, *The Reconstruction of Religious Thought in Islam*; and 'Izzu'd-Dín Maḥmúd Káshání, *Miṣbáḥu'l-Hidáyah va Miftáḥu'l-Kifáyah*.
2. Max Weber, *The Methodology of Social Sciences*, 90–112.
3. Perhaps the most effective expression of this position can be found in the writings of the great Muslim scholar and polemicist Ibn-i-Taymíyyah, who wrote extensively against varieties of "innovation" in Islam including Sufism. See, for example, Thomas F. Michel's introduction to Ibn Taymíyyah, *A Muslim Theologian's Response to Christianity*, 24–39.
4. See, for example, Káshání, *Miṣbáḥu'l-Hidáyah*; and Sells, *Early Islamic Mysticism*.

5. See Henry Corbin, *History of Islamic Philosophy*.

6. See Bernard Lewis, *The Assassins*, and Farhad Daftari, *The Ismailis*.

7. For a comprehensive scholarly commentary on Ibnu'l-'Arabí's *Bezels of Wisdom*, see Toshihiko Izutsu, *Sufism and Taoism*, 11. Ibnu'l-'Arabí has become the subject of growing interest among Western scholars. See, for example, Chittick, *The Self-Disclosure of God*.

8. Ibnu'l-'Arabí, *The Bezels of Wisdom*, 71–81.

9. Ibid., 71–81, 90–95, 249–65.

10. Bahá'u'lláh, *Majmú'iy-i-Alváh-i-Mubárakih*, 11.

11. Farídu'd-Dín 'Attár, *Muslim Saints and Mystics*.

12. Jalálu'd-Dín Rúmí, *The Mathnawí*, 5–6.

13. Bahá'u'lláh, *Áthár-i-Qalam-i-A'lá* 3:190.

14. Similarly, 'Abdu'l-Bahá speaks of the reed and unveils the spiritual meaning of the term. See *Some Answered Questions*, 45.

15. Shihábu'd-Dín Suhrawardí, *'Avárifu'l-Ma'árif*, 178–87.

16. See Shaykh Ahmad-i-Ahsá'í, *Sharhu'l-Favá'id*, 4–5.

17. The Báb, in *Safínih-i 'Irfán* 1:88–89.

18. See Juan R. I. Cole, *Modernity and the Millennium*.

19. Juan R. I. Cole, "Baha'u'llah's 'Book of the Tigris' (Sahifih-'i Shattiyyih). Translation." Cole has used the text published in Ishráq Khávari's *Má'idiy-i-Ásmání* 4:142–49. The translation of the tablet used here is based on the more accurate version in INBA 57:10–18.

20. Nader Saiedi, "Concealment and Revelation in Bahá'u'lláh's Book of the River."

21. * "Sahífiy-i-Shattíyyih," 58.

22. Ibid., 58–59.

23. Ibid., 59–60.

24. Ibid., 60–61.

25. Juan R. I. Cole, "Baha'u'llah's 'Book of the Tigris' (Sahifih-'i Shattiyyih). Commentary."

26. Cole, "Baha'u'llah's 'Book of the Tigris.'" The more accurate version of the tablet in INBA has "*Valákin chigúnih míshavad kih hích iqbál bih amrí nadáram.*"

27. Cole, "Commentary."

28. See, for example, Bahá'u'lláh, *Iqtidárát*, 71.

29. In 'Abdu'l-Hamíd Ishráq Khávari, *Má'idiy-i-Ásmání* 1:19.

30. Cole's translation of the tablet contains a number of other problems. For a full discussion, see Saiedi, "Concealment and Revelation."

31. Bahá'u'lláh, in Fádil Mázandaráni, *Asráru'l-Áthár* 3:174–77.

32. * In Ishráq Khávari, *Má'idiy-i-Ásmání* 8:62.

33. See Shoghi Effendi, *God Passes By*, 101–2.

34. Cole, "Commentary."

35. * Bahá'u'lláh, *Majmú'iy-i-Alváḥ-i-Mubárakih*, 234.

36. See, for example, Bahá'u'lláh, *Kitáb-i-Badí'*, 87–88.

37. In *Some Answered Questions*, 'Abdu'l-Bahá states that the Manifestations of God are always conscious of their station: "These words which Bahá'u'lláh said, 'I was asleep and the breeze passed over Me, and awakened me,' refer to the body"; that is, they refer "to physical condition and have no reference to the individual reality nor to the manifestation of the Divine Reality" (156, 155).

38. Quoted in Shoghi Effendi, *God Passes By*, 101.

39. See Mázandarání, *Asráru'l-Áthár* 4:22.

40. Bahá'u'lláh, in Ishráq Khávarí, *Má'idiy-i-Ásmání* 7:97–99. For Bahá'u'lláh's references to Dayyán (Mírzá Asadu'lláh-i-Khu'í) as "the third Letter to believe in Him Whom God shall make manifest," and Dayyán's recognition of Him in the early Baghdad period, see Bahá'u'lláh, *Kitáb-i-Badí'*, 102–4; and *Áthár-i-Qalam-i-A'lá* 2:34.

41. Bahá'u'lláh, *Ishráqát*, 221.

42. * Bahá'u'lláh, in 'Abdu'l-Ḥamíd Ishráq Khávarí, *Muḥáḍirát* 1:192.

43. * Ibid., 397.

44. Bahá'u'lláh, *Kitáb-i-Badí'*, 114–15.

45. Every letter of the Arabic alphabet has a numerical value (a = 1, b = 2, etc.) so that letters can also be used to denote numbers. Ḥín = (ḥ = 8) + (í = 10) + (n = 50).

46. * Bahá'u'lláh, in 'Abdu'l-Ḥamíd Ishráq Khávarí, *Raḥíq-i-Makhtúm* 1:568–69.

47. * Bahá'u'lláh, in Mázandarání, *Asráru'l-Áthár* 3:174–77.

48. '*Amá*' has many complex mystical meanings. It derives from *a'má* (the blind), and signifies the supremely inaccessible light cloud which can and cannot be seen. It represents the stage of divine invisibility and concealment and symbolizes the first expression of concealed revelation. It implies the supreme and inaccessible realm of the Primal Will and the inception of the divine Spring.

49. Bahá'u'lláh, in Ishráq Khávarí, *Raḥíq-i-Makhtúm* 2:543–45.

50. * Bahá'u'lláh, in Fáḍil Mázandarání, *Amr va Khalq* 3:353.

51. * Ibid., 443–44.

52. See, for example, Michel Foucault, *The Order of Things*; Thomas S. Kuhn, *The Structure of Scientific Revolutions*; Ludwig Wittgenstein, *Philosophical Investigations*; and Talcott Parsons, *The Structure of Social Action*.

53. Dominick LaCapra, *Rethinking Intellectual History*, 14.

54. Ibid., 35–56.

55. Ibid., 30.

56. Ibid., 31.

57. For a good discussion of different types of rationalization processes, see Jürgen

Habermas, *Knowledge and Human Interests*, and *The Theory of Communicative Action*.

58. See, for example, Bahá'u'lláh, *Majmú'iy-i-Alváh-i-Mubárakih*, 139–44; *The Seven Valleys*, 26.

Chapter 2 – The Ontological Circle

1. See Plotinus, *Enneads*.
2. Abú Naṣr Fárábí, *Al-Fárábí on the Perfect State*.
3. 'Abdu'l-Bahá, *Some Answered Questions*, 235.
4. See, for example, Aḥsá'í, *Sharḥu'l-Favá'id*, 33–89.
5. Bahá'u'lláh, in *Safínih-i 'Irfán* 1:82–84.
6. Cf. John 1:1–14.
7. The Báb, in Fáḍil Mázandarání, *Amr va Khalq* 1:99–100.
8. The Báb, *Tafsír-i-Há'*, 81.
9. ★ The Báb, in *Safínih-i 'Irfán* 1:88.
10. For example, as discussed in *Kitáb-i-Íqán*, 7–8.
11. See Bahá'u'lláh, *Iqtidárát*, 45.
12. ★ "Ṣaḥífiy-i-Shaṭṭíyyih," 59.
13. The Báb, Persian Bayán 4.3.
14. Ibid.
15. Ibid.
16. Bahá'u'lláh, *Prayers and Meditations*, 310–11.
17. Bahá'u'lláh, *Áthár-i-Qalam-i-A'lá* 3: 6.
18. Ibid., 4–31.
19. The valleys of Knowledge and Contentment are absent. At the end of the tablet, however, Bahá'u'lláh explains the reason for this omission: it was His intention to unveil all the stages of the spiritual journey and interpret all the biblical statements that He had mentioned at the beginning, but since the messenger who was to deliver the tablet to its addressee was in hurry, Bahá'-u'lláh has skipped discussion of two important stages. He terms them *taslím* and *riḍá'* (*Áthár-i-Qalam-i-A'lá* 3:87–88). These two concepts may imply different stages or they may be alternate names for the two stages in the Seven Valleys. There is no doubt that the meaning of the two sets is perfectly equivalent. *Taslím* is submission to the will of God, which is exactly the meaning of the valley of knowledge in the Seven Valleys, and *riḍá'* means contentment.
20. *Áthár-i-Qalam-i-A'lá* 3:35–76.
21. The Báb, *Selections*, 88–89.
22. Ibid., 89.
23. See *Gleanings* 153–62.
24. See Izutsu, *Sufism and Taoism*.

25. For an introduction to this subject, see Fazlur Rahman, *Islam*, 85–99.

26. This is also known as occasionalism.

27. See Núru'd-Dín A. Jámí, *Lavá'iḥ*, Lá'iḥih 24.

28. A milder version of this statement can also be found in Ibnu'l-'Arabí, *The Bezels of Wisdom*, 168–69.

29. See, for example, Mázandarání, *Amr va Khalq* 3:353, 442–46; and Bahá'u'lláh, *Ad'íyyih-i-Ḥaḍrat-i-Maḥbúb*, 391–94.

30. See Bahá'u'lláh, *Gleanings*, 329; *Iqtidárát*, 105–13.

31. See *Some Answered Questions*, 290–96.

32. The Báb, in Mázandarání, *Amr va Khalq* 1:103.

33. See, for example, Bahá'u'lláh, *Gleanings*, 46–50.

34. See Ṣadru'd-Dín Shírází, *Al-Ḥikmatu'l-Muta'álíyah fi'l-Asfári'l-'Aqlíyyati'l-Arba'ah*, vol. 1, ch. 1. For a concise account, see Shaykh Aḥmad-i-Aḥsá'í, *Rasá'ilu'l-Ḥikmah*, 156–59.

35. See 'Abdu'l-Bahá, *Some Answered Questions*, 292–93.

36. This is extensively discussed by Shaykh Aḥmad in *Sharḥu'l-'Arshíyyah*.

37. 'Abdu'l-Bahá, *Muntakhabátí az Makátíb-i-Ḥaḍrat-i-'Abdu'l-Bahá* 3: 9–10.

38. 'Abdu'l-Bahá, *Some Answered Questions*, 196.

39. See Nader Saiedi, "Antinomies of Reason and the Theology of Revelation."

40. See 'Abdu'l-Bahá, *Some Answered Questions*, 295.

41. For example, Shaykh Aḥmad is given such a title in the Kitáb-i-Íqán. See Bahá'u'lláh, *Kitáb-i-Íqán*, 66. Shaykh Aḥmad was a vehement opponent of Sufism and of the pantheistic interpretations of Islam. See, for example, Aḥsá'í, *Rasá'ilu'l-Ḥikmah*, 113–14, 153, 182–92.

CHAPTER 3 – SPIRITUAL JOURNEY IN THE FOUR VALLEYS AND THE SEVEN VALLEYS

1. *God Passes By*, 140.

2. See, for example, Bahá'u'lláh, *Majmú'iy-i-Alváḥ-i-Mubárakih*, 352–54.

3. *The Bezels of Wisdom*, 163–71.

4. 'Abdu'l-Bahá, *Some Answered Questions*, 293.

5. See Nader Saiedi, *The Birth of Social Theory*.

6. Shaykh Aḥmad discusses this idea frequently. See, for example, *Sharḥu'l-Favá'id*, 8–11.

7. Bahá'u'lláh, in Mázandarání, *Amr va Khalq* 3:472.

8. Farídu'd-Dín 'Aṭṭár, *The Conference of the Birds*, 97–133.

9. It is important to note that the word Bahá'u'lláh uses here for "heart" is not *fu'ád*—the term used for the fourth valley in the Four Valleys—but *qalb*. Arabic mystical literature uses several different terms for the English word *heart* such

as *fu'ád*, *qalb*, *ṣadr*, and *sirr*. The last one, *sirr*, also means secret or mystery. In the Four Valleys, Bahá'u'lláh uses both *fu'ád* and *sirr* to describe the fourth valley as the throne of the heart and secret (or heart because the term is *sirr*) of maturation. In light of Bahá'u'lláh's statement that the valley or city of the heart (*qalb*) consists of four stages subsequent to those of the Seven Valleys, it remains an interesting question whether this city of *qalb* is the same as the valley of *fu'ád* in the Four Valleys or not.

10.   Bahá'u'lláh, *Iqtidárát*, 107–8.

11.   See also *Gleanings*, 159.

12.   *Sharḥu'l-Favá'id*, 89–105.

13.   Weber, *The Sociology of Religion*, 138–50.

14.   See Lawrence Kohlberg, *The Philosophy of Moral Development*.

15.   See Bahá'u'lláh, *Majmú'iy-i-Alváḥ-i-Mubárakih*, 97–98.

16.   'Abdu'l-Bahá, *Makátíb* 1:85–99.

17.   See also Bahá'u'lláh *Tablets* 268.

18.   In Nietzsche's terms, Dionysian and Apollonian cultures. See Friedrich W. Nietzsche, *The Birth of Tragedy*.

19.   'Abdu'l-Bahá, *Some Answered Questions*, 120–21. See also 'Abdu'l-Bahá, *Makátíb* 2:328–29; *Selections*, 169.2.

20.   ★ "Ṣaḥífiy-i-Shaṭṭíyyih," 58.

21.   An excellent example of a Bahá'í approach to meditation and prayer is Lasse Thoresen's *Unlocking the Gate of the Heart*.

22.   The Báb, *Selections*, 41–42.

23.   ★ In Mázandarání, *Amr va Khalq* 3:445–46.

24.   In *The Bahá'í World: A Biennial International Record* 3:163.

25.   See Plato, *Collected Dialogues*, 353–84.

26.   See Immanuel Kant, *Critique of Pure Reason*.

PART II

CHAPTER 4 – THE KITÁB-I-ÍQÁN: CONTEXT AND ORDER

1.   Shoghi Effendi, *God Passes By*, 138.

2.   Ahang Rabbani, "The Conversion of the Great-Uncle of the Báb."

3.   Ibid., 34–35.

4.   Bahá'u'lláh, Tablet to Ibn-i-Aṣdaq, quoted in *Kitáb-i-Íqán* (Bahá'í-Verlag ed.), x.

5.   Muḥammad 'Alí Fayḍí, *Khándán-i-Afnán*, 40–41.

6.   Bahá'u'lláh writes in one of His tablets that the Kitáb-i-Íqán, which was requested by Afnán (Ḥájí Mírzá Siyyid Muḥammad) and was written in reply to his questions while he was present, has been attributed to someone else; yet, He adds, the travel of this Wronged One is mentioned in it and all the Afnáns bear witness to the truth (*Áthár-i-Qalam-i-A'lá* 5:148).

7. Bahá'u'lláh, in Ishráq Khávarí, *Má'idiy-i-Ásmání* 7:105. See also Shoghi Effendi, *God Passes By*, 102.

8. See, for example, Bahá'u'lláh, in Ishráq Khávarí, *Má'idiy-i-Ásmání* 7:72–73.

9. Bahá'u'lláh, *Majmú'iy-i-Alváḥ-i-Mubárakih*, 125–26.

10. Ibid., 5–10.

11. ★ The Báb, Arabic Bayán 2.7. Also quoted in Bahá'u'lláh, *Kitáb-i-Badí'*, 221.

12. ★ Bahá'u'lláh, *Kitáb-i-Badí'*, 161.

13. Baghdad was originally known as Dáru's-Salám or the Abode of Peace (or the City of God because peace is an attribute of God).

14. Qur'án 10:25.

15. Qur'án 6:127.

16. Qur'án 3:7.

17. Although present in the original, it is not included in the English translation of these tablets.

18. On the relationship of "eight unities" to Quddús, see Chapter 6.

19. Bahá'u'lláh, *Áthár-i-Qalam-i-A'lá* 3:21–32.

20. Siyyid Kázim-i-Rashtí, *Majma'u'l-Asrár*, 171–83, 306–39.

21. The Báb, Arabic Bayán 1, introduction.

22. Persian Bayán 1.1.

23. "And know thou of a certainty that every letter revealed in the Bayán is solely intended to evoke submission unto Him Whom God shall make manifest, for it is He Who hath revealed the Bayán prior to His Own manifestation" (The Báb, *Selections*, 104).

24. Persian Bayán 3.16.

25. See *Kitáb-i-Íqán*, 92–93, 256.

26. Qur'án 55:2–4.

27. Shaykh Aḥmad-i-Aḥsá'í, *Sharḥu'z-Zíyárati'l-Jámi'ati'l-Kabírah* 1:20–30.

28. Aḥsá'í, *Rasá'ilu'l-Ḥikmah*, 135, 137.

29. Qur'án 43:36, 20:124.

30. Italics added.

Chapter 5 – The Kitáb-i-Íqán: Theology Revolutionized

1. See Kant, *Critique of Pure Reason*.

2. Rene Descartes, *Discourse on Method*.

3. See, for instance, Claude A. Helvetius, *Essays on the Mind*.

4. Edmund Husserl, *Ideas*.

5. *Kitáb-i-Íqán*, 82–83.

6. See Ishráq Khávarí, *Muḥáḍirát* 2:763–73.

7. Qur'án 37:173, 9:33.

8. See Saiedi, "Concealment and Revelation."

9. See Kant, *Critique of Pure Reason*.

10. Ibid., 287–483.

11. These are discussed in Kant's *Critique of Practical Reason* and *Critique of Judgment*.

12. Saiedi, "Antinomies of Reason."

13. Qur'án 6:103.

14. See Weber, *The Sociology of Religion*, 138–83.

15. Nader Saiedi, "The Bahá'í Approach to the Environment."

16. Of course, this civilizational evolution does not occur in a simple linear form but must be viewed as cumulative and in terms of long-term trends. Because of the freedom of the human will and historical dynamics, this development is characterized by both cyclical and linear movements.

17. See *Kitáb-i-Íqán*, 195–200.

18. See Saiedi, *The Birth of Social Theory*, 30–53, 107–45.

19. Ibid., 59–159.

20. See Auguste Comte, *The Positive Philosophy* 1:1–17.

21. Georg W. F. Hegel, *The Philosophy of Right*; Karl Marx and Friedrich Engels, *Communist Manifesto*.

22. See Friedrich W. Nietzsche, *The Will to Power*.

CHAPTER 6 – THE KITÁB-I-BADÍ': THE PROMISE FULFILLED

1. Shoghi Effendi describes the book in this concise statement: "Kitáb-i-Badí', His apologia, written to refute the accusations leveled against Him by Mírzá Mihdíy-i-Rashtí, corresponding to the Kitáb-i-Íqán, revealed in defense of the Bábí revelation" (*God Passes By*, 172).

2. Ibid., 171–72.

3. Bahá'u'lláh, *Kitáb-i-Badí'*, 332.

4. Ibid., 292.

5. Ibid., 290.

6. Ibid., 124.

7. Ibid., 212.

8. Ibid., 239–50.

9. Ibid., 212.

10. ★ Ibid., 32.

11. ★ Ibid., 53–54.

12. ★ Ibid., 252.

13. ★ Ibid., 210.

14. Ibid., 38–41.

15. Ibid., 58. Quoted in Bahá'u'lláh, *Epistle*, 172.

16. Ibid., 190. Quoted in Bahá'u'lláh, *Epistle*, 165.

17. Ibid., 27. Quoted in Bahá'u'lláh, *Epistle*, 171.

18. Ibid., 66. Quoted in Bahá'u'lláh, *Epistle*, 153.
19. Ibid., 27. Quoted in Bahá'u'lláh, *Epistle*, 152.
20. Ibid., 209. Quoted in Shoghi Effendi, *The World Order of Bahá'u'lláh*, 100.
21. Ibid., 24. Quoted in Bahá'u'lláh, *Epistle*, 160.
22. Most of this tablet is published in 'Abdu'l-Ḥamíd Ishráq Khávarí, *Ayyám-i-Tis'ih*, 169–75.
23. Bahá'u'lláh, *Kitáb-i-Badí'*, 208–10.
24. Ibid., 26.
25. Ibid., 26.
26. Ibid., 26–27.
27. Ibid., 27.
28. The Báb, Persian Bayán 2.5.
29. Bahá'u'lláh, *Kitáb-i-Badí'*, 27–30.
30. Ibid., 74–82.
31. Persian Bayán 8.11.
32. Bahá'u'lláh, *Kitáb-i-Badí'*, 77.
33. * Ibid., 114–15.
34. Bahá'u'lláh has stated in many other tablets that the Beauty of Nine (that is, Bahá) appeared in the year nine as the fulfillment of the prophecies of the Bayán. See, for example, Bahá'u'lláh, in 'Abdu'l-Ḥamíd Ishráq Khávarí, *Qámús-i-Tawqí'-i-Maní'-i-Mubárak* 2:487.
35. *Kitáb-i-Badí'*, 118–19.
36. Ibid., 118.
37. Ibid., 119.
38. Ibid., 121–23.
39. Ibid., 113.
40. Ibid., 116.
41. Matt. 3:2.
42. * Bahá'u'lláh, *Kitáb-i-Badí'*, 159–64.
43. Ibid., 187–90.
44. The Nineteen Temples are included in the published version of the Báb's book Panj Sha'n (Five Modes of Revelation); see *Panj Sha'n*, 429–38.
45. Bahá'u'lláh's statement and a detailed discussion of the issue can be found in Ishráq Khávarí, *Muḥáḍirát* 1:292–308, 392–414.
46. Bahá'u'lláh, *Kitáb-i-Badí'*, 343.
47. The Báb, Persian Bayán 6.14.
48. Ibid., 3.16.
49. *Selections*, 92.
50. Bahá'u'lláh, *Kitáb-i-Badí'*, 169. Quoted in *Epistle*, 160.

51. Bahá'u'lláh, *Kitáb-i-Badí'*, 274. Quoted in *Epistle*, 160.

52. Bahá'u'lláh, *Kitáb-i-Badí'*, 237. The Báb, *Selections*, 156.

53. Bahá'u'lláh, *Kitáb-i-Badí'*, 373. The Báb, *Selections*, 155–56.

54. Bahá'u'lláh, *Kitáb-i-Badí'*, 335–37.

55. Ibid., 338.

56. Ibid., 339.

57. Ibid., 77.

58. * For a discussion of the Báb's statement addressed to Yaḥyá, see Ishráq Khávarí, *Raḥíq-i-Makhtúm* 2:187; and Muhammad Afnan, "Ayyám-i-Butún," 36.

59. * Bahá'u'lláh, *Kitáb-i-Badí'*, 227.

60. Ibid., 152.

61. Ibid., 152–54.

62. Ibid., 162.

63. Ibid., 12, 315, 407–9.

64. Ibid., 164–68.

65. Ibid., 210–18.

66. * Ibid., 219 (Arabic Bayán 2.6).

67. The Báb, Persian Bayán 4.18; also Arabic Bayán 1.1. Note that Bahá'u'lláh Himself has testified that "152" in the opening lines of the Arabic Bayán refers to Quddús. See Ishráq Khávarí, *Má'idiy-i-Ásmání* 7:86–87.

68. Bahá'u'lláh, *Kitáb-i-Badí'*, 220 (Arabic Bayán 2.7).

69. See the Báb, *Selections*, 129–30.

70. * *Kitáb-i-Badí'*, 221 (Arabic Bayán 2.7).

71. * Ibid., 224 (Qayyúmu'l-Asmá', ch. 57).

72. *Kitáb-i-Badí'*, 284–86.

73. Ibid., 218, 272.

74. * Ibid., 380.

75. Ibid., 287–90, 380.

76. Ibid., 137–58.

77. *Selections*, 104–5.

78. Qur'án 29:50.

79. *Selections*, 82.

80. Ibid., 101–2.

81. Bahá'u'lláh, *Kitáb-i-Badí'*, 301. On the battlefield, Imám Ḥusayn's forces were cut off from water by their enemies.

82. Ibid., 306.

83. Ibid., 296.

84. Ibid., 379.

85. Ibid., 328–31.
86. Ibid., 318.
87. Ibid., 402–6.
88. Ibid., 12, 402–12.

PART III

CHAPTER 7 – THE KITÁB-I-AQDAS: DATE AND CONSTITUTIVE PRINCIPLES

1. *God Passes By*, 213.
2. Ibid., 215–16.
3. Bahá'u'lláh, in Ishráq Khávarí, *Má'idiy-i-Ásmání* 7:154–56.
4. See, for example, Bahá'u'lláh, *Iqtidárát*, 185.
5. ★ Ibid., 273.
6. The Báb, Persian Bayán 2.2, 2.5, 2.19; 3.3, 3.4, 3.7, 3.8–11.
7. See *Kitáb-i-Íqán*, 139–42.
8. Anthony A. Lee, "Choice Wine."
9. Ibid.
10. Ibid.
11. Discussed by Amin Banani in a lecture on the Kitáb-i-Íqán at Landegg Academy, Summer 1998.
12. ★ Bahá'u'lláh, *Iqtidárát*, 185.
13. ★ Bahá'u'lláh, Ishráq Khávarí, *Má'idiy-i-Ásmání* 8:138.
14. ★ In Mázandarání, *Amr va Khalq* 3:445–46. See also Bahá'u'lláh, *Ad'íyyih-i-Ḥaḍrat-i-Maḥbúb*, 391–94.
15. Bahá'u'lláh, *Áthár-i-Qalam-i-A'lá* 5:91, 185.
16. Bahá'u'lláh's tablet is quoted in Muḥammad 'Alí Fayḍí, *La'álíy-i-Dirakhshán*, 19–20.
17. Ibid., 21.
18. Ibid., 19–21.
19. Bahá'u'lláh, in Ishráq Khávarí, *Má'idiy-i-Ásmání* 4:355–56.
20. Qur'án 83:25–26.
21. Suheil Bushrui, *The Style of the Kitáb-i-Aqdas*, 38–39.
22. 'Abdu'l-Bahá, *Will and Testament of 'Abdu'l-Bahá*, 20.
23. The mistake of overgeneralizing the idea of progressive revelation to such a degree that it contradicts the basic principles of the Faith was also made in my own 1987 article, "Faith, Reason, and Society in Bahá'í Perspective."
24. In the Kitáb-i-Íqán, recounting Muḥammad's apparently arbitrary change of the *qiblih*, Bahá'u'lláh explains that sometimes the sole reason for changing a law is to test the faith of those who profess belief. "Verily God caused not this

turmoil but to test and prove His servants. Otherwise, He, the ideal King, could easily have left the Qiblih unchanged...." (51).

25. Shoghi Effendi, *World Order of Bahá'u'lláh*, 23.

26. Lee, "Choice Wine."

27. Shoghi Effendi, *God Passes By*, 213.

28. Mázandarání, *Amr va Khalq* 1:11.

29. Mázandarání, *Amr va Khalq* 1: 9–11.

30. ★ Bahá'u'lláh, in Mázandarání, *Amr va Khalq* 1:10–11.

31. Kamran Ekbal, "Ágház va páyán-i-nuzúl-i-Kitáb-i-Mustatáb-i-Aqdas," 11–13; "Táríkh-i-nuzúl va nigárish-i-Kitáb-i-Mustatáb-i-Aqdas," 100–11.

32. Ekbal, "Táríkh-i-nuzúl," 107.

33. Ibid., 105.

34. Nikkie Keddie, *An Islamic Response to Imperialism*, 24.

35. Bahá'u'lláh, *Áthár-i-Qalam-i-A'lá* 5:188.

36. Bahá'u'lláh, in Ishráq Khávarí, *Má'idiy-i-Ásmání* 7:180–81.

37. Mázandarání, *Asráru'l-Áthár* 3: 255. See also Adib Taherzadeh, *The Revelation of Bahá'u'lláh* 4:337–50.

38. Ishráq Khávarí, *Má'idiy-i-Ásmání* 3:1.

39. Two tablets revealed in 1911 and published together in *Star of the West* (in Persian) give two different "dates." In one, 'Abdu'l-Bahá writes that the issue of peace among nations was established by Bahá'u'lláh "sixty years ago, namely in 1851" in Iran, until He explicated the question of universal peace in the Kitáb-i-Aqdas, which was revealed "fifty years ago." In the other tablet 'Abdu'l-Bahá writes that universal peace was commanded in the Kitáb-i-Aqdas "forty years ago" (*Star of the West*, Sept. 1911, No. 10, pp. 3, 4). *The Promulgation of Universal Peace* records Him as saying in a 1912 talk that the teaching of international language was "set forth in the Kitáb-i-Aqdas ('Most Holy Book') published fifty years ago" (435). See also 'Abdu'l-Bahá, *Majmú'iy-i-Khitábát* 3:92.

40. The law of Ḥuqúqu'lláh prescribes, as a private spiritual obligation, the payment of nineteen percent of the value of one's possessions, exempting categories such as residence and expenses. It is never solicited.

41. Bahá'u'lláh, *Áthár-i-Qalam-i-A'lá* 7: 236. In a different tablet He explains: "Before this law was revealed there was no obligation on the part of any soul. The Pen of Glory held back from revealing laws and ordinances for a number of years, and this was a token of His heavenly grace" (Bahá'u'lláh, in *Ḥuqúqu'lláh*, 9).

42. ★ Bahá'u'lláh, in Mázandarání, *Amr va Khalq* 1:10–11.

43. See, for instance, Bahá'u'lláh, *Alváḥ-i-Názilih Khitáb bih Mulúk va Ru'asáy-i-Arḍ*, 24.

44. See Bahá'u'lláh, *Tablets*, 128.

45. John Walbridge, "The Kitab-i-Aqdas."

46. Lee, "Choice Wine."

47. See, for example, ¶ 3, ¶ 5, ¶ 10, ¶ 13, and ¶ 14.

48. Bahá'u'lláh, Ishráqát, 260.

49. 'Abdu'l-Bahá's elaboration, in diverse forms, of the basic principles of the Bahá'í Faith follows Bahá'u'lláh's own further explications of these same general principles.

50. * Bahá'u'lláh, in Mázandarání, Asráru'l-Áthár 4:22.

51. See, for example, Qur'án 4:74–76; 22:40–41; 47:5–8.

52. Quoted in Shoghi Effendi, God Passes By, 198; see also Bahá'u'lláh, Áthár-i-Qalam-i-A'lá 1: 69.

53. Quoted in Shoghi Effendi, God Passes By, 238.

54. That is one of the reasons why, in some of His tablets, Bahá'u'lláh speaks of the "termination" of revelation in His manifestation, meaning that the entire promise of the Bayán has already been fulfilled. It is for the same reason that Bahá'u'lláh insists that this period is a full one thousand years, and nothing less. Bahá'u'lláh, Iqtidárát, 327.

55. * Kitáb-i-Badí', 402–3.

56. * Ibid., 403.

57. * Ibid., 403–4.

58. * Ibid., 402–6.

59. Bahá'u'lláh's tablet can be found in Ishráq Khávarí, Má'idiy-i-Ásmání 1:65–68. See also Má'idiy-i-Ásmání 4:361, and Shoghi Effendi, God Passes By, 251.

60. See Bahá'u'lláh, Tablets, 221.

61. Prayers and Meditations, 275.

62. See, for example, 'Abdu'l-Bahá, Selections 74.1.

63. Friedrich Schiller, On the Aesthetic Education of Man.

64. See Ahsá'í, Rasá'ilu'l-Hikmah, 135, 137.

65. The first systematic expression of this idea can be found in the works of Schelling. See, for example, Friedrich W. J. Schelling, System of Transcendental Idealism, 222–23.

66. Hans-Georg Gadamer, Truth and Method. See, for example, Gianni Vattimo, The End of Modernity; Julian Pefanis, Heterology and the Postmodern; and Jean F. Lyotard, The Postmodern Condition.

67. Interestingly, Shaykh Ahmad in Sharhu'z-Zíyárah and the Báb in Sahífiy-i-'Adlíyyih discuss the meaning of this and a similar Islamic tradition as means of discussing the pillars of the Faith.

68. Bahá'u'lláh, Iqtidárát, 148–49.

Chapter 8 – From the Order of the Book to the New Order

1. This is also discussed by <u>Shaykh</u> Aḥmad. See <u>Shar</u>ḥu'z-Zíyárah 3:21–23, 150–51.
2. Bahá'u'lláh, Á<u>th</u>ár-i-Qalam-i-A'lá 5:91.
3. The Báb, Persian Bayán 1.1. See also *Selections*, 102.
4. The Báb, Persian Bayán 3.13; 2.3.
5. Bahá'u'lláh, Iqtidárát, 88–89.
6. See Bahá'u'lláh, Persian Hidden Words 71.
7. Bahá'u'lláh, in I<u>sh</u>ráq <u>Kh</u>ávarí, Má'idiy-i-Ásmání 7:167–68.
8. Mázandaráni, Amr va <u>Kh</u>alq 3:442–43.
9. The Báb, Tafsír-i-Bismi'lláh. INBA 64:15–16.
10. The Báb, Persian Bayán 5.3.
11. Ibid., 6.7. Also note that in the Bahá'í marriage vow, "by the will of God" translates the Arabic word lillah.
12. Lev. 19:1.
13. Iqtidárát, 215.
14. I<u>sh</u>ráq <u>Kh</u>ávarí, Má'idiy-i-Ásmání 1:23–24.
15. * Arabic Bayán 10.3.
16. The Báb refers simultaneously to seven and to nine because the unity of the two numbers became possible only through Bahá'u'lláh. The number of categories of inheritance is seven. However, in the distribution scheme of the Bayán the seven categories are distributed as nine through three, beginning with the share of children as nine. Surprisingly, the Báb does not determine the share of the children as seven, but as nine. Similarly He assigns the share of the last group, the teachers, not as one but as three.
17. The Báb, in Safínih-i 'Irfán 1:88.
18. The Báb, Panj <u>Sh</u>a'n, 415–18, 422–23.
19. Panj <u>Sh</u>a'n, 416. The culmination of this temple is the number 540, corresponding to the number 9 (Panj <u>Sh</u>a'n, 409–10, 422–34.). The number 540 is not only 9 itself (5 + 4 + 0 = 9), it is the realization of 9 in the order of the fifth temple.
20. Ibid., 412, 350.
21. A full discussion of various aspects of this symbolism is impossible here, but these additional points are relevant. First, 540 is identified in the Persian Bayán as "the number of the letters of ṭá' (9) (Persian Bayán 5.19). This means that since 9 is composed of 5 and 4, therefore 540 is also 9. Second, the total number of inheritance shares is 42. This is the number of balá (yes), also frequently discussed by the Báb, which symbolizes acceptance of the Promised One's divine call. Third, the number 7 also is intended by the Báb to imply the word illa'lláh (save God), which has seven letters and signifies affirmation and recognition of the Promised One (in the Islamic confession of Faith, first negation appears: "There is no God"; then affirmation follows: "save God")

(Persian Bayán 8. 2). The distribution of inheritance in the Bayán is structured in terms of the numbers from 9 to 3. To arrive at this distribution, the Báb emphasizes 2520 as the highest expression of 9, because it is the first number that is divisible by all the nine numbers. Interestingly, 2520 is itself equal to 9 (2 + 5 + 2 + 0 = 9). Therefore, 2520 simultaneously represents 9 as its highest reflection. Note that 2520 and 2052 (*Huva'l-Mustaghíth,* the Báb's ultimate word for the concept of Mustaghath) are both identical in terms of 9. The number 2520, in other words, may also be a subtle reference to the fact that Mustaghath is indeed realized in the year nine. This becomes more evident when we note that the inheritance numbers are affirmations of nineteen temples which end in 2052.

22. Universal House of Justice to an individual, July 1996. In the tablet referred to, Abdu'l-Bahá writes:

> "In truth, the wisdom of this perspicuous and most mighty ordinance is that no one should draw breath without a will. Observe how, in the absence of a will, the inheritance in its entirety is divided up, distributed and dispersed contrary to the wishes of the deceased; what difficulties and disagreements are thus engendered! The will, however, is the settler of every dispute, and the cause of ease for all, for in it the testator disposeth of his property in whatsoever manner he desireth. How agreeable it is for the estate in its entirety to be disposed of in accordance with the testator's will and pleasure! Observe ye how many people during their lifetime are fearful about what will happen when they pass away. Now, with this divine commandment—the obligation and religious duty of drawing up a will before one's passing—all these difficulties are resolved."

23. ★ Bahá'u'lláh, Ishráq Khávarí, *Má'idiy-i-Ásmání* 8:138. (Italics added.)

24. Bahá'u'lláh, *Iqtidárát*, 3.

25. The Báb, Persian Bayán 6.2, 6.3; 5.13, 5.16; 8.6.

26. See the Báb, *Selections*, 101.

27. The Báb, Persian Bayán 3.16 (quoted in Shoghi Effendi, *God Passes By*, 324–25).

28. For a more detailed discussion of this issue, see Ali Nakhjavani, "Nigáhí bih Naẓm-i-Badí'-i-Iláhí."

29. Ishráq Khávarí, *Má'idiy-i-Ásmání* 7:91–92.

30. ★ Persian Bayán 3.16.

31. Ahsá'í, *Rasá'ilu'l-Ḥikmah*, 135, 137.

32. The Báb, Persian Bayán 2.3–6; 3.8–12.

33. The Báb, Tafsír-i-Súriy-i-Kawthar, 207–8.

34. See Saiedi, "Taḥlílí az Mafhúm-i-Bábíyyat dar Áthár-i-Ḥaḍrat-i-A'lá."

35. The Báb, Persian Bayán 1.1; Arabic Bayán 1, Introduction.

36. Qur'án 47:15.

37. The Báb, Persian Bayán 2.14.

38. See *Kitáb-i-Aqdas*, 246–47.

39. Arabic Bayán 6.11.

CHAPTER 9 – PHILOSOPHICAL PREMISES OF THE NEW WORLD ORDER

1. Cole, *Modernity and the Millennium*, 115–16.

2. * In Mázandaráni, *Asráru'l-Áthár* 2:17–18.

3. According to Martin Lings, Sa'd decreed the punishment according to the Jewish law for a besieged city: "When the Lord thy God hath delivered it into thine hands, thou shalt smite every male thereof with the edge of the sword. But the women, and the little ones, and the cattle, and all that is in the city, even all the spoil thereof, shalt thou take unto thyself" (Deut. 20:12–14). Lings, *Muhammad*, 229–33.

4. * In Mázandaráni, *Asráru'l-Áthár* 2:17–18. Lawh-i-Nidá' is most likely another name for the Bishárát, which begins: "This is the Call [*Nidá'*] of the All-Glorious...." (in Bahá'u'lláh, *Tablets*, 19–29).

5. *Modernity and the Millennium*, 115.

6. This is confirmed by Shoghi Effendi; see *God Passes By*, 104.

7. *Modernity and the Millennium*, 115.

8. Ibid.

9. Examples of the removal of the sword throughout the Baghdad period are found in Bahá'u'lláh, *Iqtidárát*, 8; *Tablets*, 5; *Epistle*, 21–24; *Áthár-i-Qalam-i-A'lá* 1:67; and Ishráq Khávarí, *Má'idiy-i-Ásmáni* 7:138. See also 'Abdu'l-Bahá, *A Traveler's Narrative*, 62–63.

10. See Ishráq Khávarí, *Má'idiy-i-Ásmáni* 5:140–41.

11. See James Knowlson, *Universal Language Schemes in England and France 1600–1800*.

12. Umberto Eco, *The Search for the Perfect Language*, 1–2.

13. Ibid., 339.

14. Ibid., 333 (italics added).

15. Ibid., 334.

16. Eugen Weber, *Apocalypses*, 53.

17. See, for example, Friedrich Schlegel, *The Philosophy of History*, 455–76.

18. Claude H. Saint-Simon, *Selected Writings*, 122–23, 126, 130.

19. Ibid., 80–81.

20. Ibid., 80.

21. Ibid., 99–102.

22. Ibid., 109.

23. Ibid., 78.

24. Ibid., 227–28.

25. Ibid., 229–30.

26. See also Comte, *The Positive Philosophy* 3:192–98.

27. For a classic discussion of the problem of order, see Talcott Parsons, *The Structure of Social Action.*

28. See Jeffrey C. Alexander, *Theoretical Logic in Sociology,* vol. 1.

29. Thomas Hobbes, *Leviathan.*

30. See, for example, Baron de Holbach, *The System of Nature,* 142, 264; Cesare M. Beccaria, *An Essay on Crimes and Punishments;* Elie Halevy, *The Growth of Philosophic Radicalism.*

31. This begins with Herder, is reaffirmed by the Romantics and Idealists, and is emphasized in more complex ways by Durkheim, Weber, and others.

32. Emile Durkheim, *Moral Education.*

33. See, for example, de Holbach, *The System of Nature,* 142, 280–81.

34. Eliott Currie, *Confronting Crime.*

35. James Q. Wilson, *Thinking About Crime.*

36. See Shoghi Effendi, *The Promised Day Is Come.*

37. See Bahá'u'lláh, *Gleanings,* 215.

38. Friedrich Schlegel, *Philosophy of History,* 207–10, 446–50; Friedrich Schlegel, *Philosophy of Life,* 286–87; August W. Schlegel, *Course of Lectures;* Edmund Burke, *Reflections on the Revolution;* Joseph Marie de Maistre, *Considerations on France;* Johann G. Fichte, *Addresses;* Johann G. Herder, *Reflections.*

39. Herbert Spencer, *The Principles of Sociology.*

40. Ignaz Goldziher, *Introduction to Islamic Theology and Law,* 251–52.

41. Juan R. I. Cole, "Iranian Millenarianism and Democratic Thought in the Nineteenth Century."

42. Bahá'u'lláh, in Mázandarání, *Amr va Khalq* 3:472.

43. See, for an example, Emile Durkheim, *Rules of Sociological Method.*

44. Structuralists normally emphasize this perspective. See, for instance, Louis Althusser and Etienne Balibar, *Reading Capital.*

45. Examples are the philosophers of the Enlightenment, Jeremy Bentham, and John Stuart Mill.

46. See Ernest Nagel, *The Structure of Science.*

47. Saiedi, *The Birth of Social Theory,* 1–7.

48. Marx and Durkheim are two prominent representatives of these alternative positions.

49. Bahá'u'lláh, *La'áli'l-Ḥikmah* 2:275.

50. See Immanuel Wallerstein, *The Capitalist World Economy.*

51. See Bahá'u'lláh, *Tablets,* 170.

52. Shoghi Effendi, *World Order of Bahá'u'lláh,* 42–43.

CHAPTER 10 – SPIRIT, HISTORY, AND ORDER

 1. Cole, *Modernity and the Millennium*, 29–30.
 2. Ibid., 76.
 3. Ibid., 46–47.
 4. Ibid., 76.
 5. Bahá'u'lláh, *Áthár-i-Qalam-i-A'lá* 1:85. Bahá'u'lláh mentions in the tablet that He is soon to be exiled to 'Akká.
 6. ★ Bahá'u'lláh, *Majmú'iy-i-Alváh-i-Mubárakih*, 125–26.
 7. Cole, *Modernity and the Millennium*, 60–61, 73, 191, 207 n. 39.
 8. Ibid., 207 n. 39.
 9. Quoted in Taherzadeh, *The Revelation of Bahá'u'lláh* 2:140–43. The Persian text of Panj Kanz is found in *'Andalíb* 10.40 (Fall 1991): 10–13.
10. It is for this reason that 'Abdu'l-Bahá found the parliamentary discussions in Paris power-hungry and comical and contrasted them with the norms of spiritual consultation: "In this Cause consultation is of vital importance, but spiritual conference and not the mere voicing of personal views is intended. In France I was present at a session of the senate, but the experience was not impressive. Parliamentary procedure should have for its object the attainment of the light of truth upon questions presented and not furnish a battleground for opposition and self-opinion. Antagonism and contradiction are unfortunate and always destructive to truth. In the parliamentary meeting mentioned, altercation and useless quibbling were frequent; the result, mostly confusion and turmoil; even in one instance a physical encounter took place between two members. It was not consultation but comedy…. Therefore, true consultation is spiritual conference in the attitude and atmosphere of love. Members must love each other in the spirit of fellowship in order that good results may be forthcoming. Love and fellowship are the foundation." (*Promulgation of Universal Peace*, 72–73.)
11. Cole, *Modernity and the Millennium*, 73.
12. Bahá'u'lláh, *Majmú'iy-i-Alváh-i-Mubárakih*, 125–26 (quoted in *Kitáb-i-Aqdas*, 251).
13. Accurate versions of the tablet are found in Ishráq Khávarí, *Má'idiy-i-Ásmání* 8:41 and in the authenticated INBA 26:305.
14. ★ In Ishráq Khávarí *Má'idiy-i-Ásmání* 8:41.
15. Cole, *Modernity and the Millennium*, 52.
16. See Ann K. S. Lambton, *State and Government in Medieval Islam*.
17. John Stuart Mill, *Considerations on Representative Government*, 174–90.
18. See, for example, Herbert Spencer, *The Principles of Sociology* 3:580–82; and *Social Statics and The Man Versus the State*, 356–65.
19. Cole, *Modernity and the Millennium*, 207 n. 39.
20. Mírzá Mahmúd Zarqání, *Badáyi'ul-Áthár*, 273.

21. Ishráq Khávarí, *Má'idiy-i-Ásmání* 8:60.

22. 'Abdu'l-Bahá, *The Secret of Divine Civilization*, 1.

23. Fárábí, *Al-Fárábí on the Perfect State*, 68–112.

24. Ishráq Khávarí, *Má'idiy-i-Ásmání* 7:156–60.

25. See Bahá'u'lláh, *Tablets*, 69.

26. Ibid., 144.

27. See Jürgen Habermas, *Knowledge and Human Interests*, and *The Theory of Communicative Action*.

28. *Modernity and the Millennium*, 29.

29. Ibid., 30.

30. Ibid.

31. Shoghi Effendi, *The Advent of Divine Justice*, 35.

32. Ibid.

33. Quoted in Universal House of Justice to an individual, 27 April 1995.

34. John Locke, *A Letter Concerning Toleration*.

35. Bahá'u'lláh, *Gleanings*, 232–33; *Tablets*, 125.

36. ★ Bahá'u'lláh, *Majmú'iy-i-Alváh-i-Mubárakih*, 125–26.

37. For an excellent discussion of aspects of Bahá'u'lláh's concept of politics and the Bahá'i concept of world order, see Udo Schaefer, Nicola Towfigh, and Ulrich Gollmer, *Making the Crooked Straight*.

REFERENCES

'Abdu'l-Bahá. *Majmú'iy-i-Khiṭábát-i-Ḥaḍrat-i-'Abdu'l-Bahá.* Hofheim: Bahá'í-Verlag, 1984.

———. *Makátíb.* Vols. 1–2. Cairo: Kurdistánu'l-'Ilmíyyah, 1910–12.

———. *Muntakhabátí az Makátíb-i-Ḥaḍrat-i-'Abdu'l-Bahá.* Vol. 3. Hofheim: Bahá'í-Verlag, 1992.

———. *The Promulgation of Universal Peace: Talks Delivered by 'Abdu'l-Bahá during His Visit to the United States and Canada in 1912.* Comp. Howard MacNutt. 2d ed. Wilmette, Ill.: Bahá'í Publishing Trust, 1982.

———. *The Secret of Divine Civilization.* Trans. Marzieh Gail with Ali-Kuli Khan. Wilmette, Ill.: Bahá'í Publishing Trust, 1975.

———. *Selections from the Writings of 'Abdu'l-Bahá.* Trans. Marzieh Gail et al. Comp. Research Dept. of the Universal House of Justice. Wilmette, Ill.: Bahá'í Publishing Trust, 1997.

———. *Some Answered Questions.* Comp. and trans. Laura Clifford Barney. 4th ed. Wilmette, Ill.: Bahá'í Publishing Trust, 1981.

———. *A Traveler's Narrative Written to Illustrate the Episode of the Báb.* Trans. Edward G. Browne. Wilmette, Ill.: Bahá'í Publishing Trust, 1980.

———. *Will and Testament of 'Abdu'l-Bahá.* Wilmette, Ill.: Bahá'í Publishing Trust, 1944.

Afnan, Muhammad. "Ayyám-i-Butún." *Pazhúheshnámeh* 2.1 (Autumn 1997): 3–38.

Aḥsá'í, Shaykh Aḥmad. *Rasá'ilu'l-Ḥikmah.* Beirut: Dáru'l-'Álamíyyah, 1993.

———. *Sharḥu'l-'Arshíyyah.* Manuscript. 3 vols.

———. *Sharḥu'l-Favá'id.* N.p., n.d.

———. *Sharḥu'z-Zíyárati'l-Jámi'ati'l-Kabírah.* 3 vols. Kirmán: Sa'ádat, 1397 A.H.

Alexander, Jeffrey C. *Theoretical Logic in Sociology.* Vol. 1. Berkeley: University of California Press, 1982.

Althusser, Louis, and Etienne Balibar. *Reading Capital.* London: Verso, 1979.

'Aṭṭar, Farídu'd-Dín. *The Conference of the Birds*. Trans C. S. Nott. London: Routledge & Kegan Paul, 1974.

————. *Muslim Saints and Mystics*. Trans. A. J. Arberry. London: Routledge & Kegan Paul, 1966.

The Báb. *Bayán-i-'Arabí* (Arabic Bayán). N.p., n.d.

————. *Bayán-i-Fársí* (Persian Bayán). N.p., n.d.

————. *Panj Sha'n*. N.p., n.d.

————. *Selections from the Writings of the Báb*. Trans. H. Taherzadeh et al. Comp. Research Dept. of the Universal House of Justice. Haifa: Bahá'í World Centre, 1976.

————. *Tafsír-i-Bismi'lláh*. Iran National Bahá'í Archives (INBA) 64:33–34; 60:1–56.

————. *Tafsír-i-Há'*. Iran National Bahá'í Archives (INBA) 53:81–125.

————. Tafsír-i-Súriy-i-Kawthar. Manuscript.

The Bahá'í World: A Biennial International Record. Vol. 3 (1928–1930). Wilmette, Ill.: Bahá'í Publishing Trust, 1930.

Bahá'u'lláh. *Ad'íyyih-i-Ḥaḍrat-i-Maḥbúb*. Hofheim: Bahá'í-Verlag, 1990.

————. *Alváḥ-i-Názilih Khiṭáb bih Mulúk va Ru'asáy-i-Arḍ*. Tehran: Mu'assisiy-i-Millíy-i-Maṭbú'át-i-Amrí, 124 B.E./1970.

————. *Áthár-i-Qalam-i-A'lá*. Vol. 1. Dundas: Institute for Bahá'í Studies, 1996.

————. *Áthár-i-Qalam-i-A'lá*. Vol. 2. Bombay: Náṣirí, 1314 A.H.

————. *Áthár-i-Qalam-i-A'lá*. Vols. 3–7. Tehran: Mu'assisiy-i-Millíy-i-Maṭbú'át-i-Amrí, 121–134 B.E./1965–1978.

————. *Epistle to the Son of the Wolf*. Trans. Shoghi Effendi. Wilmette, Ill.: Bahá'í Publishing Trust, 1962.

————. *Gleanings from the Writings of Bahá'u'lláh*. Trans. Shoghi Effendi. Rev. ed. Wilmette, Ill.: Bahá'í Publishing Trust, 1952.

————. *The Hidden Words of Bahá'u'lláh*. Trans. Shoghi Effendi. Wilmette, Ill.: Bahá'í Publishing Trust, 1963.

————. *Iqtidárát*. Tehran: Mu'assisiy-i-Millíy-i-Maṭbú'át-i-Amrí, n.d.

————. *Ishráqát*. Tehran: Mu'assisiy-i-Millíy-i-Maṭbú'át-i-Amrí, n.d.

————. *The Kitáb-i-Aqdas: The Most Holy Book*. Haifa: Bahá'í World Centre, 1992.

————. *Kitáb-i-Badí'*. Prague: Zero Palm Press, 148 B.E./1992.

Bahá'u'lláh. *Kitáb-i-Íqán*. Hofheim: Bahá'í-Verlag, 1998.

―――. *The Kitáb-i-Íqán: The Book of Certitude*. Trans. Shoghi Effendi. Wilmette, Ill.: Bahá'í Publishing Trust, 1950.

―――. *La'álí'l-Ḥikmah*. Vol. 2. Brasil: Editora Bahá'í, 1990.

―――. *Majmú'iy-i-Alváḥ-i-Mubárakiy-i-Ḥaḍrat-i-Bahá'u'lláh*. Ed. Muḥyi'd-Dín Ṣabrí. Wilmette, Ill.: Bahá'í Publishing Trust, 1978.

―――. *Prayers and Meditations*. Trans. Shoghi Effendi. Wilmette, Ill.: Bahá'í Publishing Trust, 1987.

―――. "Ṣaḥífiy-i-Shaṭṭíyyih (Book of the River): A Provisional Translation." *Journal of Bahá'í Studies* 9.3 (1999): 57–61.

―――. *The Seven Valleys and The Four Valleys*. Trans. Marzieh Gail and Ali Kuli Khan. Wilmette, Ill.: Bahá'í Publishing Trust, 1978.

―――. *Tablets of Bahá'u'lláh Revealed after the Kitáb-i-Aqdas*. Comp. Research Dept. of the Universal House of Justice. Trans. H. Taherzadeh et al. 2d ed. Wilmette, Ill.: Bahá'í Publishing Trust, 1988.

Beccaria, Cesare M. *An Essay on Crimes and Punishments*. Philadelphia: Philip H. Nicklin, 1819.

Burke, Edmund. *Reflections on the Revolution in France*. Indianapolis: Hackett, 1987.

Bushrui, Suheil. *The Style of the Kitáb-i-Aqdas: Aspects of the Sublime*. Bethesda: University Press of Maryland, 1995.

Chittick, William C. *The Self-Disclosure of God*. Albany: State University of New York Press, 1998.

Cole, Juan R. I. "Baha'u'llah's 'Book of the Tigris' (Sahifih-'i Shattiyyih). Commentary." 28 Apr 1997. Online posting. H-net. <http:/h-net2.msu.edu/~bahai/trans/bhshatt.htm>.

―――. "Baha'u'llah's 'Book of the Tigris' (Sahifih-'i Shattiyyih). Translation." Translations of Shaykhi, Babi and Baha'i Texts, No. 1 (April 1997). Online. H-net. <http://h-net2.msu.edu/~bahai/trans/shatt.htm>.

―――. "Iranian Millenarianism and Democratic Thought in the Nineteenth Century." *International Journal of Middle East Studies* 24 (1992): 1–26.

―――. *Modernity and the Millennium: The Genesis of the Baha'i Faith in the Nineteenth-Century Middle East*. New York: Columbia University Press, 1998.

Comte, Auguste. *The Positive Philosophy*. London: George Bell & Sons, 1896.

Corbin, Henry. *History of Islamic Philosophy*. London: Kegan Paul, 1993.

Currie, Eliott. *Confronting Crime.* New York: Pantheon Books, 1985.

Daftari, Farhad. *The Ismailis: Their History and Doctrines.* Cambridge: Cambridge University Press, 1990.

Descartes, Rene. *Discourse on Method.* New York: Liberal Arts Press, 1976.

Durkheim, Emile. *Moral Education.* New York: Free Press, 1973.

———. *Rules of Sociological Method.* New York: Free Press, 1982.

Eco, Umberto. *The Search for the Perfect Language.* Trans. James Fentress. Oxford: Blackwell, 1995.

Ekbal, Kamran. "Ágház va páyán-i-nuzúl-i-Kitáb-i-Mustaṭáb-i-Aqdas." *Payám-i-Bahá'í* 193 (Dec. 1995): 11–13.

———. "Táríkh-i-nuzúl va nigárish-i-Kitáb-i-Mustaṭáb-i-Aqdas." *Pazhúheshnámeh* 1.2 (Winter 1997): 100–11.

Fárábí, Abú Naṣr. *Al-Fárábí on the Perfect State.* Oxford: Clarendon, 1985.

Faydí, Muḥammad 'Alí. *Khándán-i-Afnán.* Tehran: Mu'assisiy-i-Millíy-i-Maṭbú'át-i-Amrí, 124 B.E./1968.

———. *La'álíy-i-Dirakhshán.* Shíráz: 123 B.E./1967.

Fazel, Seena. "Understanding Exclusivist Texts" in Moojan Momen (ed.), *Scripture and Revelation.* Oxford: George Ronald, 1997. 239–73.

Fichte, Johann G. *Addresses to the German Nation.* New York: Harper, 1968.

Foucault, Michel. *The Order of Things.* New York: Vintage, 1973.

Gadamer, Hans-Georg. *Truth and Method.* New York: Seabury Press, 1975.

Goldziher, Ignaz. *Introduction to Islamic Theology and Law.* Trans. Andras and Ruth Hamori. Princeton: Princeton University Press, 1981.

Habermas, Jürgen. *Knowledge and Human Interests.* Boston: Beacon Press, 1971.

———. *The Theory of Communicative Action.* Boston: Beacon Press, 1984–87.

Halevy, Elie. *The Growth of Philosophic Radicalism.* London: Faber & Faber, 1934.

Hegel, Georg W. F. *The Philosophy of Right.* Oxford: Clarendon, 1942.

Helvetius, Claude A. *Essays on the Mind.* New York: Burt Franklin, 1970.

Herder, Johann G. *Reflections on the Philosophy of the History of Mankind.* Chicago: University of Chicago Press, 1968.

Hobbes, Thomas. *Leviathan.* London: Collier, 1962.

de Holbach, Baron. *The System of Nature.* Trans. H. D. Robinson. Boston: Mendum, 1977.

Ḥuqúqu'lláh. Comp. Research Dept. of the Universal House of Justice. Auckland: National Spiritual Assembly of the Bahá'ís of New Zealand, 1985.

Husserl, Edmund. *Ideas: General Introduction to Pure Phenomenology.* London: Collier-Macmillan, 1969.

Ibnu'l-'Arabí. *The Bezels of Wisdom.* Trans. R. W. J. Austin. New York: Paulist Press, 1980.

Iqbal, Muhammad. *The Reconstruction of Religious Thought in Islam.* Lahore: Iqbal Academy, 1989.

Ishráq Khávarí, 'Abdu'l-Ḥamíd. *Ayyám-i-Tis'ih.* Tehran: Mu'assisiy-i-Millíy-i-Maṭbú'át-i-Amrí, 121 B.E./1965.

———. *Má'idiy-i-Ásmání.* 9 vols. Tehran: Mu'assisiy-i-Millíy-i-Maṭbú'át-i-Amrí, 128–29 B.E./1972–74.

———. *Muḥáḍirát.* 2 vols. Hofheim: Bahá'í-Verlag, 1987.

———. *Raḥíq-i-Makhtúm.* 2 vols. Tehran: Mu'assisiy-i-Millíy-i-Maṭbú'át-i-Amrí, 103 B.E./1949.

———. *Qámús-i-Tawqí'-i-Maní'-i-Mubárak.* Vol. 2. Tehran: Mu'assisiy-i-Millíy-i-Maṭbú'át-i-Amrí, 125 B.E./1971.

Izutsu, Toshihiko. *Sufism and Taoism: A Comparative Study of Key Philosophical Concepts.* Berkeley: University of California Press, 1983.

Jámí, Núru'd-Dín A. *Lavá'iḥ: A Treatise on Islamic Sufism.* Lahore: Islamic Book Foundation, 1978.

Kant, Immanuel. *Critique of Judgment.* Indianapolis: Hackett, 1987.

———. *Critique of Practical Reason.* Indianapolis: Bobbs-Merrill, 1956.

———. *Critique of Pure Reason.* New York: St Martin's Press, 1965.

Káshání, 'Izzu'd-Dín Maḥmúd. *Miṣbáḥu'l-Hidáyah va Miftáḥu'l-Kifáyah.* Tehran: Saná'í, 1946.

Keddie, Nikkie. *An Islamic Response to Imperialism.* Los Angeles: University of California Press, 1968.

Knowlson, James. *Universal Language Schemes in England and France 1600–1800.* Toronto: University of Toronto Press, 1975.

Kohlberg, Lawrence. *The Philosophy of Moral Development: Moral Stages and the Idea of Justice.* San Francisco: Harper & Row, 1981.

Kuhn, Thomas S. *The Structure of Scientific Revolutions.* Chicago: University of Chicago Press, 1970.

LaCapra, Dominick. *Rethinking Intellectual History: Texts, Contexts, Language.* Ithaca: Cornell University Press, 1983.

Lambton, Ann K. S.. *State and Government in Medieval Islam.* Oxford: Oxford University Press, 1981.

Lee, Anthony A. "Choice Wine: The Kitab-i Aqdas and the Development of Baha'i Law." Paper presented at the Fifth Annual Colloquium on Scriptural Studies, Bahá'í Studies Institute, Wilmette, Ill. <http://www.bahai-library.org/conferences/wine.html>.

Lewis, Bernard. *The Assassins.* New York: Basic Books, 1968.

Lings, Martin. *Muhammad.* London: Islamic Texts Society, 1983.

Locke, John. *A Letter Concerning Toleration.* Indianapolis: Hackett, 1983.

Lyotard, Jean F. *The Postmodern Condition.* Minneapolis: University of Minnesota Press, 1984.

de Maistre, Joseph Marie. *Considerations on France.* Montreal: McGill-Queen's University Press, 1974.

Marx, Karl, and Friedrich Engels. *Communist Manifesto.* Arlington Heights: H. Davidson, 1955.

Mázandarání, Mírzá Asadu'lláh Fáḍil. *Amr va Khalq.* 4 vols. Hofheim: Bahá'í-Verlag, 1985.

———. *Asráru'l-Áthár.* 5 vols. Tehran: Mu'assisiy-i-Millíy-i-Maṭbú'át-i-Amrí, 124–129 B.E./1968–73.

Michel, Thomas F., ed. and trans. *A Muslim Theologian's Response to Christianity: Ibn Taymiyya's al-Jawab al-Sahih.* Delmar, N.Y.: Caravan Books, 1984.

Mill, John Stuart. *Considerations on Representative Government.* New York: Henry Holt, 1873.

Muhammad-Husainí, Nusrat'u'lláh, *The Báb: His Life, His Writings, and the Disciples of the Báb's Dispensation.* Dundas: Institute for Bahá'í Studies in Persian, 1995.

Nabíl-i-A'ẓam (Muḥammad-i-Zarandí). *The Dawn-Breakers: Nabíl's Narrative of the Early Days of the Bahá'í Revelation.* Trans. and ed. Shoghi Effendi. Wilmette, Ill.: Bahá'í Publishing Trust, 1932.

Nagel, Ernest. *The Structure of Science.* New York: Harcourt, Brace & World, 1961.

Nakhjavani, Ali. "Nigáhí bih Naẓm-i-Badí'-i-Iláhi." *Payám-i-Bahá'í* 149 (Apr. 1992): 15–18.

Nicholson, Reynold A. *The Mystics of Islam.* London: Arkana, 1989.

Nietzsche, Friedrich W. *The Birth of Tragedy*. New York: Vintage Press, 1967.

———. *The Will to Power*. New York: Random House, 1967.

Parsons, Talcott. *The Structure of Social Action*. New York: Free Press, 1949.

Pefanis, Julian. *Heterology and the Postmodern: Bataille, Baudrillard, and Lyotard*. Durham: Duke University Press, 1991.

Plato. *The Collected Dialogues of Plato*. Ed. Edith Hamilton and Huntington Cairns. New York: Bollingen, 1963.

Plotinus. *Enneads*. Cambridge: Harvard University Press, 1966.

Rabbani, Ahang. "The Conversion of the Great-Uncle of the Báb." *World Order* 30.3 (Spring 1999): 19–37.

Rahman, Fazlur. *Islam*. Chicago: University of Chicago Press, 1966.

Rashtí, Siyyid Kázim. *Majma'u'l-Asrár*. Kirmán: Sa'ádat.

Rúmí, Jalálu'd-Dín. *The Mathnawí of Jalálu'ddín Rúmí*. Ed. and trans. Reynold A. Nicholson. Vol. 2. Cambridge: Trustees of E. J. W. Gibb Memorial, 1960.

Safínih-i 'Irfán: A Collection of Papers Presented at 'Irfán Colloquia. Book One. Darmstadt: Asr-i-Jadíd Publishers, 1998.

Saiedi, Nader. "Antinomies of Reason and the Theology of Revelation: Some Preliminary Thoughts." *Journal of Bahá'í Studies* 8.4 (1998): 73–84.

———. "The Bahá'í Approach to the Environment." Forthcoming.

———. *The Birth of Social Theory*. Lanham, Md.: University Press of America, 1993.

———. "Concealment and Revelation in Bahá'u'lláh's Book of the River." *Journal of Bahá'í Studies* 9.3 (1999): 25–56.

———. "Faith, Reason, and Society in Bahá'í Perspective." *World Order* 21.3–4 (Spring/Summer 1987): 9–22.

———. "Tahlílí az Mafhúm-i-Bábíyyat dar Áthár-i-Hadrat-i-A'lá." *Payám-i-Bahá'í* 222 (May 1998): 7–12.

Saint-Simon, Claude H. *Selected Writings*. New York: Holmes and Meier Publishers, 1975.

Schaefer, Udo, Nicola Towfigh, and Ulrich Gollmer. *Making the Crooked Straight: A Contribution to Bahá'í Apologetics*. Trans. Geraldine Schuckelt. Oxford: George Ronald, 2000.

Schelling, Friedrich W. J. *System of Transcendental Idealism*. Charlottesville: University Press of Virginia, 1978.

Schiller, Friedrich. *On the Aesthetic Education of Man.* New York: Frederick Ungar, 1965.

Schimmel, Annemarie. *Mystical Dimensions of Islam.* Chapel Hill: University of North Carolina Press, 1975.

Schlegel, August W. *A Course of Lectures on Dramatic Art and Literature.* New York: AMS Press, 1973.

Schlegel, Friedrich. *The Philosophy of History.* London: Bell and Daldy, 1873.

———. *The Philosophy of Life and Philosophy of Language.* New York: AMS Press, 1973.

Sells, Michael A., ed. *Early Islamic Mysticism.* New York: Paulist Press, 1996.

Shírází, Ṣadru'd-Dín. *Al-Ḥikmatu'l-Muta'áliyah fi'l-Asfári'l-'Aqlíyyati'l-Arba'ah.* Vol. 1. Najaf: Dáru'l-Ma'árifi'l-Islámíyyah, 1958.

Shoghi Effendi. *The Advent of Divine Justice.* Wilmette, Ill.: Bahá'í Publishing Trust, 1990.

———. *Dawn of A New Day.* New Delhi: Bahá'í Publishing Trust, 1970.

———. *God Passes By.* Wilmette, Ill.: Bahá'í Publishing Trust, 1944.

———. *The Promised Day Is Come.* Rev. ed. Wilmette, Ill.: Bahá'í Publishing Trust, 1980.

———. *The World Order of Bahá'u'lláh: Selected Letters.* Rev. ed. Wilmette, Ill.: Bahá'í Publishing Trust, 1991.

Spencer, Herbert. *The Principles of Sociology.* Vol. 3. New York: D. Appleton and Company, 1897.

———. *Social Statics and The Man Versus the State.* New York: D. Appleton and Company, 1893.

Suhrawardí, Shihábu'd-Dín. *'Avárifu'l-Ma'árif.* Tehran: Intishárát-i-'Ilmí va Farhangí, 1985.

Taherzadeh, Adib. *The Revelation of Bahá'u'lláh.* 4 vols. Oxford: George Ronald, 1987.

Thoresen, Lasse. *Unlocking the Gate of the Heart.* Oxford: George Ronald, 1998.

Vattimo, Gianni. *The End of Modernity: Nihilism and Hermeneutics in Postmodern Culture.* Baltimore: Johns Hopkins University Press, 1988.

Walbridge, John. "The Kitab-i-Aqdas." <Http://www.bahai-library/encyclopedia/aqdas.html>.

Wallerstein, Immanuel M. *The Capitalist World Economy.* Cambridge: Cambridge University Press, 1979.

Weber, Eugen. *Apocalypses: Prophecies, Cults and Millennial Beliefs through the Ages*. Cambridge: Harvard University Press, 1999.

Weber, Max. *The Methodology of Social Sciences*. New York: Free Press, 1949.

———. *Protestant Ethic and the Spirit of Capitalism*. London: Unwin, 1984.

———. *The Sociology of Religion*. Boston: Beacon Press, 1963.

Wilson, James Q. *Thinking About Crime*. New York: Random House, 1975.

Wittgenstein, Ludwig. *Philosophical Investigations*. Oxford: Basil & Blackwell, 1958.

Zarqání, Mírzá Maḥmúd. *Badáyi'u'l-Áthár*. Hofheim: Bahá'í-Verlag, 1982.

INDEX